JUDICIAL REMEDIES IN THE CONFLICT OF LAWS

Judicial Remedies in the Conflict of Laws

OLUSOJI ELIAS

·HART·
PUBLISHING

HART PUBLISHING
OXFORD AND PORTLAND, OREGON
2001

Hart Publishing
Oxford and Portland, Oregon

Published in North America (US and Canada) by
Hart Publishing
c/o International Specialized Book Services
5804 NE Hassalo Street
Portland, Oregon
97213-3644
USA

Distributed in Netherlands, Belgium and Luxembourg by
Intersentia, Churchillaan 108
B2900 Schoten
Antwerpen
Belgium

Hart Publishing is a specialist legal publisher
based in Oxford, England.
To order further copies of this book or to request a list of
other publications please write to:

Hart Publishing,
Salters Boatyard, Folly Bridge,
Abingdon Rd, Oxford, OX1 4LB
Telephone: +44 (0)1865 245533
Fax: +44 (0) 1865 794882
email: mail@hartpub.co.uk
WEBSITE: http//:hartpub.co.uk

British Library Cataloguing in Publication Data
Data Available

ISBN 1-901362-21-3 (hardback)

Typeset by John Saunders Design and Production, Reading
Printed and bound in Great Britain by
Biddles Ltd. www.biddles.co.uk

Foreword

WITH the increasing globalisation of trade and personal relations the subject "Conflict of Laws" becomes increasingly relevant, complex, and interesting. The greater the variety of national laws governing such matters as contracts, torts, family relations (divorce and adoption), the greater the number and types of conflicts or combinations which courts may have to consider. And it is becoming increasingly apparent, both from Court decisions and international Conventions that, as a sub-head to the determination of the substantive law to be applied in an individual case, the question of what remedy should be sought or given may be of cardinal importance and concern to the litigants, as well as of difficulty for adjudicators.

The former classical division between substance and procedure—the former to be decided according to its lex causae, the latter according to the lex fori—as long as the latter is now seen to be simplistic and, in many cases, inappropriate.

Mr Elias' book seeks to apply a deeper analysis to these issues, both in principle and through consideration of recent Conventions—Brussels, Lugano, and the Rome Convention—which will stimulate interest among academics and be of practical help to practitioners and judges. I hope that it will attract a wide range of readers.

Lord Wilberforce

Author's Preface

THIS book is a descriptive practical analysis of judicial remedies in transnational litigation and adjudication, mainly in English law. Although there are several books dealing with the topic in its domestic and comparative legal contexts, there has thus far not been a sustained effort to bridge this omission in the extensive legal literature concerning conflict of laws applications. It was therefore a matter of some personal gladness to have been offered the opportunity to take up the subject matter in 1997. Several deadlines on, it is with much pleasure that the writer offers this book to anyone with a credible interest in transnational private law, at all times having a practical and analytical perspective and detail as a primary concern.

The book is divided into five broad Parts comprised of eleven main chapters and a conclusion. The introductory chapter, which is also the first Part, sets out the general background of the subject matter of the book, comprising a thematic and structural outline of the material. The actual remedies—generally speaking, compensatory damages and other monetary remedies in personam, injunctions and interim orders, performance relief in the context of transnational agreements, restitutionary remedies—are described in Part C; declaratory relief is separately dealt with in Part D, together with some general discussion of relief in rem. Bearing in mind the central role of admiralty jurisdiction in English private international law, the appeal of devoting a separate chapter to the remedies granted thereunder was resisted because, as it happens, a good many of the rules, policies and rationales applicable in the context of other relief are derived from admiralty cases.

Right after the first Part, attention is devoted to a series of short chapters, which make up Part B, on the ramifications of applying the deceptively compressed single bright line by which remedies are characterized for conflicts purposes. Part B seeks to avoid any undue expansionism in its tenor, by looking to the broader transnationalist framework in which international litigation is to be observed. More to the point, it considers the territorialism of legal systems against a much subdued contemporary international backcloth. It should refresh the reader to go straight on from the Part, as the writer does, to the particular relief in their cast as aspects of national law, with occasional reference to the enlightening attributes of comparativism, especially in a subject area which significantly involves looking to foreign legal systems, be they those of the standard-setting European Union or from further afield in an increasingly globalized legal framework.

The writer's thanks are due to Dr Mary Welstead for her comments on the last Chapter. This book is dedicated to the writer's parents and to the "Toys" (old and new).

Contents

PART D RELIEF IN REM

PART E ENVOI

Table of Cases

Table of Legislation

Part A

Introduction

1
Background

THE LAW of civil remedies, the legal means of redressing or averting wrongs or breaches of legal obligation, plays a significant central role in every legal system. It completes the legal system's definition of the legal situation between the parties, as well in conflict of laws cases where the grant of a remedy involves the laws of different but compatible fora. There is abundant material about each remedy, be it interlocutory or final, and its own familiar well-developed governing rules, principles and policies in the ordinary domestic law of the forum in which conventional legal action for the remedy is brought.[1] Conflicts litigants necessarily present their respective claims within the normal prescribed procedures applicable to all actions determined under the jurisdiction of the forum (by writ or claim form or other originating process in English law; in French law, e.g. by assignation). This is perhaps the reason why judicial remedies in the conflict of laws have not attracted extended separate description and analysis in terms as is necessary.

Remedies collectively have been described as "the life-blood of civil justice"[2] and, individually, as "any final or interlocutory order of the court which entitles the successful party to further recourse (such as damages, debt, specific performance or injunctions); or a procedure or judicial order which disposes of the action without trial".[3] This book is about the award of these orders in the

[1] On English civil procedure see *Halsbury's Laws of England*, Vol. 37 (Practice and Procedure), (4th ed., London, Butterworths; 1982); *Halsbury's Statutes*, Vols. 13 (Damages), 21 (Injunctions), 22 (Judgments) (4th ed., London, Butterworths; Reissues 1996, 1990 respectively). General works on remedies include F.H. Lawson, *Remedies of English Law* (2nd ed., London, Butterworths; 1980); A. Burrows, *Remedies for Torts and Breach of Contract* (2nd ed., London, Butterworths; 1994); D. Harris, *Remedies in Contract and Tort* (London, Weidenfeld and Nicholson; 1988); D.B. Dobbs, *Handbook on the Law of Remedies* (2nd. ed., St. Paul, West; 1986); D.M. Walker, *The Law of Civil Remedies in Scotland* (Edinburgh, Green; 1974); P.B.H. Birks (ed.), *Wrongs and Remedies in the Twenty-First Century* (Oxford, Clarendon; 1996). Others deal with particular remedies or subject areas, e.g. R. Goff and G. Jones, *The Law of Restitution* (5th ed., London, Sweet and Maxwell; 1998); H. McGregor, *McGregor on Damages* (16th ed., London, Sweet and Maxwell; 1998); G. Jones and W. Goodhart, *Specific Performance* (2nd ed., London, Butterworths; 1996); G.H. Treitel, *Remedies for Breach of Contract: A Comparative Account* (Oxford, Clarendon; 1988); R.J. Sharpe, *Injunctions and Specific Performance* (2nd ed., London, Canada Law Book Co.; 1982); R.P. Meagher, W.M.C. Gummow and J.R.F. Lehane, *Equity: Doctrines and Remedies* (3rd ed., Sydney, Butterworths; 1992); I.C.F. Spry, *The Principles of Equitable Remedies* (4th ed., Melbourne, Sweet and Maxwell; 1990); H. Woolf *et al.*, *Zamir and Woolf: The Declaratory Judgment* (2nd ed., London, Sweet and Maxwell; 1993). A recent addition is F.D. Rose (ed.), *Restitution and the Conflict of Laws* (Oxford, Mansfield; 1995).

[2] Sir Jack I.H. Jacob, *The Fabric of English Civil Justice* (London, Stevens; 1987), at 169.

[3] N.H. Andrews, *Principles of Civil Procedure* (London, Sweet and Maxwell; 1994), at para. 14.027.

conflict of laws. It thus fills the gap, of a compendium of the solutions offered in the Courts for breaches of obligation, in the material on the subject.

A number of considerations[4] underscore and therefore differentiate the law of remedies in the conflict of laws. Consider the law of private international civil procedure, as contained for example in the United Kingdom's *Civil Jurisdiction and Judgments Act 1982* (as amended) and its implications for remedial judgments;[5] or the private international law of obligations, supranational substantive law (as will have established the given wrong or primary right to the remedy sought), which contains remedial provisions, e.g. the *Rome Convention on the Law Applicable to Contractual Obligations 1980*.[6] There are the conflict of laws dimensions of the law of unjust enrichment and its remedial aspects in restitution. To these might be added choice of law in tort or delict in the form, in Britain, of legislation in Part III of the *Private International Law (Miscellaneous Provisions) Act 1995*. Some of the most important implications of these defining developments in general jurisdiction have taken place under the clear influence or within the territorial reach of the law of the European Community, with remedial analogues and ramifications of practical and academic interest.[7]

The law of remedies in the conflict of laws is best understood in the context of the localization[8] of the legal considerations. Essentially, this means that the forum applies its normal internal law[9] for the forms of remedy and for the procedures by which they may be available, and it applies substantive law (which may not be internal law) for the legal entitlements, if any, and looks to trans-border civil procedure where necessary or in place, for its general orientation. Thus it is in the nature of the subject matter that further aptly descriptive perspectives are afforded by comparative law, for example as to the extent or absence of convergence in the relevant aspects of the laws of the interacting Common and Civil Law systems.

[4] These are identified in the course of the Chapter.

[5] E.g., Articles 24 to 26 of the *Brussels Convention on the Jurisdiction and Enforcement of Judgments in Civil and Commercial Matters 1968* (Schedule 1 of the 1982 Act) provide for the free movement of interlocutory and final judgments among the Member States of the European Community.

[6] This Convention is incorporated into English law as Schedule 1 of the *Contracts (Applicable Law) Act 1990*; Article 10(1)(c) provides for the assessment of damages in accordance with lex causae rules on the point, and is an example of a rule of the conflict of laws on remedies.

[7] Cf. P.M. North, "Is European Harmonization of Private International Law a Myth or a Reality? A British Perspective" in his *Essays in Private International Law* (Oxford, Clarendon; 1993), especially pp. 5–18 on the applicability of the British *Civil Jurisdiction and Judgments Act 1982* (as amended) in all actions brought in the forum, rather than only in cases brought there within the scope of the *Brussels Convention* on which the Act is based. This compelling view has not been and seems unlikely to be immediately expressed in the courts.

[8] *Oxford English Dictionary* (2nd. ed., Oxford, Clarendon; 1989), Vol. VII, at 1080 where localization is defined as: "To make local in character; to invest or imbue with the characteristics of a place or district, or in a particular part or point of any whole or system. Usually with limitative force; to restrict or confine to a particular place or area; to make local in range or currency"; *The Chambers Dictionary* (Edinburgh, Chambers Harrap, 1993), at 983: "local action (*law*): a legal action that relates to a specific place and must be brought there".

[9] The term, internal law, bears the same meaning or sense as that in which it is used, e.g., in the various Conventions of the European Communities; that is, the domestic law of the forum.

The ease with which judgments can be applied between jurisdictions is, in the final analysis, the formal interface between legal systems, and perhaps reflects some of the rudiments of international or globalized administration of civil justice apace of the increasingly harmonized private international legal order. In view of the various international judgment enforcement régimes,[10] further invaluable perspectives are provided by considerations of regionalism, internationalism or globalization which form a separate emerging legal framework for the conflict of laws on remedies. The remainder of this introduction expatiates the background factors, the pervading sources, influences and implications of characterization, and then the classifications, of judicial remedies.

LOCALIZATION, CHARACTERIZATION, SUBSTANCE AND PROCEDURE

Judgments generally, especially those which contain remedial orders, are the most telling reflection of the influence of form or procedure in the legal system. In an early treatise on the conflict of laws and in the course of descriptive comparison between the matter of form or procedure and the matter, in contemporary terminology, of essential validity or substance, Bartolus noted that "when there is a difference of place, different reasons exist for different results . . . So the law has provided that so far as form is concerned its effect is recognized everywhere . . . [In rendering a judgment] the judge disposes about a right . . . which follows the person everywhere; therefore execution is allowed by another judge."[11] Much has transpired in the refinement of conflict of laws theory and practice in the centuries since these observations, unimbued with contemporary factors (e.g. the recognizing forum's public policy) were made. But the observations continue to be of value not least in the important area of distinguishing procedure or form from substance or essence (the remarks take even sharper relief in the context of extra-territorial enforcement).

The conflict of laws is facilitated by legal fictions[12]—such as "procedure" or "substance"—which serve to assist the forum in the rationalization and resolution of disputes, including disputes which have decisive elements which will have

[10] Generally, C. Platto and W.G. Horton (eds.), *Enforcement of Judgments Worldwide* (2nd ed., London, Graham and Trotman; 1993). P.M. North, *Essays in Private International Law* (Oxford, Clarendon; 1993), at 226) has observed that "conventions designed to improve the international administration of justice, i.e. conventions which are primarily of a procedural or administrative nature, have proved to be amongst the most successful".

[11] Bartolus de Saxoferrato, *Commentary on Justinian's Code*, c. 1450, para. 41 (translated by J.H. Beale (Harvard University Press, 1914) as *Bartolus on the Conflict of Laws* (repr. Westport Conn., Hyperion; 1979), at 42–44).

[12] *Mostyn* v. *Fabrigas* [1774] 1 Cowp. 161 at 174 per Lord Mansfield, on the fundamental conflict of laws' legal fiction of non-forum law being construed as fact rather than as law in conflict of laws cases; P.B. Carter, ("Priorities of Claims in Private International Law") [1983] Vol. LIV *BYBIL* 207, at 212 on the procedural but rather different subject of forum prioritization of creditors' claims: " . . . Indeed for a *forum* automatically to apply its own domestic rules could only be explained in terms of the unwarranted fiction that the fact situation contained no significant foreign elements".

arisen outside the scope of application of forum internal law, and which are not necessarily applied in the internal or domestic jurisprudence of the forum or at least are not necessarily applied there in the same way. In either of the domestic law or the conflict of laws settings, the one pervasive facilitating legal fiction at issue in the conceptualization and application of remedies in the Common Law is that they necessarily have a predominantly "procedural" characterization and construction. This is certainly correct, as noted at the outset of this conspectus, in so far as the decision on the remedy ultimately rests with its governing law as forum law.[13] But it does not mean that, as a rule of fixed deployment, the forum's apparatus provided by "procedure" exclusively delivers all the terms of reference as to the manner in which remedies are in fact conceptualized and applied. Current editions of *Dicey and Morris on the Conflict of Laws*[14] or *Cheshire and North's Private International Law*[15] contain uniform authoritative classical commentary on remedies in the conflict of laws being subject to internal law, as do other leading works:[16] the lex fori as it provides for remedies has its framework in the legal system to which the forum belongs.

The theories of the conflict of laws – for examples, Cook's influential "local law"[17] or Dicey's territorial "vested or acquired rights"[18] theories or Savigny's more scientific theory which emphasizes the role of all relevant circumstances in determining the legal system to which a case is to be subjected[19] – would also broadly accommodate the basic idea of localized adaptation of internal remedial law as the keystone to the law of wrongs and remedies in the conflict of laws. The present work is not the place to dwell at length on the intricacies of the theories (they hardly feature in the courts' contemporary jurisprudence if at all they do) as they may aid the definition of remedies in the conflict of laws. It is more useful to note and examine the importance of what the forum regards as pragmatically falling within its remedial competence, wherein interaction on the issues as may exist with other legal systems assists or affects adaptation or

[13] At the time of writing, an example of a legal system that would regulate things otherwise (e.g. by adopting another forum's machinery) could not be found.

[14] L. Collins *et al.* (12th ed., London, Sweet and Maxwell; 1993), at 169 *et seq.*, particularly at 171–172 (on "nature of remedy and method of enforcement"), 183-184 ("Damages"), 189–199 (on injunctions).

[15] P.M. North and J.J. Fawcett (eds.) (London, Butterworths; 1992), at 74 *et seq.*, especially 91–106 (on "The nature and extent of the remedy", "Damages" and "Judgments in foreign currency").

[16] E.g., J.G. Collier, *Conflict of Laws* (2nd ed., Cambridge, CUP; 1994), at 68–71; A.E. Anton, *Private International Law: A Treatise from the Standpoint of Scots Law* (Edinburgh, Green; 1967), at 548 *et seq.*

[17] *Logical and Legal Bases of the Conflict of Laws* (Cambridge, Mass., Harvard Univ. Press; 1949), Chapter I. Cook's theory was compatible with English lawyers because of its reliance on the courts' experience rather than on jurists' extrapolations.

[18] *Conflict of Laws* (5th ed., London, Sweet and Maxwell; 1932), at 17, 43. This theory was adapted and imported from earlier writings of Huber. Dicey did for the theory in England what Beale did in the United States in his *Treatise on the Conflict of Laws* (Cambridge Mass., Harvard U.P.; 1935, 3 Vols.), at 1967–1969, Vol. 3.

[19] *Cheshire and North*, *op. cit.*, at 21–23.

purposive refinement. This is illustrated for example by the Anglo-American experience and case law on international antisuit injunctions.[20]

The dichotomy is of particular significance to the study of remedies because although, not surprisingly, they are formally characterized in general terms as matters of procedure, they also typically involve non-procedural, even substantive, law. The adage is *ubi ius ibi remedium* or *ubi remedium ibi ius*. As Sir Jack Jacob observes,[21] "[a]t the stage at which remedies are awarded by the court there exists the closest connection between civil procedural law and substantive law", and "the importance of civil remedies lies in the inseparable connection between the legal right, claim or interest and the judicial remedy, relief or redress provided by the court". A digression might be permitted at this point: conflict-of-laws' characterization[22] will refer only to the general definitional issue of "remedies as procedure" in order to avoid any confusion that could arise from the alternative conflict-of-laws' term, classification, or its derivatives, the use of which will be limited to references later in the Chapter to the types of remedy.

International remedial competence derives from forum (i.e., judicial) convenience and practicability.[23] In terms which relate well to remedies (for the present, it is immaterial that the following description is made about convenience as a justificatory basis for the likewise jurisdictional (or procedural) but rather different issue of service of process out of the jurisdiction), Collins describes judicial convenience in terms, first, of the identification of the forum best suited (in the different sense of being conveniens) to dispose as to the facts and their proof and as to the law applicable to the merits and of the objectivity and effectiveness of forum jurisdiction.[24] Forum convenience in relation to remedies simply means that the considerations must necessarily be localizable; that is, the considerations be construed in the terms with which the forum is jurisdictionally equipped or in which the forum has adequate procedural machinery. For example, the English forum will not automatically order its own discretionary remedy because the claimant sues for it, not even if the remedy's analogue under the lex causae is characterized as such. Forum competence as it pertains to remedies is elaborated in the next Chapter.

The general law of procedure includes a variety of attitudes, policies, rules and descriptive characteristics of litigation systems. Collectively, these provide a fair measure of the effectiveness of procedure, which itself extends to several types of topic besides remedies.[25] In the case of remedies, procedure is conceptually distinguishable from the substance or content of the judicial decision

[20] E.g. T.C. Hartley, "Comity and the Use of Anti-suit Injunctions in International Litigation" (1987) 35 *AJCL* 487. This article discusses the *Laker* cases litigated between the courts of England and those of the US See also his, "Antisuit Injunctions and the Brussels Jurisdiction and Judgments Convention" (2000) 49 *ICLQ* 166.

[21] *Op. cit.*, at 169–170.

[22] Dicey and Morris, *op. cit.* (1993), Chapter Two, especially at 45–46.

[23] Cf. Dicey and Morris, *op. cit.* (1993), at 169–170.

[24] *Essays in International Litigation and the Conflict of Laws* (Oxford, Clarendon; 1994), at 231–234.

itself. Dissimilar remedial forms can be applied to the same wrong, in which situation the correct choice of procedure for redress depends on forum law on the remedy and on the type of relief the claimant seeks. In much the same way, the same form can apply to otherwise unrelated causae or substantive issues: the question of the defendant's liability for a particular type of breach does not necessarily presuppose an exclusive procedure or remedy; nor can an action for, say, damages automatically denote the precise cause of action. What "procedure" does enable in a way that is beneficial to a study of remedies in the conflict of laws is for jurisdiction and judgments to be considered together, more so in the light of localized international civil procedure in the *Civil Jurisdiction and Judgments Acts 1982* and *1991* based on the *Brussels* and *Lugano Conventions on Jurisdiction and the Enforcement of Judgments in Civil and Commercial Matters 1968* and *1988*.[26] The implications for remedies are variously discussed in this book, as aspects of the transnational jurisdiction.

From the comparative point of view, it is noteworthy that in Civil Law systems, judicial intervention does not emphasize remedy-based forms of action according to the legal rationality which is familiar to Common Law. The Civil Law's equivalents, by which rights arising from the established non-performance will determine the nature of judicial intervention, are rather different. Civil Law primarily turns on the subjective right itself, "with the law of actions having been confined to "technical" (and, in the legal community's mind, secondary) codes of procedure".[27] Localization is differently reached but it nonetheless comparably institutionalizes the forum's remedial intervention. Judicial relief in the Common Law turns just as much upon considerations of how fittingly a formal remedy the claimant seeks can be co-ordinated with the forum's findings. These findings can be based on the application of substantive rules which, significantly, are not necessarily rules of forum law.

In *Phrantzes* v. *Argenti*,[28] Lord Parker C.J. held that the liability of a bride's father to pay dower under non-forum law was not remediable, on the grounds that although English law gave jurisdiction as to the merits it provided no procedure apposite to the primarily foreign right. Nor did the lex causae provide a remedy having a sufficiently precise comparator in forum law. The

[25] J.A. Jolowicz in I.R. Scott (ed.), *International Perspectives on Civil Justice: Essays in Honour of Sir Jack. I.H. Jacob* (London, Sweet and Maxwell; 1990) at 27–45 (in this paper, the nature and purposes of general civil procedure are discussed, alongside the need for unification), and "On the Nature and Purposes of Civil Procedural Law" (1990) 9 *CivJQ* 262); also, N. Andrews, *op. cit.*, Chapter two generally, and also at 455–462; on the effectiveness of remedies, see Jacob, *op. cit.*, at 63–67.

[26] Cf. text carrying n. 5 above, and A. Briggs "Which Foreign Judgments Should We Recognize Today?" (1987) 36 *ICLQ* 240.

[27] P. Legrand, "European Legal Systems are not Converging" (1996) 45 *ICLQ* 52, at 71; also, R.C. van Caenegem, *History of European Civil Procedure, International Encyclopedia of Comparative Law*, Vol. XVI (Tübingen, Siebeck; 1971), Chapter Two, para. 15, where the origin of procedural rules in the civilian tradition is located in the particular court's methods and not in different forms of action or of remedy. The differences are part of the basis in comparative method in the rest of the book.

[28] [1960] 2 QB 19, at 35.

domestic case analogue is illustrated in *Trawnik's Case*[29] in which the neighbours of a Royal Air Force base were refused the judicial remedy of declaration because the remedy was unavailable for Crown liability in nuisance. Interpretations of the same ratio were applied in other decisions on which the law is based: in refusing to grant an injunction in *Baschet* v. *London Illustrated Standard Company*[30] in respect of the publication in France of an alleged libel, Kekewich J held that the grant could be governed only by forum law. In *Boys* v. *Chaplin* Lord Wilberforce identified the role of the judicial policy of flexibility in the interpretation of remedies in the conflict of laws.[31] In *National Bank of Greece and Athens SA* v. *Metliss*,[32] the remedy of recovery (from a third party) of a contract sum due was ordered on the basis of the House of Lords' flexible constructive interpretation of the remedy as it applied under differing forum and non-forum laws. The sums would not have been recoverable on a rigid interpretation of either set of laws.

For a further example, consider the judicial enforcement of a term in an international contract for the sale of land situated outside the jurisdiction of the forum as in *Penn* v. *Baltimore*,[33] or more recently in *Richard West and Partners Limited* v. *Dick*,[34] in which the remedy sought was specific performance of a term providing for the pre-sale inspection of the land. The English lex fori gave the forum jurisdiction, to order service out even, as well as the competence to order extra-territorial performance of the contract term in issue, subject to regulations imposed by the situs.[35] The remedy was awarded since the applicable forum and situs laws at issue were sufficiently co-ordinated. In the conflict of laws, the questions of jurisdiction and of the choice of applicable law provide the main bases for interpretation and analysis, as illustrated in the development of the conflict of laws on damages through the cases.[36] Heads of damage, the items which comprise the claimant's loss, are sub-characterized, as a matter of procedure, and they are established together with the fact of breach which is deemed substantive. Damages and the other remedies are individually presented in the chapters of Parts C and D. The presumption there is of course that there is effective substantive liability on which meaningful discussion of the remedies' aspects depends. The general choice of law aspects of remedies will have been dealt with in Chapter Four, and the enforcement aspects in Chapter Five.

29 [1985] 1 WLR 532.

30 [1900] 1 Ch. 73, at 77–78 (cf. also *Warner Brothers Pictures Incorporated* v. *Nelson* [1937] 1 KB 207). The older cases include *Liverpool Marine Credit* v. *Hunter* (1868) LR3 ChApp 479, at 486.

31 [1971] AC 356, at 391, 394.

32 [1958] AC 509, especially at 524–525, per Viscount Simonds (followed in *Adams* v. *National Bank of Greece and Athens SA* [1961] AC 255 on identical facts); cf. R.H. Graveson, *Comparative Conflict of Laws: Selected Essays* (Amsterdam, North-Holland; 1977, 2 Vols.), especially at 65 (Vol. 1).

33 [1750] 1 Ves Sen 44 .

34 [1969] 1 All ER 943.

35 Cf. *Tito* v. *Waddell (No.2)* [1977] Ch 106, at 322 (per Megarry V.-C.)

36 These cases are analysed in the Chapter on the remedy of damages. An outline preview is provided at the place cited at n. 14 above in *Dicey and Morris*.

SOME COGNATE MATTERS: LIMITATION, EVIDENCE

The characterization of remedies as procedure, and the localizing design of general procedure in particular, would be more complete with some discussion of cognate procedural matters which are generically discussed with remedies in the general textbooks. The discussion begins with the limitation of actions which, fairly recently in English conflict of laws, has been radically re-characterized by statute as substantive, with a host of important implications arising from this separation from procedure.

The *Foreign Limitation Periods Act 1984* significantly re-defines the English conflict of laws' approach to the interpretation and application of relevant foreign limitation periods.[37] The case law in force before the Act meant that the approach of the forum was to strictly adhere to its own internal law limitation provisions.[38] This was in furtherance of the definition of the lex fori as exclusively internal law. According to Section 1 of the *1984 Act*, the matter of limitation has to all intents and purposes been re-defined to be substantive in line with the substantive defence function of the matter.[39] This gives rise to several implications with respect to actions begun after 1 October 1985. The main one is that choice-of-law method now applies to limitations much as it does to liability on the merits of the case. A conflict of laws defendant can now rely on a live (substantive) defence available under relevant and applicable non-forum law even though forum law provides to the contrary to disallow the reliance. The same claimant may likewise not sue in the forum if the time for the initiation of suit has expired under the applicable (non-forum) substantive law.[40] Discretionary aspects of the limitation under the applied non-forum law now vest in the English forum, in so far as the practical exercise of the discretion will reasonably compare with its definition under the original non-forum corpus of case law and jurisprudence[41] (in comparison, since non-forum remedies are not granted in the conflict of laws, the binding relevance or applicability of any discretionary aspects of such remedies does not arise). The only circumstances in which forum internal limitation law applies are where forum law is the governing substantive law, where the issue for determination is the date of

[37] Cf. Law Commission Working Paper No. 114 "The Classification of Limitation in Private International Law" (London, H.M.S.O.; 1982); P.B. Carter, "The Foreign Limitation Periods Act 1984" (1985) 101 *LQR* 68.

[38] Ibid. The cases include *Huber* v. *Steiner* [1835] 2 Bing NC. 202, *Phillips* v. *Eyre* [1870] LR 6 QB 1, p. 29, and more recently *Black-Clawson International Ltd* v. *Papierwerke* W.-A. AG [1975] AC 591, at 630, the US decision in *Chase Securities Corporation* v. *Donaldson* (1945) 325 US 304, at 313, and the Canadian case of *Clark* v. *Naqvi* (1990) 63 DLR (4th) 361. For an overview, *Dicey and Morris op. cit.* (1993), at 186.

[39] This attribute of time limitations (i.e., whether the limitation in question extinguishes both the right and remedy, or just the remedy) was noted in the early case of *Williams* v. *Jones* [1811] 13 East 439). On the point that in civil law systems limitations have always been characterized as substantive: O. Lando in *International Encyclopædia of Comparative Law* (Tübingen, Siebeck; 1971), Vol. 3, Chapter Twenty-four at 123–124.

[40] S. 1(1)(2) of the Act. [41] S. 1(4).

commencement of proceedings or of the running of the actual periods concerned,[42] or where forum public policy excludes the application of relevant non-forum law.[43] The old Common Law rules continue to apply to actions begun before the coming into force of the statute. Thus, while forum internal law of remedies applies mandatorily, the application of its internal law of limitation arises either by default or as a result of choice of law. Within the new framework, non-forum limitations are displaceable on no other bases.

The leading inference for conflicts remedies concerns the applicability of non-forum law in a non-typical[44] choice-of-law situation. Remedies clearly are juridically different from limitations as is illustrated in the fact that remedies do not wholly attract "choice-of-law", as contrasted with "procedural", considerations as limitations now do. The idea of wholesale application of non-forum remedial law (i.e., that remedies law is definitionally substantive law) would be mistaken if it were proposed as the general rule. Consequently, whatever deductions one makes from the foregoing will remain simply descriptive of the remedies issue in situ. Despite the considerable parallels arising from the fact that neither limitations nor remedies in domestic cases are necessarily considered in terms of whether they are substantive or procedural, remedies are typified by considerations of form because remedies emphasize forum process in a way that limitations do not. The closer association of remedies with procedure emphasizes the important underlying policy which favours certainty, practicability and flexibility, the hallmarks of durability and continuity in the procedural lex fori.[45] For the purpose of clarity in defining remedies in the conflict of laws, it would be unnecessary to make more of the fact that the lex causae rather than the lex fori now applies to the topic of limitation once deemed to be irrevocably procedural or subject to internal law[46] in the way that remedies are predominantly cast, not least in terms of post-judgment enforcement.

In contrast with limitation, trial evidence is characteristically a matter for the procedural law of the forum. It includes the permitted or required forms of proof, of admissibility, and the law governing witnesses and the burden of proof.[47] It is a procedural matter also subject to the internal law of the forum in the way that remedies are. The unassailable rationale is that there is no justification for subjecting the forum for litigation to the evidential rules of procedural law of another jurisdiction. Likewise, in the case of remedies it is

[42] S. 1(3). [43] S. 2(1); *The Komninos S* [1990] 1 LlRep 541.

[44] Cf. ss. 1(1) and 5. It is described as non-typical because the subject area with which limitation is juridically associated is that of procedure (cf. e.g. Atiyah and Summers, *op. cit.*, at 10) rather than substance, the latter being the category which typically attracts choice-of-law considerations. It is a matter of supreme interest that limitation is categorized as a contract law remedy in *Chitty on Contracts* (28th ed., London, Sweet & Maxwell; 1999), Chapter Twenty-nine.

[45] Cf. n. 25 above.

[46] E.g., A.V. Dicey, *The Conflict of Laws* (6th ed., London, Stevens; 1949), at 859 *et seq.*

[47] E.g. *Dicey and Morris*, *op. cit.* (1993), at 174–181, 211–212; on the respective aspects identified in the main text, *St. Pierre* v. *South American Stores Ltd.* [1937] 1 All ER 206 is in point, at 209. See also *Bain* v. *Whitehaven & Furness Junction Ry.* 3 HLC 1 (1850); *In re Fuld (No.3)* [1968] P 675, at 696–697.

effectively mandatory that forum remedial process cannot be displaced from the core of the considerations relevant to remedial adjudication.

The law of evidence is materially procedural. It secures compliance with the forum's scientific process of proof, determines precisely what constitutes evidence, and confirms the implicit immutability of the forum when the question is indubitably procedural. Indeed, according to Article 1(2)(h) of the *Rome Convention*, Convention rules do not apply to matters of evidential procedure. Like remedies, these are left to the various leges fori. This does not mean, however, that the only law the forum recognizes as potentially at issue is its own internal law. In *South Carolina Insurance Co. Ltd.* v. *Assurantie Maatschappij "De Zeven Provincien"* NV,[48] over-ruling Griffiths L.J. in the Court of Appeal,[49] Lord Brandon upheld the view in *Dicey and Morris*[50] that a party before the English forum may take any evidence-procuring steps, e.g. seek a discovery order available in a relevant jurisdiction other than the forum, as this would nevertheless not detract the forum from applying its internal law to the evidential issues arising before it. It is of course not the case that the forum itself applies the non-forum rules in question. The analogous remedies' principle is illustrated by inter-jurisdictional interlocutory relief procedures: the litigant in either case seeks to rely on the process of another forum, to assist the ultimate realization of the English action. It is inconsequential that the non-forum evidential rules on which an English litigant might rely (in the relevant forum elsewhere) are radically different provisions from the comparable rules, if any, of the forum's internal law, as were the US rules vis-à-vis the English rules in the *South Carolina* decision.[51]

Indeed the English lex fori itself contains provisions to govern the taking of evidence within its jurisdiction for use in other fora in the *Evidence (Proceedings in other Jurisdictions) Act 1975*[52] and in Order 70 of the *Rules of the Supreme Court 1965* (as amended).[53] *The Hague Convention on the Taking of Evidence in Civil and Commercial Matters 1970*[54] contains well developed rules on similar and other issues. The main analogy for the matter of remedies is of forum independence in civil procedure. The lex fori is the inclusive category of rules, principles, and policies of which a good few are irrelevant in the domestic case. There are of course some evidential aspects of a conflicts case which are referred to non-forum law: the status of a litigant's spouse, as to competence, compellability or privilege might need first to be determined by the appropriate

[48] [1987] AC 24. [49] [1985] 3 WLR 739, at 746–747.

[50] *Op. cit.*, at 175; and *loc. cit.*, at n. 47 above.

[51] The English rules were *Rules of the Supreme Court 1965* (as amended) Orders 24 (disclosure and inspection of documents), 26 (interrogatories) which avail only the parties to the dispute. The comparable US District Courts Rules avail non-parties as well, as in *John Deere Ltd. and Deere & Co.* v. *Sperry Corporation* 754 F.2d 137 (1985).

[52] Cf. K. Lipstein "The Evidence (Proceedings in other Jurisdictions) Act 1975: An Interpretation" (1990) 39 ICLQ 120; *Dicey and Morris*, *op. cit.*, at 212–218.

[53] Ibid.

[54] Ibid.; also L. Collins, "The Hague Evidence Convention and Disclosure" (1986) 35 *ICLQ* 765, on the applicability of the Convention to the issue of discovery.

lex causae before the lex fori rule as to admissibility of the witness's evidence can be applied where necessary. Other procedural topics, such as the rules to identify the proper parties to the litigation, the service of process, security for costs, the law of set-off and counterclaim, and the law on priorities of creditors' claims, could also be discussed. Doing so would not necessarily enhance an appreciation of remedies as procedure.

CLASSIFICATIONS OF RELIEF

The range and variety of types of remedial order with particular reference to the decisive classificatory scheme will now be described. It is of course the case that by and large conflict of laws' classifications follow the categories in internal law. At any rate, invariably the same ample rationales of remedial justiciability will be seen to be broadly applicable to either the domestic or the conflict of laws settings, for the reasons given at the outset of this overview.

Within the general characterization of remedies as procedure for the purposes of private international litigation and adjudication, there are further classifications or sub-classifications in the practical jurisprudence on the subject,[55] based on the practice and procedure of the courts. Of these classifications, Burrows offers an encompassing function-derived ordering which centres on compensation, restitution, punishment, compelling performance of positive obligations, preventing wrongful acts, compelling the undoing of a wrong, and declaring rights.[56] Andrews sets out a reasonably exhaustive form-based list of the actual remedies themselves.[57]

Of the breadth of individual procedures available, it is on eminent authority that "[t]he effectiveness of the system of English civil justice may be attributed to the vast number, variety, diversity and flexibility of its judicial remedies".[58] Classifications are to be found in different contexts, at respective levels of analysis and to differing ends. The categorizations identify the types and assortments of remedy available in the forum (the typology), define the given remedy's apposition to the particular obligation alleged to be in breach (the practical jurisprudence), or, significantly, will indicate the best course of action for the aggrieved claimant or for the defendant's response thereto (the operative and more strictly procedural choice of remedy). The remedy (or consolidated remedies) selected by the claimant can of course not be revoked once the action proper is under way.[59]

The main classificatory themes include the hierarchy of remedial norms of

[55] This is the basis upon which Lawson's work cited at n. 1 proceeds, as do most works including Treitel, *op. cit.*, Chapter One; cf. D. Laycock, *Modern American Remedies: Cases and Materials* (Boston, Little Brown; 1985), at 2–6.

[56] *Op. cit.*, at 8.

[57] *Op. cit.*, paras. 14–029 to 14–037. A few are omitted, e.g., damages in trover.

[58] Jacob, *op. cit.*, at 171.

[59] Jolowicz in Scott (ed.), *op. cit.*, at 32.

the internal law of the given system amongst the substitutional or pecuniary, the coercive, the constitutive or declaratory and so on. By far the most widespread or even primary remedy in the courts in practically every jurisdiction are money remedies, albeit that in the Civil Law, where "the vast majority of judgments are coercive" rather than substitutional as in the Common Law, the theory runs that the first remedy is performance.[60] This is returned to later in this book as is the situation by which the Civil Law's general remedial rule for performance rather than substitution nevertheless results in the expediency of the latter, as in the Common Law.

The general importance of classification is illustrated by the decisive choice of remedy that has to be made in any given fact situation. That choice can be as conceptually basic as between an action for liquidated or compensatory damages on the one hand and penalty clauses on the other;[61] or as avant garde as between the obsolescent action for money had and received[62] and one which involves considerations either of the proper law of a restitutionary remedy[63] or the contemporarily topical concept of restitutionary damages.[64] In *The Puerto Buitrago* the recovery of a liquidated sum was compared with an award of specific performance as well as with property rights.[65] Thus, these engaging overlaps and differences from classification can be concrete but responsive to fairly straight-forward interpretation and application. Needless to say, the practical point thereby emphasized is that the choice of remedy, be it the claimant's or the defendant's, must be the right one else the action fails or is, at best, less than optimized.

There is as much a plethora of types of process or remedial action as there are groupings which accord to the essentials of particular remedies, just as there are classes which really serve analysis rather than the strict pragmatic aspect. Further unprecedented rights and forms of action can also be introduced by legislation or judicial interpretation to supplement the jurisdiction where new

[60] Lawson *op. cit.*, at 13; 12–14, on the classification of judgments and the comparisons in German (i.e., leistungsklagen (performance), festellungsklagen (declaration), gestaltungsklagen (constitutive orders)) and French (i.e., *donner* (to give), *faire* (to do)) laws respectively; cf. Treitel, *op. cit.*, at 75.

[61] Cf. Treitel, *op. cit.*, at 228–233.

[62] *Moses* v. *Macferlan* 2 Burr. 1005 (1760), at 1012; *Sinclair* v. *Brougham* [1914] AC 398; *Rover International Ltd.* v. *Cannon Film Sales Ltd. (No. 3)* [1989] 1 WLR 912. On the matter of obsolescence, see Hon. Sir Peter Millett "Tracing the Proceeds of Fraud" (1991) 107 LQR 71, at 85: "the common law action for money had and received should be abolished".

[63] Cf. *Baring Brothers & Co. Ltd.* v. *Cunninghame District Council* [1996] TLR 538 (Scots Court of Session (Outer House), per Lord Penrose).

[64] Cf. Law Commission Consultation Paper No. 132 "Aggravated, Exemplary and Restitutionary Damages" (London, H.M.S.O.; 1993), at 155–172, 177–178; also, Burrows, *op. cit.*, at 293–299; and *dicta* in *Surrey C.C.* v. *Bredero Homes Ltd.* [1993] 3 All ER 705, at 710–711: "The classic illustration is a claim for the return of goods sold and delivered where the buyer has repudiated his obligation to pay the price".

[65] [1976] 1 Ll Rep. 250; Jones and Goodhart, *op. cit.* (2nd ed.; 1986), at 262. So have the common ground between orders in personam and in rem, and the constitutive aspect of coercive awards: W.H. Hohfeld, *Fundamental Legal Conceptions as Applied in Judicial Reasoning* (ed. W.W. Cook, New Haven, Yale Univ. Press; 1964), at 13 *et seq.*

circumstances arise.[66] A number of these self-descriptive classes have already been touched upon in the course of this introduction: the civil, rather than the criminal; the judicial, rather than the extra-judicial which equally arise by the operation of law; those which operate ad personam, rather than ad rem; the interlocutory (e.g. discovery of documents, undertakings as to costs or as to damages) as distinguished from the final or permanent, and from the ancillary; the pecuniary or substitutional, the coercive, the declaratory, even the substantive or primary, rather than the procedural (in the pre-trial and post-judgment senses) orders.

Others have provided subtexts: the self-enforcing (e.g., status decrees), the non-self-enforcing; the strictly domestically applicable (e.g. declarations of title to land within the jurisdiction), the strictly transjurisdictionally applicable (e.g., by express/contractual or implied (e.g., by submission to jurisdiction) consent as to the applicable remedy); the comparativist domestic and/or comparativist conflict of laws types, be they convergent or divergent; the equitable or discretionary (in English law, injunctions and performance), rather than the strictly legal that are available as of right (i.e., damages); indeed, the discernible system-specificities of remedies law, for example vis-à-vis the regionally aspirated as in the case of the relevant aspects of the law of the European Community with the novelty of remedial rights accruing to individuals as against the Member States.[67] Some, for example damages against Community institutions under E.C. law[68] or damages in foreign currency (as was groundbreakingly applied on the basis of specific provision in Article 106 of the *Treaty of Rome 1957* in *Schorsch Meier GmbH* v. *Hennin*[69] and soon afterwards in *Miliangos* v. *George Frank (Textiles) Ltd.*[70] and *The Despina* R),[71] are particularly apposite to the conflict of laws, others are not quite so (e.g., negative declarations of title which affect proceedings in progress elsewhere).[72] Most are generally applicable either way (e.g. Mareva injunctions).

To reiterate, this book specifically concerns the judicial remedies of damages, injunctions, specific performance of contracts, restitution, remedies in rem, admiralty remedies, and certain other types of judicial award, e.g., in matrimonial cases, as these are available to resolve private international litigation in the courts, primarily in England.

[66] Cf. Hon. Sir Leonard Hoffmann, "Changing Perspectives in Civil Litigation" (1993) 56 MLR 297.

[67] Generally R. D'Sa, *E.C. Law and Civil Remedies in England and Wales* (London, Sweet and Maxwell; 1994), Chapter Ten; M. Brealey and M. Hoskins, *Remedies in E.C. Law* (London, Longmans; 1994), Chapters Five to Nine on the remedies in English courts for breaches of Community Law. The remedies are much the same in form as those applied to other breaches.

[68] Cf. *Francovich and Bonidaci* v. *Italy* [1991] ECR 1-5357.

[69] [1975] QB 416.

[70] [1976] AC 443.

[71] [1979] 1 All ER 421 (the decision extends such awards to tort damages and to unliquidated damages for breach of contract).

[72] Collins, *op. cit.*, at 274 *et seq.*, discussing the *Marc Rich* case, [1989] 1 LlRep. 548, (C.A.)

SCOPE AND PERSPECTIVE OF A BOOK ON CONFLICTS REMEDIES

International, transnational or transjurisdictional civil procedure is clearly an important legal phenomenon, is integral to the perspective of the conflict of laws on remedies adopted in this book. A clear idea is now had of the typification of procedure and its instrumentalism, of the inclusiveness or exclusiveness of the lex fori, and of the frequently statutory localization of the relevant and applicable law. Thus remedies in the conflict of laws are necessarily subject to a functional realistic localization of the legal considerations. These considerations depend on what is practicable by the forum. Remedies law has been shown to be intrinsically inseparable from procedural law, although a literal comprehension of the usual "procedure" characterization would be mistaken. In the conflict of laws, there are identifiable judicial policies which are extracted from, therefore are identical to, much the same policies and considerations in the local dimension. They include sustaining forum jurisdiction as far as is possible, the validation of obligations or the regulation of autonomy, efficiency, and effectiveness, and conflict avoidance. These and others are collectively identified in the Part on theory and policy. The policies characterize the legal system's general remedial jurisprudence, and are derived from the general competence of the forum. Little or nothing is to be said of extra-judicial solutions to obligational breach situations, e.g., rescission or the termination of contracts in the event of fundamental breach or avoidance of litigation by agreement, except as they may explain or be relevant to an action for one or other of the main judicial remedies discussed in Part C. The best way to fulfil the descriptive aims herein is to present the law as it treads the fine lines between theoretical explications and practical considerations of internal law as it adapts to private international law, without either sacrificing the salient features of the one for those of the other or belabouring matters which are not directly consequential to these aims.

COMPARATIVE LAW DIMENSIONS

Profound conceptual and epistemological differences exist between the different legal systems at legal system and subject area levels. Legrand persuasively points out some of these "irreducible differences" between the main legal traditions.[73] Diversity in remedial interventionism in comparative perspective is an invaluable resource to the purpose of the book while recognizing that, in the domestic action in any national system, only occasional or casual (rather than binding) reference is made to the provisions of comparable legal systems. Characteristically, the same internal law applies to breach of obligation as does to

73 *Loc. cit.*, generally.

specified remedial liability and to the available remedy. Indeed the same body of law or the same legal system governs all the questions of remedy which arise. Needless to say, there is no transjurisdictional aspect. In English law, a law of actions, remedies as procedure is a subtle presumption. In other legal systems, the same presumption barely exists in the much less explicit sense in which recourse to judicial procedures itself may be construed as remedial. In any event, the same legal system regulates all matters arising right up to the point of enforcement of awards where necessary. The present writer is unaware of a legal system that realistically or possibly can operate otherwise. In either the Common or Civil Laws, the remedy sought will generally either determine the cause of action, or determine the nature of remedial judicial intervention. This provides the requisite presumption of similarity for comparative legal method.[74] As Koopmans has put it, because all courts whatever the national system are dans le même bain as far as the general nature of the legal issues they face is concerned, comparative law can provide bases for new directions for the courts.[75] It may well be that some of the procedurally imposed limits on remedial adjudication—e.g. whether the forum has a remedy as in the area of international intellectual property litigation as discussed by Trooboff[76]—can be refined in this manner.

Another basis for the comparative law dimension is that several contemporary aspects of English conflict of laws owe some of their origins or derivations to the jurisprudence of either the Civil Law jurisdictions or to those of other Common Law systems. Because they are an independent source of information, rather really than because applicable non-forum remedial law (excluding the forms) may bind the forum, are comparable laws referred to in passing.[77]

[74] Cf. K. Zweigert and H. Kötz, *An Introduction to Comparative Law* (2nd ed. translated by T. Weir, Oxford, Clarendon; 1992), at 36.

[75] "Comparative Law and the Courts" [1996] 45 ICLQ 545, especially at 548–550, 555–556.

[76] In C. McLachlan and P. Nygh (eds.), *Transnational Tort Litigation—The Jurisdictional Principles* (Oxford, Clarendon; 1996), especially at 128–132, where he argues for new forms of action and remedies for transjurisdictional intellectual property cases in localized international law of civil procedure; cf. also *Pearce* v. *Ove Arup and Partners*, *The Times*, March 17th, 1977.

[77] A number of the works relied on for the comparativist aspects have already been cited in this introduction. Apart from those in note 1 (viz. Lawson, Treitel in particular, Zweigert and Kötz, Dobbs), other citations mentioned thus far include Atiyah and Summers (eds.), the *International Encyclopedia of Comparative Law*; Platto and Horton, and Markesinis (ed.). Further leading works include E.J. Cohn, *A Manual of German Law* (2nd ed., B.I.I.C.L.-Oceana; 1968), 2 Vols.; G. Dannemann, *An Introduction to German Civil and Commercial Law* (London, B.I.I.C.L.; 1993); D. Harris and D. Tallon, *Contract Law Today: Anglo-French Comparisons* (Oxford, Clarendon; 1989); O. Jauering *et al. Bürgerliches Gesetzbuch* (Munich, Beck; 1991); B. Rudden, *A Source-Book on French Law* (3rd ed., Oxford, Clarendon; 1991); *The Italian Civil Code* (translated by M. Beltramo, G.E. Longo, and J.H. Merryman; Dobbs Ferry, Oceana; 1969).

STRUCTURE AND COMPOSITION OF THE BOOK

The next Part takes up remedialist theory and policy in brief chapters, viz.: international civil procedure and the remedial judgment; remedial dimensions of judicial policy; choice of law and the nature of applicable remedial law; non-self-executing remedies, extra-territoriality and the issue of non-predeterminability of the place of enforcement. A limited alternative thesis to the procedurally inclusive paradigm makes up the last chapter of the Part. A practical orientation is adopted throughout. Part C is on the main individual remedies, the detail of their respective governing principles and policies (procedural and substantive) in conflicts cases, plus supplementary comparative analysis from Civil Law systems. Declarations are separately discussed in Part D. Part E is a concluding chapter.

Part B

Remedialist Theory and Policy: Exploring Single Bright Line Logic

2

The remedial judgment

THE ULTIMATE LOCAL FORM AND THE TRANSNATIONAL CONTEXT

THIS CHAPTER EXAMINES the remedial judgment in private international adjudication by considering the formal or procedural aspect of the remedial jurisprudence of English law. A comprehensive view of the exercise of general judicial jurisdiction is not, as a general rule, necessarily always rendered in terms that differentiate or emphasize transnationalism in litigation and adjudication – nor need it do so. The best explanation of this is that the procedural law of which, for want of a better expression, "judgments law" is part and parcel is necessarily expressed to be forum or internal law, whatever be derivation of the substance of the decision.

The Chapter is by no means intended to be overabundant as to the conflicts dimensions, where such be the case, of a remedial judgment. The forms of judgment are precisely those used in domestic law. Or at least it does not seek to represent them other than as one type of formal result of forum jurisdiction and competence where, emphatically, there is a valid legal dispute according to forum procedural law.

Rather than make more than is justified from the special contexts of transnational litigation and the conflict of laws, this necessarily brief Chapter keeps with the basis for the book itself–it offers a descriptive analysis of its topic in terms which respond to contemporary practical circumstances. It takes up the (conflicts) judgment as the dispositive remedy, as the enforceable product of forum jurisdictional jurisprudence, whether its enforcement be territorial or to be executed in another forum state.

To reiterate, the main object is to describe and to emphasize some of those aspects which may require cautious analysis if any accretion is to be made to the globalization of civil justice, so that any cavil in the writer's tenor is put down to the fact that, for the most part, it does not really draw on conflicts judgments in which the preponderance of the factors point to internal law. For the present purpose, "remedy" excludes "procedural right of action" and, perhaps less questionably, how the claimant's entitlement will have been rationalized to have justified the grant of substantive legal relief in the form of a judgment.

As Sir Jack Jacob put it, "[f]rom the procedural point of view, the importance of civil remedies lies in the inseparable connection between the legal right, claim or interest and the judicial remedy, relief or redress provided by the court."[1] Any forum's jurisdictional rules and jurisprudence (acquisition; declination; exercise) secures the role of territory in the application of its remedial judgment having or without a procedural impact beyond the forum state. In most cases, other than those obtaining under bilateral or regional jurisdiction and judgments arrangements, there is little basis for formal—i.e., in contrast with substantive—misgiving as to the nature or consequences of a remedial decision reached on proper jurisdictional competence. Attention to general transnational judicial jurisdiction unites several perspective levels: local or internal; convention-based; reciprocity-based; abstractly, *ius gentium*-derived.[2]

To begin at the basic local level, as it is explained by Lord Diplock:[3]

> "[*i*]n its narrow and very strict sense, the "jurisdiction" of a validly constituted court connotes the limits which are imposed on its power to hear and determine issues between persons seeking to avail themselves of its process by reference (i) to the subject matter of the issue, or (ii) to the persons between whom the issue is joined, or (iii) to the kind of relief sought, or any combination of these factors. In its wider sense it embraces also the settled practice of the court as to the way in which it will exercise its power to hear and determine issues which fall within its "jurisdiction" (in the strict sense) to grant, including its settled practice to refuse to exercise such powers or to grant such relief in particular circumstances."

Contemporary transnational norms, for example as they are found in international jurisdiction and judgments conventions[4] or under statutory provisions for cross-border application, are neither so urgent nor ambitious as to override the relevant pre-existing forum state law as encapsulated in his Lordship's statement. Remedies and the jurisdictional competence by which they are to be made available are first and foremost provided for under national law. There is an important relationship between local and transnational attitudes. How well this relationship is served or accommodated by the jurisdictional rules of the forum is, more often than not, a direct function of the localizing matrix of the process of characterization. Jurisdictional connecting factors can vary widely among forum states,[5] though they do not directly influence the exercise of remedial jurisdiction, other than in terms that there is a recognized jurisdictional

[1] *The Fabric of English Civil Justice* (London, Stevens; 1987), at 170. On the pertinent legal rules, see Vol. 22 *Halsbury's Statutes* (4th ed., London, Butterworths; 1995 Re-issue).

[2] See, e.g., A.F. Lowenfeld, *International Litigation and the Quest for Reasonableness: Essays in Private International Law* (Oxford, Clarendon; 1996), Chapter One, especially at 1–5.

[3] In *Garthwaite* v. *Garthwaite* [1964] P. 356, at 387–388.

[4] The paradigm has to be the E.U. *Brussels Convention on Jurisdiction and the Enforcement of Judgments in Civil and Commercial Matters 1968* and the *Lugano Convention 1988*; Art. 25 provides that "judgment" refers to any decision of a Member State forum, including decrees, orders, execution orders, costs awards, interest, specific (non-money) orders, be any of these final or interlocutory, with or without subject matter jurisdiction (Art. 24), with or without notice; for identical efforts in South-East Asia, see P. Koh, "Foreign Judgments in ASEAN-A Proposal" [1972] 45 ICLQ 844, especially at 854–859.

[5] Cf. H. Smit, "Common Law Rules of In Personam Adjudicatory Authority: An Analysis of Underlying Policies" (1972) 21 *ICLQ* 335: "The danger of leaving one's umbrella in Sweden is known the world over..."

relationship between the formal bases for adjudicatory jurisdiction and the measures that may be taken to enforce or execute substantive relief.[6]

The substantive taxonomy of remedies follows the patterns under internal law: e.g., personal/proprietary; legal/equitable; provisional/final; substitutional/coercive/restitutional; substantive/enforcement. These sub-classes of relief are not merely for the convenience of description; there is an important functional dimension which does not necessarily always travel well between different legal traditions, especially, but by no means only, outwith Convention-based arrangements. One conceptually difficult result is that it is, in principle, possible for a forum to reach a decision which, according to its own overall jurisprudence, settles the questions raised as to legal liability to the extent that the particular forum can conveniently do so, but which for any number of formal reasons (non-recognition; inadequate enforcement procedures) does not completely materialize the substance of the claimant's entitlement to relief. Judicial jurisdiction makes this possible result reasonably remote: such actions will probably not be subsumable under forum procedure at all. Similarly, the reverse situation, by which a compromising defendant is rendered more vulnerable is much less frequent if not constructively undermined by the accepted jurisdictional norm by which the defendant is to be sued, all things being equal, in his or her forum state.

The important connection between jurisdiction and territory means that, even in situations in which techniques for resolving jurisdictional jurisprudential differences are built into the design of the applicable rules (e.g., Article 16 of the *Brussels Convention* dealing with the allocation of exclusive jurisdiction in cases concerning proprietary interests in immovable property (jurisdiction in rem); Articles 24 and 25 of the *Brussels Convention* which provide for cross-enforcement and a definition of "judgment" for the *Convention's* purposes), the rendition of a remedial judgment does not necessarily mean that substantive justice in accordance with an applied non-forum governing law necessarily follows. This imperfection is not one to be circumvented without some measure of discrimination. There may be no analogues in the local jurisprudence of the forum which grants the particular conflicts relief. Blomeyer has written[7] that the unpacking of these difficulties, arising by far more as an exception than as a norm, may well have to be pursued from comparativist methodology, rather than by insisting on inter-jurisdictional dialogue that merely recognizes an insurmountable presumption of similarity,

Effective application of non-forum procedural (remedial) law by the forum, as a simple solution, is ostensibly already much in the offing without resort to

[6] See, e.g., C. McLachlan, "The Influence of International Law on Civil Jurisdiction" [1993] HYBIL 125, at 140; this article is an elegant study of the *ius gentium*-derived level at which judicial jurisdiction relating to remedies can be observed.

[7] "Types of Relief Available (Judicial Remedies)" in *International Encyclopaedia of Comparative Law* (Tubingen, Paul Siebeck; 1974), Chapter XVI (Civil Procedure), Chapter Four; also, see generally B.S. Markesinis, *Foreign Law and Comparative Methodology: a Subject and a Thesis* (Oxford, Hart; 1997).

comparativism. There is talk of a substantive remedy having a proper law in the report of the decision of the Outer House of the Scots Court of Session in *Baring Brothers and Company Limited* v. *Cunninghame District Council*.[8] The topicality of a codified international law on civil procedure is also variously and realistically commented on, for example, by Tetley.[9] One inference is that international civil procedure is cogent, harmonistic,[10] and, from the standpoint of dualist Common Law jurisprudence, ineluctably intuitive in terms of its practical application.[11] There are structural issues and problems which require operable responses. One concerns the Civil Law's analogue for the Common Law's resort to contempt proceedings in public law to support its personal jurisdiction;[12] the Civil Law reaches the same juridical result through inter-party proceedings only,[13] it imposes a fine (in French law, the astreinte; in Austrian and German law, the geldstrafen). It has always been part of Common Law judgments jurisprudence that "[i]t is not the habit of [its] courts in considering whether or not it will make an order to contemplate the possibility that it will not be obeyed."[14] Conversely, actual enforcement is part of the discretionary jurisdiction of the Common Law, for example, in the grant of injunctions, such as in the local case of *James North & Sons Textiles Limited* v. *North Cape Textiles Limited*.[15]

These and other characteristics of a typical remedial judgment properly belong to the discussion of the nature of the applicable remedial law and of the question of enforceability in subsequent chapters of this Part of the book. It is sufficient to say that there are the universal features of finality, recognizability and enforceability, and transnationalism, in every remedial judgment in international adjudication, whatever be the granting forum state. The particularized substantive remedies are taken up individually in Parts C and D. The remaining aspects of remedial law and enforcement are discussed in the rest of the present Part to complete the backdrop of remedialist theory and policy. The next Chapter illustrates some of the considerations which significantly complete the necessary interpretive context by which black-letter statements of the law—

[8] [1996] TLR 538.

[9] In *International Conflict of Laws: Common Civil and Maritime* (Montreal, International Shipping Publications; 1994), at 868; see also J.A. Jolowicz, "On the Nature and Purposes of Civil Procedural Law" in I.R. Scott (ed.), *International Perspectives on Civil Justice* (London, Sweet & Maxwell; 1990), 27, especially at 36–39 (the effectiveness of procedure) and 39–43 (the creation of procedural jurisprudence).

[10] Cf. P.M. North, *Essays in Private International Law* (Oxford, Clarendon; 1993), Chapter One generally; also A. Lowenfeld, *International Litigation and the Quest for Reasonableness* (Oxford, Clarendon; 1996).

[11] Cf. the Lord Goff of Chieveley *The Future of the Common Law* (1997) 46 ICLQ 745, e.g. at 754.

[12] Cf. G.H. Treitel, *Remedies for Breach of Contract: A Comparative Account* (Oxford, Clarendon; 1987), at 59 *et seq*.

[13] See, e.g., J.H. Merryman *The Civil Law Tradition: An Introduction to the Legal Systems of Western Europe and Latin America* (2nd ed., Stanford, Stanford Univ. Press; 1985), e.g., at 130.

[14] *Re Liddell's Settlement Trusts* [1936] Ch 365, at 374 (per Romer J.)

[15] [1984] 1 WLR 1428 (C.A.)

procedural law, for the present—are to be construed and interpreted. It is to be shown that the process of interpretation in transnational litigation and adjudication significantly involves considerations that are not necessarily always manifest from the form and text of a remedial judgment.

3

Forum policy

PROCEDURAL JUSTICIABILITY AND POLICY IN THE CONFLICT OF LAWS: REMEDIAL DIMENSIONS

IT IS AN aphorism that "[t]he entire conflicts process is, in a broad sense, forum policy . . . [I]t represents the forum's approach to a situation containing a foreign element."[1] It is moreover the case that the types of internationalist response to these situations depend on which legal regime systemizes the forum's remedial disposition to a particular conflicts case. In cases arising in the scheme of the European Community Conventions, the forum does not discriminate, for example, as between money judgments and coercive orders in the way that it must in cases arising outside the European Community, even where adjudicatory jurisdiction is not lacking. Of itself, this is not necessarily an issue because this illustrative context primarily concerns the recognition and enforcement of foreign judgments rather than the grant of relief as an aspect of original jurisdiction. It is more important to recognize "policy" as "a term that can be made to cover all sorts of factors, such as the need for action, a choice of alternatives, the danger of collision with public opinion, shortage of material resources, and expense. Many of them are too imponderable or too 'political' to be really 'justiciable'."[2] Indeed, it is not always the case that judicial reliance on policy in the common law will precisely indicate its formulation or foundation.[3] At any rate, it provides a rationale or justification, away from particular remedial principle, for the availability of a given judicial remedy. Without doubt, judicial policy imbues transnational adjudication with an ampler scope for the dispensation of justice, on occasion with some difficulty.[4]

[1] D.C. Jackson, *The Conflicts Process: Jurisdiction and Choice in Private International Law* (London, Oceana Publications-British Institute of International and Comparative Law; 1975), at 279. See also P.M. North and J.J. Fawcett, *Cheshire and North's Private International Law* (12th ed., London, Butterworths, 1992) at 4: "The policy [of entertaining actions in respect of foreign claims]".

[2] F.H. Lawson, *Remedies of English Law* (2nd ed., London, Butterworths; 1980), at 253, albeit in the context of appeals in their constitutive cast.

[3] See generally J. Bell, *Policy Arguments in Judicial Decisions* (Oxford, Clarendon; 1983), e.g., at 53: "[J]udicial rule-creation operates in a kind of creative continuity within the existing law, rather than be radically innovating"; also see generally T. Murphy and R. Rawlings, "After the Ancien Regime: The Writing of Judgments in the House of Lords 1979/1980" 45 *MLR* 34 (1981).

[4] Cf. T.C. Hartley, "The European Court, Judicial Objectivity and the Constitution of the European Union" (1996) 112 *LQR* 95.

To be clear, this Chapter analyses the theme of policy without looking to itemize the range of considerations that can be allocated to the topic other than at a rather generalized level. Individual policies which run with particular remedies (e.g., how the coercive jurisdiction responds to transnational tort/delict duty situations arising in the context of environmental law and policy; how exemplary or punitive damages are viewed in the contexts of compensation and the public interest; how intellectual property rights may be localizable; how, as a matter of policy, the quantum of damages is linked to local values, and so on) are best dealt with in the respective chapters on the various remedies in succeeding Parts. Apart from the foregoing, other standards of adjudication (e.g., requirements of legal certainty, predictability, consistency, uniformity, and so on) which may also be subsumed with policy are taken as known in the present Chapter.

In principle, any form of relief can be awarded by the forum if proper jurisdiction is had, if the facts and the proof of substantive liability are right, and if the other general issues do not counteract the grant of the particular remedy. These policy factors may be read from or into the formal texts of the schemes under which judicial jurisdiction is exercized, rather as is the case with what is involved in extracting the policy bases for adjudication from the text of the judgment. The contemporary, and foreseeably defining, example of jurisdictional policy in its broadest sense must be the Preamble to the *Brussels Convention on Jurisdiction and the Enforcement of Judgments in Civil and Commercial Matters 1968*, as this is incorporated into forum law via the *Civil Jurisdiction and Judgments Act 1982* (and *1991*). The *Convention's* stated central objective is to implement Article 293 of the *Consolidated Version of E.E.C. Treaty*.[5] The legal foundations are territorial, in the interests of harmonizing the relevant legal aspects of the Community.[6] A pervading element of regional consolidation at a profound level is therefore not to be excluded from careful observation of the applications of the transaction-facilitating scheme to which judicial relief necessarily belongs. It gives the scheme a subtext, and the courts' interpretive attitudes are inexorably dynamic, in line with increased familiarity with the requirements of the scheme.

Similar but perhaps less intensified transnationalist policy criteria are present in other arrangements subsisting beyond,[7] entailing, e.g., the Commonwealth. There are many bilateral agreements contained in statutory instruments; these are properly raised in the Chapter on post-judgment enforcement and execution. What must reasonably not be left out of a broader view of transnational

[5] This provision is the old Art. 220 of the original *Treaty of Rome*.

[6] See, e.g., M. Bonell, "The 1968 Brussels Civil Jurisdiction and Judgments Convention and the 1980 Rome Convention on Applicable Law" in B.S. Markesinis (ed.), *The Gradual Convergence* (Oxford, Clarendon; 1994), 146, at 163–164.

[7] See, e.g., the *Administration of Justice Act 1920*, the *Foreign Judgments (Reciprocal Enforcement) Act 1933*. The proposed but unfinished UK/US Judgments Convention also deserves to be mentioned, as to which, see, e.g., P.M. North, "The Draft U.K./U.S. Judgments Convention: A British Viewpoint" (1979) 1 *NwJInt'l L & Bus* 219.

remedialism beyond Europe is that perhaps, in keeping with trends in the international process by which substantive and procedural legal norms are globalized, a more universally consistent geographical spread of the relevant dispositive norms may come about, that the regional context of the European Union may be confirmed to be a definite prototype or matrix. An injunction, albeit in the form of a constitutive declaration, granted by the Bangalore (India) High Court in *Airbus Indistrie G.I.E.* v. *Patel and Others*[8] was not enforceable in England, even though the interests of procedural efficiency could have been served; the result, by which the English forum was non conveniens, was nevertheless asserted by the forum on other bases. The *Rome Convention on the Law Applicable to Contractual Obligations 1980* was applied by Cresswell J. in *Sierra Leone Telecommunications Limited* v. *Barclays Bank plc*,[9] between a non-domiciliary claimant and a local defendant, without the need (properly, the present writer submits) for enquiry as to whether the territorial rules are applicable to a foreign suitor. One would presume that, by the policy of localization, the same law would apply if the hypothesis was that the defendant was not otherwise connected with the jurisdiction other than by reason of the place of performance of the contractual obligation.[10]

The short point for the standpoint of judicial policy as it specifically relates to relief is that there is an (abstract) extra-legal interpretational context to be brought together from these international instruments relating to general jurisdiction, that context is more than perfunctory in the influence it has on the forum's remedial jurisprudence. While its discernible impact on judicial remedies is rather subtle but prevalent as to jurisdictional competence, it is nevertheless at least necessary and reasonable that it be noted because, as one consequence of policy, res judicata does not always automatically cross jurisdictional borders.

Whilst an enduring liberal internationalist policy or attitude may be noticed in judicial resolution of agreement-derived disputes (contracts; personal or marital relations),[11] wherever these may have originated, transnational trends are ostensibly expanding to disputes in which party autonomy and its consequences (e.g., vindication of legal relations freely assumed; protection from wrong as far as is feasible), which itself is a matter of policy the courts are keen to sustain, are not necessarily a prominent characteristic. Judicial objectivity is on the increase.[12]

Alongside this group of generalized considerations, it is worthwhile to take account of further juristic factors such as those discussed by Graveson in the

[8] [1998] 2 All ER 257 (H.L.) [9] [1998] 2 All ER 821.

[10] Cf. The reasoning by which Lord Denning MR applied English law in *Sayers* v. *International Drilling* [1971] 1 WLR 1176 which concerned an offshore tort in Nigerian waters where the claimant was British and the defendant was Dutch.

[11] For example, there is a distinct presumptive policy in favour of marriage or of validating marriages, especially where there is no avoiding law that may be relevant to facts that are themselves indicative of conjugal status in good faith: *Collett* v. *Collett* [1968] P. 482, at 492.

[12] Hartley, *loc. cit.* (n. 4).

contexts of the philosophy of private international law and judicial justice,[13] and of the relevance of the wholly separate matter of public policy. These discrete batches of policy justification (transnational adjudication as policy; specific policy considerations; public policy) influence private international law in a general sense which deserves and has received worthwhile discussion in the literature.[14] The aim of the present Chapter is not to review these general issues of forum policy, although it is natural or inevitable to look to distil or to isolate themes or issues of or pertaining to generalized remedial policy from them. Aware that a different approach or nomenclature could be just as justifiable, the particular intermeshed policies are these: convenience and practicability; rational and judicial justice; efficiency (as the minimization of procedural conflicts); forum and public interest. A recurring policy of localization deserves to be reckoned with. It has been discussed in the second section of the first Chapter. It is manifest in the forum's attitude to forum-shopping as this is encapsulated in the jurisdiction allocation or declination rules. It also features in the next section below. As Carter notes, "[e]very rule of law, and this is no less true of private international law, should, of course, be based upon, and reflect, policy considerations."[15] Such influence as public policy (e.g., as justice and morality), legal mandation or inderogability, and state or governmental interest analysis may have on private international law in relation to judicial relief closes the Chapter.

CONVENIENCE (AS PRACTICABILITY) IN REMEDIAL ADJUDICATION

Convenience[16] or the lack of it may be illustrated in circumstances in which formal redress of proven liability involves undesirable consequences analogous to, but not quite in the sense of, contrariness to public policy. This present discussion takes further the relevant portion of the first Chapter. Consider that ownership of a copyright properly registered under the laws of country A is proved to have been infringed by an English domiciliary in an English claim, that the claim goes as far as proof of liability because the sole issue contested by the defendant is the propriety of having been sued, it being the case that there

[13] *Comparative Conflict of Laws: Selected Essays* (Amsterdam, North-Holland; 1977), Two Vols., Vol. 1, at 14–50 ("Philosophical Aspects of the English Conflict of Laws") and 51–65 ("Judicial Justice as a Contemporary Basis of the English Conflict of Laws").

[14] A fair selection must include J.J. Fawcett "Policy Considerations in Choice of Law"(1984) 47 *MLR* 650, A.J.E. Jaffey, "Foundations of Rules for the Choice of Law" (1982) 2 *OJLS* 368, especially at 372 *et seq.*, F.V. Harper, "Policy Bases of the Conflict of Laws" (1947) 56 *Yale LJ* 115.

[15] "The Role of Public Policy in English Private International Law"(1993) 42 *ICLQ* 1.

[16] It is possibly necessary to avoid misgivings or association between "convenience" and the jurisdictional doctrine of forum (non) conveniens, the latter being concerned with jurisdiction acquisition or declination on the basis that the forum concerned (and no other) is the most appropriate court in which trial ought on all good principle to take place. That the forum is jurisdictionally conveniens is far from the issue of what the forum can conveniently, in the sense of practicably, do in furtherance of a claimant's substantive entitlement. Cf. Chapter One, text at nn. 23–24.

are co-infringers, not domiciled in the jurisdiction, who are subject to similar proceedings elsewhere. In order for the forum to grant relief against the English defendant, there would be involved the question whether English copyright law, local or territorial by definition as it is, can be interpreted so as to accommodate the claim originating from foreign law;[17] that is, whether the claim can be localized in terms that would, e.g., set a precedent for other subsequent claims of the same type.[18]

This interpretation and its result would involve an inconvenience, even if it has to be conceded that the claim was in fact justiciable according to forum procedural law in the sense that the forum was able to reach a result based on the relevant substantive foreign law having satisfactorily been proved. It is impracticable for the forum to formally proceed to award redress on the basis of analogy simply because substantive liability is accepted and, had the circumstances been wholly local, there could have been relief under forum procedural law. As Aldous L.J. maintained in *Plastus Kreativ A.B.* v. *Minnesota Mining and Manufacturing Company*,[19] "[a] finding of infringement is a finding that a monopoly granted by the state is to be enforced . . . That result should . . . come about from a decision of a court situated in the state where the public have to pay the higher prices." The question why wholly foreign circumstances should otherwise be subject to the convenience of the forum and, likely subtly, of its domestic legal precepts is not easily answerable other than in terms that, from a practical perspective, the action be pursued elsewhere because of structural lacunae in private international legal relations and adjudication.

Where jurisdiction is properly had and exercised in a particular cause, the question whether a particular remedy is to be made available follows affirmative response to the primary question of justiciability (i.e., that there is legal liability in the defendant). It may not be formally possible to take remediability further; the available remedial forms may not precisely co-ordinate with the liability where the liability originates under a different legal system.[20] The conceptual apparatus of forum jurisprudence is not elastic enough—nor must it be—to accommodate certain kinds of substantive liability, so that there are inherent limitations on what the forum can do in terms of legal redress in those situations where the nature of the applied law is inapposite to the forum's machinery. In either set of circumstances, the convenience with which the forum can adjudicate is curtailed; it is inconvenient for the forum to exercise its

[17] Such were the facts in *Pearce* v. *Ove Arup Partnership Ltd. & Others* [1997] Ch. 293; see the present writer's Note in 9 AJICL 673 (1997) (prepared before the subsequent appeal in the case). See also L. Collins *et al. Dicey and Morris' The Conflict of Laws* (12th ed., London, Sweet & Maxwell; 1993), 4th Supplement (1997), at 232; at 170 of the main text (discussing Rule 17): convenience also concerns the conduct of "the trial of a case containing foreign elements in a manner with which the court is unfamiliar."

[18] Cf. R.A. Posner, *The Problems of Jurisprudence* (New York, OUP; 1990), at 86: "[U]nless the precedent is authoritative in announcing a major premise that cannot be questioned, it can be a source only of data that are anecdotal in character or of reasons, considerations, values, policies..."

[19] [1995] RPC 438, at 447.

[20] *Phrantzes* v. *Argenti* [1960] 2 QB 19 (per Lord Parker C.J.)

prescriptive jurisdiction. Without putting too fine a point on it, the scope of this book cannot admit of legal or legalistic relationships which are naturally alien to the legal system either because of the type of norms involved in such relationships or because they cannot be conveniently characterized.

As to remedialism, the reaches of convenience so described may be taken as manifest in the positive terms of flexibility in the forum's dispute resolution mechanisms where this can be reasonably accomplished without undue expense to legal system and litigants. The present writer submits that the declaratory jurisdiction discussed in Section D, in contrast with the constitutive, must in this light be a unique item in the remedial armoury, availing a claimant of an enabling minimal formal confirmation of legal rights capable of transnational application where all else would fail. But there remains an innominate lacuna. The explanation of the type of notional incapacitation imposed by other local rights' enforcement machinery is not necessarily always convincing or satisfactory. Claims which would fail under local law could just the same be brought if they would succeed under the applicable law. To extrapolate from what Mann said in relation to an ostensible wholly local context, "[o]ne cannot help feeling that there exists at present a certain tendency towards expediency, expedition, efficiency, economy, streamlining. Any measure which is liable to prejudice the quality or the dignity of the judicial process for the sake of reaching any of these aims, praiseworthy in themselves, is bound to give rise to misgivings."[21]

So much for a description of the judicial policy of convenience or practicability. It suffices to recognize it as a cognitive juridical benchmark for pragmatism, that its roots and foundations are in forum jurisprudence, mutable or adaptable as that jurisprudence reasonably is in response to requirements from the relevant other legal system. It transpires in succeeding sections of the Chapter that there may well be other policy considerations which could positively influence the availability of relief where, in particular, flexibility of positive response is not to be withheld by the forum.

RATIONAL OR JUDICIAL JUSTICE

A pair of House of Lords' decisions which have, in principle as well as in actuality, not quite since been repeated illustrate the berth of the forum's international competence based on the policy of doing rational justice.[22] The flexibility of approach, redolent of the Lord Wilberforce's speech in *Chaplin* v. *Boys*,[23] "to take account of the varying interests and considerations of policy which may arise when foreign elements are present", is not necessarily the type which is generally to be identified in the case law. *National Bank of Greece and Athens S.A.* v. *Metliss*[24] and *Adams* v. *National Bank of Greece S.A.*[25] respectively

[21] "Reflections on English Civil Justice and the Rule of Law" (1983) 2 *CivJQ* 320, at 335–336.
[22] Graveson, *op. cit.*, at 33 ("the dominant principle of rational justice").
[23] [1971] AC 356, at 391. [24] [1958] AC 509. [25] [1961] AC 255.

involved claims to recover contract sums due from a third party where the proper law of the contract could have been either forum law or a foreign lex causae. If it was the latter, which incidentally was also the third party corporation's lex domicilii, the result would have been that the defendant-respondent third party would have been statutorily protected from having to pay the sums if the claims had been brought in its domiciliary forum. If the proper law was forum law—as it was held by Sellers J. at first instance and by the House of Lords (reversing the the Court of Appeal)—then the lex domicilii had no effect whatever with the result that the sums claimed were perfectly recoverable from the third party qua the "universal successor"[26] of the contractual party. More to the present policy of judicial justice, had the respective alternative governing laws been separately construed, the result would have been an inflexible policy-excluding application which would make little of the claimant's provable and recognizable substantive right.

It sounds in the much-quoted passage from the judgment of Cardozo J. in *Loucks* v. *Standard Oil Company of New York*[27] that:

> "[i]f aid is to be withheld here, it must be because the cause of action in its nature offends our sense of justice or menaces the public welfare . . . The courts are not free to refuse to enforce a foreign right at the pleasure of the judges, to suit the individual notion of expediency or fairness. They do not close their doors unless help would violate some fundamental principle of justice, some prevalent conception of good morals, some deep-rooted tradition of the common weal."

Chaplin v. *Boys* rests on identical explanations which, however, are more giving to conceptual rationalization and therefore more readily lend themselves to precedent than their Lordships' dicta in *Adams* and in *Metliss*. Indeed, perhaps it simply means that the policy of rational justice is best understood as substantively different from that judicial flexibility. For one thing flexibility may result in the application of foreign law, just as it may indicate the scope for internal law in a conflicts case in which foreign law might otherwise be deemed to be the correctly applicable law.[28] What the respective sets of remedial decision may be described to have in common is that neither was precedented, so that much was left to judicial inventiveness in the absence of conceptual certainty.

[26] *Metliss*, at 524–525.

[27] [1918] 224 NY 99, at 110–111.

[28] For a critique which is essentially an eloquent plea for flexibility, see P.B. Carter, "Priorities of Claims in Private International Law" (1983) *LIV BYBIL* 207, based on *Bankers Trust International Limited* v. *Todds Shipyards Corporation, The Halcyon Isle* [1981] AC 221 (P.C.), in which their Lordships' House was divided as to the scope for the *lex fori* in determining questions of priority where the claims in rem were conflictive. To have proceeded on the basis that these questions were procedural, as the majority did (per Lord Diplock, e.g., at 229), and thus for the lex fori, involved the notion that the issues were wholly domestic. Lords Salmon and Scarman (e.g., at 246) thought otherwise, that the affirmative issue was whether English law recognized the foreign construction of the same concept of English law, with a view to resolution by English law on that basis. The same approach can be advanced as to remedial concept; indeed, the issue in *The Halcyon Isle*, the (maritime) lien, is itself remedial.

Whether, for example, this may connote a substantivist or proper law approach specifically for remedies and, if at all so, how it does so is properly part of the Chapter on applicable remedial law because its resolution hinged on the identification and selection of the proper law as forum law from which (restitutionary) relief followed. The residual point by which relief would have been denied if relevant non-forum law was applied was conveniently displaced—as it was in *Chaplin* v. *Boys*—by the policy of providing relief (returning money to the right owner) in circumstances in which it was rational to have done so. The desirability of ascertaining the dimensions of particular policy, especially in the case of foreign rules, was not better illustrated.

EFFICIENCY: MINIMIZING PROCEDURAL CONFLICTS

On the premiss that the law of remedies is procedural law, it is rudimentary that, in the transnational context, a minimum enforcement formality of judgments is necessary, either because its objective is to conclusively ratify normative facts sourced in non-forum law or because the relief the forum is aiming to dispense is interlocutory and thus not likely to alter rights which may originate elsewhere. Further, principles of comity require that the legal process of the relevant foreign jurisdiction(s) in which the relief is to be applied be a feature, at some decisional level which depends on the enforcement requirements of the particular relief.

If one asserts with Kramer[29] that "[c]onflicts between the forum's procedural policies and another state's substantive policies are especially likely with respect to rules that serve both substantive and procedural purposes", that "[a forum's] preference for forum procedural interests contrasts sharply with the treatment of substance/procedure conflicts", and that "the ultimate purpose of procedural law is to implement substantive law accurately and efficiently", then, in relation to remedies as procedure, one is identifying the substantive element in formal relief as well as asserting that the minimization of procedural conflicts is much less of an issue in the case of final or substantive relief. Choosing the legal system or environment from which one is to obtain a remedy necessarily implies a substantive trade-off: the remedy available in a relevant but uncontested forum is, for whatever valid reason, not favoured by the claimant in England. But this is the substantive conflict which may or may not be usefully separable from the procedural conflict at issue in this section.

Consider this example: should the circumstances of an equitable wrong be capable of giving rise to compensation and restitution, the former restoring loss and the latter re-directing the wrongdoer's gain, it has happened that judgment is entered on both counts without the need for directions as to election having been considered necessary. Such were the circumstances in *Tang Man Sit*

[29] "Rethinking Choice of Law" (1990) 90 *ColumLRev* 277, in the order in which the passages appear above, at 326, 327 and 329.

(deceased) v. *Capacious Investments Limited*[30] in which a performed building contract led on to the buildings subsequent user having caused them to degenerate. Relying on decisions like those of Lightman J. in *Island Records Limited* v. *Tring International plc*[31] in which the need for election of relief to be made before judgment was clarified, the Privy Council (Lord Nicholls of Birkenhead's speech) went further to recognize the possibility that, exceptionally,[32] election may not be finalized or substantive relief may reduce the claimant's entitlement even after election may have been made. The policy issue being that double recovery is to be discountenanced and prevented at all cost, the solution must be that, in the case of final remedies in which there is an undeniable substantive core, there is little in the nature of a substantively justified policy—local or foreign—by which the procedural policy that runs with the matter of the form of relief opted for can be affected one way or the other. Therefore, a cautionary note is necessary in the context of the policy of minimizing procedural conflicts, mindful that such conflicts do arise where the forum's relief is so discrepant from the remedy afforded by the applied substantive law. The redeeming factor is that the claimant will, in selecting the forum for adjudication, have made a trade-off, and any improbable consequences ought really not be attributed to the legal structure. In the best context, of international procedural unification,[33] in which substantive entitlement can be quite divergently reasoned out among systems and in which integration is not appreciated in consistent terms, the necessity for minimization cannot be accomplished simply for its own sake nor, as far as the present writer is aware, has it been so postulated.

Minimizing procedural conflicts, as a policy factor, is integral to the conflict of laws and is probably best illustrated in the discussion of antisuit injunctions in Chapter Eight. A different facet of the same policy is the question of remedial effectiveness, the extent to which relief forthcoming from the forum tangibly relieves the aggrieved claimant whose substantive entitlement is settled; the material aspects of jurisdictional effectiveness are discussed in the context of post-judgment enforcement in Chapter Five.

LEGAL MANDATION, PUBLIC POLICY, STATE INTEREST

The application of the forms of forum law is mandatory if the claimant is seeking relief from the forum. It is trite that certain types of relief are not available for particular kinds of infringement. English law regards some types of monetary award as contrary to policy. Foreign laws characterized by the forum as

30 [1996] 2 WLR 192.

31 [1995] 3 All ER 444.

32 E.g., in *Mahesan* v. *Malaysia Government Officers Co-operative Housing Association Ltd.* [1979] AC 374 for alternative but inconsistent relief claims from a fraudulent agent selling property at an undervalue.

33 Cf. K.D. Kerameus, "Procedural Unification: The Need and the Limitation" in I.R. Scott, *International Perspectives on Civil Justice* (London, Sweet & Maxwell; 1990), 47, at 55 *et seq.*

penal or as relating to revenue cannot, directly or otherwise, be enforced in England.[34] An illegal contract may be declared void from its inception so that no award of damages can flow from its supposed breach. However, no marriage can be pronounced void from its inception whatever be the background circumstances, nor can pronouncements of illegitimacy be made about extra-marital offspring. Breach of a valid contract primarily attracts relief in compensation rather than in performance. A contract not typically specifically enforceable cannot be the subject of a mandatory injunction to compel performance. A settlor's incapacity under a penal foreign law will not be upheld because the basis is in penal, thus inapplicable foreign, law, nor can concubinary status be upheld even if it is valid by a foreign law. There is a distinctive attitude to upholding marital relationships whether they are celebrated under local law or otherwise, as Part II of the *Private International Law (Miscellaneous Provisions) 1995* suggests in its provisions on potentially polygamous unions. There is an unpejorative expansionist policy in adapting longer-standing forms of relief to the requirements of the pace of international or global civil and commercial activity, as the relevant parcels of the Chapters on damages (e.g., under European law), restitutionary and injunctive relief indicate.

Less accepted in English conflict of laws is the notion that the interest a state has in its laws can be resorted to by the conflicts forum, for example, to justify exclusive application of those laws.[35] But it is said on some authority that, in the context of transnational torts, "[t]he state which has the greatest interest is the state where both parties are resident",[36] from which it is reasonably harmless to infer the unsurprizing axiom that the exclusively applicable remedial forms are those of that state. Thus, policy considerations which ordinarily arise in connexion with choosing the law by which to resolve causae are also pertinent to the formalism of relief, in line with contemporary trends in objectifying rationales for relief away from the exclusive application of forum law.

It is practically undebatable that public policy is different from, broader than, the scope of judicial policy, and that a useful context for appraising or being appraised of the latter is the former. Therefore, if, as it has been persuasively argued,[37] the commendable internationalism (i.e., reckoning with foreign law and policy) of English conflict of laws has subtly produced an altogether more refined application of public policy-based exceptions to issues of private

[34] Cf. *Empresa Exportadora de Azucar* v. *Industria Azucarera Nacional SA (The Playa Larga)* [1983] 2 LlR 171, at 190 (per Ackner LJ): "[T]he Court must look at all the circumstances, and then consider whether the law is so far-reaching in its scope and effect as *really* to offend againsy public policy".

[35] Cf. J.J. Fawcett "Is American Governmental Interest Analysis the Solution to English Tort Choice of Law Problems?" (1982) 31 *ICLQ* 150, especially his concluding remarks at 166.

[36] C.G.J. Morse *Torts in Private International Law* (London, North-Holland; 1978), at 286; cf. Lowenfeld, *op. cit.*, as he identifies a compelling nexus between state law and private law as a basis for refining the quality of private international law.

[37] N. Enonchong "Public Policy in the Conflict of Laws: A Chinese Wall Around Little England?" (1996) 45 *ICLQ* 633; but see generally P.B. Carter, "Rejection of Foreign Law:Some Private International Law Inhibitions" (1984) LV *BYBIL* 111.

transnational legal liability, then there is little need to deliberate whether and to what extent public policy unduly impacts upon remedial competence. Public or state policy does not significantly reach the remedial competence of the forum, other than in connexion with the regulation of transactions that are, for grounds of public policy, not justiciable. A recent example is the ruling of Mance J in *Kuwait Airways Corporation* v. *Iraqi Airways Company and Another*.[38] It is more useful to look to contemporary aspects of transnational adjudication—substantivist rationales and objective judicial remedialism which does still not lose sight of formalism—to which attention turns in the next Chapter.

[38] *The Times*, 12th May 1998.

4

Applicable remedial law

WHERE ARE WE NOW?

THE GENERAL DESCRIPTION of the law on remedies, as comprising elements of both adjectival and substantive law, has been discussed in various places in this book. This well-supported interpretation[1] of Dicey and Morris' Rule 17[2] epitomizes remedies as procedure and thus for the lex fori, is neither to be regarded as heretical nor taken to be expansionist or suggestive of remedial law as random or any less predictable. Perhaps what needs to be clearly stated is that "remedies as procedure" ought really to be understood as referring to forms, that any type of relief is first recognizable from its formal attributes. There is little that is formal about remedial policy. There is likewise not much that is procedural or adjectival, for example, about the rule that effective substantive rationalization of most forms of equitable (coercive) relief depends on whether recompense should reasonably conciliate the claimant. Indeed, the ostensibly restrictive cast of Rule 17 is perhaps best appreciated, even by the uninitiated foreign litigant, as a prime example of legal formalism of the kind which makes interpretive requirements of anyone seeking to rely on or to apply its verbal fixity.

The Comment to the text of Dicey and Morris' Rule 17 and its equivalents in the Common Law world,[3] as well as the elaboration of particular relief in the relevant Chapters of this book, make this requirement clear. The requirement is strengthened by a standpoint[4] which advocates minimal restraint as to the scope of applicability for foreign law in respect of nominally procedural issues in the conflict of laws. Because remedies are significantly substantive, it is, within reason, fair to seek to rationalize the availability of formal relief in terms of a non-forum lex causae by which substantive liability is established, not simply because therein lies the intellectual venture that is the conflict of laws in international litigation but because, the present writer submits, the exercise prescribes the limits of convenience-based adjudication.

[1] Jurisprudence texts as well as textbooks on remedies make this much clear.

[2] L. Collins *et al.* (eds.), *Dicey and Morris' The Conflict of Laws* (12th ed., London, Sweet & Maxwell; 1993), at 169.

[3] Notably the American Law Institute's *Restatement of the Conflict of Laws: Second* (St. Paul, Minnesota, A.L.I. Publishers; 1971), e.g., at paras. 122 *et seq*. and 171.

[4] See generally R. Fentiman, *Foreign Law in English Courts* (Oxford, Clarendon; 1998), e.g., at 286 *et seq*.

Where better for a contemporary practical analysis to prudently begin, relatively uncontradicted and abreast of today's conflicts litigation, than in the conceptually substantivist area of transnational restitution law, drawing from the range of types of remedy. What transpires as sauce for remedial restitution is also sauce for other conflicts relief, because notional analogues—liability and relief—are equivalent in general remedial adjudication. The context for discussion is propitiously provided by the decision of the Outer House of the Scots Court of Session in *Baring Brothers & Company Limited* v. *Cunninghame District Council*,[5] hereafter *Barings*. The rest of the Chapter consists of a case study of the facts and decision.

BARINGS: A CASE STUDY

Every legal subject has its own distinct basic concepts and terminology, to facilitate judicial resolution of causes of action belonging to the given subject and to provide tenets for describing or dealing with the issues arising. So it is that the Common Law concept of "the proper law" has been applied to elements of disputes which are beyond the scope of forum law. Jurisdictional and procedural matters, which broadly conceptualized must include remedies, have never been resolved by reference to the proper law. However, Briggs has shown that an analogous notion of propriety can be used to describe justifications for other types of question, e.g. recognition and enforcement of foreign judgments,[6] that are notionally related to jurisdiction; remedies are granted or withheld in the form of a judgment. It is therefore a matter of importance that the term, proper law, was deployed in the context of relief in the report of the decision in *Barings*, much to the disinterest of the extensive and stimulating commentary generated in response to the decision as to the substantive issues of choice-of-law in agreement-related unjustifiable enrichment conflicts.[7] These issues involved resort to "the proper law of the obligation" to restore under a contract void from its inception. The full facts are presently described.

In its characteristic form, the concept of the proper law is relevant, according to the courts, in relation to contract conflicts, and it is typically expressed

[5] [1996] TLR 538 (Lord Penrose). The writer would like to thank the editors of the Denning Law Journal (1998), for permission to adapt portions of his article in which much of the ensuing comment was expressed. Further, he wishes to acknowledge the generous edifying response of The Right Honourable The Lord Mackay of Clashfern to the writer's humble request for better comprehension of Scots law. The present Chapter affords a most welcome opportunity to refine, as may be useful, some of the ideas contained in that article.

[6] In "Which Foreign Judgments Should We Recognise Today?"(1987) 36 *ICLQ* 240, especially at 250 *et seq*. His propositions are derived from reciprocity, rather than obligation, as the foundation for the relevant jurisdictional competence.

[7] E.g., generally, J. Bird, "Choice of Law and Restitution of Benefits Conferred Under a Void Contract: Baring Bros. *v*. Cunninghame DC" [1997] *LMCLQ* 182. Other more genralized commentary on restitution/enrichment conflicts well before the *Barings* case include H. Gutteridge and K. Lipstein, "Conflicts of Law in Matters of Unjustifiable Enrichment" 7 (1941) *CLJ* 80. Others more recent turn up in the course of the Chapter.

in the terms of objective ascertainment of the law which, either by the parties' express choice or by considered circumstantial implication from the contract, is to govern issues arising. The contract is then taken to be "most significantly connected or related" to one particular substantive jurisdiction rather than another, without necessarily implying that every conceivable issue relating to the contract is to be referred to that jurisdiction. The conclusive attractions of proper law doctrine have been embraced outside the Common Law world, notably by states signatory to the *Rome Convention on the Law Applicable to Contractual Obligations 1980*, the *Rome Convention*. Subject to some modification and reservation,[8] the Convention applies in Britain via the *Contracts (Applicable Law) Act 1990*. Proper law doctrine is the subject of considerable scholarly literature, e.g. as to its enduring character,[9] its severability,[10] indeed as to the indebtedness of general private international law's progress to it. Its main feature, its flexibility,[11] is at once the main reason for its approval as it is a basis for its possible misapprehension, as may have been occasioned in *Barings*.

There have been various approaches to extending the scope of the doctrine beyond its reach in transnational contract law. Morris[12] persuasively argued in favour of its conceptual potential in tort conflicts situations as this was subsequently taken up in United States' courts, for example, in the celebrated case of *Babcock* v. *Jackson*.[13] English courts have not accepted the concept of a proper law of a tort. Indeed, the scope of the contractual proper law hardly extends to tort issues arising in concurrent liability cases where a tort coincides with breach of contract (with the further incidence of liability limitation) as was maintained in *Sayers* v. *International Drilling Company S.A.*[14] At the Court of Appeal stage of *Chaplin* v. *Boys*,[15] an issue-specific version (i.e., in contrast with one that is broadly specified by the cause-of action) of the proper law of a tort was applied but over-ruled on appeal to the House of Lords.[16] But for express inversion in *Red Sea Insurance Limited* v. *Bouygues SA*,[17] there are dicta in the leading opinion in the case which might be construed to suggest some acknowledgment of the scope for an unprotracted issue-specific version of the doctrine in the context of transnational torts, founded on a policy of

[8] One of these is contained in s. 2(2) of the *1990 Contracts Act*, to the effect that art. 10(1)(e) of the convention—that the proper law applies to "the consequences of nullity of the contract"—is without force of law in the UK.

[9] Pace F.A. Mann, "The Proper Law of the Contract—An Obituary" (1991) 107 *LQR* 353.

[10] Cf. C. McLachlan, "Splitting the Proper Law in the Conflict of Laws" (1990) LXI *BYBIL* 311.

[11] E.g., F.A. Mann, "The Proper Law in the Conflict of Laws" (1987) 36 *LQR* 437. Fentiman's is pretty much a lone voice that has usefully related the term to matrimony, in, "The Validity of Marriage and the Proper Law" (1985) 44 *CLJ* 256.

[12] In "The Proper Law of a Tort" (1951) 64 *Harv L Rev* 881, and previously (1946) 62 *LQR* 180.

[13] 191 NE 279 (1963); see also *Kilberg* v. *Northern Airlines Inc.* 9 NY (2d.) 34 (1961), and for a discussion of the broader jurisdictional framework, see K. Siehr, "Traffic Accidents" in C. McLachlan and Hon. Peter Nygh (eds.), *Transnational Tort Litigation: Jurisdictional Principles* (Oxford, Clarendon; 1996), at 192.

[14] [1971] 3 All ER 163. [15] [1968] 2 QB 1. [16] [1971] AC 356, at 389 and 391.

[17] [1995] 1 AC 190, at 206 (per Lord Slynn of Hadley).

flexibility in identifying the applicable substantive law.[18] On the issue of relief, one might be inclined to presume that were the lex delicti to contain remedial rules, such rules would be applicable where no other reason (e.g. public policy, incompatibility of forum and lex delicti forms) dictates otherwise.

What is most important is that there is neither judicial nor other authority for extending proper law rationales to questions other than those arising contractually. Mindful of a distinct substantivist characteristic of issues of jurisdiction (e.g., those aspects which involve the exercise of judicial discretion or which are not strictly to be defined as pertaining to judicial administration or the management of litigation) which does not necessarily receive much attention, and of the truism that judicial relief is an ultimate test of the efficacy of the judicial process, it is proposed to explore the particular circumstances of the *Barings* case in point.

THE FACTS AND THE CONTENTIONS

Barings is one of many cases[19] which arose from agreements between a number of local authorities acting ultra vires on the one hand and several banks on the other, with the exception of the decision of the Court of Appeal in *Macmillan* in which the parties were a communications company and an investment company, and the subject matter was confined by the court to whether the lex situs governs issues of priority to ownership of shares in the wider framework of restitution conflicts.[20] In *Barings*, the pursuers were a bank who with the defenders had made a forward-rate swap agreement, defined in *Barclays Bank plc* v. *Glasgow City Council*[21] as being essentially "a futures contract, the financial outcome of which depends on future movements in interest rates." The British Bankers Association's standard form specifically developed for these agreements was used, providing for English law as the lex causae. In furtherance of the supposed contract, the defendants had paid monies to the pursuers and, on this basis, the latter had paid back larger sums which both

[18] Ibid., especially at 207–208: "The exception [to the application of English law] is not limited to specific isolated issues but may apply to the whole claim, for example, where all or virtually all of the significant factors are in favour of the *lex loci delicti*." Cf. S. 11(2) (c) *Private International Law (Miscellaneous Provisions) Act 1995*, the *1995 Act*, by which multi-locality torts are subject to the law of the country in which the most significant element(s) of the events constituting the tort or delict in question occurred.

[19] Other similar fact cases include *Barclays Bank plc* v. *Glasgow City Council; Kleinwort Benson Ltd* v. *Glasgow City Council* [1994] 4 All ER 864; *Westdeutsche Landesbank Girozentrale* v. *Islington London Borough Council* [1994] 4 All ER 890; *Kleinwort Benson Ltd.* v. *Sandwell Borough Council; Kleinwort Benson Ltd* v. *South Tyneside Metropolitan Borough Council* [1994] 4 All ER 972; *Morgan Guaranty Trust Co.* v. *Lothian Regional Council* 1995 SLT 299 (in which the earlier English case of *Hazell* v. *Hammersmith and Fulham Borough Council* [1990] 2 QB 697 is examined); *Macmillan Inc* v. *Bishopsgate Investment Trust plc (No.3)* [1996] 1 All ER 585.

[20] Cf. J. Stevens, "Restitution or Property? Priority and Title to Shares in the Conflict of Laws" (1996) 59 MLR 741 and A. Dickinson, "Restitution and the Conflict of Laws" [1996] *LMCLQ* 556.

[21] *Loc. cit.* above, at n. 19, at 882–883, per Lloyd LJ.

parties had believed to be due under the contract. The transaction was subsequently agreed as having been ultra vires the defenders and, therefore, void from its inception, following the decision in *Morgan Guaranty Trust Company* v. *Lothian Regional Council*, hereafter *Morgan*. These transactions were first held to be void in England in *Hazell* v. *Hammersmith and Fulham Borough Council*. From the perspective of practical advice, it may be questioned why a Scottish local authority had agreed to subject the vires aspects of its activities to rules other than those of its parent legal system. This was not an issue in the case.

The pursuers in the case in hand had asserted English law, the supposed governing law of the agreement, as the only legal system which not only applied but did so to allow a restitutionary remedy. The policy basis for the assertion was simple: that the legally regulated obligation ought in all good conscience to be remediable, the presumption being, as the record of the case infers, that English law would literally allow the Scots forum to avail them of the Scots restitutionary remedy of payment. More of this aspect of the overall circumstances in due course. The pursuers had derived their entitlement to restitutionary relief from the restitutionary right to recover the excess by which the defenders were unjustifiably enriched. By Scots law, the defenders' lex domicilii, the claim was extinguished by prescription under Section 6 of the *Prescription and Limitation (Scotland) Act 1973*. The action had persisted ostensibly because, limitation being substantive and to be referred to the lex contractus, English law as the supposed proper law did not extinguish it. That the claim had been brought in the defenders' forum domicilii, rather than in England as the jurisdiction of the parties' supposed choice of governing law, was ostensibly well within the defendant-protecting policy of the applicable jurisdictional rule contained in Article 2 of the *Brussels Convention on Jurisdiction and the Enforcement of Judgments in Civil and Commercial Matters 1968*, the *Brussels Convention*.[22] The defenders argued that in accordance with *Morgan*, there was no claim to restitution, even though they did not implicitly deny that they were enriched nor did they assert any defence to the enrichment.

The main questions arising concerned, first, the extent to which the issues and ratio in *Morgan*—a case pleaded, argued and decided as a domestic case although there was a choice-of-law clause in favour of English law—could apply to *Barings*, the latter to all intents and purposes being a conflicts case. This issue was disposed of by distinguishing the cases further on the point that the wholly domestic Scots circumstances and, consequently, the test applied in the former did not divulge the best deployable methodology for the latter case in identifying the legal system with which the quasi-contractual obligational situation was most closely related.

[22] The question of the right forum turns up in due course of the Chapter. It strengthens the basis for considering "procedure" (as jurisdiction and (remedial) judgment) in identical terms, differently from "substance" or "merits" of an obligational situation. To reiterate, the latter are the typical subjects of proper law theory.

The second and more interesting question, as was expressed by the court, was whether the proper law which validates a contract also determined the nature and extent of an available restitutionary remedy. It is to be noted that, in the present case, the contract itself was incapable of being validated howsoever (not even by the parties' supposed choice of law), because it was void. The jurisdictional reason why the litigation took place in Scotland may be recalled but it need not be repeated.

THE ISSUES: "PROPER LAW", "REMEDY"

The ratio in the decision of the Lord Penrose, allowing a proof before hearing[23] in the action, was that the law of the remedy sought (of payment) was not necessarily also the supposed contractual lex causae. The result, by which Scots law of payment applied, was consistent with his judgment in *Morgan*. His Lordship proceeded to entertain proof of the relevant provisions of the law of the physical locus of the contract (England, by reason of the material connexions) which might or might not have been the proper law of the (void) agreement. The result, technically his answer, was that the proper law did not, qua validating law, necessarily apply to the availability of the given remedy. This finding is neither difficult to grasp nor, by analogy, different from the conceptual separation of enrichment as causa from restitution as relief, the first being governed by the substantive law of the enrichment and the latter by forum law of forms. These laws could of course overlap where forum law is also lex causae.

Invitingly significant considerations for the ripening law of enrichment conflicts are raised, mostly because of the frequent and even casual references to considerations of propriety of the typically procedural matter of remedial forms. His Lordship rightly observed that these and related questions had been "the subject of debate among eminent jurists and other commentators, but had received little attention from the courts", that "there was no binding authority and that there was a lack of convincing analysis in such authority as existed on the critical issues in the case."[24] He opted for a flexible approach[25] which was reminiscent of Lord Wilberforce's predilection for flexibility in *Chaplin* v. *Boys* as to the different matter of the lex delicti for tort conflicts, as well as of Blaikie.[26] Similar open-ended application may, in general terms, be identified in Sections 6 and 221 of the American Law Institute's *Restatement of the Conflict of Laws Second*. Of itself, his Lordship's decisive preference (as to substantive liability law, the writer submits) may well have explained the use of the term "the proper law of the restitutionary remedy", not least because he did not

[23] Under S. 72 *Court of Session Act 1868*, to enable the facts in issue to be established before trial on the merits.

[24] At 13 of the transcript.

[25] At 16 of the transcript.

[26] J. Blaikie, "Unjust Enrichment in the Conflict of Laws" [1984] *JR* 112.

consider the non-enrichment ramifications of his preference, nor was he required by counsel to have done so.

It is neither unusual nor necessarily incorrect to associate "claim" or "action" with "remedy", without referring to the discrete formal aspects of "remedy". Bird observes that "[t]he reality is that restitution actions which arise out of void contracts are, in a sense, merely contractual remedies and the law which declares the contract to be void is the most suitable to regulate the consequences of that finding."[27] Thus, "action" and "remedy", the latter construed in its weaker sense to be synonymous with the former, both go to the redress of the deleterious effects of a contract or other obligational situation. Furthermore, the ongoing unpacking of the law of restitution conflicts is pervaded by its choice-of-law aspects mostly because of the novelty of the subject area in English conflicts law[28] and because of the important divergences of approach between restitution systems,[29] so that in comparativist terms, the disparacy of origins, applications and policies between or among systems makes flexibility of approach in the judgment or decisional forum particularly attractive. All the same, an "action" is for a "remedy" and the remedy can be analysed of itself without necessarily requiring its being related to the particular underlying causa which itself may deserve separate attention.

Granted that the term "the proper law of a restitutionary remedy" may simply have been a misnomer for the law applicable to the substance of the enrichment, ampler discussion is nonetheless worthwhile because of the sheer but unacknowledged novelty of the use of the term, with a host of implications. For instance, the use of this term might signify that the type of question which arises in connexion with a remedy could be analysed in greater detail to determine whether one aspect or other could be governed by the law of another state. Herein lies the difference between conceptualizing remedies in the conflict of laws and developing a "proper law of the remedy". Either goes to applicable remedial law, but the former is the present writer's preference. The forum-oriented consequentialism of the decision (i.e., the long-standing association of "remedies as procedure" with forum law, as with Dicey & Morris' Rule 17) makes the decision the ideal medium for the discussion that now follows, beginning with the responsive intersection between "substance" and "remedy". The added factor is that the circumstances were balanced between Scotland and England, and these respective legal systems did have significantly well-founded claims to being applicable to the dispute.

[27] *Loc. cit.*, at 186.

[28] Cf. F.D. Rose, *Restitution and the Conflict of Laws* (Oxford, Mansfield; 1995); A. Briggs, "Restitution Meets the Conflict of Laws *(Macmillan v.* Bishopsgate*)*" [1995] *RLR* 94; J. Bird, "Restitution's Uncertain Progress—Macmillan *v.* Bishopsgate" [1995] *LMCLQ* 308. Departures which attend to remedial restitution in local law are discussed by K. Barker, "Rescuing Remedialism in Unjust Enrichment Law: Why Remedies are Right" (1998) 57 *CLJ* 301, especially at 304–306, 318–326, and G. Virgo, "What is the Law of Restitution About?" in W.R. Cornish, R. Nolan, J. O'Sullivan and G. Virgo (eds.), *Restitution Past, Present and Future: Essays in Honour of Gareth Jones* (Oxford, Hart; 1998), 305. Chapter Ten of this book refers.

[29] See, e.g., B. Dickson, "Unjust Enrichment Claims: A Comparative Overview" (1995) 54 *CLJ* 100.

THE DECISION AND ITS CONSEQUENCES AND IMPLICATIONS

The decision was based on the differentiation of the pursuers' enforceable restitutionary right to recover from the defenders' enrichment. As the defenders argued, the respective concepts could in a suitable case be conveniently governed by different legal systems: for example, the former would have to be subject to forum law and the latter would be governed by the lex causae. This would accord with normal conflicts methodology which co-ordinates remediability by the forum with the substantive law, and by which ascertainment of a legal entitlement originating from a non-forum lex causae does not automatically convert the entitlement into a remedially enforceable right. Thus, if the right to recover and the form of recovery are considered to be one and the same issue because they may have been established by reference to the same law, then there can be little analytical or practical difficulty. As was the case in *Barings*, the precepts need to be conceptualized as separate and subject to the correct law(s). There being a forum remedy, and proof of unjust enrichment, are best considered disjunctively lest they be taken to be one and the same issue, which they invariably are in a purely domestic case (e.g. *Morgan*), whilst in a conflicts adjudication they might well be separated out.

If by definition either issue were exclusively governed by the lex causae, especially where the underlying contract is void, then the result, as given in the report, would be to produce:

> "a fundamental difficulty to be overcome in seeking within what was ex hypothesi a nullity the solution to the choice of law aspects of the problem of restitution. The proper law had exhausted its purpose in dictating that solution and it was not attractive to proceed then to give effect to a term of that contract when the contract had ceased to have any validity between the parties."[30]

His Lordship did thus not apply the parties' chosen lex causae.

To have disapplied that choice as he did was to serve the ends of "substantial" logic and justice.[31] This did not mean, as his Lordship recognized in allowing for any fortuity as to identifying the locus of the enriched and the enrichment, that the chosen law could not ultimately be relevant and material to the restitutional issues, "but will not per se be determinative of that connection";[32] or, indeed, by civil analogy, that substantive law may generally be relevant and material to other relief in a different cause of action. The judgment also stated[33] that:

> "(a) the restitutionary obligation [not the restitutionary remedy] or quasi-contractual obligation is governed by the proper law of that obligation; and (b) that the proper law of the obligation is the law of the country with which, in light of the

[30] At 13 of the transcript. [31] At 13–14 of the transcript. [32] At 16 of the transcript.

[33] Ibid.; see also C. McLachlan and Hon. Peter Nygh *op. cit.*, especially at 230–231, and *Chase Manhattan NA* v. *Israel-British Bank (London) Ltd.*[1981] Ch. 105, in which the law of the place of enrichment was applied.

whole facts and circumstances, the critical events have their closest and most real connection."[34]

This means that the substantive restitutionary obligation involves choice of law, but not that availability of a given remedy similarly does. This is because the available remedy need not be that which is indicated by the law which establishes that the enrichment concerned was unjustifiable.[35]

The view that choice-of-law method could be applied to remedies is not really new. It is perenially relied on, for example, in *Baschet* v. *London Illustrated Standard*[36] where French law of injunction founded argument for the particular remedy from an English court. The view tends to over-emphasize the scope of relevance of the causa as it is resolved by choice of law, apart from circumstances in which forum and foreign law are practically on all fours as often happens in litigation involving Common Law jurisdictions.[37] As it applies to the restitution conflicts circumstances in *Barings*, the view has been thoroughly examined by Bird in terms which criticize the actual decision. She argued that the application of the supposed proper law of a void contract, as the lex causae of an action for restitution, is in fact neither illogical nor unjust—at least not where the contract is correctly nullified for other types of reason such as fundamental mistake, misrepresentation, or duress—because "[w]hile from the point of view of strict legal theory the question of whether a contract is void falls under a different category to the question of what the consequences of that finding are, from all other points of view it is the same question."[38] In effect, she was opposed to his Lordship's application of a forum-oriented approach, basing her perspectives in common sense and judicial convenience and recognizing that flexibility of approach in fact meant that there was not a world of difference between his Lordship's view and hers. For the sake of discussion of the appositeness of liability and relief, the voidness of the contract in *Barings* and the prescription of the claim by Scots law may be temporarily suspended to permit substitution of these questions with that of the parties' live voluntary and legally regulated (remediable) relationship.

[34] Ibid., citing Blaikie, and *Dicey and Morris*'s Rule 201, *op. cit.*, at 1471–1478, especially at 1473 10, transcript); cf. *Arab Monetary Fund* v. *Hashim* [1996] 1 LlR. 589, at 597: "The obligation to restore an enrichment obtained at another's expense is governed by the proper law of the obligation."

[35] On the point of "substantial logic" (text at n. 31, above) as the basis for having applied Scots law, it would appear to have been sound advice if the parties had in fact made provision for agreed remedies partly for the purpose of removing practical policy problems, e.g., whether the legal entity neither constituted, domiciled and managed in nor normally subject to the relevant foreign law did in fact wish to be subject to that (non-forum) law, especially where the issue is the validity and consequence of its transactions. The parties could have agreed that an English forum should have exclusive jurisdiction over matters arising under the agreement.

[36] [1900] 1 Ch 73.

[37] Cf. The *Pakistan National Shipping* case (*Times Law Reports*, 17th December 1997) concerning the application of identical injunctive laws between the English and Pakistani legal systems. For an example from beyond the Common Law, cf. the *AMF* case, above, n. 34.

[38] *Loc. cit.*, at 184–186 (see also art. 8(1) *Rome Convention*). This appears to conflate contract validity with its effects without distinguishing the question of the form of relief applicable to an enrichment consequent to nullification of the underlying contract. Further detail from her commentary resurfaces in Chapter Six.

A(N INTERIM) CONCLUSION: THE PROBLEM

The writer's view is based on systems' differentiation as to remedies and remedial forms, on flexibility being an appealing proposition in theory as well as in practice because it (flexibility) reconciles the divergences between Lord Penrose's view and Bird's, by emulating the judgment's conflation of remedial law with a flexible forum-oriented approach and her likewise flexible premiss that legal obligation and its governing law are often quite inseparable. The writer attempts to differ in that in *Barings*, the respective issues ought to have been governed by the same law but for different reasons, given the unavoidable importance of forms. Pared of his Lordship's adjudgment in response to parties' arguments as to applicable law, the decision itself could be described as being the result of applying forum law to all the issues of obligation and relief on the bases that forum substantive law was applicable in default of the chosen law; i.e., that the void contract could not select its applicable law. Bird's flexibility would leave significantly underplayed the conceptual differentiation of "obligation" from "remedy" and from "proper law", at some cost to theory and practice: English law would directly apply to establish an obligation to disgorge which would then be converted by the forum into an enforceable forum right, but she stopped short of the issue of the actual remedy the forum would grant.

The problem of applicable remedial law requiring a response then is this: if the forum of adjudication, therefore the nature and extent of the available remedy, is to be Scottish, the prospect exists that the pursuers would, in the hypothetical scheme by which limitation is not an issue, unjustifiably go without relief because the same law would settle the obligation to provide relief (in *Barings*, to disgorge). According to the Scots forum, English law did not automatically apply to give that relief nor did it found an enforceable restitutionary obligation. This result would be as difficult as rigidly separating substance from remedy in a way that sallows the merits of deliberating their intersection and, more to the point of the present discussion, would associate forum forms exclusively (inflexibly) with forum law on liability. It does not, it is submitted, objectively localize the circumstances.

The writer's response is provided in the last chapter of this Part, following the next short chapter on how relief that is not self-executing may be enforced. The intermission between problem and response is deliberately aimed at bringing salient other non-restitutional relief into view, to enable a fuller appreciation of the response the writer calls "objective localization". It is a scheme he suggests for conflicts situations in which none of the aspects of forum policy discussed in Chapter Three could be sufficient to justify the grant of relief, in those cases where local forms would, by reason of the cross-border circumstances, need not be rationalized in precisely the same way as their domestic case counterparts.

5

Enforcing non-"self-executing" remedies

ENFORCEMENT, EXECUTION

TALK OF JUDICIAL enforcement may, in a generalized sense, refer to formal acknowledgment or recognition of rights, or, as it applies in the present Chapter, it may mean ensuring a recalcitrant defendant's compliance with a remedial judgment. Strictly speaking, the narrower sense, of post-judgment execution, is not remedial in the way that money awards, substitutional relief or judicial coercion are remedies. It is dealt with in this book because it entails a distinctively non-substantivist type of remedial jurisdictional proceduralism, no less a matter invoked at a successful claimant's option, and because there is a territorialist sub-theme which may be of importance to the forum's remedial competence, viz. the relevance of identifying the jurisdiction(s) in which a forum judgment may need to be enforced and (or) executed; given or not the role of reciprocity in determining which (remedial) judgments may be recognized and (or) enforced. It is similarly of interest, to conflicts doctrine, that this present topic capably further amplifies the substance/procedure dichotomy, albeit that post-judgment execution is normally local, in the sense of being relevant or applicable within the territory of the forum state.

There are several preliminary issues of definition. For a start, as the Chapter heading[1] indicates, not all relief requires execution in order for the goal of substantive effectiveness to be accomplished. Indeed, execution may be indirect in that giving legal consequence to substantive judicial relief may involve recourse to procedural measures not necessarily directly related nor exclusively apposite to the res judicata. Further, effective execution may still not guarantee actual redress against the original defendant, in which situation the claimant has either to waive full or partial substantive relief in the event of the defendant's remedial incapacity or to require some other non-interventionist remedial arrangement with the defendant. Secondly, it is part of the exercise of

[1] The appellation, "self-executing", is sometimes given to have its origins in American legal parlance. This is noted, for example by F.H. Lawson, *Remedies of English Law* (2nd ed., London, 1980), at 240. The reasons given in the main text above suffice to explain its terminological relevance, as a description of one of a set of chapters, to remedial theory and policy in the conflict of laws.

forum discretion to grant equitable relief that such a remedy will not issue if it is incapable of execution, that facility of executory enforcement significantly determines the availability of specific (equitable) relief. Thirdly, for (money) judgment debts, execution follows normal rules and process prescribed by internal law, and this necessitates a fourth point regarding the limits of this proceduralism as it is prescribed by substantive liability settled by non-forum law.[2] This is presently discussed to illustrate substance and procedure in the present context, with a view to further preparing the backdrop for objective localization. A final point which also prepares the reader for the last Chapter of this Part is that it is necessary and useful to recognize that while declarations or decrees of legal status which clarify but do not change the parties' legal relations and are self-effectuating are distinctly not directly relevant to the substance of the Chapter, they nevertheless significantly assist demonstrating precisely how well res judicata can cross national legal borders. The Chapter comprises illustration and analysis of immutably procedural rules of post-judgment execution in transnational context, without at all seeking to itemize or to exhaust the range of the type of rule. Of greater interest is the wide range of interacting autonomous territorial jurisdictions, at their most topical in the context of res judicata and territory.

THE ROLE OF THE LEX FORI

The enforcement of judgments and orders in general is regulated by Order 45 of the *Rules of the Supreme Court*, the tenor of which primarily attends to local judgments for the recovery or payment of money, for possession of land, for delivery of goods, for injunctive action, for third party execution, waiver, post-judgment stays. (It is important to bear in mind that the provisions of the R.S.C., as Schedule 1 of the Civil Procedure Rules 1998, continue to be relevant today; the remainder of this book uses the R.S.C. unless the context does not so permit). Order 46 deals with writs of execution. In conflicts adjudication, a classic case illustration of the role of the lex fori in the enforcement of (foreign) awards is the Court of Appeal's decision in *Minister of Public Works of Kuwait* v. *Sir Frederick Snow and Partners*,[3] albeit an arbitral award under the *New York Convention on the Recognition and Enforcement of Foreign Arbitral Awards* to which the United Kingdom acceded by its *Arbitration Act 1975*. The issue before Stephenson, Kerr and Fox L.JJ. was whether the definition of "Convention award" contained in Section 7(1) of the statute could be retrospectively applied. Reversing the judgment of Mocatta J. at first instance, it was held that an award made within the territory of a state party did not necessarily

[2] See, e.g., L. Collins *et al.*, *Dicey and Morris' The Conflict of Laws* (12th ed., London, Sweet & Maxwell; 1993), at 172.

[3] [1983] 1 WLR 818, at 829; at 830, cf. S. 1(2)(c) *Foreign Judgments (Reciprocal Enforcement) Act 1933*, per Stephenson LJ.

require reference to whether the state was a signatory at the time of the award, relying on Lord Brightman's view in *Yew Bon Tew* v. *Kenderaan Bas Mara*,[4] that rule construction depends on whether a narrow interpretation "would impair existing rights and obligations", however procedural a particular rule is given to be. Settling this question of definition as being a matter for forum law then enabled the levying of execution.

The rule, by which the mode of judgment execution follows forum rules, founds in the necessity of keeping with the choice of forum. The main corollary of the rule is that forum law which goes to the defendant's substantive liability is inapplicable, so that (mortgage) debts affirmed according to a foreign lex causae which specifies how the debt liability is to be removed will be literally enforced by the forum without recourse to forum law restrictions applicable to local facts, because the substantive law (as it is ultimately expressed as res judicata) qualifies to be given full effect: *Sigurdson* v. *Farrow and Others*.[5] The mode of satisfaction—whether in land or goods, whether receivership (Order 51) or defendant constraint following contempt proceedings is necessary or to be authorized (Order 52), whether particular items of the debtor's property are chargeable (Order 50), garnishable (Order 49), subject to *fieri facias* procedure (Order 47) or attachable—is what underlies the distinctive proceduralism the writer has referred to previously in this Chapter. Likewise, under Order 52 *R.S.C.*, for coercive judgments, the almost obsolete and drastic[6] "ultimate sanction", Burrows reminds us,[7] is "imprisonment" should contempt proceedings be ineffective. These examples of execution rules would, all things being equal, apply to registered, recognized and enforced foreign judgments. Little is to be gained from protracted consideration of preponderantly local conflicts cases, as these may be looked up in domestic law texts. Such cases, however, are just as much part of conflicts adjudication as are those that preponderantly involve foreign elements.

So far so straight-forward. A recapitulation is necessary. It was said at the outset that local legal substantivism has no place in the processual scheme of execution; if any substantivism is identifable, to do so would exaggerate the conflicts context by classifying as substantive, not only, e.g., monetary liability established under foreign law but also local rules which methodically systematize or categorize executable property. Doing so serves neither the ends of practicability nor those of reasonable, acceptable or worthwhile legal abstraction. The limits of substantivism are those set out in the decisions discussed early on in the present section. The topic of the Chapter is incontrovertibly

[4] [1983] 1 AC 553, at 563.

[5] 121 DLR (3d) 183 (1981), concerning execution of a British Columbia order in Ontario. See also the Canadian decision, *243930 Alberta Ltd.* v. *Wickham* 73 DLR (4th) 474 [1990], which is authority that *lex causae* provisions—as to how, e.g., a mortgage debt is primarily but not exclusively to be satisfied—do not mean that the forum cannot make a more general order; see also the earlier Ontario Appeal, *Northern Trusts Co.* v. *McLean* [1926] 3 DLR 93.

[6] Cf. F.H. Lawson, *Remedies of English Law* (2nd ed., London, Butterworths; 1980), at 9.

[7] In *Remedies for Torts and Breach of Contract* (London, Butterworths; 1993), at 2.

procedural. It may not necessarily consist of what a litigant is concerned about whilst in the throes of substantive litigation, but it most certainly features either pre- or post-trial, in seeking to preserve the full and effective justiciability of the merits. It must be noted that some of the injunctive interim relief discussed in Chapter Eight, as falling outside the scope of substantive relief, also avail ancillary post-judgment execution. So it must be that a practical factoring of the rules of the type in view must objectively feature as part of litigants' overall disposition. There is an important subtext of territorialism in this context and, as the next section shows, it has several relevant points of reference which, as far as the writer is aware, have not necessarily been amplified.

TERRITORY AND RES JUDICATA

A remedial judgment may need to be enforced by execution outside the territory of the judgment forum state. Some of the relevant considerations were raised in describing the remedial judgment in Chapter Two. Typically, the enforcement forum state is identified or identifiable from prior stages of litigation and adjudication of a given fact situation. In the case of declaratory judgments which do not require execution, predictability is not an issue: defendant compliance takes the form of enforcement jurisdiction being subject to public policy, to queries of judgment forum competence or to some other context of transnational compatibility; the res in such judgments is just as judicata as it is in the other types of legal relationship with which this section may be said to be primarily concerned.

Received practice is that every conflicts judgment involves, to a greater or lesser extent, some indication of its "end zone", where enforcement is extraterritorial. *Henderson* v. *Henderson*[8] carries dicta to the effect that courts of equity require proof that a foreign court will co-operate before an order requiring its execution will be made. These dicta are certainly consonant with the generally restricted availability of recognition and enforcement jurisdiction for coercive or non-debt judgments outside the scheme of the *Brussels Convention*.[9] The local law position in England survives whatever mutation may have become *Castanho* v. *Brown and Root (U.K.) Limited*.[10] As to the extraterritorial interlocutory injunctive jurisdiction, Lord Scarman stated then that, in prescribing the avoidance of injustice, "[t]he English court . . . does not pretend to any interference with the other court; it acts upon the defendant by punishment for his disobedience to the order of the court."[11] It may be said that resort to rules regulating original jurisdiction may provide the same result, of res judicata which effectively compels or restrains a defendant, by leaving the probability of necessary judicial intervention to the best forum, at least in respect of coercive judgments which have a negative legal effect as, for example, with the Indian injunction in the *Airbus* decision raised earlier in this Part.

[8] [1843] 3 Hare 100. [9] Arts. 25 *et seq.*, of Part V. [10] [1981] AC 557. [11] Ibid., at 572.

At any rate, if the view of standard practice is to be fully received (this writer's view is that it should not be, at least not necessarily), none of the immediately foregoing should be of interest to the claimant either in pressing his substantive and formal case or in formulating it, where (and because) he does not have a pre-determined idea of where the relief he seeks is to be realized. However one may be disposed to the issue of pre-determination, it seems that enquiry as to its denying application is not likely to go far at all. Transnational law in action, beyond the territory of the European Community wherein the issue has no impact, has other substantial or consequential preoccupations. Localism and its amplitude in regulating the non-compliant defendant need, or deserves, not be couched so vulnerably as would make its fora less defended from foreign remedial orders than its present shape prepares it to be. Why an extraterritorial injunction, which may proveably return to the judgment forum for actual enforcement, should not be available requires some rationalization in the existing scheme for remedial competence.

Let it be assumed that there is no issue of comity wanting. Lack of juridical foundation for a variant arrangement of general application is not necessarily absent, nor does the variant as it is presently described necessarily attribute an unwanted or insupportable competence or omnipotence to the forum. The example of final, in contrast with anticipated, substantivism—as the primary and substantial difference of theory between the respective so-called perpetual and the interlocutory types of injunction—provides a starting point.[12] The latter is well-known to be grantable extraterritorially (worldwide), e.g., the Mareva, wherever the defendant's assets may be, without the imperative for either the claimant to have indicated in which jurisdiction(s) those assets actually are or for a substantive cause before the forum, as was once thought to be the case.[13] Non-compliance is supported by the full measure of the forum's executory machinery. The writer is unaware of final injunctive relief operating in this way as a general rule. Final injunctions are dispositive in a way in which interlocutory relief cannot be, not even under colour of post-judgment enforcement. It is juridically absurd to go so far as to suggest that non-money judgments be treated as though they were money judgments, especially since they neither involve arithmetical evaluation nor lack a dedicated back-up scheme in default of compliance.

The question the writer would ask, with the principle of reciprocity as a considered basis for cross-border judgment jurisdiction, is why it is to be regarded as heretical that non-money final judgments be more generally cross-enforceable. The question is asked not for any reason other than its own sake. It is no more open to abuse than are the span of money judgments, nor is the generation of limiting principle intractable be such principles founded in local law, public policy or any other of the type which can prevail against money judgments. That more is required to be done in an enforcement forum in

[12] Cf. *Dicey and Morris*, *op. cit.*, at 194–197.

[13] See *The Siskina* [1979] AC 210, reversing Lord Denning MR in the Court of Appeal.

furtherance of judicial coercion arising in the one state accounts for a consequential divergence from remedial declarations, when perhaps it ought not necessarily to do. And all this remedial diversity running with a forum which does not lack either original or prescriptive jurisdiction in any of the possible fact/liability permutations.

Formal judicial transnationalism has an historically discrete pedigree in English law. For convenience, the *Judgments Act 1838* can be taken to start up its statutory or textual chronology. At the present time, there are very many bilateral and other instruments which either are devoted to international administration of civil justice or contain provisions pertinent to the topic in their particular contexts.[14] Local statutes include: the *Administration of Justice Act 1920, 1956, 1970* and *1977*; the *Foreign Judgments (Reciprocal Enforcement) Act 1933*; the *Protection of Trading Interests Act 1980*; the *Supreme Court Act 1981 (Admiralty)*; the *Civil Jurisdiction and Judgments Acts 1982* and *1991*; the *Contracts (Applicable Law) Act 1990*. International conventions include: the *European Convention on the Recognition and Enforcement of Decisions Concerning Custody of Children and on the Restoration of Custody of Children 1980*; the *Hague Conventions on the Recognition of Foreign Divorces and Legal Separations 1970*, and *of Decisions Relating to Maintenance Obligations 1973*. The inter-governmental dimensions further afield have produced a plethora of bilateral instruments directly in point, mostly through Orders-in-Council relating to specified countries or jurisdictions including those which now form the membership of the European Community. Indeed, the makings of the EC rules are to be found in one such instrument (S.I. 1972/1590). Today, the *Brussels Convention*, which firmly belongs to and predominates the sample of the present paragraph, provides (Section 26) that any judicial judgment or order of whatever description (as long as it is not procured without notice to the party against whom it is directed) is automatically to be recognized in other Member States, subject only to limited exceptions outwith a regionalist justification. The writer submits that the juridical reason, to be actively differentiated from the philosophical basis for the *Brussels Convention* as is possible,[15] for the present geographical elision of enforceable relief permits furthering practical enquiry.

The framework is necessarily general and internationalist, and is not limited to the law of obligations. It proceeds on the understanding that there are juris-

[14] A useful manual is G.S. Graham and R.D. Mackay, *Butterworths Jurisdiction, Foreign Judgments and Awards Handbook* (London, Butterworths; 1994). See also *Halsbury's Statutes*, Vol. 22 (4th ed., London, Butterworths; 1995 Reissue). The EC conventions have attracted a large amount of intellectual traffic which need not be considered here.

[15] See, e.g., P.M. Storm, "Europe" in C. Platto and W.G. Horton (eds.), *Enforcement of Foreign Judgments Worldwide* (2nd ed., London, Graham & Trotman; 1993), 150, at 153: "The Conventions are by far the most modern and liberal in existence. They are a natural consequence of the basic philosophy underlying the EEC Treaty: in a common market there should be no internal frontiers hampering the free movement of persons, goods, services and capital. Likewise, there should be 'free movement of judgments' to secure adequate legal protection of individuals and enterprises throughout the Community. Such free movement of judgments is only possible between countries who trust each others' legal systems and judiciaries."

dictions in which money judgments are not the only types of recognizable and enforceable judgment,[16] without necessarily thus inferring that the English forum reciprocates by granting the type of judgments if the enforcing forum is predetermined. However, it proposes that the English forum should be so disposed where the types of issue itemized below are affirmatively answered by the party seeking to rely on the disposition, that there are unconvincing reasons of inconvenience in current practice. At its most venturesome, the set of questions takes in both situations in which the enforcement forum is and is not so easily pre-determinable, thereby objectifying the single bright line logic of contemporary procedural formalism which firmly excludes cross-enforceability as an applicable rule or policy norm, and presents it rather as being draconian or recommendatory of exorbitant judicial jurisdiction. Above all it emphasizes transnational proceduralism as a reflexive concept in response to the diffusion of its substantivist counterpart in contemporary conflict of laws. Its irreducible minimum standards are those forthcoming from comparativist reference to various jurisdictions' laws on recognition and enforcement of (remedial) judgments, wherein typical contextual considerations (of the jurisdictional competence of the judgment forum; the finality of the award; the absence of judgment vitiating factors; public policy of the judgment forum state and the judgment enforcement state; and so forth) are reasonably consistently brought to bear in practically every national jurisdiction. If a claimant is permitted to raise and have affirmed the following questions, the writer should say that there is justification for making less of the place of enforcement as a hindering factor. The picture thesis is completed in the last Chapter. The questions are whether there are rules which:

- define the forum's judgment as a foreign judgment for the purpose of formal recognition and enforcement;
- determine the given foreign forum's competence to decline recognition and enforcement;
- provide for the foreign forum's indicia of judgment finality,
- indicate the foreign forum's domestic competence;
- refer to the fulfilment of dispute resolution clauses;
- describe the foreign forum's proclivity to re-open foreign judgments;
- precisely stipulate enforcement/execution procedures;
- ensure that execution will be stayed in the event of substantive (or other) appeal.

[16] Cf. Art. 200 of the Japanese *Code of Civil Procedure* (Law No. 29, 1980) and Art. 24 *Code of Civil Enforcement of Japan* (Law No. 4, 1979), the main pre-requirement being reciprocity with the judgment forum state.; S. 3B(1992) of the *New Zealand Reciprocal Enforcement of Judgments Act 1934* brings non-money judgments within the jurisdiction, subject to Orders in Council for the purpose, with the usual other factors (competent jurisdiction; finality; public policy etc.) applying; Paras. 441–442, 481(1) *Restatement (Third) of Foreign Relations Law* (US); Cantonal civil procedure laws on the enforcement of non-money judgments apply in Switzerland; Art. 552 of the Bolivian *Civil Procedural Code*; S. 44A Indian *Code of Civil Procedure 1908*; For a general overview, see C. Platto and W.G. Horton (eds.), *op. cit.*

Responses to the above, and they may be differently or more fully expressed, would enable the judgment forum to determine whether and how far its possible order is likely to be applied abroad. The extraterritorialist thesis of the present Chapter is but a template for deliberation which ensures the policy against procedural conflicts. Its use may well indicate that the forum's judgment may well conform with the relevant foreign enforcement machinery,[17] for example but not necessarily only (i.e., as long as it meets a discernible minimum standard of enforcement formality in the enforcing forum state) where the foreign jurisdiction has also produced the lex causae. For descriptive convenience, the set of questions may be referred to, as inverse choice of law, as being indicative of a law of (the place of) enforcement. It does not involve any re-invention of the conflict of laws since it merely indicates a less prominent aspect of the forum's overall jurisdictional competence. Its absence from the mainstream of contemporary transnational litigation is mostly a consequence of its not typically forming a significant part of the parties' statements of cause in contemporary transnational litigation. But it is from this, and from its underlying received reasons, that the devil in its detail makes it fitting. Perhaps as far as it can go is determined by pre-determination of the relevant other jurisdicton(s), in which case it would be the claimant's bonus that such an enforcement forum state's rules in point would recognize and enforce.

In closing, consider that a claimant seeks an injunction to prevent foreseeable acts in contravention of a transnational contract, that the judgment forum has properly acquired jurisdiction, that either litigant is substantially connected to a pre-determined enforcement forum state in which the contract at issue was made and the lex causae of which is applicable.[18] The writer's scheme above suggests that the types of question therein be stated as part of the cause for extraterritorial relief in the judgment forum. It is to be noted that, within the scheme and territory of the *Brussels Convention*, non-EC coercive orders against a domiciliary may be directly applied in any Member State's courts.

[17] Cf. *Sigurdson*, at 185–187 (per Medhurst J.).

[18] The hypothesis is but a slight variation of the facts in *Warner Brothers Pictures Incorporated* v. *Nelson* [1937] 1 KB 209.

6

Objective localization

BARINGS RESUMED: REMEDIES AND THE CENTRE OF GRAVITY

CHAPTER FOUR ENDED with a problem posed and a response deferred. This present Chapter takes up the observational response. At its barest, it is based on the issues raised in *Barings*, and, generally speaking, it consists in the writer's exploration of the forum's objective exercise of its single bright line logic, of remedies as procedure but not necessarily entirely or literally for internal law. With its attention to forum remedial forms, the response posits the rationalization of those forms in the terms of the applied non-forum substantive law where, as an exception, particular transnational circumstances necessitate this and the machinery of the forum permits it, without the need for justificatory recourse to the type of expansionism that could remove the justiciability-based exercise from the limits of feasible co-ordination of lex causae and lex fori.

In any set of facts giving rise to a cause of action, enquiry as to whether those facts centre upon a particular legal system is normal in seeking to correlate a finding on remedial liability with how and how far that liability is to be redressed. Indeed, where the relief is not in money, the metaphorical plot must thicken. That it was restitutional liability in *Barings* can, for the sake of hypothesis, be regarded as random enough to afford an adequate basis for generalized obligational and remedial analogy. Had the facts been different, such as if they had included a positive genuine affirmation of the pursuers' as to their contractual capacity, a tort action based on negligent misrepresentation would have produced factually different but thematically related factors.

By way of illustration, consider an award of damages: the substantive right thereto and the remedial or procedural amount comprise remediability, by which the former is referred to the lex causae and the latter to the lex fori with the possibility that both laws may be found in the same legal system in the right case. From the perspective of the convenience of the forum, quantification of damages can involve the forum's application of the rules of quantum of another legal system, even though such rules (where they are to be found) are to be taken to be procedural, for example, under Article 10(1)(c) of the *Rome Convention on the Law Applicable to Contractual Obligations 1980*. That this is conceptually different from the standard approach of the forum to these issues—for example, as it was applied by Lord Upjohn in *Boys* v. *Chaplin*[1] at the Court of Appeal stage or, previously, by McNair J in *NV Handel Maatschaapij J Smits Import-Export* v. *English Exporters*[2]—is to be noted with regard to the limitation that forum law must allow reference to the lex causae on this issue,[3] as, however, must be a view that perhaps it is somewhat promethean to interpret the *Rome Convention* provision in this way so removed from the Common Law.[4]

In a general context not directed at the *Convention*, Kramer opines that "[a] choice of law problem exists only if the different laws relied on by the parties can plausibly be construed to govern the case"[5] and:

> "[o]ne might . . . object that this imposes a substantial burden on forum courts to learn and apply foreign rules of procedure, an objection reminiscent of the justification for the traditional approach [of applying only forum procedural rules]. But the court need learn only foreign procedural rules that serve substantive [purposes] . . . Moreover, the adversarial system naturally limits this burden, since the court will consider only foreign rules that are properly raised by the parties. Finally, finding and applying foreign procedural rules is no more difficult than finding and applying foreign substantive law . . . Indeed, the premise of this canon is that some procedural rules should be applied because they are in reality part of another state's substantive law."[6]

This passage emphasizes the decisional judicial policy of practicability and convenience with which non-forum rules may be applied, whether they be characterized as procedural or as substantive.

The *Barings* facts gravitated towards a foreign (English) legal system, thereby accentuating the point that there is much to commend in the view, albeit in the context of tort claims based on intellectual property rights, that "courts have been asked to moderate the effect of the limitations on their jurisdiction fostered by the operation of local-action or territorial principle cases."[7] A remedial decision based on non-forum substantive law exclusively depends on forum law for its form. Form dictates the extent to which lex causae (procedural) rules may be applicable by the forum, is the "homeward trend and the result orientation"[8] in Lord Penrose's ruling. It is consideration of the form of

[1] [1968] 2 QB 1, at 31. [2] [1955] 2 LlR 69, at 72.

[3] L. Collins *et al.*, *Dicey and Morris' the Conflict of Laws* (12th ed., London, Sweet & Maxwell; 1993), at 172; see also *Chitty on Contracts* (28th ed., London, Sweet & Maxwell; 1999), at para. 31–139. The present writer refers to it as "the Article 10(1) gloss", mainly in Chapter Seven, and thereafter.

[4] See, e.g., C.M.V. Clarkson and J. Hill, *Jaffey on the Conflict of Laws* (London, Butterworths; 1997), at 241.

[5] In "Rethinking Choice of Law" (1990) 90 *Colum LRev* 277, at 283.

[6] Ibid., at 328–329.

[7] P. Trooboff, "Intellectual Property" in C. McLachlan and Hon. Peter Nygh (eds.), *Transnational Tort Litigation: Jurisdictional Principles* (Oxford, Clarendon; 1996), at 128–129; see generally 128–132 ("Broadening the Scope of Claims Asserted and Relief Granted").

[8] J. Bird, "Choice of Law and Restitution of Benefits Conferred Under a Void Contract: *Baring Brothers* v. *Cunninghame DC*" [1997] LMCLQ 182., at 192.

relief that limits the narrower restitutional rules to the subset of "procedure", and which, by definition, must determine the bounds of policy considerations of propriety of application of these rules. A precondition for this interpretation may be that the remedial rules of a non-forum lex causae, if any, would need to be practicably applicable from the forum's point of view, especially where the place of litigation (the forum) is all that is not determined by the lex causae. A corollary of this view is that remedial rules are applicable at all, that applicability is ever only not an issue if remedies are narrowly characterized as being but tacitly part of forum process which typically depends on forum law.

The remedies issue belongs, as it has been indicated to do in Chapter Two, to the wider matter of jurisdiction wherein substantive entitlement must deterministically feature. It has been settled law, since *Re Bonacina*,[9] that lex causae categories need not precisely mirror those of internal law, so that, in that case, lack of contractual consideration, in the sense of English law, in the agreement having an Italian proper law did not prevent rights thereunder being enforced by the English forum. Each remedy that makes up the forum's armoury of relief need not, or cannot, individually be expanded upon in this Chapter, nor does the writer wish to follow such a course in view of the discussion of particular relief in the ensuing Parts of this book. But the *Barings* facts have been shown to be adaptable to cover further broad remedial considerations and indicators.

Substantivist adjudication runs with legal relationships in which party autonomy is an over-arching consideration. Autonomy does not feature in relation to forum procedure in general. As Jolowicz, points out, "[s]ubstantive law is, procedural law is not, 'self-executing' ",[10] so that autonomy ends with the parties' subjection of their legal relationship to the procedural rules of the forum. Although autonomy does feature in contract law, its scope does not extend to judicial relief in formal terms (other than in relation to consensual relief) but, in having resolved the applicable substantive law, it will have indicated the law the (remedial) provisions of which are to be considered for remedial applications. So it is that, in *Penn* v. *Baltimore*[11] or in *Richard West & Partners (Inverness) Limited* v. *Dick*,[12] the English forum was able to grant decrees of specific performance of contracts relating to foreign land. The respective awards complied with the leges siti in which actual enforcement was to take place. That the defendants were forum domiciliaries meant that basic personal jurisdiction was effectively exercizable, as is the case in *Barings* except that the relief (payment) lies in restitution. The circumstances by which enrichment actions are substantive and procedural necessitate identification and application of lex causae and lex fori rules for the respective types of issue. The form of remedy is unavoidably and self-evidently for forum law.

It may be said that effectiveness in remedial orders and its intersection with

[9] [1912] 2 Ch 394.

[10] In I.R. Scott (ed.), *International Perspectives on Civil Justice* (London, Butterworths; 1990), 169, at 33–34.

[11] 1 Ves Sen 444 (1750).

[12] [1969] 2 Ch 424.

subsequent recognition and enforcement (including formal execution) is unassured because of the relative novelty of the foregoing emphasis on substantive res judicata. But, because effectiveness is a direct function of the autonomous judgment forum's competence as it may be accepted by the enforcing court, the theory of (internationally effective) remedies, especially those which accurately reflect causa established by non-forum law, must be as operable as the conflicts policy of entertaining foreign suit at all; conflicts relief is the central aim of transnational administration of civil justice.

The intersection of "substance" with "remedy" can matter little even when the issue is the form of relief. In point of fact, the interchangeability of "action" and "remedy" may perhaps extrapolate as "original jurisdiction" and (remedy-awarding) "judgment".[13] If it is necessary to consider jurisdictional propriety in connexion with whether an action is to be entertained, then it ought reasonably to be relevant to whether remedial considerations are localizable so as to avoid unduly domesticized relief or remedies; localization may not be possible because the lex causae is so predominant that existing lex fori forms should be regarded as inelastic to enforce the underlying rights. Forum-oriented as judicial policy must be, in keeping with the forum's jurisdictional competence, it would further an interest in coherence of adjudication if conflicts remedies were conceptualizable to reflect their jurisdictional foundations, neither sacrificing the substantive liability dimensions nor under-valuing the error of requiring a forum to make an order alien to its legal structure. By and large, the bulk of conflicts cases the forum determines will not require such gymnastic remedial adjudication such, further, as could affirm the viability of a "proper law of a remedy".

Were the claim in *Barings* not barred by prescription, the remedy of payment would have needed to sustain a (sound) right to restitution originating in English law, thus harking back to the need to dismantle the unnecessary "fundamental difficulty" referred to in Chapter Four, in discussing the restitutionary right to recover. Recent and current trends (e.g., in the way that the lex loci delicti has in principle superceded dual actionability according to Part III of the *Private International Law (Miscellaneous Provisions) Act 1995*) make it unwise to rule out now or foreseeably the seductive possibility of restitutionary remedies in the conflict of laws being referrable to non-forum law, significantly, where the circumstances correctly point to that law for resolution. This approach is not so removed from Carter's reference, in relation to the old forum-oriented tort conflicts rule, to "technique[s] of forum control . . . [the] significance and value [of which are] to be assessed in the context of established (if not always legitimate) forum control techniques of general applicability, such as resort to public policy or the manipulation of the characterization rules."[14] It remains to be seen of course whether the exception to the lex loci delicti rule will accommodate referral of remedial issues of a tort case to its lex

[13] Cf. A. Briggs, "Which Foreign Judgments Should We Recognize Today?" (1987) 36 *ICLQ* 240.
[14] P.B. Carter, "Choice of Law in Tort and Delict" (1991) 107 *LQR* 405, at 408–409.

delicti as other issues may be under Sections 11 or 12 of the 1995 Act, public policy permitting. Conflicts remedies may, in some fact situations, need to be conceptualized and articulated in a way that responds to the governing law of the particular obligation and (or) to the law of enforcement.

Objectifying remedial considerations in transnational adjudication might not be as straight-forward or palatable in the terms in which this Chapter has set them. But it is reasonably obvious that deceptively laconic as a literal interpretation of Rule 17 must be, it would be just as unproductive to look away from the amplitude of the forum's jurisdictional (including remedial) localizing matrix, as this is illustrated by non-pecuniary (therefore, non-self-executing) restitutionary orders where the place of application of such orders is difficult to ascertain, e.g., because the place is not within the scope of the *Brussels Convention*. But is this really a restrictive issue, in view of the forum's observable extraterritorial competence? In *Barings*, the likely places of enforcement of a final order of payment are Scotland or England. The remedy of payment is reasonably consistent with the English remedy for the recovery of money paid, as in *Exall* v. *Partridge*[15] and, indeed, in the similar facts case of *Kleinwort Benson Limited* v. *Glasgow City Council*.[16] Nor would the recognition of confluent remedial forms amount to "[treating] all enrichment actions as matters of remedy rather than right, or procedure rather than substance."[17] In *Batthyany* v. *Walford*,[18] a case concerning rights running with real property in Austria, the forum's characterization of the substantive issues accorded with the lex situs rather than with internal law. The relief sought and granted was an account of profits on the basis of Austrian law.

In *Barings*, Lord Penrose's elimination of the apparent bearing of English law and his convenient application of internal law of jurisdiction and relief was in line with his ruling in *Morgan*, a wholly domestic case, and with uniform resolution of other identical cases before the forum. The quintessence of localization is that a judgment forum is capable of enforcing non-forum rights without necessarily taking the lex causae to be its own law and without being part of the legal system from which that law originates. The remedy of payment would justiciably support the entitlement to disgorgement under English law. Because national systems are interconnected only by rules to which they subscribe, the plausibility of legal objectivity in transnational adjudication is difficult to denounce. The reasonably clear possibility of applicable remedial law being comprised of a non-forum lex causae and distinctive procedures is not merely beyond the plausible. It is likely to underscore the shape of any developments.

[15] 8 TR 308 (1799).

[16] [1997] 3 WLR 923.

[17] T.W. Bennett, "Choice of Law Rules in Claims of Unjust Enrichment" (1990) 39 *ICLQ* 136, at 144.

[18] 36 Ch D 269 (1887), especially at 278–279, 281; since followed in *BP Exploration (Libya) Ltd.* v. *Hunt (No.2)* [1979] 1 WLR 783, at 838–835 (affirmed [1981] 1 WLR 232) and in *Chase Manhattan Bank NA* v. *Israel-British Bank (London) Ltd.* [1981] Ch 105.

CONCLUSION

Having reflected on some of the abstract aspects of the English conflicts forum's remedial theory and policy—no doubt these aspects can be radically differently presented by another commentator—the relevant law as it applies in the various forms are described and discussed in the remainder of this book. What has featured in this closing Part has a variable bearing on what remains, based as the actual remedies need to be in forum practice in actual cases. Should the content of this Part not have satisfied or convinced the reader, it is at least to be hoped that it may have provided some food for thought about the nature and scope of the conflict of laws relating to remedies and, perhaps, it may have provided some pointers on some of the issues in international civil procedure relating to remedial judgments in particular.

Part C

Particular Relief in Personam

7
Compensatory damages and other money awards in personam

PRELIMINARY

THIS CHAPTER DEALS with forum awards which require the defendant to pay a sum of money because he is found to be in breach of civil obligation to the claimant. The courses of action for these awards originated from the old Roman private law tranches of actions in personam and those in rem.[1] In English law, the distinction has substantially been preserved—with the jurisdiction in rem now limited to admiralty cases—for as much continues to fasten upon whether the particular claim arises from a legal relationship of which at least one of the parties is a res, in which case the judicial remedies in rem amplified in Chapter Eleven are characteristically applied against exclusive title and derived rights to the res, now usually a ship; or whether, on the other hand, it is in the nature of the breached relationship that its redress is immediately administrable only against the defendant personally. In the latter case of remedies in personam, the award of money in the form of damages or in one or other of a diversity of forms[2] is regarded in nearly every legal system—Common Law or Civil Law—as leading final relief in general, and international, civil litigation.[3]

While it may be of some interest that not all jurisdictions have necessarily retained this classification of actions, not least the Italian legal system which is the modern successor to the Roman, it should be noted that a separate in rem category does not really exist in the general jurisdictional rules of those systems.[4] As regards the practical enforcement or effectiveness of awards

[1] W.M. Gordon and O.F. Robinson (tr.), *The Institutes of Gaius* (London, Duckworth; 1988), Book Four, at 402 *et seq*. For an incidental note on the different basic uses of the distinction (the claim running against a person or against property; territoriality of jurisdiction; the form of the forum's final order; the matter of enforcement), see D. Laycock, *Modern American Remedies: Cases and Materials* (Boston, Little Brown; 1985), at 697–699.

[2] H. McGregor, *McGregor on Damages* (16th ed., London, Sweet & Maxwell, 1997), paras. 2–6 which identify some other traditional common law actions, inter alia for contract sums due, in quasi-contract, independently in equity.

[3] Cf. G.H. Treitel, "Remedies for Breach of Contract" in *International Encyclopædia of Comparative Law* (Tübingen, Paul Siebeck; 1976), Vol. VII, Chapter 16, s.III, para. 40; cf. S. Cromie, *International Commercial Litigation* (London, Butterworths; 1997), Chapter II, at 92 *et seq*.

[4] Cf. M. Cappelletti and J.M. Perillo, *Civil Procedure in Italy* (The Hague, Martinus Nijhoff; 1965), at 83, para. 4.03b; but see the recent *Reform of the Italian System of Private International*

between disparate legal systems, this is a relatively easy issue to surmount even in circumstances where procedural competence is less straight-forward,[5] because "[i]t is the substance of what is claimed that matters. Thus it is not relevant whether the action is in personam or in rem or in what branch of the law the claim arises".[6] In this narrow sense, it can be said that the core idea of civil justice—differently conceptualized among countries as it must be—is itself recognizably global.[7] Indeed, Common Law actions and remedies in personam will amply accommodate proprietary (real or personal) considerations. In any case, it is the same encompassing lex fori or forum jurisdiction, rooted in statutes (including those which incorporate international Conventions) and case law, which will invariably avail or deny claimants of the relief they seek.[8]

Modern examples of the result of the exercise of jurisdictional competence in personam are judicial awards in foreign currency[9] and the worldwide *Mareva* injunction or freezing order against the defendant's assets, albeit a non-money remedy.[10] In all cases, proceedings begin by service of the appropriate process in the way prescribed by the amended *Rules of the Supreme Court 1965*[11] (for the purpose, reference is to be made to Schedule 1 of the *Civil Procedure Rules* in effect from 26th April 1999) or by comparable means in other legal systems. The wide-reaching nature of personal remedial jurisdiction is illustrated by the different types of action sounding in money for substitutional compensation, for literally enforceable actual or liquidated sums due or for penalties,[12] or the action for, say, equitable damages. There are several other types of money action in personam, and they are to be distinguished from personal or propri-

Law (Law No. 218 of May 31st 1995), Articles 5, 51–55 (Vol. XXXV(3) 765, May 1996), which makes several references to the jurisdiction, in light of the classification in *Brussels Convention* provisions which refer to the jurisdiction.

[5] See e.g. *The August 8* [1983] 2 AC 450; *The Deichland* [1990] 1 QB 361. In these admiralty cases, the same action proceeded in personam and in rem; for the Scots law parallel position by which admiralty cases may be brought in rem, in personam or both, see R.E. Aird and J.N. Jameson, *The Scots Dimension to Cross-Border Litigation* (Edinburgh, W. Green/Sweet & Maxwell; 1996), paras. 15.77–15.82.

[6] C.F. Forsyth *Private International Law: The modern Roman-Dutch law including the jurisdiction of the Supreme Court* (3rd ed., Juta, Cape Town; 1996), at 191. This is so as long as parallel actions are barred (*Republic of India and Another* v. *India Steamship Co. Ltd. (Indian Endurance and Indian Grace) (No. 2) The Times*, October 23rd 1997; House of Lords).

[7] V. Gessner (ed.), *Foreign Courts: Civil Litigation in Foreign Legal Cultures* (Aldershot, Dartmouth; 1996), generally, and particularly H. von Freyhold, V. Gessner, V. Olgiati, "The Role of Courts in Global Legal Interaction", at 269, and especially 275–280.

[8] See generally C. McLachlan and Hon. P. Nygh (eds.), *Transnational Tort Litigation: Jurisdictional Principles* (Oxford, Clarendon; 1996), especially the introductory sections of the first four chapters.

[9] Cf. the text accompanying notes 69–71 in Chapter One.

[10] E.g. in *Republic of Haiti* v. *Duvalier* [1990] 1 QB 202, at 213–214.

[11] Order 5, rules 2–4; s. 151(1) *Supreme Court Act 1981* defines "action" as "any civil proceedings begun by writ or in any other manner prescribed by the rules of court"; *Dicey and Morris, op. cit.*, at 270–271.

[12] These are discussed as performance remedies in Chapter Nine; on this classification, cf. P.J. Cooke and D.W. Oughton, *The Common Law of Obligations* (London, Butterworths; 1989), at 225–230.

etary restitutionary remedies discussed in the eponymous Chapter Ten, especially those in money (e.g. actions for the recovery of money paid, of money had and received, or for account of profits). Because restitutionary damages are damages qualified by measure or type of liability, they are discussed in the present Chapter. Status and succession awards in money are subsumed under the forum's so-called jurisdiction quasi in rem,[13] and are to be included in the discussion in the chapter on remedies in rem.

The typical money award in personam is often in place of an order to impose or to restrain obligational performance, which performance itself may be the payment of money. The contrast between the money remedies discussed in the Chapter and performance remedies taken up in the ninth is, however, bound to raise a number of fundamental questions. One is the question whether foreign money obligations arising contractually are generically specifically enforceable as of right. The English authorities seem to be not necessarily at one, but to no real disadvantage.[14] Such an obligation in a wholly domestic case was stated to be so enforceable, "by the ordinary methods of execution" against even the successor of a deceased contractual party, in *Beswick's Case*.[15] The contrast also raises the different but related question whether claims based on simple foreign debt continue to be pervaded by the obsolescent action in detinet (for the delivery up of unlawfully retained personal property)[16] despite a foreign debtor's conceivably precarious position as against a creditor's assignee of the debt.[17] Although the ultimate object of the exercise of jurisdiction is the claimant's pecuniary situation in either question arising from the contrast, legal systems place considerable emphasis on the characteristic difference between substitution and performance as is done in this Part.

The difference is prominent in the conflict of laws: where the (non-forum) lex causae form of remedy for a wrong lies in performance but the lex fori relief is in substitution, the latter will always prevail.[18] At the level of interaction between respective systems as is facilitated by the conflict of laws, it should hardly be surprising that several important areas of the subject (e.g. the substance of obligations; the recognition and enforcement of judgments) have developed from or been influenced by the enforceability of money obligations.

13 E.g. s. 18 *Matrimonial Causes Act 1950*.

14 E.g. *Lloyd Royal Belge* v. *Louis Dreyfus & Co.* [1927] LlLRep 288, at 293 (Romer J). Ideally, the claimant in pursuit of such a claim and who has suffered non-compensatory loss would be advised to seek equitable damages as well. See also F.A. Mann, "Specific Performance of Foreign Money Obligations?" (1968) 31 MLR 342 , *inter alia* (at 343) criticizing the contrary view that "a decree of specific performance for the payment of foreign money will [most likely] not be granted in any circumstances" in *Dicey and Morris* (8th ed., London, Stevens; 1967), at 889, n. 90.

15 [1968] AC 58.

16 *Re United Railways of The Havana & Regla Warehouses Ltd.* [1961] AC 1007, at 1043.

17 Cf. *New York Life Insurance Co.* v. *Public Trustee* [1924] 2 Ch 101. at 119 per Atkin LJ (a debt is deemed to be located at the debtor's residence on the assumption that his assets are there); see also P. Rogerson, "The Situs of Debts in the Conflict of Laws—Illogical, Unnecessary and Misleading" [1990] *CLJ* 441, at 442–443, 453–460.

18 *Halsbury's Laws*, *op. cit.*, para. 886; but see *Chitty on Contracts: Volume I, General Principles* (27th ed., London, Sweet & Maxwell; 1994), para. 30–099.

To be sure, textbook restatements of the law of conflicts damages are frequently given some pride of place within the standard renditions on remedies in general in the same works, often with little about the other remedies.[19]

The Chapter primarily deals with the ersatz or compensatory type of monetary award,[20] and does so mindful of at least two things: authoritative observations that "[t]he hegemony of compensation for loss is an illusion"[21] and, second, that compensatory damages are by no means the only type of money award, indeed that the internal strengths and weaknesses as well as the future of the entrenched jurisprudence on damages are the renewed current subject of persuasive scholarly debate, notably by Atiyah[22] and also by Hepple.[23] Other types of damages in view include the equitable (in their own right and in some recognition of in personam jurisdiction lying quintessentially in equity), the nominal, the frequently higher punitive (or exemplary) and the aggravated (which are also substantially compensatory).[24]

For policy reasons, some of the non-compensatory remedies are not easily applied in domestic cases[25] mainly because the awards are not based on the claimant's actual (including future) loss, let alone in conflicts cases where they do not necessarily fall satisfactorily within the private law scope of the subject. Put differently, it will likely be either inconvenient or impossible under the machinery of the forum for a non-compensatory head of damage to be applicable in a conflicts case.[26] The domestic law bases for conflict of laws applications of some of the non-compensatory types of award are up for reform[27] and have assisted in identifying and eliminating a few of the problem areas from the considerations in the inter-governmental effort to convene procedures to facili-

[19] E.g. L. Collins *et al.*, *Dicey and Morris' the Conflict of Laws* (12th ed., London, Sweet and Maxwell; 1993), at 169 *et seq.*; P.M. North and J.J. Fawcett *et al.*, *Cheshire and North's Private International Law* (12th ed., London, Butterworths; 1992), at 91–106; see also *Halsbury's Laws of England* (4th ed., London, Butterworths; 1996 reissue), Vol. 8(1) paras. 1066 *et seq.*, especially at para. 1078.

[20] *The Shorter Oxford Dictionary* describes damages as "a sum of money claimed or awarded in compensation for loss or injury" (Oxford, Clarendon; 1993), Vol. I, at 588.

[21] P. Birks, *Civil Wrongs: A New World* (London, Butterworths; 1992), at 57; cf. n. 29 below (Cane).

[22] *The Damages Lottery* (Oxford, Hart Publishing; 1997), with main points, especially at 2, 189–193, to do with the inefficiency and unfairness of third-party (rather than first-party) insurance which is the source of the vast bulk of damages pay-outs in the English legal system. A predecessor for some of his ideas is the Australian Woodhouse Reports which advocated state compensation systems to replace some types of damages actions.

[23] In M.D.A. Freeman (ed.), *Current Legal Problems* (Oxford, Clarendon; 1996–1997), at 69–94.

[24] Cf. e.g. A. Ogus, "Exemplary Damages and Economic Analysis" in K. Hawkins (ed.), *The Human Face of the Law: Essays in Honour of Donald Harris* (Oxford, Clarendon; 1997), at 85, and 88–93 (on compensation as deterrence).

[25] Cf. Law Commission of England and Wales "Aggravated, Exemplary and Restitutionary Damages" Consultation Paper No. 132 (London, H.M.S.O.; 1993), e.g. at Part VIII.

[26] But see *SA Consortium General Textiles* v. *Sun and Sand Textiles Ltd.* [1979] 2 QB 279, at 299–300; cf. L. Collins, *Essays in International Litigation and the Conflict of Laws* (Oxford, Clarendon; 1994), at 347–349, especially on the related context of recognition and enforcement.

[27] Ibid., *loc. cit.* at n. 23 above, and at paras. 6.21, 6.48, 7.21–22; also A. Burrows, "Reforming Exemplary Damages" in P.B.H. Birks (ed.), *Wrongs and Remedies in the Twenty-First Century* (Oxford, Clarendon; 1996), 153 *et seq.*, and N. McBride, "Punitive Damages" in the same work, at 175 *et seq.*

tate international enforceability of judicial awards generally.[28] The non-compensatory types are elaborated later in the Chapter particularly in the knowledge that "[t]he traditional insistence that compensation occupies a peculiarly privileged position in the law of obligations gives too little weight to the disapproval and deterrence functions of civil [non-criminal] law."[29]

In the comparativist context, the clear case is that broadly identical money remedies are in reality differently conceptualized by different systems as to their availability and measure. Take the general basis for damages: "For damage in our law, for *damnum* in Roman law, for *dommage* or *dommage-interêts* in French law".[30] This version of the general basis understates the divergence of doctrine which becomes a divergence of approach or of emphases. Treitel has encyclopædically placed the salient differences in comparative analysis in the particular circumstances of breach of contract.[31] The most frequent of the differences between systems is the broad one by which, in the doctrine of the Civil Law, the primary remedy for breach of obligation is given to lie in enforced performance whenever possible, as expressed for example in Paragraph 241 of the German Civil Code (the *Bürgerliches Gesetzbuch* (*BGB*)). There are identical provisions in Articles 1143–1144 of the French *Code civil*, and in further Articles of the *BGB*.[32] Articles 43–44 and 49 of the Swiss *Obligationenrecht* (Code of Obligations) allow the claimant the option to claim performance, subject to the forum's discretion as to the best relief.

Thus, civilian practice variably produces identical courses of action as in the Common Law where the primary legal remedy lies in the adequacy of damages, with performance being the exceptional discretionary (i.e. equitable) alternative.[33] Nonetheless, the respective traditions recognize, in not too disparate terms, the legal substance of obligations, the desirability of the defendant's personal freedom from the hardship of a bad bargain, the costs to the machinery of law enforcement, and the benefit to the claimant of substitute relief in money.[34] The reasons for the realistic practical similarities in the face

[28] The Lord Chancellor's Department, *Proposed Convention Between the United Kingdom and the United States for the Reciprocal Recognition and Enforcement of Judgments in Civil Matters, Third Consultative Paper*, March 1979, see e.g. Art. 2(2)(b) Draft Convention (cf. P.M. North, "The Draft UK/US Judgments Convention: A British Viewpoint" *NJILB* 1 (1979), at 219–239); S. Cromie, "A Choice Between Evils" *NLJ Practitioner* (16th August 1996) 1244. He discusses inter alia the difficulties with regard to US multiple and punitive damages awards being enforced elsewhere, especially in view of the awarding courts' inability to agree, bilaterally even, as to limits on the enforceability of these awards.

[29] P. Cane, "Exceptional Measures of Damages" in P. Birks (ed.), *op. cit.*, 301, at 325; cf. *Smith New Court Securities Ltd.* v. *Scrimgeours Vickers (Asset Management) Ltd.* [1996] 3 WLR 1051, at 1072–1073 (per Lord Steyn, on punishing intentional tortfeasors); see also D.G. Owen (ed.), *Philosophical Foundations of Tort Law* (Oxford, Clarendon; 1995), Chapter One.

[30] McGregor in Birks (ed.), *loc. cit.*, at 203.

[31] *Remedies for Breach of Contract: A Comparative Account* (Oxford, Clarendon; 1987), Chapters Three and Four.

[32] E.g. Arts. 250–51, 283, 326, 633(3), 651c(3) of the German *BGB* (there are exceptions).

[33] Treitel, *op. cit.*, at 63–65.

[34] Ibid., at 47 *et seq.*; cf. B. Chapman, *Wrongdoing, Welfare and Damages* in D.G. Owen (ed.), *op. cit.*, at 409–10.

of theoretical divergence are concerned with the claimant's position in the final analysis which, pragmatically, should be seen to represent fulfilment of the ultimate immutable object of international civil justice.

A further illustration of divergence of approaches is that, even in other Common Law systems, it is not unusual to find that damages may be awarded in multiple (punitive) sums.[35] Conversely, Civil Law systems do not generally recognize punitive sums,[36] not even in Scotland. Similarly, dispositions vary across and within legal traditions as to the bases for and limits to awards, e.g. for exemplary damages in the Common Law, just as there are different conceptual interpretations, for example of the relatively newer area of restitutionary damages,[37] or with regard to damages administered by English (as well as other national) courts and the European Court of Justice in European Community cases, as has been discussed for example by Brealey and Hoskins.[38] These and remaining issues are examined in the course of the Chapter. Of the "encompassing" underlying personal jurisdiction, there is some comparativist consensus that it does not go far enough as regards several so-called "transitory" aspects of trans-jurisdictional litigation which affect claims including those from intellectual property rights and their infringement,[39] product liability,[40] defamation[41] and environmental damage.[42] The net effect of the current local (internal law) character of the jurisdiction is that it either reduces (or rules out altogether as may be the case) the trans-jurisdictional remediability of such wrongs, and it is to be hoped that this can be improved upon whenever possible.

It is proposed to discuss first the compensatory principle generally, and then in the respective categories of breach of contract, tort, and unjustified enrichment, covering the typical issues from characterization, particularly whether the given issue is substantive or procedural and whether (and when) foreign or forum law applies to it. In this connexion, it may be recalled that the Civil Law operates on the back of a general organic private law of obligations, and court process does not typically categorize causes of action in contract, tort or restitution.[43] The

[35] Some US state anti-trust and similar laws (Minnesota, North and South Dakota, Montana, Oklahoma), and federal *Fair Labor Standards* and *Truth in Lending Acts*; *Desforge* v. *West St. Paul* 231 Minn 205 (1950), on multiple damages for the tort of trespass to land; but see *Re Westinghouse Uranium Contract* [1978] AC 547, at 594, for British views on recognition and enforcement. S.M. Waddams, *The Law of Damages* (Toronto, Canada Law Book Co; 1983), Chapter eleven.

[36] The Sri Lankan Roman-Dutch system appears to be an exception: cf. C.G. Weeramantry, *The Law of Contracts*, (Private publication, 1967), Vol.2, para. 932.

[37] For a sound preview of the internal law dimensions, see H. McGregor, "Restitutionary Damages" in P.B.H. Birks (ed.), *op. cit.*, 203 *et seq.*; also, in the same edition, P. Cane, *loc. cit.*, especially at 312–23.

[38] *Remedies in E.C. Law* (London, Longmans; 1994), Chapter Six.

[39] P. Trooboff in McLachlan and Nygh (eds.), *op. cit.* 125, at 128–134; also, A. Briggs, "Two Undesirable Side-Effects of the Brussels Convention?" (1997) 113 *LQR* 364–368, and G.W. Austin, "The Infringement of Foreign Intellectual Property Rights" (1997) 113 *LQR* 321, especially 324–335.

[40] P. Schlosser, ibid. 59, at 79–81. [41] P.B. Carter, ibid. 105, at 105–107, 121–123.

[42] F.K. Jeunger, ibid. 201, at 208–209, 213.

[43] Treitel, *op. cit.*, 9–10, on the French distinctions (with direct remedial implications) between types of obligations *de moyens* and *de résultat* (cf. B. Nicholas, *The French Law of Contract* (2nd

Civil Law does however set considerable store by the concept of "fault" which is neither required nor excluded in the Common Law and which moreover is not applied only to the matter of liability—as negligence or other excuses (or defences) for wrongs are, in the Common Law—but is also directly applied to remedies in cases where fault can be a head of damage. This is illustrated in the general principle expressed in Paragraph 276 of the German *BGB* (that "the debtor is responsible for deliberate acts of negligence"),[44] in Article 99 of the Swiss *Obligationenrecht* previously encountered above, in Article 1147 of the French *Code civil* and Paragraphs 920 and 1295(1) of the Austrian Civil Code (*ABGB*) which all connect fault with damages.

The irrelevance of fault in English internal law is possibly reflected in the identity of the ultimate payer of damages: insurance companies and the public, rather than the actual wrong-doer.[45] Nevertheless, the terminology is decidedly familiar and, as one commentator has remarked, "[i]n the field of private law, the similarities in the substantive contents of legal rules are so significant that there are grounds [for] an assumption that the legal rules in different countries are normally similar in their contents";[46] so that although there are far-reaching fundamental systemic differences as to the nature and consequences of remedial liability, there is at least a reducible comprehensibility of respective systems' concepts of "obligation" and "remedy", what Treitel means by a "considerable common core of meaning".[47]

COMPENSATORY DAMAGES

General

Damages are defined on notable authority in *Broome* v. *Cassell & Company*[48] as "the pecuniary compensation, obtainable by success in an action, for a wrong which is either a tort or a breach of contract, the compensation being in the form of a lump sum which is awarded unconditionally and is generally, but now not necessarily, expressed in English currency".[49] Naturally, the definition

ed., Oxford, Clarendon; 1992), 50 *et seq.*, where he adds obligations de guarantie); P. de Cruz, *Comparative Law in a Changing World* (London, Cavendish; 1995), 289–290.

[44] It is worthwhile to note the characterization of the defendant as "debtor" in the pro-performance-as-the-primary-remedy language of formal civilian jurisprudence. In English law, similar characterization is used in judgment awards.

[45] Atiyah, *op. cit.*, 108 *et seq.*

[46] M. Bogdan, *Comparative Law* (Stockholm, Kluwer Norstedts Juridik; 1994), at 97–98.

[47] *Op. cit.*, at 45.

[48] [1972] AC 1027 at 1070, per Lord Hailsham L.C.; see also *Halsbury's Statutes of England and Wales* (4th ed.,
Vol. 13, London, Butterworths; 1996 Re-issue), at 648.

[49] Cf. McGregor, *op. cit.*, para. 1. Other specific leading works include A. Ogus, *The Law of Damages* (London, Butterworths; 1970), D. Kemp (ed.), *The Quantum of Damages* (6th rev. ed., London, Sweet & Maxwell; 1995–6); H. Street, *Principles of the Law of Damages* (London, Sweet & Maxwell; 1962).

equally applies in the conflict of laws, and it is also the case that an action for damages may involve a claim for other non-money relief as in domestic litigation when the rules as to the claimant's election of relief often make it appropriate to do so, as in *Johnson* v. *Agnew*:[50] e.g., where the claimant can claim performance as well as damages for delay in the delivery of working goods (e.g. unique personal property), or where the claimant in an action of private nuisance may be granted a negative injunction plus damages. This section describes the compensatory principle and its corollaries.

The remainder of the Chapter begins with the rules of assessment or quantification which re-emphasize the "procedural" quality of the remedy; i.e., the sum of money awarded is the remedy in view. The definitional importance of the issue of quantum lies clearly in the influence it can have on choice of jurisdiction or forum, it being the case that the claimant may choose to sue in the forum which, in the circumstances, is expected to make the higher award.[51] For this reason and because effective substantive liability can for the most part be presumed in a work on remedies, these procedural rules are separately analysed first in each category of obligation discussed below, beginning with breach of contract.

The substantive right to damages itself, i.e. the type of liability or wrong the proof of which leads to a judgment for compensation and upon which the quantum need not necessarily directly depend,[52] is then discussed in the setting of the question of heads or items of liability or damage, the proof of which substantiates the right. Compensatory damages in the general area of tort (or delict) and, in the Common Law, in the fast-growing area of restitution will be seen to manifest the increasing influence of the lex causae upon traditional interpretations of procedure and, as a result, to have begun to favour the applicability—to be differentiated from the mere relevance—of rules of non-forum law qua lex loci delicti where necessary, in the way that contract conflicts cases have objectively done in principle for much longer through the theory of the proper law of the contract,[53] e.g. in Paragraphs 171 (torts) and 207 (contracts) of the American Law Institute's *Restatement Second of the Conflict of Laws*.[54] Identical views,

[50] [1980] AC 367, at 392–394, 397–399; also, e.g. *Oakacre Ltd.* v. *Claire Cleaners (Holdings) Ltd.* [1982] Ch 197 (specific performance at breach, with additional damages accruing between breach and judgment, pursuant to the *Chancery Amendment Act 1958* (*Lord Cairns' Act*)); contra *Advanced Portfolio Technologies Inc.* v. *Ainsworth*, *The Times*, 15th November 1995, in which foreign, rather than forum, proceedings were stayed.

[51] *Castanho* v. *Brown & Root (U.K.) Ltd.* [1981] AC 557; the decision survives on the point.

[52] By analogy, in the same way that a right to specific performance depends on nothing but the underlying contractual obligation, as pointed out by Lord Upjohn in *Beswick* (above, note 14), at 102; cf. S.A. Smith, "Rights, Remedies and Normal Expectations in Tort and Contract" (1997) 113 *LQR* 426, especially at 432.

[53] Cf. P.R.H. Webb, "Some Thoughts on the Place of English Law as Lex Fori in English Private International Law" (1961) 10 *ICLQ* 818, at 838–842. Although this insightful article does not isolate remedies for discussion, its focus on the *lex fori*, the law with which remedies are identified, lends itself to analogy.

[54] (Rev. and enlarged ed., St. Paul, Minnesota, American Law Institute Publishers; 1971), including the Comments; also, H. McGregor, "The International Accident Problem" (1970) 33 *MLR* 1, at 5–8, 21–26.

which rest on the merits of the connexion between relief and the lex causae, have been expressed by Beale,[55] Goodrich[56] and Leflar.[57] To ignore this connexion would be, as a relatively recent edition of *Salmond on Jurisprudence* states, "[t]o define procedure as concerned not with rights, but with remedies, [and] is to confound the remedy with the process by which it is made available".[58]

The remedy in view will be seen as an interpretive dynamic feature of conflicts remedies generally, in terms of whether and, if so, to which circumstances or class of issues it is convenient (and just) for the forum—by its lex fori rules, simpliciter (i.e. as internal law) or by legislative incorporation of international Conventions' provisions, rather than because the lex causae requires that application—to apply the rules of a relevant law which is, in neither form nor content, the same as the internal remedial law of the forum. These terms are very much a recent expansion of the jurisdiction-reflecting norms of practical conflicts jurisprudence by which internal law would otherwise apply exclusively.[59]

Useful analogues can thus be identified for the conflict of laws aspects and analyses of other types of remedy, particularly from the functional "substance" and "procedure" framework which is as responsive to the conflict of laws as it is to general remedial jurisprudence. For a start, the conflict of laws on damages shows the flexibility with which the procedural characterization of a remedy is to be approached. Also, by implicitly ruling out the initiation of suit for a foreign form of monetary remedy within the forum, the law of conflicts damages illustrates and is underscored by the inevitably localized definition of the limits of forum process in general. Perhaps more than anything, it assists the definition of remedies law on its own as being discrete from but overlapping with substance and procedure. The considerations may be distilled into a sequence of basic questions, viz.:

(a) has the defendant breached a loss-causing compensable obligation to the plaintiff?;[60]
(b) is the forum competent by its own law conveniently to proceed to remedy the breach?;

[55] J.H. Beale, *A Treatise on the Conflict of Laws* (New York, Baker Voorhuis; 1935), Vol. II, para. 412.1.

[56] H.F. Goodrich, *A Handbook of the Conflict of Laws* (4th ed. (E.F. Scoles), St. Paul, Minn., West; 1964), 159, emphasizing the consistency of awards regardless of choice of forum, recognizing the limits imposed by forum machinery.

[57] R.A. Leflar, *American Conflicts Law* (3rd ed., New York, Bobbs-Merrill; 1977), at 250–251, 253.

[58] (12th ed., by P.J. Fitzgerald, London, Sweet & Maxwell; 1966), at 461–464 (emphasizing the purposes and subject-matter of litigational processes).

[59] On the point, see the present writer's, "A Critique of the Orthodoxy of Excluding Foreign Law in the Evaluation of Compensatory Damages in the English Conflict of Laws: Considerations of Propriety of Quantum": an LL.M. dissertation in the University of Hull (1986) which accurately predicted the presently discussed applicability of foreign quantum law.

[60] Where there is breach but no unrecovered loss, nominal damages are awardable: *D Almeida Araujo Lda.* v. *Sir Frederick Becker & Co. Ltd.* [1953] 2 QB 329.

(c) by which law does the forum decide how, and how far, it should go in providing relief?

From the following discussion of breach situations, several factors of judicial policy concerned with fairness between the partes, certainty and uniformity in the law will be seen clearly to bear on the forum's responses to these questions.[61]

It is useful first to clarify the compensatory principle as it obtains in the conflict of laws.

The compensatory principle in the conflict of laws: general issues of terminology

In English law generally, the basic principle in domestic and conflicts cases alike is that damages—and no other money award—are compensatory (i.e. substitutional). The gist of the principle runs that "in almost all actions for breach of contract, and in many actions for tort, the principle of restitutio in integrum is an adequate and fairly easy guide to the estimation of damage, because the damage suffered can be estimated by relation to some material loss";[62] that "there must be some injury to [the claimant's legally protected] interests";[63] that "where any injury is to be compensated by damages, in settling the sum of money to be given for reparation of damages you should as nearly as possible get at that sum of money which will put the party who has been injured, or who has suffered, in the same position as he would have been in if he had not sustained the wrong for which he is now getting his compensation".[64]

These definitions emphasize different aspects of the broad tenet and make clear the central importance, especially in conflicts cases, of the difference and the inter-relation between (substantive) "damage"[65] and (procedural) "damages" made prominent by Cheshire and subsequently judicially affirmed in the cases which illustrate the principle.[66] A recent example of these is the House of Lords' decision in *Dimskal Shipping Company SA* v. *International Transport Workers Federation*,[67] in which it was held, inter alia, that proper law method applies to the solution of (all) questions of substantive obligation (thus avoiding the problem of terminology faced in a few earlier authorities, e.g. *NV Handel Maatschaapij J Smits Import-Export* v. *English Exporters*, in

[61] Cf. Lord Wilberforce in *Boys* v. *Chaplin* [1971] AC 356; also, e.g., P. Nygh, *Conflict of Laws in Australia* (6th ed., Sydney, Butterworths; 1995), at 263.

[62] *Broome* v. *Cassell & Co*, note 48, above, at 1070.

[63] Treitel, *op. cit.*, 76.

[64] *Livingstone* v. *Raywards Coal Co.* [1880] 5 AC 25, at 39 per Lord Blackburn.

[65] This is defined as "the disadvantage which is suffered by a person as a result of the act or default of another": *Halsbury's Laws op. cit.*, (1991), Vol. 12., para. 1102; see also, A. Ogus, *op. cit.*, 2; D.M. Walker, *The Law of Contracts and Related Obligations in Scotland* (2nd ed., London, Butterworths; 1985), paras. 33.23 *et seq.*

[66] E.g., in *D'Almeida Araujo Lda.* v. *Sir Frederick Becker & Co. Ltd.* [1953] 2 QB 329, at 292–293, per Pilcher J., citing G.C. Cheshire, *Private International Law* (4th ed., London, Butterworths; 1952), 659–660, and following the Canadian Supreme Court in *Livesley* v. *Horst Co.* [1925] 1 DLR 159.

[67] [1992] 2 AC 152.

which McNair J. did not necessarily distinguish measure of damage from measure of damages).[68] The general position elsewhere is more or less the same: for example, Paragraphs 122 (on rescission), 249 (on situations where no wrong has occurred), 254 (on the duty to mitigate losses), and 325–326 (on timeous performance) of the *BGB*.[69]

Damages will typically protect a claimant's positive expectation (loss of bargain or of the expected performance)[70] and status quo-negating (reliance, out-of-pocket expense)[71] interests, as well on occasion as the restitutionary, when the defendant benefits without actual loss to the claimant (as long as the liability depends on either of the two earlier types of interest and, if it relates to a contract, the contract must have been validly terminated by the claimant, rather than, e.g., is frustrated).[72] The award in restitution cases is for an undue shift of wealth, rather than as simple compensation.

At its core the versatility of damages is the limited but real versatility of the principle itself. The issue of other non-compensatory types of award is often really whether the over-riding principle can accommodate the head(s) under which those other types may be claimed, as was inferred by Lord Steyn in the *Smith New Court* litigation.[73] This can raise issues of conceptualization, e.g., of how to distinguish between straight-forward compensatory damages from, say, the punitive or the restitutionary, particularly in view of the general restorative tenor of the principle be the loss pecuniary or not.[74] Inter-related though they may be, these interests generate differing interpretations and consequences for damages, depending on the type of cause of action.[75] In *Inverugie Investments Limited* v. *Hackett*,[76] the claim to mesne profits was taken into account in quantifying the "restitutionary compensation"[77] for deliberate trespass to landed property (in the Bahamas) but, unhelpfully perhaps, the judgment shied from expatiating the mutual exclusivities of the compensatory and the restitutionary principles. The decision is returned to in section of the present Chapter, on restitutionary damages.

The language of "adequacy" (as "appropriateness" or "suitability") of damages goes to the factual basis for compensation in any given case. Substitutional

[68] [1955] 2 Ll Rep. 69, at 72.

[69] Cf. Article 1149–1151 French *Code civil*.

[70] *Robinson* v. *Harman* [1848] 1 Exch. 850: to put the aggrieved party in the position he would have been in had the contract been performed.

[71] *Anglia Television* v. *Reed* [1972] 1 QB 60: to put the claimant in as good a position as before the contract was made; cf. also *McRae* v. *Commonwealth Disposals Commission* [1950] 84 DLR 377.

[72] *Wrotham Park Estates* v. *Parkside Homes* [1974] 1 WLR 798.

[73] Ibid. (note 29, above), at 1076.

[74] Consider the definition in *Trayner's Latin Maxims* (Edinburgh, W.G. Green & Sweet and Maxwell; 1993), at 558–559: "Entire restitution; restoration to one's former condition"; cf. Cooke and Oughton, *op. cit.*, 98–99; Watts, *loc. cit.*

[75] Treitel, *op. cit.*, at 82–105.

[76] [1995] 1 WLR 713; cf. P. Watts, "Restitutionary Damages for Trespass" (1996) 112 LQR 39–41.

[77] Watts, ibid., at 40.

compensation can compare with actual performance itself only up to the point at which money can replace the agreed performance, as has been eloquently discussed by Spry,[78] and elaborated in Chapter Nine. In a recent paper, Ogus points out that the adequacy of compensatory damages also serves a deterrent purpose, particularly where the harm at issue is not fully covered by the compensatory award.[79] Thus, dicta, for example in *Radford* v. *De Froberville*[80] to the effect that general statements of the compensatory principle can be imprecise, should draw attention to the fact that the precedents can be misleading if the factual bases between the supposed authority and the facts in hand do not coincide.

The simple rationale is that the established wrong and the material imbalance it generates between the parties cannot be factually undone, so that the award satisfactorily re-adjusts that tangible imbalance such as it can. Subject to exceptions soon to be discussed, the inclusive principle—*restitutio in integrum*—applies varyingly in all the types of case of breach of obligation be they founded in contract, in tort or in other wrong, although the "remoteness" or "reasonable foreseeability" rules necessarily diverge according to the requirements of the choice of law rule which applies to the particularized wrong: in contract, the claimant usually recovers for loss of bargain and, in tort, for the defendant's failure to leave him alone.[81] The (dispositive) inclination away from applying the forum's internal law adds to the contrast between tort and breach of contract.

Indeed, the object of the principle is full and fair, rather than impossibly perfect, compensation.[82] These are presently explained further in discussing the respective wrongs. It is very much a principle that is qualified (in the sense of negating some types—therefore, some extents—of recovery) by circumstances to be elaborated below:[83] for example, rules as to exemplary awards, the remoteness rules encrypted in the celebrated case of *Hadley* v. *Baxendale*,[84] the rules applicable where the claimant is contractually entitled alternatively to liquidated or to unliquidated damages, as was established in *Dunlop Pneumatic Tyre Co. Ltd.* v. *New Garage & Motor Co. Limited*,[85] and the rules on mitigation of damage.[86] Thus, the materiality of loss is given the context of legal principle and practical reason.

[78] I.C.F. Spry *Equitable Remedies* (London, Sweet & Maxwell; 1990), at 58–73; cf. text at nn. 32–33 above.

[79] *Loc. cit.*, at n. 24 (in Hawkins (ed.)), 94–100, especially at 96–97.

[80] [1977] 1 WLR 1262, at 1272 (per Oliver J.).

[81] Cf. McGregor, *op. cit.* (14th ed.; 1980), para. 573; also, *Liesbosch Dredger* v. *Edison S.S.* [1933] AC 449, at 463 (per Lord Wright).

[82] *Pickett* v. *British Rail Engineering Ltd.* [1980] AC 136, at 168 per Lord Scarman; Treitel, *op. cit.*, at 174–179.

[83] For an overview, McGregor, *op. cit.*, Chapters Ten to Twelve; Treitel, *op. cit.*, at 146 generally.

[84] (1854) 9 Ex 341, at 354–355 (per Alderson B.); cf. *Liesbosch Dredger*, *loc. cit.* (note 81, above).

[85] [1915] AC 79.

[86] E.g. in *British Westinghouse Electric & Manufacturing Co. Ltd.* v. *Underground Electric Railways Co. of London Ltd.* [1912] AC 673, at 688–689.

What the principle signifies in the conflict of laws is fairly well settled, and it is to the illuminating types of cause to which consideration now turns. To recapitulate, the measure of damage or of liability is ever governed by the legal system which ascertains the breached obligation (qua lex causae) because the kind of compensable loss is integral to the obligation, as is the measure of damages in *Rome Convention* contract cases; in tort and in the few remaining types of contract case, the latter would appear to continue to depend on forum law. In the English legal system, general (i.e. naturally consequential) and special (usually non-pecuniary) damage, as distinguished in *B.T.C.* v. *Gourley*,[87] must, according to Order 18, rules 8(3), 12(1) and 15(1) *R.S.C.*,[88] now be specifically pleaded or stated as part of the causa. Between judicially calculated awards and simple compensation made under an applicable national statute,[89] no strict demarcation is to be drawn in the Chapter except where the contrary is indicated. The matter of awards other than in sterling is also taken further in the present Chapter, apropos of quantum. In all cases, the over-riding compensatory policy is tempered by a policy in favour of containing the defendant's remedial liability.

Breach of Contract

A breach of contract arises when there is no lawful excuse for a failure to perform one or more of the conditions (capable of giving rise to rescission and damages), warranties (giving rise to damages only) or other intermediate and (or) fundamental terms of a given contract.[90] A contract can be breached by a refusal to perform, defective performance, delayed performance or the prevention of performance. Recovery for breach is impossible or a misnomer in situations where a contract is re-negotiated following part-performance of the contract, in frustrated contracts, in agreements which deal with breach situations and in statute-barred claims. Non-judicial types of relief (e.g. rescission (termination); repudiation) do not fall directly within the scope of this book.

The last forty to fifty years have witnessed progressive development in the cases involving damages for breach of contract. A lean body of fairly settled conflicts case jurisprudence highlights the elements of the compensatory principle, although the scope of application of forum law to the issue of quantum remains somewhat elusive.[91] The ground-breaking developments which make for the applicability of non-forum rules of assessment are thus far unsupported

[87] [1956] AC 185, at 206 (per Lord Goddard).

[88] See also *Practice Directions* at [1976] 1 WLR 83, [1977] 1 WLR 197.

[89] See e.g. *Re The Herald of Free Enterprise* (The Guardian newspaper 2nd May 1989; arbitration), in which fixed payments inter alia under the Fatal Accidents Acts were applied to awards made to the successors of accident victims.

[90] Cf. J. Steyn, "Contract Law: Fulfilling the Reasonable Expectations of Honest Men" (1997) 113 *LQR* 433, at 441–2 (on the implications of the different types of term).

[91] The point appears in *Chitty on Contracts*, *op. cit.*, para. 30–098 (at text following note 27).

by judicial authority in England, and there are a few older decisions to the contrary. Therefore, it is useful first to clarify the compensatory principle on the issue of quantum in the light of the decisions, and to add that for self-evident reasons the now-relevant incidental matter of proof—in the standard way in conflicts cases[92]—of applicable foreign remedial law (with the burden resting on the claimant) should realistically be appended to these terms as where appropriate should the issue of foreign recognition and enforcement of forum damages awards. On the standard of proof, it can safely be said that the onus as to damage and damages is the claimant's, and the standard is one of reasonable certainty or "evidence from which the existence of damage can be reasonably inferred and which provides accurate data for calculating the amount".[93]

Damages are assessed at the time of breach or when it is no longer probable that the party in breach can make good the default (in other words, when performance ought to have taken place), unless to do so would "give rise to injustice, [and] the court has the power to fix such other date as may be appropriate in the circumstances";[94] in *Wroth* v. *Tyler*, the date of judgment for damages for breach of a contract for the sale of land[95] was held to be the operative date. In assessing damages, the court must consider all possible information on the losses suffered, and Order 59 rule 10 *R.S.C.* empowers appellate courts to admit evidence of any new circumstances.

The actual once-and-for-all[96] assessment is done by the judge (or by a jury in appropriate cases),[97] but may be referred to the Chancery or Queen's Bench Master under Order 37 of the *R.S.C.* In making the evaluation, the considerations may extend to the reason for performance, the impact of mitigation, and the likelihood of actual curative steps being taken where the basis is the cost of cure. The main reasons for the single assessment rule are the finality, necessity and convenience of an unconditional[98] single but broken-down sum which will show the composition of the heads of award and the awardee(s). Should there be an appeal as to quantum, any re-assessment in the appeal will be made easier, although it is out of the question that a subsequent larger award can be ordered in the case of subsequent realization of an awardee's true loss being greater than what comprised the initial award (to be distinguished from recoverable future losses), as in the tort case of *Buckland* v. *Palmer*;[99] a genuine separate cause of action would be the solution in the circumstances. It is noteworthy

[92] *Cheshire and North*, *op. cit.*, Chapter Seven generally.

[93] McGregor, *op. cit.* (1980), para. 261; cf. *Monarch SS Co. Ltd.* v. *Karlshamns Oljefabriker A/B* [1949] AC 196.

[94] *Johnson* v. *Agnew* [1980] AC 367.

[95] [1974] Ch 30.

[96] McGregor, *op. cit.*, paras. 1, 1794–1812; Cheshire & North (10th ed., London, Butterworths; 1979), 712; *Dicey and Morris* (10th ed., 1980), at Rule 209, 1175 *et seq.*

[97] McGregor, *op. cit.*, para. 1794.

[98] *Banbury* v. *Bank of Montreal* [1918] AC 626 (an award, to depend on contract subject-matter was first to be returned, was overturned in this case).

[99] [1984] 3 All ER 554; see also the old case of *Fritter* v. *Veal* 12 Mod Rep 542 (1701).

that Section 2 of the *Damages Act 1996* allows periodic payments; Sections 4–6 provide for structured settlements.[100]

Quantum

Broadly speaking, assessment is of the value of the loss sustained, as the objectively quantifiable (i.e., by a third party, if necessary[101]) cost of completing the contract (or the re-instatement of the rights infringed).[102] Difficulties encountered in the course of estimation, e.g. of non-compensatory harm, prospective loss or the liable defendant's poverty will not bar relief. Whenever the claimant seeks damages for reliance on a contract in breach, the normal basis is that party's expenses bar heads of damage which are not recoverable; for recovery of consequent losses incurred on the basis of expectation, the correct basis is either the claimant's reparative cost or the difference in value between the original subject-matter and its replacement, although it may be both bases if an earlier curative attempt fails (in reality, two separate causes) as it did in *Harling* v. *Eddy*[103] where a claimant who had bought a heifer which then died was entitled to its value plus veterinary costs (the award outstripped the value of a healthy heifer); for restitution, the basis is the defendant's unearned benefit.

A claimant can generally not recover more than one type of interest for the same loss and where the loss flows from having made the contract rather than from its breach only the lower expectation loss is recoverable.[104] Subject to the claimant's duty to mitigate, all proximate and incidental losses can be recoverable as expectation losses. Reliance losses are, however, usually easier to recover where the expectation losses are too conjectural.[105] The Court of Appeal in *Sealace Shipping Company Limited* v. *Shipping Limited* re-affirmed the view that a claimant "is fully entitled to be as extravagant as he pleases but not at the expense of the defendant",[106] although the decision in *The Rijn* holds that the defendant is presumed to have performed in the ways least burdensome to himself and least beneficial to the claimant.[107]

A rule as to quantum aims "to quantify in terms of money the sum payable by the defendant in respect of the injury, for which his liability has already been determined by the proper law".[108] It is important to understand the narrow (calculation) and wide (causal) senses of such a rule. The former sense (of sums

[100] Cf. Law Commission Consultation Paper, "Structured Settlements and Interim and Provisional Damages" No. 125 (London, H.M.S.O.; 1992), Part V.

[101] Cf. *Shearson Lehman Hutton Inc.* v. *Maclaine Watson & Co. Ltd.* [1990] 3 All ER 723 (on evidence of a market where the goods could have been sold); in the civil law, a very high degree of uncertainty of damage will bar an award: Treitel, *op. cit.*, at 192–193.

[102] D. Harris, A. Ogus, J. Phillips, "Contract Remedies and the Consumer Surplus" (1979) 95 *LQR* 581, 589–594.

[103] [1951] 2 KB 739.

[104] See e.g. *CCC Films (London) Ltd.* v. *Impact Quadrant Films* [1994] 3 All ER 298.

[105] Cf. the cases at note 71 above.

[106] *The Times*, 25th September 1990 ([1991] 1 LlRep 120; Neill, Ralph Gibson and McCowan L.JJ., C.A.)

[107] [1981] 2 LlRep 267, at 271.

[108] *Cheshire and North*, *op. cit.* (1979), at 711.

to be included in or excluded from the award) monifies the injury in a pretty direct way, the latter (that the quantificatory process is subject to choice-of-law) places the evaluative exercise in the fuller context of the process and machinery applicable to the cause of action in breach of contract. The lex causae determines the limits to compensation, the definition of the award and the legal principles for calculation, insofar as the lex fori will accommodate these lex causae positions.[109] Thus, these senses simplify what would otherwise be a rather mixed bag of rationales.

A forum quantum rule goes to the methodology which converts the lex causae right into a forum process right to relatively precise recompense; the required degree of precision in the English courts has been described by Lord Diplock as idiosyncratic (in *Boys* v. *Chaplin*)[110] but empirical.[111] In *Lim Poh Choo* v. *Camden Area Health Authority*, Lord Scarman said that "[a]s long . . . as the sum awarded is a substantial sum in the context of current money values, the requirement of the law is met".[112] The point about monetary values is presently expanded in the context of foreign currency awards. Considerations such as the foregoing complete the picture of the quantificatory method by which a conflicts wrong is monetized either because the governing law is forum law or because relevant non-forum law is either unsatisfactorily proved or is lacking in rules to monetize the loss. For reasons of the convenience of the forum, the method excludes resort to actuarial evidence: in English internal law, the point is contained in *Watson* v. *Powles*[113] or to extra-ordinary risks of inflation and interest and, in another decision, capital depreciation rates.[114] The Giuliano-Lagarde Report on the *Rome Contracts Convention* also excludes factual or other non-legal arithmetic assessment.[115]

The assessment of damages in contract cases is given[116] to be a matter for the lex causae (in so far as the lex causae has rules in point) because of Article 10(1)(c) of the *Rome Contracts Convention 1980*:[117] "The law applicable to a contract . . . shall govern in particular:..within the limits conferred on the court by its procedural law, the consequences of breach, including the assessment of damages in so far as it is governed by rules of law." This provision is part of English law contained in Schedule I of the *Contracts (Applicable Law) Act 1990*, and it forms a radical exception (but it is submitted, correct and perhaps overdue because it emphasizes the almost inseparable link between the nature of loss and its monetary value) to the pre-existing rule to the effect that it is a

[109] Cf. *The Indian Grace* [1992] 1 LlRep 124.

[110] [1968] 2 QB 1, at 41 (Court of Appeal).

[111] I.e. previously in *Hennell* v. *Ranaboldo* [1963] 1 WLR 1391, at 1393–1394.

[112] [1980] AC 174, at 189–190.

[113] [1968] 1 QB 596, at 604 (per Lord Denning) and 605 (per Winn L.J.)

[114] *Mallett* v. *McGonagle* [1970] AC 166, at 176 (per Lord Diplock, since known as "the Diplock assumption").

[115] At 33.

[116] *Halsbury's Laws*, *op. cit.*, para. 1078; *Dicey & Morris*, *op. cit.*, at 183.

[117] I.e. S. 2 and Article 10(1)(c) of Schedule 1 thereof.

matter for the lex fori, as propounded for example in *Kremezi* v. *Ridgway*.[118] While most of the older authorities involved practically similar substantive provisions in both the English and the other relevant law(s), it should be noted that they also involved, as an unexplored issue, different remedies for breach; i.e., the issue of conflictive relief was not taken as far as it can now be.

It is interesting that other legal systems (e.g. the South African, in *Stewart* v. *Ryall*,[119] and the Australian, in *Breavington* v. *Godleman*)[120] have applied the lex causae to the procedural matter of quantum for some considerable time. In the present English law, the vast majority of contracts concluded after April 1 1991 is to be regulated by the *Rome Convention*[121] in force for ten years, and is then implicitly renewed every five years if there has been no abrogation. The few excepted types of contract (e.g. insurance contracts which, by the internal lex fori, cover risks within the territory of the Convention (Article 1(3)) are governed by the old Common Law rules,[122] or by specified régimes which need not be taken further here.

There are several general factors affecting the process of assessment.[123] As is the case with much of the conflict of laws, much is owed to admiralty cases for the development and texture of the law in these areas. The following points apply where English law is the contractual lex causae. Limits to the application of a different lex causae will be imposed by the public policy of the forum. In the case of taxation, presently discussed (a matter of revenue law), which is definitionally inapplicable in conflicts cases, foreign lex causae tax considerations will generally be inapplicable,[124] subject to expert evidence as in *Juliet Praet et Cie* v. *H.G. Poland*[125] as to the excepting circumstances of the claimant otherwise being a taxable private legal personality. It is equally important to note that the same considerations apply to non-compensatory, especially liquidated, sums where appropriate and will not be repeated in discussing those awards.

All the rules pertaining to assessment now to be discussed are procedural *par excellence* (for the lex fori, but not simpliciter), in that their application is not necessarily to be construed conjunctively of the rules applicable to the substantive issue[126] particularly because, as an observer notes, "it is the actual amount of damages awarded, not the "measure of damages", that provides the relevant evidence" of the obligation the court upholds.[127] A legitimate consideration

[118] [1949] 1 All ER 662 (breach of promise of marriage), at 664.

[119] (1887) 5 SC 146 (per Smith J.); but see *Parker, Wood & Co.* v. *Bullard, King & Co.* [1876] NLR 18.

[120] [1980] 80 ALR 362, at 373.

[121] Articles 1(2) and 17 of the *Convention*; section 7 *1990 Act*.

[122] *Halsbury's Laws* (Vol. 8(1)), paras. 844–845, 855, 857–858, 886.

[123] E.g., McGregor, *op. cit.*, paras. 573–615; Ogus, *op. cit.*, Chapter four generally.

[124] *Government of India* v. *Taylor* [1955] AC 491 (on foreign capital gains tax accruing to a foreign government following the English voluntary liquidation of the defendant).

[125] [1962] 1 LlRep 566 (on wrongful termination of cross-border motor insurance agency).

[126] *Cheshire and North*, *op. cit.*, at 100.

[127] Smith, *loc. cit.* (1997) (LQR), at 432. Thus a (further) terminological distinction can be drawn between quantum and measure of damages, the latter being limited to the literal, rather than the pecuniary, protection offered.

which restrains an analytical description of these factors from being regarded as pertaining to the measure of damage is that to do so is not unlikely to becloud the issue as being one for a liquidated claim.

(a) Interest

The first of these factors is liability for, and the rate of, interest[128] (claimed separately) on the compensatory award itself. Interest accrues in full with the cause of action, as in *Nicholson* v. *Hall*,[129] and applies, where it does, until the date of judgment, as was held in *Cook* v. *Kier*.[130] These considerations are aimed at making the compensation full by restoring to the claimant "the use of the money which was due to him".[131] As with interest on contract sums due (Article 10(1)(b) *Rome Convention*, on performance being governed by the lex causae), interest on compensation is substantive and for the lex causae, as was found in the early case of *Arnott* v. *Redfern*[132] and more recently in *Mount Albert Borough Council* v. *Australasian Temperance & General Mutual Life Insurance Society*.[133] Mann persuasively argued that interest is really a form of damage,[134] not least because the different heads of damage attracting interest are to be itemized; typically, non-pecuniary losses (e.g. in defamation) cannot attract interest because the claimant would not have been deprived of the use of his money. Pecuniary losses include sums for breach of an insurance contract (in *Edmunds* v. *Lloyd Italico e L'Ancora Compania di Assicurazioni e Riassicurazioni SpA*).[135] Section 35A of the *Supreme Court Act 1981*[136] leaves the rate of interest on debts and liquidated damages to the (internal) lex fori when the governing law is English law.

It is difficult to conceive of liability for the interest due on a foreign debt—the payment of which the English forum orders to be made in foreign currency—being governed by English rates, especially where the (foreign) lex causae stipulates a rate. However, when the award in foreign currency is to be paid in sterling, the separate interest which accrues on the sterling payment should be calculated at the rate applicable to sterling at the date of payment. The

[128] Cf. *Halsbury's Laws*, *op. cit.* (Vol. 8(1)), at para. 1078.

[129] [1963] 3 All ER 849 (in this case, the date of the wrongful dismissal).

[130] [1970] 2 All ER 513.

[131] *BP Exploration Co. (Libya) Ltd.* v. *Hunt (No. 2)* [1982] 1 All ER 925, at 974 (per Robert Goff J.)

[132] 2 C & P 88 (1825).

[133] [1938] AC 224; and from Canada, *Montreal Trust Co.* v. *Stanrock Uranium Mines Ltd.* [1966] 1 OR 258 (Ontario High Court, on the issue of payment of interest on interest); but see *Midland International Trade Services* v. *Sudairy* (Financial Times, 2nd May 1990) where, strangely, the lex fori was applied.

[134] "On Interest, Compound Interest and Damages" [1985] 101 *LQR* 30, e.g. at 31, 34–37 and 47; in *Tehno-Impex* v. *Gebr van Weelde Scheepvartkantoor BV* [1981] QB 648, the Court of Appeal held that interest on sums paid before the beginning of proceedings were claimable as damages for loss of use of the money (the House of Lords later over-ruled this decision in *La Pintada*, below, in the text which carries note 132).

[135] [1986] 2 All ER 249.

[136] See the providing statute, S. 15(1) *Administration of Justice Act 1982*; cf. *Westdeutsche Landesbank Girozentrale* v. *Islington LBC* [1996] 2 WLR 802.

applicable rate is the average rate on current short-term investment accounts, laid down (in admiralty) in *The Funabashi*,[137] but the forum may not apply a rate where the contract itself has stipulated one. The rates of interest are fixed periodically by the Lord Chancellor.

In English law, the right to interest is limited to when the defendant fails to make payments due, to special damage and in admiralty.[138] Thus, in *The President of India* v. *La Pintada Compania Navigacion*, no interest was awarded on any sums already paid before issue was joined[139] (rather than on sums paid after proceedings began but before judgment),[140] although the Law Commission had recommended that interest should be added to such sums.[141]

Section 3(1) of the English *Law Reform (Miscellaneous Provisions) Act 1934*[142] first formalized the earlier Law Revision Committee's recommendation that the courts have a general discretion (without specific principles, as found in *Jefford* v. *Gee*,[143] with the onus for refusal on the defendant) as to when interest should be awarded or refused.[144] The discretion does not extend to moneys not forming part of the compensatory award, e.g., post-judgment interest (governed by Section 17 *Judgments Act 1838*, which makes the award a judgment debt), interest on interest, compound interest,[145] or interest payable by operating law.[146]

(b) Currency of award

The forum will award damages in the currency which best expresses the loss and, where liability is best expressed in foreign currency (e.g. because, as in *Miliangos*, the claimant, the lex causae, and the currencies of account and of payment were Swiss, and because sterling depreciated between breach and judgment and was thus onerous to a foreign creditor), the sum in sterling to be paid is fixed by reference to the applicable rate of exchange on the date of payment.[147] In *Miliangos*, Lord Wilberforce made a number of basic

[137] [1972] 2 All ER 181. [138] McGregor, *op. cit.*, paras. 575–584. [139] [1985] AC 104.

[140] Section 35A(3) *Supreme Court Act 1981*.

[141] Law Commission Paper, "Law of Contract: Report on Interest" No. 88 (London, H.M.S.O.; 1978), Cmnd. 7229, para. 114.

[142] It is now superseded by S. 15 of the *Administration of Justice Act 1982* which introduces a S. 35A to the *Supreme Court Act 1981* (for the High Court) and a Ss. 69 and 97A of the *County Courts Act 1959* (for county courts).

[143] [1970] 2 QB 130, at 143.

[144] Law Commission Second Interim Report "Statute Law Revision: Third Report" No. 37 (London, H.M.S.O.; 1934), Cmnd. 4546, Para. 8: "In practically every case a judgment against the defendant means that he should have admitted the claim when it was made and have paid the appropriate sum as damages"; in *London Chatham & Dover Railway Co.* v. *South Eastern Railway Co.* [1893] AC 429, the House of Lords reluctantly denied a power to award interest (437, per Lord Herschell L.C., in considering the earlier ruling to that effect in *Page* v. *Newman* 9 B.& C. 378 (1829)).

[145] Cf. *Ferguson* v. *Fyffe* [1841] 8 ER 49, per Lord Cottenham L.C. (citing Lord Eldon in *ex parte Bevan* [1803] 9 Ves 324); cf. F.A. Mann, *loc. cit.* at note 134, especially at 42–46. The reason for excluding compound interest awards is that to do so is unduly complex.

[146] Ibid. (Mann), e.g. at 32.

[147] *Miliangos* v. *George Frank & Co. (Textiles) Ltd.* [1976] AC 443; *Commerzbank A/G* v. *Large* 1977 SC 375.

observations[148] which assist clarification: that the form of the relevant rules of practice (Orders 42 rule 1 and 45 *R.S.C.*) in fact, favoured the making of such awards where appropriate; that there were no problems of their enforcement, indeed, that such awards were typically enforceable after arbitration (citing *Jugoslavenska Oceanska Plovidba* v. *Castle Investment Co. Inc*,[149] *The Teh Hu*,[150] *The Halcyon the Great*)[151] and only needed to be converted into sterling at the date of payment. The directly enabling Article 106 of the EEC *Treaty of Rome* was also relied on by his Lordship, as was the *Schorsch Meier GmbH*[152] decision in point, the only other case in which an English forum had at the time made such an award on the basis of the same Article.

In line with the rapid expansion of the new rule (originated in debt in *Miliangos*) to cover unliquidated damages, e.g. in *The Folias*[153] and in the tort circumstances of *The Despina R*,[154] the lex causae in a case in hand need not have been English law in order for the award in foreign currency to be made, nor does the currency need be more than that in which the claimant normally does business. The issue is redolent of remoteness. Interest may follow the rates available under the lex causae as it did in *The Pacific Colocotronis*,[155] rather than follow the rates available in the forum system. *Miliangos* has been applied to a restitutionary claim, in *B.P. Exploration Co. (Libya) Limited* v. *Hunt (No. 2)*.[156]

The underlying explanatory object is that the claimant, who is almost invariably the party seeking an award in foreign currency, be shielded from changes in the external money value of the obligation or loss, and not from changes in the internal value of his (foreign) currency. The question itself, i.e. whether a foreign currency award is to be made, is a procedural one, although the law to be referred to in the actual calculation is the lex causae[157] (which will give way to forum law where the relevant lex causae rules are not pleaded or are excluded by forum policy).

Once the rule of decision has determined that an award in foreign currency is not available, no other cognate considerations should survive. Where English law is the lex causae, first reference is to the contract terms to see whether a currency is expressly or tacitly provided for as in *Jugoslavenska*[158] and, more recently, in *Metaalhandel JA Magnus BV* v. *Ardfields Transport Limited*[159] in

[148] Especially at 463 *et seq*. For the comparable New York state law, which stands in isolation from the remainder of the United States, see S. Stern, "The Courts and Foreign Currency Obligations" [1995] *LMCLQ* 494, where he discusses the enabling S. 27(b) amendment of the *New York Judiciary Law* of July 20th 1987 as against the otherwise prevalent so-called "home currency rule" enshrined in S. 20 *Currency Act 1792*.

[149] [1974] QB 292. [150] [1969] 3 All ER 1200, at 1206–1207.

[151] [1975] 1 All ER 882. [152] [1975] QB 416.

[153] *Services Europe Atlantique Sud* v. *Stockholms Rederiaktiebolag SVEA* [1979] A.C. 685; see also, *Kraut AG* v. *Albany Fabrics Ltd.* [1977] QB 182.

[154] *Owners of MV Eleftherotria* v. *Owners of MV Despina R* [1979] AC 685.

[155] *Shell Tankers (U.K.) Ltd.* v. *Astro Comino Armadora SA* [1981] 2 LlRep 40; cf. Law Comm Paper No. 124 (London, H.M.S.O.; 1983), Para. 4.15, which leaves the rate to the forum's discretion instead of tying the rate to that which applies locally.

[156] [1983] 2 AC 352. [157] *The Folias*, at 700; *Miliangos*, at 465.

[158] Above at note 149, at 298. [159] [1988] 1 LlRep. 197.

which the parties' reasonable contemplation operated in the absence of a choice of currency. Needless to say, if the claimant in using his own currency has done the reverse of mitigate his losses, then the evaluation of those losses should not be referred to that currency. In contractual restitution, the correct currency, according to *BP Exploration*,[160] is that of the defendant's unearned gain. Further points particular to torts are raised incidentally in the course of quantum of tort damages.

(c) Taxation

Deductions for taxation comprise another set of considerations which may be central to the issue of quantum[161] and typically, but by no means exclusively, in wrongful dismissal cases. Where deductions are made, the basis for the deductions is that the claimant may recover for lost net earnings (or profits), past or future, which otherwise would have been taxable; the issue is redolent of a remoteness-of-damage issue. The leading case in point is the tort case of *British Transport Commission* v. *Gourley*.[162] The decision applies whenever a damages award is not taxable in the claimant's hands and, therefore, applies to damages for breach of contract as well.[163] The *Gourley* ratio is that, in assessing damages for loss of income in the past and future, tax savings must be taken into account where the damages award itself is not taxable but the lost income would have been taxable were it not lost (or replaced). It has since been followed as far afield as in South Africa[164] and, as far as the present writer is aware, has been departed from only in Canada;[165] it was followed in New Zealand in *Smith* v. *Wellington Woollen Manufacturing Co. Limited*[166] and in Australia in case of *Hamlyn* v. *Hann*.[167]

The basic requirements for the application of the ratio are, first, that the compensable wrong should otherwise have been taxable in the normal way, e.g. higher rent payments than were actually due as in *Sykes* v. *Midland Bank*[168] and, secondly, to the defendant's relief, that there should be no legislation to prohibit the deductions. According to *Riches* v. *Westminster Bank*,[169] damages themselves may be taxable depending on the kind of loss and on whether there is legislation on the point. Non-pecuniary losses are usually not taxable in reflection of the central idea of the *Gourley* principle that damages ought to be reduced on the basis of tax-saving considerations. When the *Gourley* principle applies, the assessment is made on broad lines, as was stated by Earl Jowitt in

[160] Ibid. at note 156, at 355.

[161] Cf. McGregor, *op. cit.*, paras. 571–608, 610–613, 619–621; Street, *op. cit.*, at 88–104.

[162] [1956] AC 185 (first encountered above in differentiating general from special damage); see also *Rajah's Commercial College* v. *Gian Singh & Co. Ltd.* [1977] AC 312.

[163] Cf. *Chitty on Contracts* (27th ed. London, Sweet & Maxwell; 1994)), paras. 26–073 to 26–078.

[164] See e.g. *Ministry of Defence* v. *Jackson* 1991 (4) SA 23 (Z.S.); but see *Whitfield* v. *Phillips* 1957 (3) SA 318 (A).

[165] *R.* v. *Jennings* [1966] 57 DLR (2d.) 644. [166] [1956] NZLR 491. [167] [1967] SASR 387.

[168] [1969] 2 QB 518 (since rent is not taxable, no deduction was made in this case).

[169] [1947] AC 390.

the judgment itself,[170] and at the prevalent rate at the date of judgment.[171] Consideration is to be given to the claimant's tax relieving, mitigating or compensating circumstances, if any, e.g., other private moneys as was found by Pilcher J. in *Beach* v. *Reed Corrugated Cases*.[172] In *Rosenberg & Son Limited* v. *Manchester Corporation*,[173] the damages for a lessee's removal expenses made allowance for the lessee's tax savings thereon.

When the award of damages is taxable in the claimant's hands, quantum will likely not be affected by taxation. Therefore, *Gourley* is inapplicable in its direct form, and quantum will rise accordingly, as it did in *The Telemachus*,[174] to shift the tax incidence (of what would have been the claimant's tax liability) to the defendant (the distinguishing judicial policy considerations of promoting emergency salvage which were particular to that case should be noted).

If there are tax liability issues for both claimant and defendant, overwhelming considerations of forum convenience will discourage the forum from what would otherwise be a thorough method of settling the issue of the propriety or accuracy of apportioning the deductions to be made.[175] It would be helpful to ignore any inferences of punitive, impractical, or non-distributive aspects to tax-deducted damages which might arise in these regards, and to note that for these reasons the notion of subjecting all awards to tax considerations is indeed persuasive in the interests of propriety of quantum.[176]

The considerations differ slightly when the tax in issue is capital gains tax. *McGregor on Damages*[177] (the lex causae being English law) provides a magisterial survey and analysis.[178] The gist of these considerations is that, by the introduction of capital gains tax in the *Finance Act 1965* and now consolidated in the *Capital Gains Tax 1979*, this tax does not bring on a reduction in the size of awards as does income tax. The incidence, in the award, of capital gains tax (determined by Section 1 of the latter statute) is likely only if the loss is of a disposable capital asset which is subject to taxation under Section 20(1)(a) of the *1979 Act* which defines disposal. Thus the question is of taxability and not of reduction of the award.

(d) The claimant's contributory negligence

This can be differently expressed as the apportionment of losses between the parties where the proven liabilities in damages are to be shared. The basis for the forum's apportionment is not causal, strictly speaking, but relates more directly to the actual harm. Whether there is a basis for apportionment clearly

[170] [1956] AC 185, at 203 (see also Lord Goddard, at 207 and Lord Reid, at 215).

[171] Ibid., at 209. [172] [1956] 2 All ER 652, at 658. [173] [1971] 23 P & CR 68.

[174] [1957] P 47 (on salvors' compensation).

[175] But see the Scots case of *Stewart* v. *Glentaggart* 1963 SLT 119 in which such an award was followed; in the English case of *Bold* v. *Brough, Nicholson and Hall* [1963] 3 All ER 849, a "golden handshake" case in which the tax-free portion of the money involved was subjected to *Gourley* by Phillimore J., and was deducted.

[176] Cf. Ogus, *op. cit.*, at 115 (he suggests legislation to this end).

[177] *Op. cit.*, at places referred to in n. 161, above.

[178] *Op. cit.*, paras. 614–615, and 619–621.

depends on what the lex causae says about whether contributory negligence is, not just a defence, but also a quantum-limiting consideration. In *Forsikringsaktieselskapet Vesta* v. *Butcher*,[179] the claimants had re-insured the underlying insurance of their fish farm in Norway. They instructed their brokers, the defendants, to expunge a clause imposing a duty on the claimants to monitor the farm round the clock, under the original insurance, from the re-insurance (and to confirm having done so). The brokers did not comply with either instruction. The re-insurers were held liable by the House of Lords, regardless of the clause at issue, for fish lost. The defendants were not liable for the loss, indeed their Lordships did not discuss contributory negligence in the way that it had been in the Court of Appeal and at first instance, at which stages it was held that the defence was available in the case of (tortiously negligent, rather than strict) breach of a contractual duty of care.

It therefore appears that unless and until breach of contract itself, including consideration of the issue of fault, is specifically addressed, a sufficiently unyielding statement of the law in this regard will not yet be forthcoming particularly in conflicts cases. It must be said that the matter of apportionment of liability is redolent of other factors of the right to damages to which attention presently turns.

In *Butcher*, the lex causae was English law. The defining law is the *Law Reform (Contributory Negligence) Act 1945* which does not directly go to breach of contract or the consequences; in principle, it recognizes simultaneous tort liability. The Law Commission has recommended that contract defences should include contributory negligence,[180] and the need to implement the recommendation, provisional as it is, could hardly be clearer than in the result subsequently reached in *Schering Agrochemicals Limited* v. *Resibel NV SA*[181] in which the claimant chemical manufacturers' unreasonableness in not investigating a defect-revealing occurrence or to discontinue operations until the already bad situation had been checked was held to deny them any damages for consequent losses; in other words, there was a complete defence to the assertion of the right to damages, rather than any admission of a basis for apportionment. It is therefore probably easier to rely on a foreign lex causae if that law has clear rules of apportionment.

Thus examined and analysed, the forum's fulfilment of the assertion of a right to damages conveniently brings the discussion to the separate question of the right itself, with reference to the items or types of loss which are taken to substantiate that right. It cannot be over-emphasized that there are considerable overlaps between the respective questions since either question answered affirmatively will limit or exclude the cause-disposing quantum; if a particular type of loss is not compensable, there will be no award for it. The overlaps

[179] [1988] 2 All ER 43.

[180] "Contributory Negligence as a Defence in Contract", Working Paper No. 114 (London, H.M.S.O.; 1990).

[181] An unreported Court of Appeal decision of 26th November 1992.

certainly make analysis possible and sometimes easier, but cannot necessarily be described as ever-useful for intending litigants.

Heads or measure of damage

In the present discussion, concern is with the variety of types of injury for which an award of compensatory damages for breach of contract may be granted. As long as the harm is consequential, compensable (in the sense of not being too remote as was first laid down in the *locus classicus* of *Hadley* v. *Baxendale*)[182] wrongs are, in general, either pecuniary or non-pecuniary (the latter having some affinity with considerations of property)[183], with the possibility of sub-categorization in terms of whether the loss generated is primary (general) or additional (special). An award can consist of more than one item, indeed more than one category, of damage. In point of fact, and as would confirm the fine lines between quantum and liability, a fair number of the cases which illustrated the former will be seen to re-surface in the present analysis in terms of how quantum is explained and constituted.[184]

As has previously been pointed out, the law by which damage is measured has long been recognized as the lex causae. The denominator is the type of sufficiently proximate interest, also previously outlined (i.e., expectation, reliance or restitutionary), which the claimant seeks to have the forum protect, and there is no legal system within the purview of this book which is not adequately thoroughly familiar with the application of the relevant specified rules of another legal system in the context of international contracts where it is appropriate to do so. It goes without saying that the interests protected in breach situations are, by and large, commercial losses.[185]

The law of contract conflicts is owed a fair deal by the present level of development of the law. If the foreign governing law requires the application, or indeed the disapplication, of a particular kind of loss, then the forum will apply that law unless its own rules (or the wider public policy to which the forum must defer) prevent it from doing so for reasons to be discussed here after the description of the types of loss. The considerations will accordingly have no place in the obligational situation sounding in contract which does not involve an unliquidated sum, and will include the law on mitigation of damage (or vorteilsausgleichung in the Civil Law).[186]

In contract conflicts, it is crucial to distinguish between remoteness which goes to the cause of breach (i.e., fault) and remoteness which relates to the actual damage which results from breach. This is because these concepts are

[182] Above, at text carrying n. 84.

[183] Cf. McGregor, *op. cit.*, generally, Part one, as it concerns contract; A. Burrows, *Remedies for Torts and Breach of Contract* (2nd ed., London, Butterworths; 1994), at 137.

[184] Cf. *Chitty on Contracts*, *op. cit.*, paras. 26–043 to 26–049. These paragraphs illustrate remoteness vis-à-vis quantification using the contexts of the sale of goods, the carriage of goods, contracts concerning land, contracts to lend or pay money and the sale of shares.

[185] *Sunley* v. *Cunard White Star* [1939] 2 KB 791, at 799 (per Hallett J.)

[186] Cf. Treitel, *op. cit.*, at 179, 184 and 187–188.

quite different even though they are both closely related to the parties' reasonable contemplation and may be subject to whether or not matters extraneous to the contractual relationship (e.g. the independent acts of the claimant or of a third party) are a factor. The former usage falls outside the scope of this book in that it refers exclusively to non-remedial liability (or to the pre-judgment obligation), and particularly because the conflict of laws adds its own dimension in that the same law need not apply to either concept. In the latter, as described in *Chitty on Contracts*, the decisive point is whether "the promisor implicitly accepts responsibility for the usual consequences of a breach of the promise in question, while the promisee implicitly accepts the risk of any other consequence".[187]

When English law is lex causae, the rule in *Hadley* v. *Baxendale* has been applied with some modification in the respective decisions in *Victoria Laundry (Windsor) Ltd.* v. *Newman Industries Limited*[188] and in *Koufos* v. *Czarnikow Limited, The Heron II*.[189] In *Hadley*, the claimants sought to recover prospective profits from their mill which had become inoperable. The defendants were carriers who had unreasonably delayed the delivery of the mill for repair. Recovery was refused because the facts within the defendants' knowledge did not reasonably show that the profits would cease on the basis of the delay; in other words, the loss of profits was too remote a consequence of the breach. Lord Scarman summarized the test as follows in *H. Parsons (Livestock) Limited* v. *Uttley Ingham & Co. Limited*: "The court's task . . . is to decide what loss to the plaintiff it is reasonable to suppose would have been in the contemplation of the parties as a serious possibility had they had in mind the breach when they made their contract".[190] Thus the breach itself need not actually have been within the contemplation of the parties. It need only be the case that a reasonable man could have foreseen the particular type, rather than the extent, of loss. The decisive consideration depends on the forum's discretion as to the broad categorization of losses, and includes nothing by way of the cause or the factual details of the loss.[191] The general rules are dealt with in detail in standard works like *Chitty on Contracts*.[192] It is sufficient to identify the types or heads of loss as follows beginning with basic pecuniary losses, depending on the contract party in breach.

(A) Natural pecuniary loss (excluding exchange contracts)[193]

(i) Benefit transferor's breach: This can be in the form of breach identified at the outset of the present section. Briefly, where the party obligated to transfer a contractual benefit (be it property, money or services) does not perform, or delays or gives inadequate performance, the benefit-receiving party is to be

[187] *Op. cit.*, paras. 26–021 and 26–022.

[188] [1949] 2 KB 528, especially at 539–540.

[189] [1969] 1 AC 350.

[190] [1978] QB 791, at 807.

[191] *Uttley Ingham*, above, at 811.

[192] *Op. cit.*, paras. 26–021 *et seq.*

[193] I.e., contracts which do not involve the payment of money in return for the benefit of the agreement.

compensated. The natural loss is the price the wronged party would pay for the benefit with deductions for the unpaid agreed price. In *Monarch S.S. Company* v. *Karlshamns Oljefabriker*,[194] a contract of carriage of goods failed because the carrier did not carry the goods to the correct destination and was liable for the market price reduced to the extent of the agreed rate. The same applies to construction contracts in which case the defaulting contractor will pay to get the work done less the contractual rate as in *Mertens* v. *Home Freeholds*.[195]

When performance is delayed, the natural loss is well illustrated by contracts of sale with basic loss being the market value of the subject matter on the date at which delivery was due but reduced to the extent of market rates when delivery does take place as in *Elbinger Aktiengesellschaft*;[196] but *Crondace Construction* v. *Cawood Concrete Products*[197] involved an award which excluded the reduction. Authorities distinctly favouring the proposition that the same applies elsewhere—for example to the sale or lease of land, to the hire or hire-purchase of goods and the sale of securities, loan agreements, services and building contracts involving delay in performance of the contractual obligation at issue in these contracts—are hardly available, but mutatis mutandis will most likely be the case on the basis of analogy from the foregoing.[198]

In the case of defective performance, natural pecuniary loss comprises the represented value of the contractual subject matter (excepting defective services) without its factual value. If however the required but defective performance consists of defective service (e.g. damage to goods in transit) the loss is really consequential rather than natural, as in *Lister* v. *Romford Ice Company*.[199] Where proprietary benefit is lost as a result of breach, the natural loss is the reduction in the value of the property. In cases involving the sale or lease of land, the rule in *Bain* v. *Fothergill*,[200] which denies the buyer or lessee the right to damages for loss arising from defective title, does not apply.

The wider issue, for which there can be no generally applicable statement as to how the claimant's natural loss (i.e. the reduction in the value of the property) is to become a right to compensation, is whether the claimant is to be awarded the reduction in the market rate or the cost of restoring the property.

(ii) Benefit transferee's breach: This typically involves the payor not paying for the benefit of the contract; the effect of the breach consists of non-performance, and the natural loss is the contract price reduced by the market price, i.e. it mirrors a natural loss that may arise from the transferor's non-performance. McGregor has suggested[201] that the alternative[202] recovery of any expectation (or post-contract reliance) interest-based out-of-pocket expenses already

[194] [1949] AC 196; for the similar measure as regards a contract for the carriage of persons, see the observations of Blackburn J. in *Hinde* v. *Liddell* (1875) LR 10 QB 265, at 268.
[195] [1921] 2 KB 526. [196] (1874) LR9 QB 473, per Blackburn J. [197] [1978] 2 LlRep. 55.
[198] Cf. McGregor, *op. cit.*, paras. 36 and 37. [199] [1957] AC 555.
[200] (1874) LR 7 HL 158. [201] *Op. cit.*, paras. 45 *et seq*.
[202] *CCC Films (London)* v. *Impact Quadrant Films* above, n. 104, is authority that the claimant must elect (per Hutchinson J., at 14).

incurred by a claimant, be it in preparation or in part-performance (therefore, really part of the price), should be possible because the reality is that the claim is rather different from the basis for recovery of natural loss; the basis is that, as with a tort claimant he be restored to his pre-contract position (rather than the agreed position examined thus far in (i) above).

It is the self-evidently acceptable basis in situations where *Bain* v. *Fothergill* applies to enable recompense for deposits paid or for investigation of title, instead of recompense for loss of bargain. In *Lloyd* v. *Stanbury*,[203] the claimant purchaser of a farm who failed to prove loss of bargain was awarded sums inter alia for conveyancing, relocation expenses and loss of earning capacity for the time being (the circumstances of title to land make this a precedent requiring caution in its application in a conflicts case because of the *Moçambique* rule against forum jurisdiction in cases involving title to foreign land; the lex causae would have impossibly to be English law for the usefulness of the decision to survive mere analogy).

In *Anglia Television* v. *Reed*,[204] it was tacit in the Court of Appeal's decision that frustrated expenses incurred after and not before the formation of the contract were recoverable. Likewise, in *Suse* v. *Pompe*[205] where a bill of exchange was dishonoured in a foreign country at a time when sterling appreciated from the time of issuance of the bill, damages for making the contract were refused because there was no nexus between the breach and any losses while there was such a connexion between formation and loss. The constant thread in relation to reliance expense is that if it is not directed at performance and thus cannot relate to breach nor the effects of breach, it cannot be recovered as damages.[206]

(B) Consequential pecuniary loss

This comprises the transferee being deprived of rights of user, profits or interest until he mitigates the deprivation by repair or finding a replacement, and in these cases the proximacy of the loss determines the availability of a sum in compensation as is typical in contracts of sale as in *G.K.N. Centrax Gears* v. *Matbro*[207] and to a lesser extent in those of carriage (e.g. in *The Pegase*).[208] Where recovery is refused it is because of remoteness and not because the item of loss itself does not qualify as a recognized head of damage.

Loss of reputation, publicity or credit are generally not recoverable heads in English law if pecuniary loss cannot be established as being a consequence of these types of loss. However, it must be noted that failing to pay money produces an entitlement to nominal damages only, following the general rule in point as was laid down in *Trans Trust S.P.R.L.* v. *Danubian Trading Company*.[209] Loss of the services of a relative (including e.g. a wife, as in *Jackson* v. *Watson*)[210] is

203 [1971] 1 WLR 535. 204 [1972] 1 QB 60. 205 (1860) 8 CB (N.S.) 538.
206 Cf. *Chitty on Contracts*, *op. cit.*, Para. 26–034. 207 [1976] 2 LlRep 555.
208 [1981] LlRep 175. 209 [1952] 2 QB. 297. 210 [1909] 2 KB 193.

also recognized as a head of damage even though there would have been no express contract.

Breach-induced expenditure within reason is recoverable, so that in *S.S. Ardennes (Cargo Owners)* v. *S.S. Ardennes (Owners)* recovery was allowed for an increase in the claimants' import duties payable which resulted from delayed carriage;[211] by analogy this extends to the other ways in which breach arises because the losses incurred are consequential, for example where a lessee of real property incurred costs for alternative accommodation for the duration of lack of repair by the lessor as in *Calabar Properties* v. *Stitcher*.[212]

In similar vein, compensation paid to a claimant for the carriage of goods by a third party has been held to be recoverable as against a defendant in *The Ocean Dynamic*,[213] as were claimant's litigation costs in suing the defendant for breach irrespective of the success or failure of the suit.[214]

Instead of seeking to recover on the bases of breach-induced expense or of the broad types of breach-preventing gains thus far identified, a recovery for breach-frustrating expenditure as was discussed above in relation to natural damage arising from breach is allowed. The expectation, and not the pre-contract reliance, expense in view is similarly a component of the price of ensuring the benefit of the contract or, as Fox L.J. put it in the slightly different factual context (in licensing) of *C.& P. Haulage* v. *Middleton*,[215] "the waste resulted from what was, on the [transferee's] side, a very unsatisfactory and dangerous bargain." To allow recovery in these circumstances would place the wronged party in a better position than if the contract had been performed.[216] As with the position in regard to natural loss, double recovery is to be avoided by the forum, and it would appear that in the election of head of damage the onus is his to prove that the preferred type of recoverable loss outstrips the other.[217]

(C) Non-pecuniary loss[218]

This, inasmuch as it is substantial and reasonably foreseeaable, can take any of the forms of physical inconvenience and discomfort arising from breach (indeed the substantial inconvenience arguably need not be physical, as was dissentiently suggested by Denning L.J. in the professional negligence case of *Griffiths* v. *Evans*),[219] pain and suffering, loss of amenity and of expectation of life. The House of Lords' decision in *Addis* v. *Gramophone Company Limited*[220] established the rule that damages for mental distress, occasioned in that case by injured feelings arising from harsh wrongful dismissal of an employee, do not form a compensable head of damage nor does loss of society

211 [1951] 1 KB 55. 212 [1984] 1 WLR 287. 213 [1982] 1 LlRep 88.
214 Cf. *Bowmaker (Commercial)* v. *Day* [1965] 1 WLR 1396.
215 [1983] 1 WLR 1461, at 1468–1469. The insertion is the present author's.
216 McGregor, *op. cit.*, para. 61.
217 Cf. *T.C. Industrial Plant Pty.* v. *Robert's Queensland Pty.* (1964) 37 ALJR 289.
218 An excellent survey appears in *Chitty on Contracts*, *op. cit.*, paras. 26–040 *et seq.*
219 [1953] 1 WLR 1424, at 1432. 220 [1909] AC 488.

not even of relatives because the loss is not financial. The loss can be financial and therefore recoverable under a different head of loss of opportunity to gain an enhanced reputation,[221] or in respect of a contract which specifically aims "to provide peace of mind or freedom from distress" like the employment contract in *Bliss* v. *South East Thames Regional Health Authority*.[222]

Having now discussed the typical heads of damage known to English law—it would serve little purpose to reproduce them other than as they may conform to the generally accepted broad classes (say) in the form of a list—it is to the mitigation rules to which consideration now turns.

The law on mitigation of loss or damage

The law on mitigation of loss can be described as that part of the law of substitute performance from a third party following breach but before forum intervention, and which part is contained by the original contract in breach; in effect, the theory of efficient breach.[223] It forms a separate set of considerations in the reckoning of the heads of damage, and the reason for the mitigation rules is to further determine or limit the loss for which a defendant is to be held liable or damage by which the right to damages is to be constituted. The rules of mitigation share the general incidence of reasonableness mutatis mutandis upon which remoteness of damage depends, and aim to "prevent the waste of [limited] resources in society".[224]

There are three broad rules of mitigation viz.:

(a) with the onus on the defendant, there can be no recovery for any part of the breach-generated loss which a claimant's objective reasonableness in the normal risk-free course of things could have negated[225] (it is important to note that the claimant is not required to be reasonable as to which pre-trial remedy to follow);
(b) the claimant's mitigating steps must be reasonable lest the loss thereby avoided be excessively in his favour;[226] and

[221] E.g. in *Joseph* v. *National Magazine Co. Ltd.* [1959] Ch. 14 (breach of an authorial contract).

[222] [1987] ICR 700, at 718; see also *Hayes* v. *Dodd* [1990] 2 All ER 815, at 824.

[223] Cf. P.S. Atiyah, *An Introduction to the Law of Contract* (Oxford, Clarendon; 1995), at 428, 454.

[224] Chitty on Contracts, *op. cit.*, para. 26–050; for a fullsome discussion of the policies in mitigation law, see J.W. Bridge, "Mitigation of Damages in Contract and the Meaning of Avoidable Loss" (1989) 105 *LQR* 398. The present author's reservations are to do with his "duty" description.

[225] *British Westinghouse Electric Co. Ltd.* v. *Underground Electric Railways* [1912] AC 673; *Sotiros Shipping Inc. & Aeco Maritime SA* v. *Samiet Solholt, The Solholt* [1983] 1 LlRep 605 is authority that this rule limits quantum by assumption of the claimant's net gain via reasonableness, rather than impose a literal duty on him; see also, *Anglo-African Shipping Co. of New York Inc.* v. *J. Mortner* [1962] 1 Ll Rep 81, at 94, and *Youell* v. *Bland Welch & Co. Ltd.* [1990] 2 LlRep 431, at 461–462. It is similar to a contributorily negligent tort claimant as given in the main text following note 229, above.

[226] For an excellent discussion see A. Burrows, *op. cit.*, at 70–74, in which he deploys the terms "unreasonable inaction" (e.g. refusing the defendant's offer of loss-reducing alternative performance as in *The Solholt* above, note 225) and "unreasonable action" (e.g. a loan at exorbitant interest charges in order to gain release of a ship detained in breach of contract as in *Compania Financeria Soleada SA* v. *Harmoor Tanker Corporation Inc., The Borag* [1981] 1 All ER 856).

(c) the claimant may recover further losses incurred in the course of his mitigation as long as the further losses were reasonable.[227]

Perhaps the most important theme is that the original benefit-transferee's damages are likely to be lower when substitute performance is handy.[228]

The meaning ascribed to mitigation in the English Common Law as has just been outlined involves a slightly narrower idea than obtains in the Civil Law where there is an additional heading, *Mitverschulden*, or the fault of both parties which requires the forum to go beyond the compensating advantage(s) which pervades the Common Law; in the Common Law, the additional heading exists but is resolved altogether differently but to the same effect by reference to contributory negligence.[229] In French law, it is called *faute de la victime*, and works in much the same way, but has a wider scope of application in that the defendant is not exonerated by the claimant's breach-causing fault,[230] as does contributory negligence for which there is no parallel in the *Code civil*. It is similar to the English rule described at (b) above, and illustrates an interesting divergence in the Common Law world in the shape of the American courts not being likely to uphold such a transferee's liability where lesser or exploitative terms are offered in substitution by a transferor in breach, as in *Shirley Maclaine Parker* v. *Twentieth Century Fox Company*.[231] The German rule in the Commercial Code (*HGB*) Paragraph 324 and, by derivation, Paragraph 615 which applies to employment and service contracts, is similar and it applies to putative as well as actual gains and recuperations; in other words, *vorteilsausgleichung* requires sufficient causal connexion between the breach by the transferor and the gain of the suing transferee, so that the latter's extraneous entitlements (e.g. insurance or pension pay-outs) are not factored by the forum.

A great deal more may be said of compensatory awards particularly from the comparativist point of view but would arguably not enhance the foregoing not least in the very practical terms of how best intending litigants may best proceed in a conflicts situation involving the relevant legal systems. This is partly because the comparable systems' formal and substantive procedures work in radically different ways; for example, there is no doctrine of precedent in the Civil Law as would make similar fact cases determinable in the same way even though the various codes' provisions would frequently bring on the same consistency of legal applications as avails by the Common Law doctrine.

The same considerations apply adaptively in the case of mitigation of losses suffered in tort cases.

The remaining types of damages and the ambiguity which surrounds the

[227] Ibid.

[228] Cf. D. Harris, *Remedies in Contract and Tort* (London, Wiedenfield and Nicholson; 1988), 6–7 and 78–87.

[229] Cf. Treitel, *op. cit.*, 179–180.

[230] See the *Lamoricière* case (fatal injuries): Cass.civ., June 19 1951, S. 1952.I.89 (note Ripert); note Bequé to Cass.com. June 19 1951; J.C.P. 1951.II.6426; and note Mezaud and Mezaud, Rev.trim. dr.civ. 1951, at 515.

[231] [1970] 474 P 2d 689.

notion of restitutionary damages are amplified after the breach-of-duty situation in tort which now follows.

Tort

General considerations

In concise terms, a tort is the cause of personal injury, financial loss or property damage. In order to recover tort compensatory damages, proof is required of the tort situation in question (i.e., the combined effect of the internal lex fori and the law of the place where the tort is committed) and that it is the cause of the legally recognized loss or damage. As with their domestic basis and counterpart, torts in English private international law mainly derive from the tort of negligence but by no means is this their only aspect. For example, a breach of contract is recognizedly apt to produce tortious liability such as where defective goods provided under a contract of sale cause harm. Others include intentional torts such as conversion of property, and torts of strict liability (e.g. defamation; employers' liability) and product liability. Bar torts of strict liability and the tort of deceit, the test of what is proximate damage is of the parties' reasonable foreseeability of the effects of the breach situation.[232]

The law of the place of the tort, the lex loci delicti commissi, is the governing law in most jurisdictions[233] including the English where it is made all the more relevant by Section 11 of the *Private International Law (Miscellaneous Provisions) Act 1995*. For the majority of tort conflicts, the Section stipulates this law in place of the lex fori-oriented rule of double (civil) actionability (now abolished by Section 10 of the same Act) first laid down by Willes J. in *The Halley*,[234] in *Phillips* v. *Eyre*.[235] Section 13 excludes actions for defamation from the ambit of the new provisions. The new statute has attracted much commentary,[236] the least favourable of which is that it does not change a great

[232] Generally, *Clerk and Lindsell on Torts* (11th ed., London, Sweet & Maxwell; 1995), Chapters Six and Twenty-seven; *McGregor*, *op. cit.*, Book II, Part II; *Dicey and Morris*, *op. cit.*, Chapter Thirty-five generally.

[233] Cf. Appendix A of the Law Commission, "Private International Law: Choice of Law in Tort and Delict" Working Paper No. 87 (1984); *Dicey & Morris*, *op. cit.*, 1480; but see e.g. Article 62(1) of the *Reform of the Italian System of Conflict of Laws 1995*, or Articles 130–142 of the *Swiss Private International Law Act 1987*; also C.G.J. Morse, "Choice of Law in Tort: A Comparative Survey" 32 *AmJCompL* 51 (1984). See especially, e.g., Art. 38 German *EGBGB* (introduced by the *Revision of Private International Law* statute of July 25th 1986); Art. 3(1) French *Code civil*; the Dutch Supreme Court decision in *Stichting Centraal Orgaan Vooraadvorming Aardolieprodukten (COVA)* v. *Banque Générale du Luxembourg (Suisse) SA en Nederlandse Middenstandsbank NV*, Hogeraad 19 Nov. 1993, no. 15066, N.J. 1994, no. 622; Para. 48 Austrian *IPR-Gesetz*; Belgian Cour de Cassation 10 Mar. 1988, *La Patriotique* c *Meuser*, *Pas.* (1988) I 829, further to Art. 3(1) of the Civil Code. There is generally a proper law type of exception, plus provision for public policy or ordre public.

[234] (1868) LR2 PC 193.

[235] (1870) LR6 QB 1. Incidentally, for a vigorous judicial critique of the rule (in the Court of Appeal), see *Metall und Rohstoff AG* v. *Donaldson Lufkin & Jenrette Inc.* [1990] 1 QB 391, at 440–441 *et seq*.

[236] E.g. C.G.J. Morse, "Torts in Private International Law: A New Statutory Framework"

deal of the law in practical terms. As Morse noted, it enhances the likelihood of a clarifying re-statement of the law of international torts by providing a legislative framework for judicial reformulation.[237] McLachlan and Nygh have recently produced a commendably delightful set of papers to critically address the general jurisdictional principles and aspects of international torts,[238] a leading characteristic of which is the territoriality thereof as can be observed in the remedial aspects of the jurisdiction.[239]

Much of what was said earlier in the present Chapter about the compensatory principle as it explains contract damages generally applies mutatis mutandis to tort damages.[240] Indeed, in distinguishing tort from crime (the lack of conceptual discrimination between them significantly underlied the old rule of double actionability),[241] it is to be observed that under modern conditions, the law of tort, like the law of contract, serves the purpose of adjusting economic and other interests, that it is increasingly an instrument of distributive rather than of retributive justice. It is also the case that the terminology of propriety of applicable law, in terms of the jurisdiction most closely related to any issue arising in connexion with an action, has been persuasively recognized in the tort context[232] albeit to a markedly much lesser extent than is the case with contract. This terminology is now contained in section 12 of the *1995 Act* in the form of exception to the law of the place of commission, and is especially useful when identification of the locus delicti (the connecting factor)[243] is elusive or when an identified *lex loci delicti* refuses damages wholly or partly as did Maltese law in *Boys* or in *M'Elroy* v. *M'Allister*[244] where Scots law provided to similar effect.

The problem appears to be whether the "particular issue between the parties [which] may be governed by the law of the country which, with respect to that

(1996) 45 *ICLQ* 888; A. Briggs, "Choice of Law in Tort and Delict" [1995] *LMCLQ* 519; P.B. Carter, "Choice of Law in Tort: The Role of the Lex Fori" [1995] *CLJ* 38 and "The Private International Law (Miscellaneous Provisions) Act 1995" (1996) 112 *LQR* 190; P. Rogerson, "Choice of Law in Tort: A Missed Opportunity ?"(1995) 44 *ICLQ* 650.

[237] *Loc. cit.*, above, at 902.

[238] *Op. cit.* (*Transnational Tort Litigation . . .*); for example, on defamation excluded from the British statute, see P.B. Carter's paper on the subject at 105 *et seq.*, especially 121–122, to the effect that the lex loci delicti commissi should, subject to forum public policy, be applicable to these actions as well. See the present writer's comment in Vol. 25 *International Business Lawyer* (London, International Bar Association; 1997) on the topic based on the compilation.

[239] See e.g. P. Trooboff's paper, "Intellectual Property", 125, especially at 128–134.

[240] Cf. *British Anziani (Felixstowe) Ltd.* v. *International Marine Management (UK) Ltd.* [1979] 2 All ER 1063, at 1068.

[241] Cf. P.B. Carter "Choice of Law in Tort and Delict" (1991) 107 *LQR* 405, at 409.

[242] See *Scott* v. *Seymour* (1862) 1 H & C 219; *McLean* v. *Pettigrew* [1945] 2 DLR 65; *Babcock* v. *Jackson* 12 NY 2d. 473 (1963); Lord Denning in the Court of Appeal in *Chaplin* v. *Boys* [1968] 2 QB 1, and subsequently a House of Lords' minority on appeal in the same case; *Johnson* v. *Coventry Churchill International Ltd.* [1992] 3 All ER 14. Academic writing on the subject includes J.H.C. Morris, "The Proper Law of A Tort" (1951) 64 *Harv L Rev* 881; P.M. North, "Torts in the Dismal Swamp: Choice of Law Revisited" (1991) 42 *Northern IrLQ* 183.

[243] *Metall und Rohstoff*, above (note 235), at 446 *et seq.*, is authority that the interpretation of the connecting factor is for the lex fori. The type of difficulty of identification is illustrated torts occurring on board a ship as in *MacKinnon* v. *Iberian Shipping Co.* 1955 SC 20.

[244] 1949 SC 110 (on the right to solatium under Scots law but unknown to English law).

issue, has the most significant relationship with the occurrence and the parties"[245] includes the issue of damages. Remedies are not specifically included in any of the scholarly commentaries on the exception. A claimant in an English action will sue for the forum's award since the award itself is but a(n) (analysis-facilitating) part of mandatory forum procedure. In line with the contract conflicts position, it is submitted that policy (including public policy) permitting they are likewise to be included, not least because to do so may be compatible with the internationalizing principles (such as under the *Brussels Convention*) of the relevant jurisdiction.

However, it is useful to note Lord Slynn's dicta, which so convincingly presaged the new statute, in his judgment in the Privy Council in *Red Sea Insurance Co. Ltd.* v. *Bouygues SA* that "[t]o limit the [tort choice of law] rule so as to enable an English court only to apply English law will conflict with the degree of flexibility envisaged by Lord Wilberforce [in *Chaplin* v. *Boys*], though the fact that the forum is being required to apply a foreign law in a situation where its own law would give no remedy will be a factor to be taken into account when the court decides whether to apply the exception", and that "the exception is not limited to specific isolated issues but may apply to the whole claim, for example, where all or virtually all of the significant factors are in favour of the *lex loci delicti*".[246]

These dicta could be interpreted to imply that considerations of the allowable damage under the lex loci must be viewed as representing the policy of forum flexibility away from applying internal tort law especially, on the issue of remedies, when a non-forum lex delicti contains rules as to relief. This possible interpretation can persist notwithstanding the provision of Section 14(3)(b), that any procedural rules must necessarily accord with forum law; in other words, the remedial analogues from (say) contract conflicts are to be discerned in international tort situations whenever the non-forum remedial positions are contained in the definition of applicable law, and insofar as the preservation of forum public policy[247] in Section 14(3)(a)(i) or other definitionally inapplicable foreign law (i.e. "penal, revenue or other public law". Section 14(3)(a)(i) and (ii)) are not thereby infringed.

Thus had the lex delicti or the law with which the events, for example, in *Johnson* v. *Coventry Churchill* were most closely related been German law (qua lex loci delicti commissi) and not English law (as the applied proper law of the contract involved in the personal injury there), then the relevant rules of the German legal system allowing recovery for negligent, rather than wilful, breach of duty to provide a safe working system could have applied, insofar as the rules can be deemed applicable by the English forum.

245 *Dicey and Morris*, *op. cit.*, Rule 203(2), 1498–1499, as with S. 12 *1995 Act*.

246 [1995] 1 AC 190, at 206–207. Earlier on at 206, the proper law of a tort is rejected, but not a policy of flexibility as to applicable law.

247 For an analogy for public policy in international tort situations, cf. Collins, *op. cit.* (*Essays* . . .), 402–406 on the forum's application of its public policy against the defence of common employment even in the international contract context.

The meaning and scope of policy

Policy will be seen to play a much greater part in tort conflicts awards[248] so that it is not necessarily always easy or perhaps even necessary to categorically state whether proximacy of damage or loss, rather than policy, forms the basis for the awards in some of the cases in view. For reasons which will become clear, a preference for the over-riding role of policy is desirable not least because the trans-jurisdictional context and the relevance therein of closeness of connexion between any facts in hand and a particular jurisdiction makes it necessary to determine the reason or policy for a particular relevant rule in a given system and thus whether the application of the rule at issue is easily justifiable between the particular parties. By way of illustration, Article 508 of the Portuguese Civil Code sets a fairly low ceiling for travel accident liability but in practice allows its courts to award for claimant's out-of-pocket expenses but not for pain and suffering nor for loss of amenity of life, in effect there is a policy there of not providing a remedy for personal injuries. It seems unlikely that when an English court, whose law and public policy provides for these items, is faced with an international tort claim which involves the respective leges delicti (and where there are sufficient points of contact with English law, beyond the adequacy of tangible bases for having acquired jurisdiction), that the English forum will apply the Portuguese rules to deny relief.

Similarly, comparative conflict of laws will indicate that the lex fori is just as attractive to most legal systems where it protects forum state nationals, residents or domiciliaries. This is so despite the general predilection in favour of the lex loci delicti commissii or, in exceptional cases, in favour of the most closely related jurisdiction or, for example, under the Italian conflicts reforms, of the jurisdiction of the claimant's choosing. A recent illustration is to be found in the acclaimed Swiss Act of 1987. These preferences for forum law are soundly based on realistic considerations such as the avoidance of compensatory awards which offend forum policy.

There are some important points which arise from the fact that the legally protected duty situation which typifies torts, foreseeable though it must be, is not pre-determined as between the parties. *Restitutio in integrum* is not literally applicable to torts insofar as a strictly restorative aim in tort cannot be imputed, for example, to personal injury compensation: i.e., for example, a lost limb cannot be restored.[249] One of the clearest illustrations of the difference of substantive principle between contractual and tortious liability exists in the general jurisdictional rules in the area of product liability, as in *Kalfelis* v. *Bankhaus Schroeder, Münchmeyer, Hengst & Company*[250] in which a product

[248] See e.g. *TransTrust S.P.R.L.* v. *Danubian Trading Co.* [1952] 2 QB 297 (Romer L.J.'s closing remarks at 307); B.S. Markesinis (ed.), *op. cit.*, Chapter Twelve, generally, on policy in general tort law in the comparative context with analogues which clearly can extend to the issue of remedy, e.g. administration, value systems, the environment, system internal balance, insurance.

[249] Cf. *H. West & Son* v. *Shepherd* [1964] AC 326, at 346 (per Lord Morris).

[250] (Case 189/87) [1988] ECR 5565 (E.C.J.)

liability claim sounded in contract and tort before the German courts between predominantly German parties. Paragraph 823(2) of the German *BGB* classifies breaches of statutory duty in product liability with torts whereas others, like the French system, classify the same breaches as contractual. In any case, the fact that the place of adjudication has the decisive word on the acceptable cause of action may be seen as helpful on the remedial issue, but in the absence of full uniformity among different systems there remains some scope for synchronizing the practical aspects of differing systems' formulations and methods in the international context.[251]

The English decision in *Carlogie* v. *Royal Norwegian Government*[252] is authority that foreseeability is central to the matter of scope of recoverability. In that case, foreseeability actually explained the negligence damages award away from the defendant's act. Likewise, it stands to reason that the typical loss in tort cases is non-monetary and must be specially pleaded as resulting from other damage which is actionable by itself. Of these the characteristic examples are presently discussed as the heads of loss. The pertinent observable theme is that tort personal injury compensatory damages normally protect personal safety and good reputation and consequently basic monetary losses feature primarily in property torts. The law of torts can also be described as affirming expedient (as distinct from ethical) values, and this may be the reason for the wide-ranging diversification of relief in the forms of disgorgement, exemplary, vindicative, control and deterrence measures to be discussed later in this and in later Chapters.

There are economic torts which are not necessarily differently reflected in the typical measures of damages for torts in the way that their "economic"[253] description might suggest. Of the economic interests, Cane has provided an excellent extensive study.[254] In English law, the general measure for economic (property) loss is the diminution in the value of the loss in line with the reasonable market cost of repair with no reference to any improvement to the property because of the repair.[255] Thus, *restitutio in integrum* becomes the value of loss at the time of commission of the tort, with allowance for subsequent and for consequential loss.[256] For personal injury, this includes the loss of subsequent or future earning capacity. In these terms can it be said that the issue of remoteness of damage or factual prevision remains the thread that is common to every breach situation. Directness of consequence alone, as laid down by the Court of Appeal in *Re Polemis*,[257] has since been superseded by foreseeability in

[251] Cf. P. Schlosser, "Product Liability" in McLachlan and Nygh, *op. cit.*, Chapter Five.

[252] [1952] AC 292.

[253] See generally e.g. J.D. Heydon, *Economic Torts* (2nd ed., London, Sweet & Maxwell; 1978).

[254] *Tort Law and Economic Interests* (2nd ed., Oxford, Clarendon; 1996).

[255] *Clerk and Lindsell*, *op. cit.*, Para. 27–04.

[256] Cf. *Liesbosch Dredger*, 460 (per Lord Wright); also *The Gazelle* [1844] 2 WRob (Adm) 279 at 281: "The right against the wrongdoer is for restitutio in integrum and this restitution he is bound to make without calling upon the party injured to assist him in any way whatsoever".

[257] [1921] 3 KB 560.

Overseas Tankship (U.K.) Limited v. *Morts Dock and Engineering Company*[258] in which the Privy Council set down the larger measure since followed in the Scots appeal to the House of Lords in *Hughes* v. *Lord Advocate*.[259] More is to be said of this in discussing the heads of damage.

According to recent commentary,[260] there is a bias in the measure of tort damages toward the contract-as-promise measure of damages, in which the former would require radical re-definition in the terms of "normal expectancies" as would re-emphasize the ultimate position in money terms as the general aim of compensatory damages. The object of the commentary in question was to give remedies, tort damages in particular, the separate consideration they deserve and reward as analytical tools in the law of obligations. Although the commentary serves to reiterate that the concept of an obligational situation, be it in tort or in contract, is generic and is the creature of the same legal system, in practice it introduces a different generalized name for the measure of tort damages.

The conflict of laws' incidence of difficult substantive overlaps between contract and tort reaches further than, but is considerably determined by, the likelihood of liability in tort being a consequence of a breach of contract. Collins has discussed these at some length.[261] The focus of his comments has not been the strictly remedial, rather the obligational, situation between parties. Yet, they have given much assistance as to the choice of action when these overlaps arise, and as to the central importance of parties' expectations in any obligational situation, thus arguably giving a slight edge where a hard preference needs to be made to contract conflict actions instead of tort conflict actions. Usefully, he reminds that where remedies in tort and contract concur, it is to be anticipated that the flexibility of the mandatorily applicable (procedural) lex fori rules of pleading provides some assurance for a claimant who prevaricates as to the preferable measure of damages to pursue.[262] It is nevertheless the case that where the applicable law is not English law, the outcome of contract-related tort litigation can be affected by the incidence of proper law rationales.

The decision in *Banque Bruxelles Lambert SA* v. *Eagle Star Insurance Co. Limited*[263] sustains the intersection of quantum or measure of damages in breach of contract with the measure in tort when, as Cane put it, "performing

[258] [1961] AC 388. [259] [1963] AC 837.

[260] J. Stapleton, "The Normal Expectancies Measure in Tort Damages" (1997) 113 *LQR* 257; but see also D. Friedmann, "Rights and Remedies", in the same volume at 424–426, and S.A. Smith, *loc. cit.*

[261] First in, "Interaction Between Contract and Tort" (1967) 16 *ICLQ* 103, and in "Exemption Clauses, Employment Contracts and the Conflict of Laws" (1972) 21 *ICLQ* 320. Both are contained in his previously cited *Essays*. See also *Dicey and Morris*, at 1198–1200, 1314–1316, and 1487.

[262] *Op. cit. (Essays)*, at 394, citing *Clark* v. *Kirby-Smith* [1964] Ch 506 (that the action in solicitors' professional negligence sounds only in contract) and *Lister* v. *Romford Ice & Cold Storage Co. Ltd.* [1957] AC 555, at 579 (per Viscount Simonds).

[263] [1995] 2 WLR 607, at 616–617 (on changes in objective property values as these affect mortgagees' and purchasers' entitlements as against valuers).

the contract and not committing the wrong add up to the same thing".[264] When this happens, the defendant's obligation (thus the recovery of the value of what would have been transferred but for the breach situation) is the factor having exclusive relevance over and above the way the action proceeds. As will be seen in the context of the recognized heads, proximacy of loss simultaneously unites and differentiates the respective measures because, by and large, the same interests—including the basis in opportunity costs sometimes said to be excluded from tort compensation (they are not, not even in personal injury cases)[265]—obtain in either case.

More detailed consideration of tort compensatory damages now turns to the respective matters of quantum and heads of liability (or the type and scope of legal protection afforded) in that order. It may be noted by way of observation at this stage that there is a compelling case based on economic analysis of legal remedies for compensatory damages to be more widely applied to tort liability instead of mandatory remedies in performance (i.e. injunctive relief) than they currently are, not least because money will by and large be a more useful means of redress from the wronged party's point of view especially in property torts such as trespass.[266]

Quantum

The lump sum rule applied in nearly all English tort actions is set out in Order 18 rule 12 *R.S.C.* and Order 6 rule 1(5)-(7) *C.C.R.* and is classically rendered for torts in *Fournier* v. *Canadian National Railways*.[267] Departure from a single assessment is permitted in out-of-court, and in structured, settlements,[268] as well as where the wronged party is a minor or a mental patient, generally when the forum has cause to be concerned about how best to meaningfully apply the award. Damages are assessed as at the time when the cause of action arose, at the date of damage, or for personal injuries at the date of trial since the forum must advert to all the relevant events leading up to trial. Flexibility as to the date is also necessarily significant in the case of proprietary or economic loss which loss is fixed at the point when it was reasonable for the claimant to have made repairs.[269] For personal injuries, the cost of care for life or the value of lost earnings for the remainder of the injured party's working life are the bases for the calculation of awards, and allowance is made, at the time of trial, for unpredictable supervening events like death, redundancy or disease, as in

[264] *Op. cit.*, 144.

[265] E.g. H. Collins, *The Law of Contract* (2nd ed., London, Butterworths; 1993), at 184–185, 372–376 and 381–384.

[266] Cane, *op. cit.*, 49–56.

[267] [1927] AC 167, a Canadian Supreme Court appeal to the Privy Council. The German *BGB* disapproves lump sums where the circumstances do not indicate a "serious reason" for making them.

[268] See Part III Law Commission Report, "Structured Settlements and Interim and Provisional Damages" No. 224 (London, H.M.S.O.; 1994).

[269] *Dodd Properties* v. *Canterbury City Council* [1980] 1 All ER 920.

Jobling v. *Associated Dairies*.[270] The forum's non-actuarial and fairly low figure produced by the multiplication of the annual sum by the relevant number of years is the subject of current review by a working party of legal and actuarial experts convened by the Lord Chancellor to make considered and more realistic re-appraisal of the size of these awards.[271]

Admiralty Commissioners v. *SS Susquehanna*[272] confirms that general as against special damages are to be distinguished. An example of special damage is the loss of opportunity to begin independent business as in *Domsulla* v. *Barr*.[273] In *Slater* v. *Mexican National Railway Company*,[274] the United States Supreme Court upheld a state (Texas) court's refusal, having applied the Mexican lex loci delicti, to award either a lump sum or periodical sums as damages for unlawful death in Mexico because there was no express or inherent procedure to have done so, even though Mexican law provided only for the latter type of award. It is noteworthy that some international instruments contain attractive solutions to a few of the typical problems of actual valuation in the process of quantification itself. Examples are Article 11(4) of the *EEC Draft Convention on Contractual and Non-Contractual Obligations 1972* and Article 8(4) of *The Hague Convention on Product Liability 1971* which respectively refer the process, even in cases of actual monetary losses, to the lex causae, rather than to the lex fori as is characteristic of the Common Law. Were these instruments incorporated into forum law, it is not entirely inconceivable that actions brought in the scheme of these provisions would nevertheless be for an award of forum damages.

For English personal injury litigation, the general roughly pre-determinable sizes of compensatory awards derive their legal basis solely from the fact that they are judicially conventional. That they are unregulated by any doctrine of precedent[275] is the most obvious likely justification for the forum's firm position as to the inapplicability of foreign systems' typical award sizes. The process of actual estimation is as follows: the quantification, in this order, of special

[270] [1982] AC 794.

[271] See Sir Michael Ogden Q.C. in *The Times*, 30th September 1997, at 37. The article describes the basis for the Ogden tables the strength of which lies in accuracy rather than expert advice. These tables are admissible without proof under the *Civil Evidence Act 1995*. The tables give the injured party an investable capital sum towards costs of care or lost earnings. The *Damages Act 1996* sets the rate of return with the Lord Chancellor in consultation with the Government Actuary and the Treasury. Up for consideration alongside the Ogden tables is the so-called Duxbury Method in use in the Family Division of the High Court for the capitalization of maintenance payments and which are perhaps inaccurately based on the error that a person has a pre-determinable expectation of life from which an income for life can then be estimated. What unites the respective approaches is that if they are applied to general compensation, they will bring about increased levels of damages awards. Cf. R. Lewis, "Personal Injury Compensation: How Much is Enough?" [1995] *LMCLQ* 324.

[272] [1976] AC 655, at 661 (per Lord Dunedin).

[273] [1969] 1 WLR 630.

[274] [1904] 522 P 2d 666, at 672.

[275] See e.g. J. Munkman, *Damages for Personal Injuries and Death* (10th ed., London, Butterworths; 1996), at 188 and Appendix A thereof which is the *Official Guidelines for the Assessment of General Damages in Personal Injury Cases 1993*.

damages and general damages (explained below as admissible heads of damage), followed by necessary deductions (e.g. social security benefits)[276] and the addition of interest.[277]

The claimant's financial weakness, to be differentiated from the negligible value of his property where the tort is proprietary, can increase the level of the award as long as the financial weakness is within the parties' purview and insofar as the loss afoot is not down to the claimant's own financial unreasonableness as was so found by the Court of Appeal in *Compania Financiera "Soldeada"* v. *Hamoor Taber Corporation, The Borag*.[278] Precision as to loss and any future contingency is required by Section 32A of the *Supreme Court Act 1981* (except where the damages are provisional). The pleaded damage must not be speculative or nonsensical.[279] Awards for personal injury are itemized according to whether they are pecuniary or otherwise, for the same reasons as with contract damages. Similarly, identical factors of interest, the currency of the award,[280] taxation,[281] collateral benefits,[282] mitigation,[283] and contributory negligence[284]—which otherwise

[276] E.g. *Coupland* v. *Arabian Gulf Oil Co.* [1983] 1 WLR 1136; also *Nabi* v. *British Leyland Plc.* [1980] 1 All ER 667 (unemployment receipts); *Hodgson* v. *Trapp* [1988] 3 All ER 870 (attendance and mobility allowances). Insurance and pension benefits of any sort are not deductible: see, respectively, *Hussain* v. *New Taplow Paper Mills* [1988] 1 All ER 541 and *Smoker* v. *London Fire Authority* [1991] 2 All ER 449.

[277] I.e., applying the *Gourley* principles elucidated in the context of breach of contract.

[278] [1981] 1 WLR 274.

[279] *Moeliker* v. *Reyrolle & Co. Ltd.* [1977] 1 WLR 132, at 142; cf. Burrows, *op. cit.*, at 31–36.

[280] I.e., *Miliangos* (a negligence damages case, as were *The Despina R*, and *Schorsch Meier* (q.v.)) applies e.g. where an ameliorative medical operation in a personal injury case is conducted in foreign currency irrespective of the currency of expense as was held in *The Transoceanica Francisca & Navios V* [1987] 2 LlRep 15. However, non-pecuniary losses have to be in sterling and the typification of the loss will follow the particular circumstances of a case: *Perestrello e Companhia Limitada* v. *United Paint Co. Ltd.* [1969] 1 WLR 570, at 579.

[281] Cf. *Clerk and Lindsell*, Para. 27–16; for a comparativist dimension, see the American Law Institute's *Restatement Second of the Law of Torts* (St. Paul. Minnesota, American Law Institute Publishers; 1977), Para. 914 (on the non-taxability of compensatory awards and the taxability of punitive awards).

[282] Cf. *Clerk & Lindsell*, Paras. 27–17 to 27–21; cf. *Social Security Administration Act 1992*, Part IV and the *Social Security (Recoupment) Regulations 1990*, as well as the Court of Appeal's decision in *Hassall* v. *Secretary of State for Social Security* [1995] 1 WLR 812.

[283] I.e. of damage or expenses brought onto the claimant by the tort (e.g. managerial time used for restorative work: *Tate and Lyle Food and Distribution* v. *G.L.C.* [1982] 1 WLR 149; funeral expenses under S. 1(2)(c) *Law Reform (Miscellaneous Provisions) Act 1934*); cf. *Clerk and Lindsell*, *op. cit.*, Paras. 3–09 *et seq.*; not recoverable, e.g., are the pensions of drowned crew: *Admiralty Commissioners* v. *SS Amerika* [1917] AC 38. Mitigation is hardly ever raised in tort conflict actions perhaps because of its convenient redolence of remoteness or recoverability. It is clearly substantive and for the lex delicti, and is analogous to contractual mitigation which has always been accepted to be substantive: *D'Almeida*.

[284] See the Privy Council decision in *Sigurdson* v. *British Columbia Electric Railway* [1953] AC 291; also P.M. North, "Contributory Negligence and the Conflict of Laws" (1967) 16 *ICLQ* 379, especially at 391–392, where he raises the valuable point that where a lex loci delicti bars, rather than reduces, relief (e.g. French law) but a doctrinally independent lex fori makes it a ground for apportionment of loss, it would seem inevitably to follow that a forum policy of flexibility must result. It is also noteworthy that *Barclays Bank plc.* v. *Fairclough Building Ltd.*, [1994] 3 WLR 1057, is authority that the incidence of contributory negligence makes irrelevant the basis of a given action being in tort or in contract since the awardable measure will reflect the extent of the liabilities between the parties.

would be res inter alios acta—bear mutatis mutandis upon the awardable sum. It is to be observed that these related issues are also deemed to be substantive and for the lex delicti or lex causae (the latter expression is used here as an alternative expression to identify the law governing the substantive tort).

In view of the *1995 Act* and its sufficiently clear inclination away from applying the internal lex fori when necessary, it appears that the rule would now no longer be automatically applicable by which English domestic law would exclusively determine quantification, nor would it seem necessarily to follow that a foreign tort quantum which would be applicable in the interests of propriety (e.g. as may arise under a statute of the applicable law) needs be the same as the English sum as in *M'Elroy* v. *M'Allister*. The advantageous import for an action relying on the rule, in that it provided in most cases for higher awards than would be forthcoming under the lex loci delicti (e.g. in *Boys*), can of course not be ignored. Nonetheless, for reasons of system specificities about the foundations and the predictability of the range of compensatory awards even in conflicts cases, it is not likely that it will come to pass that an English forum will ever make awards which might be consonant with the type of size for similar awards (say) in United States' courts.[285] A claimant in a case in which the governing law of a tort is the law of a US state will, for reasons that would be jurisdictionally well-grounded, probably not choose to sue in England any way.

Morse's general remarks[286] about the possibility of a forum applying procedurally compatible non-forum relief under the lex delicti to the remedy appear to ring truer in the light of the internationalization[287] of tort conflicts. For the present writer, it is to be hoped that whenever quantum may be due under the rules of the applied lex causae, then the forum can apply those rules if they do not offend forum judicial practice and policy or public policy.

Heads of damage

The House of Lords in *Boys* v. *Chaplin* put to rest the notion that the topic of this subsection is subject in the final analysis to the lex fori, because the topic is properly substantive and not procedural. The law of liability (i.e. of the locus delicti or otherwise) is also the law of recoverability. Apart from the broad classifications into natural or basic non-monetary or non-pecuniary losses and consequential losses which can be translated into an award of money (and the illustrations of these), the more useful dimensions to pursue are those of the items of damage available for particular torts.

The breach-of-duty situation can give rise to different types of damage:[288] unrecognized (i.e. not legally recoverable); recognized; and restricted. There

[285] See e.g. J.G. Fleming, *The American Tort Process* (Oxford, Clarendon; 1988), at 224 *et seq*.

[286] *Torts in Private International Law*, (New York, North-Holland Publishing Co.; 1978), at 195–196.

[287] The days when Lynskey J. refused to apply any law but the lex fori to remoteness and heads of damage in *Kohnke* v. *Karger* [1951] 2 KB 670, are long gone; the decision remains authority that quantum is for the lex fori.

[288] *Clerk and Lindsell*, *op. cit*., (Supplement; 1994), Para. 1–45.

are, as with breach of contract, significant intersections among the matter of the heads that may be applied to quantum, the matter of awards or composite parts thereof which are not materially compensatory (e.g. exemplary awards), and the matter of the requirement upon the claimant that the recoverable money be mitigated. The reference to heads is to the items of the compensatory quantum, the first of these.

Generally speaking, typical heads recognized under forum law include severally or collectively in the same suit, personal injury about which there is extensive legislation[289] and any of consequential economic loss, personal non-financial damage, property damage, interference with property, and pure economic loss. Each of these carries a significant body of law and is best discussed individually.

As Cane has pointed out, for recovery for non-pecuniary damage apart from nervous shock (i.e. mental distress), there has first to be some other damage actionable by itself, and for "pure loss of a [financial] chance"consequent upon some other automatically actionable loss, such as personal injury, the recoverable head is the discounted underlying primary claim.[290] The reason is that this type of damage by itself is difficult to assess. Therefore, the award is assessed according to the likelihood of the opportunity materializing, as in the Australian High Court decision in *Sellars* v. *Adelaide Petroleum*.[291] The celebrated cases in point in the English courts include *Ross* v. *Caunters*, in which Megarry V.-C. allowed a testamentary beneficiary to recover damages for the negligent draftsmanship of a solicitor which caused the beneficiary the loss of a legacy,[292] and, more recently, in *White* v. *Jones*[293] on identical facts.

The main kinds of recoverable personal non-pecuniary loss—viz.: (a) loss of liberty (e.g. false imprisonment, malicious prosecution, negligence); (b) injured feelings (e.g from personal injury, assault, defamation, malicious prosecution, false imprisonment, or nuisance); (c) damage to reputation (e.g. including defamation of goods, negligence, deceit, misrepresentation, breach of copyright); and (d) inconvenience (e.g. from practically every tort)—will naturally be easier to obtain in tort because they are much the rule, than they are in contract where they are the exception. The awards for (a), (b) and (d) may overlap, in which case they may be assessable together. Awards for (b) are dealt with as awards for pain and suffering, and for (c) the award is dealt with as future economic loss where the cause of action is not in defamation. For (d) the sum is rather modest where it does not form part of a loss of amenity claim in personal injury.

[289] E.g. the *Fatal Accidents Acts 1846, 1959* and *1976*, the *Law Reform (Contributory Negligence) Act 1945*, and the *Law Reform (Personal Injury) Act 1948*.

[290] *Op. cit.*, 136–137; see also, e.g., *Behrens* v. *Bertram Mills Circus* [1957] 2 QB 1, at 28 (per Devlin J.)

[291] (1994) 179 CLR 332.

[292] [1990] Ch. 297; the decision was not followed in the Australian case of *Seale* v. *Perry* [1982] VR 193.

[293] [1995] 2 WLR 187.

To these may be added the recoverability of consequential economic loss such as with unreplaced or unrepaired property for which, if it is profit-earning, money is awardable under the cost-of-repair mode of assessment, for loss of profits for the duration of repair or for the reasonable lapse before the property at issue is replaced. Under the market value mode, recovery for loss of profit is pre-included so as to avoid double recovery.[294] In the case of conversion and trespass (generically, interference with property), the judicial view of recoverability is that the goods were destroyed and the date of assessment is generally the date of loss as was held in *BBMB Finance (Hong Kong) Ltd.* v. *Eda Holdings Limited.*[295]

In the case of trespass to land, including foreign land insofar as the applicable substantive law is English law, proof of loss is unnecessary; for example, because loss of user infers financial loss. An alternative approach is to grant an amount corresponding with fairness as to the loss incurred, as in *Bracewell* v. *Appleby*[296] concerning an award for the grant of an easement. Pure economic loss is financially evaluated, however difficult the evaluation might be, and may necessitate informed speculation where the loss or part of it is yet to arise. In the English forum, items of loss available under an applicable non-forum law will be applied to the award but subject to forum policy and interpretation of the item, for its compatibility with the form of forum awards.

Personal injury awards serve a dual role: to compensate for loss caused by the injury and to put the injured party in the position he would have been in but for the injury. Of the general streams of damage, special (i.e. incidental) and general, the former includes the following: lost earnings and related fringe benefits (by far the most usual item), associated property damage, medical and related expenses (including relations' expenses in point), and increased normal expenses. The heads of general damage include pain and suffering, lost amenity, lost present and future earnings and earning capacity, lost pension rights, and future expenses. In English law, Section 1(1)(a) of the *Administration of Justice Act 1982* abolished the separateness of the head of loss of expectation of life; the head is now subsumed with pain and suffering in Section 1(1)(b) of the same legislation. Similar heads, of loss of society of relatives and loss of social consortium of a wife, are abolished by Sections 4 and 5 of the *Law Reform (Miscellaneous Provisions) Act 1970* and Section 2 of the *1982 Act* respectively, although damages continue to be awarded for bereavement of a spouse or the parent of a person tortiously killed, under Section 1 of the *Fatal Accidents Act 1976* (as given by Section 3 of the *1982 Act*). Where any of the foregoing heads overlap, recovery more than once for each item is to be avoided.

[294] *Dominion Mosaics and Tile Co. Ltd.* v. *Trafalgar Trucking Co. Ltd.* [1990] 2 All ER 246.

[295] [1991] 2 All ER 129. The basis is different where, e.g., under S. 3 *Torts (Inteference with Goods) Act 1977*, a later date is appropriate because the better basis is the return of the goods: *IBL Ltd.* v. *Coussens* [1991] 2 All ER 133.

[296] Previously referred to in connexion with contract damages.

Concerning claims by a defendant for contribution, a matter regulated in English internal law by the *Civil Liability (Contribution) Act 1978*, it is the unfortunate case that domestic law invariably applies in conflicts cases in which the issue arises. A case in point is the unreported recent decision of Chadwick J. in *Arab Monetary Fund* v. *Hashim*.[297] Because the substantive aspects of the underlying cause will, in some cases, have been determined by non-forum law, it appears to be an extension of the jurisdictional basis in the forum's personal jurisdiction that forum law on contribution will also apply. Further, it must be noted that the statutory basis for the existing position implies that the old view persists by which domestic statutes bear upon conflicts cases regardless of the internalized policy behind such statutes.[298] The solution may be suggested here that statutes which not infrequently surface in conflicts cases be augmented with the "most-closely-related jurisdiction" exception[299] in the interests of ensuring that conflicts claimants' substantively legitimate expectations be sustainable.

In the eyes of the English forum, the policy-defined scope of recoverability means that because certain torts and types of damage are not actionable of themselves but rather upon proof of special damage (e.g. malicious prosecution;[300] slander),[301] that recoverability is substantively speaking not directly dependent on a subjectively conceptualized view of remoteness, but on want of legal protection such as is to be inferred from the parties' contemplation. According to *Schneider* v. *Eisovitch*,[302] in which nervous shock resulting from a motor-car accident was a basis for compensation, damage is remote and thus is irrecoverable whenever it is not admittedly foreseeable by the parties.

It is submitted in closing that in the same way that common ground between systems' tort or delict laws on compensatory damages makes cross-border court process possible, the formal and substantive differences between the same systems explain the particular disposition within each jurisdiction. Enough has been said by way of illustration of these differences. It is further submitted that harmonization in these respects, as distinct from unification,[303] would be perhaps a little utopian for the simple reason that the inter-system convergence which is pre-required as a foundation for harmonization is not easily justified let alone strived for. The application of forum rules, internal and specifically for

[297] 29th July 1994 (CH 1988 A No. 9317).

[298] Cf. A. Briggs, "The International Dimension to Claims for Contribution: Arab Monetary Fund *v.* Hashim" [1995] *LMCLQ* 437.

[299] See e.g. *Dicey and Morris*, *op. cit.*, 1533–1534.

[300] E.g. in *Quartz Hill Gold Mining Co.* v. *Eyre* [1883] 11 QBD 674, in which a plaintiffs costs in defending an earlier civil action (which costs exceeded the taxed costs for which he got judgment) were held not to be recoverable.

[301] *Allsop* v. *Allsop* 5 H & N 534 (1860).

[302] [1960] 2 QB 430. On the point, see also *Thursgood* v. *Van der Bergh* [1951] 2 KB 537, at 552, per Asquith L.J. on directness of causation as the sole basis for recoverability, and *The Daressn* [1971] 1 LlRep 60 where loss of profits, arising from delay in port of a chartered vessel, was held to be recoverable only if the profits lost were not unreasonably high, nor was the loss to have arisen from profits yet to be realized from later charterparties as in *The Liesbosch Dredger*, at 463–464.

[303] See generally Morse, *op. cit.*, Chapter Eleven.

tort conflicts, in furtherance of a balance between general and specific tort conflicts has served well the ends of developing and more effectively localizing the rules and principles which govern tort compensatory damages. Even where the tort in question has been committed abroad and English internal substantive tort law does not apply, any difficulties associated with the forum's process of selecting the law to apply, e.g. those identified by Briggs,[304] will be easily contained by the incidental matter of the basis upon which the forum will have taken jurisdiction in the first place: that the cause of action in tort sounded within recognized forms of action. The remedial issue, it is finally submitted, will also be determined by the prescribed forum procedure but may well develop into the situation in which the form of award will expressly accommodate the substantive compensation afforded by the non-forum lex delicti.

In terms which may be seen fundamentally to accentuate divergence among systems, remarking a while ago on the attorney-claimant relationship in the American tort context, O'Connell proposed in culturally-specific terms (i.e., to US legal practice) the abolition of awards for pain and suffering and suggested that funds to be dedicated to that head be directed instead to the payment of attorney's fees.[305] This type of proposal not likely to take ground in the English legal system in the way that, for example, the so-called "no-win-no-fee" (or conditional fee) scheme also derived from US practice, can to enable less well-off tort victims access to the courts.[306] There is no better indication of the part played by certainty and predictability (rather than (say) parochialism) of forum approach in containing the desirability of flexibility in these trans-jurisdictional situations.

RESTITUTIONARY (OR DISGORGEMENT) DAMAGES

Breach of Contract

What are restitutionary damages?

Applying Birks's self-admittedly inchoate definition of restitution as "the response which consists in causing one person to give back something to another"[307] as a starting point in discussing the relatively newly-coined remedy of restitutionary damages,[308] it is inevitable for a number of doctrinal reasons

[304] [1995] LMCLQ 519, at 521 *et seq.*; i.e. whether a foreign tort not recognized under internal forum law is nevertheless actionable in the forum under the *1995 Act*. The forms of action will of course provide a negative response.

[305] D.P. O'Connell, "A Proposal to Abolish Defendant's Payment for Pain and Suffering in Return for Payment of Client's Fees" *Univ Ill LR* 333 (1981).

[306] *BBC Radio*, 17th October 1997; also, N. Hilborne, *The Times*, 21st October 1997, at 41.

[307] P. Birks, *An Introduction to the Law of Restitution* (revised reprint, Oxford, Clarendon; 1994), at 11.

[308] A. Burrows, *op. cit.* (1994), at 293: "The suggestion that damages can be restitutionary will appear to many as a heresy". There is an enormous body of work on the subject especially in the last fifteen years or so, e.g. D. Friedman, "Restitution of Benefits Obtained Through the Appropriation

(e.g. the considerable terminological intersection with compensation[309] previously mentioned in the present Chapter; the radical divergences in the concept of restitution between legal systems as were expounded by Bennett;[310] that inward-looking choice-of-law has definitionally been integral to the topic since it began to crystallize in English law; that in reality, "the matter which the law of restitution seeks to organize developed long before anyone thought of calling it restitution"[311]) that enquiry becomes the present appraisal, once the definitional aspect of the umbrella remedy[312] is clarified. It is important also to lay aside wholly substantive restitution (or unjustified enrichment analogous to (say) the contractual breach situation) and to make clear that the subject here is remedial restitution (or unjustified enrichment flowing from an obligational situation in breach) with exclusive reference to so-called disgorgement (rather than compensatory, or any other) damages, which nevertheless includes the substantive aspects of the remedy.

Burrows' definition suggests that restitutionary damages are primarily concerned with or are best typified by tort-generated enrichments.[313] Cane's justifications[314] for restitutionary damages are in situations where the defendant is a purely passive or a negligibly active recepient in the liability-generating

of Property or the Commission of a Wrong" 80 *Colum LR* 504 (1980) generally, and, "The Efficient Breach Fallacy" 18 *J Leg Stud 1* (1989), 18 *et seq*.; G. Jones in A. Burrows (ed.), *Essays in the Law of Restitution* (Oxford; Clarendon; 1993), 7–8. The decision of the Court of Appeal (per Lord Woolf M.R.) in *Attorney-General* v. *Blake and Another* [1998] 1 All ER 833 contains obiter dicta, especially at 843–846, recognizing serious necessity for the remedy of restitutionary damages for breach of contract where (a) "the defendant fails to provide the full extent of the services which he has contracted to provide and for which he has charged the plaintiff...and the amount of expenditure which the defendant has saved by the breach provides an appropriate measure of damages" (at 845), and (b) "where the defendant has obtained profit by his doing the very thing which he contracted not to do" (at 846). In view of the pendency of appeal at the time of writing and in view of his Lordship's statements (at 846g) that "[o]nly time will tell whether these distinctions [between compensatory and restitutionary principles] are tenable" and that "[t]hey may not hold", the present writer respectfully prefers to retain the descriptive analysis which follows in the remainder of this Section of the main text above. The writer's previously published commentary on *Blake* is appended at the end of this Chapter.

[309] Cf. B. Nicholas, "Unjustified Enrichment in the Civil Law and Louisiana Law" (1962) 36 *Tulane LRev* 607, at 609 where he views restitutionary relief in general as supplementary alternatives to other main types of remedy.

[310] T.W. Bennett, "Choice of Law Rules in Claims of Unjust Enrichment" 39 *ICLQ* 136 (1990).

[311] Birks, ibid. at note 304 above; see also *Lamine* v. *Dorrell* [1705] 92 ER 303 on conversion, *Lightly* v. *Clouston* 127 ER 774 (1808) (breach of contract); latterly, *Whitwham* v. *Westminster Brymbo Coal & Coke Co.* [1896] 2 Ch 538, and *Watson Laidlaw & Co. Ltd.* v. *Pott, Cassels & Williamson* [1914] 31 RPC 104, per Shaw L.J., at 119–120.

[312] The other types of restitutionary remedy are discussed en bloc in Chapter Ten, and are all, to a greater or lesser extent, concerned with bringing about a re-direction of an unearned or unjustified enrichment at someone else's expense. Some legal systems, notably the German (Paras. 812 *BGB et seq.*), have a separate, unified actively applied restitutionary remedy. In England, the available remedies were once considered to sound in quasi-contract (cf. Birks, *op. cit.* (*Introduction . . .*, 29–39); also S. 1 of the American Law Institute's *Restatement on Restitution* (St. Paul, Minn., American Law Institute Publishers; 1937)).

[313] *Op. cit*, 293–299 (on contracts, 307–311); see also his *The Law of Restitution* (London, Butterworths; 1993), 386–390, and McGregor, *loc. cit.* (Birks (ed.), 206–210.

[314] *Loc. cit.*, in Birks (ed.), above, n. 27, 301, at 321–323.

event, and where the optimization of limited social resources by resort to the forum would be a good thing: "If we accept expressing disapproval and giving deterrence signals as proper goals for civil law, there is no generally conclusive reason why disgorgement damages should not be available for breaches of civil law, although there may be good arguments against their award which outweigh the arguments for them in certain types of case".[315] The leading decisions are discussed in the course of this section. Beale has concluded that "while restitutionary awards [generally] are justified when a proprietary right has been infringed or there is a fiduciary obligation, they should not be applied to contracts generally", although it is worth considering whether to allow the contract parties to truly freely and equitably make specific provision for damages or penalties which are not related to the loss in question.[316]

It is accepted that damages are not co-extensive with compensation and that the contractual interest protected can be equitable, i.e. restitutional. Contractual restitutionary damages can be said to be typified where for example goods have been paid for in full but are defective at the time of delivery at which time the market value of the goods has become less than the drop in their value which has arisen because of the defect(s). For reasons now to be adduced it is submitted that the encroachment upon the pre-eminence of compensation by the notion of restitutionary damages requires a great deal more caution, indeed that it encourages their disconsideration for those reasons: that they do not go to claimant's damage suffered, but rather to the defendant's gain or saving. Restitutionary damages are supposed basically to reverse a defendant's ungrounded gains (so-called autonomous restitution[317]), be the gains at the claimant's expense, rather than by wrongs against the him. It is implicit in the division that breach of contract is not a wrong for which general restitution is exclusively apposite. This is so only insofar as the distributive policy served by restitution is not displaceable by compensation.

In expanding the reasons, it is important to look at the pivotal decision in *Wrotham Park Estate Co. Limited* v. *Parkside Homes Limited*[318] in which Brightman J. awarded a sum which did not compensate for any loss from a breach of restrictive covenant enforceable in equity (thus sounding in a contract-type proprietary action or in tort), but rather was a small but fair proportion (five per cent) of the defendants' profit made on the back of the claimants. The policy basis for the award of damages was that the sum avoided "an unpardonable waste of much needed houses".[319] The approach was followed in *Bracewell* v. *Appleby*,[320] although in neither case did the courts explicitly nominate the award in one way instead of the other.

[315] Ibid, at 323.

[316] In "Exceptional Measures of Damages in Contract" in Birks (ed.), *op. cit.*, 217, at 247.

[317] Birks, *op. cit.* (Introduction), at 314–315. This distinction has been acknowledged e.g. in *Macmillan Inc.* v. *Bishopsgate Investment Trust Plc (No. 3)* [1995] 3 WLR 978, at 988; cf. J. Bird "Choice of Law" in F.D. Rose (ed.), *Restitution and The Conflict of Laws* (Oxford, Mansell; 1995), 64, especially at 67–70.

[318] [1974] 1 WLR 798.

[319] Ibid., at 811; cf. Cane, in the text accompanying note 254 above.

[320] [1975] Ch. 408.

The absence of judicial application of the term is particularly important when one considers Steyn L.J.'s dicta in *Surrey County Council* v. *Bredero Homes Limited*: that the *Wrotham Park Estate* award was defensible because a claim for a similar sum as a separate head of loss, of bargaining opportunity, was exceptional since such a sum may have been fixed by the parties' agreement.[321] By and large the same reasoning had been applied by Lord Denning in the tort case of *Penarth Dock Engineering Co. Limited* v. *Pounds*.[322] However, he related the award to compensation[323] though there was a less clear-cut line between the compensatory and the restitutionary principles in the estimation of the gains that were repayable and of the loss-unrelated sum. In Beatson's words, "[i]n general, the gain to a defendant from a breach of contract is irrelevant to the quantification of damages",[324] but not in contracts for the sale of land the effect of which is to vest the buyer with an equitable interest in the price of a wrongful sale to a third party in breach of the original contract as in *Tito* v. *Waddell (No. 2)*.[325]

Damages in restitution appear to depend on the indeterminacy or difficulty of compensation with the result that they were not the form of restitutionary award in *Attorney-General* v. *Guardian Newspapers (No.2)*[326] where a claimant's substantial charitable donation had been disclosed, nor in *Stoke-on-Trent City Council* v. *W. & J. Wass Limited*[327] in which there had been a deliberate infringement of a right to hold a market. The infringements in the respective cases coincided with the policy in such awards as described at the start of the section.

It was the consideration of situations like the foregoing which led the Law Commission to acknowledge general (i.e. pre-differentiated) restitutionary awards in money—of which there can be little doubt that damages are the prominent feature—replete with a clarifying definition to provisionally conclude their deliberations in the following terms: "[R]estitutionary damages are prima facie justified if there has been either interference with a proprietary right or with an analogous right, and the gains made by the defendant are attributable to the interest infringed".[328] The present writer's interpretation of the position as to restitutionary damages is this: given the existing English law on restitution and restitutionary actions (which admits, for example, of the possibility of an action for money had and received independently of trespass where a defendant burgles a claimant's mother's house and takes the claimant's money) and because restitutionary damages are damages, they are explicable in

321 [1993] 3 All ER 705, at 714. 322 [1963] 1 LlRep 359, at 361–362.

323 So did Lord Donaldson M.R. in *Universal Thermosensors Ltd.* v. *Hibben* [1992] 2 All ER 257, in which the claimant had lost no profits (272) but was entitled to the defendant's gains (of time, trouble and expense: 274) from the wrongful use of the plaintiff's confidential information.

324 J. Beatson, *The Use and Abuse of Unjust Enrichment* (Oxford, Clarendon; 1993), 15; *The Siboen* [1976] 1 LlRep 293, at 337; also, the US decision of *Hospital Products Ltd.* v. US Surgical *Corporation* (1984) 156 CLR 41.

325 [1977] Ch. 106, at 332. 326 [1990] 1 AC 109, at 255–256. 327 [1988] 1 WLR 1406.

328 *Op. cit.*, above, note 25, at Para. 8.19 (the arguments for and against these awards are previously made at Paras. 7.18 *et seq.*).

terms of the type of case cited above in terms of being different from compensatory damages and from other non-compensatory types.

Thus if so-called restitutionary damages are independent of actions for restitution (terminologically and causatively speaking, they are not) as well as of compensation (yet again no decided breach of contract case gives them to be so), then their acceptability and concretization may well depend on what the House of Lords may make of an opportunity to pronounce on *Wrotham Park Estate* or, perhaps, on the development of a unified restitution action—in equity as was suggested in principle in the context of tracing e.g. by Millett J.[329]—which would be led by or include the current judicially accepted basis for awards in the discussed cases above and which action would not necessarily depend on the abolition of exemplary damages (with which so-called restitutionary damages at present have a distinct affinity insofar as the policies they respectively further may coincide, as was observed by the Law Commission).[330] The Law Commission had also concluded provisionally that restitutionary damages should not be associated with breach of a fiduciary relationship nor with a contract for which specific performance may be available.[331] Claimants' choice of monetary restitution can possibly bring about the unification because the aims and ultimate position of claimants who successfully sue within the variety are consistent, as presently demonstrated in the apposite Chapter of this book.

The conflict of laws offers a dimly-lit medium for the best way forward. The facilitating consideration is the substance of the remedy rather than its form so that, whether or not damages themselves may correctly be called restitutionary, a well-founded action for money sounding in restitution will likely always succeed. It is better to wait and see how the courts or Parliament clarify the situation which has provided as exciting and intellectually fulfilling a legal topic as can be hoped for. The only available work, edited by Rose,[332] comprehensively deals with the pervading jurisdictional and substantive (trial) aspects of restitution under the traditional Common Law and the *Brussels Convention* rules. The fact of the matter is that remedial restitution (as a separate concept from the underlying jurisdiction), especially in conflicts cases, is far from being clearly resolved in the way that compensatory damages have been.

The over-riding but, in the academic literature, increasingly eroded reason, that there is not one English case in which restitutionary damages have explicitly been awarded or refused, scores a palpable hit. While it may be acceptable to rest content with the interpretation that the emerging distinct class of restitutionary damages augment (in the sense of neither replacing nor adding to, but are compatible with) compensatory damages, to do so can run counter to the spirit of an overall legal system which in formal terms does not individuate the term. It is therefore yet another quirk of terminology, all the same neither entirely surprising nor discomfiting given the pervading analysis of choice-of-law

[329] "Tracing the Proceeds of Fraud" (1991) 107 *LQR* 71, 85.

[330] *Op. cit.*, e.g. at Para. 7.18 (at 167).

[331] *Op. cit.*, Para 7.22(3).

[332] *Op. cit.*, at n. 242 above.

methodology with restitution in the conflict of laws, that at least one case—*Baring Brothers & Co. Limited* v. *Cunninghame District Council*[333]—appears to have involved the deployment of a similarly previously unused expression, the proper law of a restitutionary remedy; by analogy, the expression proper law of compensatory damages is acceptable but is not characteristic parlance. Nor do the writer's views on restitutionary damages (in the sense of particularized forum process for the purpose) as rendered so far change appreciably in the tort or delict context, not least because the difference of context is just as synonymous with compensatory damages albeit on a different basis.

It is a bonus to the present work that a good few of the defining cases on general restitution did in point of fact arise from cases having a foreign element, not least *Fibrosa Spolka Akcyjna* v. *Fairbairn Lawson Combe Barbour Limited* in which Lord Wright laid down the advent of unjust enrichment pretty much as a coherent basis having comparativist application for liability away from tort or contract.[334] In that case, however, no foreign law was pleaded. Rose's seminal work veritably reduces the gap and friction produced by the difference between substantive restitution on the one hand and formal or remedial restitution on the other. As Bird stated, the difference between legal systems' approaches is but one of labelling, thus explaining the British reservation to the elsewhere typical contractual (and not restitutional) characterization of unjustified enrichment generated by breach of contract in Article 10(1)(e) of the *Rome Convention* on the consequences of breach)[335] which is based on a sound insistent preference for descriptive accuracy, and which reservation is contained in Section 2(2) of the *Contracts (Applicable Law) Act 1990.*

In cases where the applicable restitutional lex causae is not English law, it would stand to practical reason that, on principle the English forum makes an award which is not inconsistent with the substantive law. Because a claim for an award which can be seen to be one for restitutionary damages is possible, the main apparent reason for not leading a claim for such an award in the form of a head of special damage is that, even though the particular facts on which the claim is based and on which a calculation may be based can be pleaded under Order 18 rule 12(1) (q.v.), the formulation of the basis is at best a very rare proprietary exception such as Lord Steyn admitted of in *Wrotham Park Estate*; it simply is not generally known to forum substantive law, nor are the forum's jurisdictional grounds sufficiently clear for entertaining international contract restitution cases, e.g., in *Dimskal Shipping Co. SA* v. *International Transport Workers Federation*[336] in which the proper law of the underlying contract was accepted as being applicable to the restitution claim.

333 *The Times*, 30th September 1996, before Lord Penrose (Scots Court of Session (Outer House)).

334 [1943] AC 32, at 61.

335 Ibid., at 87–88 (see also her "Choice of Law and Restitution of Benefits Conferred under a Void Contract" [1996] *LMCLQ* 183); cf. B.S. Markesinis, *Foreign Law and Comparative Methodology* (Oxford; Hart; 1997), at 137.

336 [1992] 2 AC 152; cf. H. Mather, "Restitution as a Remedy for Breach of Contract" (1982) 92

Assuming that restitutionary damages do develop into a refined class of non-compensatory damages, in line with and as a reflection of the quality of the response and comment they have attracted thus far, as they should (since it will be of practical necessity to categorically differentiate them from e.g. equitable damages discussed next, and from account of profits—which does not depend on a breach of contract—in Chapter Ten), it can safely be said that their assessment can be left to the informed but unregulated discretion of the forum as may be taken to have been illustrated in *Wrotham Park Estate*. The more the remedial forms the better perhaps. Alternatively, the unlikely issue of recognizable heads if such be the path of their elaboration may well require legislative intervention, in view of the dicta already referred to.

A summary overview of the present law

This much can be garnered from the existing literature about damages which protect the contract-based restitutionary interest:

(a) where the defendant's unjust enrichment in money is autonomous of his wrong, there may be other restitutionary remedies available against him, but not restitutionary damages;
(b) where the unjust enrichment in money flows from a breach of contract (i.e., a gain or a saving), the claimant must prove that the defendant would not have been so enriched but for the breach and that the contract has been validly terminated (rather than that consideration has totally failed, in which case, the action will lie in money had and received and not in restitutionary damages; i.e., there would have to be an overlap between the reliance and (or) expectation interest in order for a restitutionary interest to be protected by an order for disgorgement);
(c) where the interests do not overlap, compensatory damages will be the correct form of relief because they will be sufficient to restore the contractual interests in breach;
(d) where they can be said to be available, the measure of restitutionary damages for breach of contract would appear to have a narrower range than in torts. The tort position is now discussed.

Yale LJ 14. It is perhaps a further expression of the unyielding intersection between compensation and restitution that Treitel (*op. cit.*, 82–105) discusses comparative contractual restitution in money in the context of substitution, albeit recognizing that the interest protected is neither expectation nor reliance but is usually taken to depend on their being at issue. The beginnings of the resolution of this type of case may well have been set in motion by Lord Goff's leading judgment in *Kleinwort Benson Ltd.* v. *Glasgow City Council* (*The Times*, October 31st 1997) in which it was held—"beguilingly simply" (per Lord Nicholls) but conclusively, it is to be hoped - that a claim for restitution is to be distinguished from one in either contract or tort, so that in the context of the *Brussels Convention*, the correct jurisdictional basis is the general one of defendant's domicile (Art. 2), rather than special bases deriving from the matter being one "relating to a contract" (Art. 5(1)) or "relating to tort, delict or quasi-delict" (Art. 5(3)); but, cf. the dissent of Lords Nicholls and Mustill, as to Art. 5(1) necessarily being pragmatically construed widely because of the variety of contract issues that may need to be resolved, as intended by the European Court of Justice, e.g., in *(Case 38/81) Effer SpA* v. *Kantner* [1982] ECR 825.

Tort

The practical and analytical amplitude of tort-induced restitutionary damages

The relatively wider range of judicial dicta about the remedy in consideration in actions in tort would appear to make for more fodder than is available in contract cases. But even then, the fodder summons a great deal of caution from anyone who may be keen to see the award proliferated. For example, Nourse L.J. in the Court of Appeal said that "[i]t is possible that the English law of tort, more especially the so-called "proprietary torts", will in due course make a more deliberate move towards recovery based not on loss suffered by the plaintiff but on the unjust enrichment of the defendant . . . I doubt whether [that process] can begin at all at this level of decision".[337]

With the advantage of the definition of the kernel of disgorgement damages, it is convenient to proceed to examine the equally definitional issue of the measure of this type of judicial award such as has been identified in the academic literature. Indeed, as will be seen, a reassuring basis for clearer definition of the particular relief is forthcoming from the present type of obligation even though the present author nevertheless persists in his preference, for the sake of the accuracy of conceptualization of the underlying cause of action in autonomous or dependent unjust enrichment and of clarity of terminology, that the "damages" description of these particular restitutive awards is a seductive but significantly unacknowledged misnomer; there is no comparable extended reference in the courts or in the literature to expectation(ary) or reliance damages,[338] at least not in the way that so-called restitutionary damages have attracted attention.

Needless to say, the tort aspects which were discussed above in the context of contract will not be raised anew in the present sub-section save for emphasis or for re-appraisal as may be necessitated by the new context. The Law Commission's Consultation Paper provides a fairly finite list of torts which, under the existing law, can attract or have attracted restitution as well as those which have not done so.[339] Of the former set are proprietary torts (conversion; trespass to goods and to land; intellectual property rights infringed), fraud or deceit, passing off, breach of confidence or of fiduciary duty, intimidation and nuisance. The latter are given to exclude assault and battery, although the reason in principle (i.e., that other relief, e.g., an exemplary award will be forthcoming) as to why this must be so are not clear. The basis for tort-generated

[337] I.e., in the *Wass* case, at 1415; see also *Clerk and Lindsell*, op. cit., para. 1–13.

[338] Cf. L.L. Fuller and W.R. Purdue, "The Reliance Interest in Contract Damages" (1936–1937) 46 *Yale LJ* 52 and 373 in two instalments. Seminal as their academic exposition remains, it is to be noted that it did not quite generate extended judicial acceptance of non-compensatory reliance damages.

[339] Paras. 7.5 and 7.6 especially, and on to Para. 7.17. Other relief, e.g. exemplary awards have often availed claimants where restitution has not.

disgorgement awards supposes that any tort-generated enrichment of the defendant which enrichment exceeds the claimant's loss is an unjustified enrichment to be extracted from the tort-feasor and reversed to the victim;[340] in other words, that tort does not pay. Thus, as McGregor has indicated,[341] not only do the typical cases relied on, for example, by the Law Commission not necessarily involve an unjust enrichment in these terms, these cases can not all found restitutionary damages as they are given to do.

The property trespass cases are in point.[342] The net effect is that though awards in these cases may and often will be associated with the restitution interest, it seems closer to the mark to identify them with non-damages restitution or with a damages-in-compensation basis such as an account of profits. The commanding decision on the point, and one in which restitutionary damages were withheld for their inappropriateness, is *Stoke-on-Trent City Council* v. *Wass* cited earlier;[343] nominal damages were awarded in recognition or affirmation of the claimant's position in the eyes of the law.

One remaining fundamental flaw in the term as it relates to tort is that the basis for the claim for disgorgement being an unjustified enrichment is not quite readily met in tort situations; in other words, the enrichment could have been (but will not have been) without justification as is the case in other cases of restitution. However, where this requirement is met there might be a basis for the restitutionary description.

Burrows persuasively set out the situations[344] in which it is tenable in the same areas of enrichment-based (i.e. in terms of the defendant's savings made) wrongful interference with goods, trespass to land, nuisance and breach of confidence. Lord Denning stated, in *Strand Electric Engineering Company Limited* v. *Brisford Entertainments Limited*, in which action for detinue of a defendant who had wrongfully retained theatre equipment, that such an action "resembles therefore, an action for restitution, rather than an action of tort".[345] His Lordship also went further to say that he could imagine the owner of the retained goods being entitled to any profits such as there might be; there were none involved in the case itself, nor were any pleaded as the cause of action there.

At least two points must be made about these dicta possibly furthering the case for restitutionary damages. First, that an action of tort is to be contrasted with an action for restitution does not exhaustively imply that the former cannot result in an award of the latter; the one is the cause of action and the

[340] R. Goff and G. Jones, *The Law of Restitution* (4th ed., London, Sweet and Maxwell; 1993), at 721.

[341] *Loc. cit.* in Birks (ed.), at 207.

[342] Cf. *Inverugie Investments Ltd.* v. *Hackett*, discussed above in the setting of the compensatory principle and general issues of terminology. By no means are property trespass cases the only type of case that drive home the point; cf. McGregor, *loc. cit.*, 208 *et seq*.

[343] For an authoritative critique of the decision, see R. Goff and G. Jones, *op. cit.*, 723.

[344] *Op. cit.* (*Remedies . . .*), 294–299.

[345] [1952] 2 QB 246, at 254–255.

other is a remedy among others for it. Second and further to the first, his Lordship made clear the issue of semblance not of unyielding characterization. Lords Somervell and Romer preferred to rest their otherwise concurring views on more general compensation rather than on monetary restitution per se. To reiterate, when the award is in damages, it protects the restitution interest, and where it is restitution the award may be any of the various forms of restitutive award (not damages) as may correspond to the advantage (wrongfully received according to the particular facts) that is to be referred to as may be the case. Much the same thread should run through the other types of situation as these have already been raised in clarifying contract-based awards.

These considerations apply as a matter of course in a conflicts case in which the applicable substantive law is English law. It being the case that the English rules on restitution are comparatively emergent, it is perhaps a little too early to proffer practically realistic indicia of the direction in which the sophistication of the conflict of laws rules will go. And this is substantiated by the fact that at the stage at which choice-of-law considerations arise, i.e. after the forum's assumption of jurisdiction to adjudicate, the basis for that assumption will variably infer the applicability of the forum's apprehension of the enrichment situation in the ways foregoingly described. These are given more of an exposition in the Chapter on restitutionary remedies to which supposed "restitutionary damages" would belong but for the reasons given earlier on. As will be explained in Chapter Ten, restitution conflicts as a whole must wait for the clarification of the domestic law in these respects and, if anything is to be made of the course of the conflict of laws, the notion of the applicability of restitutionary conflicts damages would seem to be rather remote.

Of the remaining types of damages available,[346] namely equitable damages, exemplary, aggravated and nominal damages, a few words will now be said, starting with the latter. The closing discussion is of damages under the law of the European Community.

EQUITABLE DAMAGES

It was previously pointed out in setting the scene for the contrast between compensation and performance that it would be good advice to a party who had suffered non-compensatory loss to seek equitable damages as well.[347] Section 50 of the *Supreme Court Act 1981* provides for the discretionary rather than legal power to award these damages as a direct supplement to an equitable (i.e. discretionary) performance remedy, as well as on their own when access to the

[346] *Addis* v. *Gramophone Co. Ltd.* [1909] AC 488 is authority that exemplary or punitive damages are unavailable for breach of contract; but see *McMillan* v. *Singh* (1985) 17 HLR 120 a housing law case in which no reference was made to the *Addis* rule nor to decisions based on it, and *Warner* v. *Clark* (1984) 134 NLJ 763 where the Court of Appeal applied a basis in tort to a breach of contract case and made an exemplary award.

[347] Above, n. 14.

performance relief is barred because of any of the equitable principles, discussed in Chapter Nine, which govern the main remedy. The sole pre-requirement in the latter case is that the case be one in which the court could grant the underlying but unavailable relief which this type of damages would then replace. It is the latter situation which calls for comment at the place reached in this book. The issue is necessarily whether to insist on access to a given performance remedy without which there can be no equitable damages. In other words, the question is whether the thus described right to the particular equitable remedy subsists.[348]

These damages will stand on their own even though the enforcement of the accompanying specific order has been disregarded by the claimant owing to the defendant's default of compliance, as in *Malhotra* v. *Choudhury*.[349] Because of the rule of election of relief, in Section 49 of the same statute, by which the claimant can add a compensatory damages claim to one for enforced performance as in *Johnson* v. *Agnew*,[350] equitable damages—assessed in the exactly the same way as compensatory damages[351]—operate clear of legal damages because they will avail the claimant in the absence of a cause of action at Common Law. The type of cause is illustrated by a continuing breach which generates prospective loss[352] and which would not have been covered by injunctive relief, as in *Bracewell* v. *Appleby*.[353]

Arguably the best characterization of underlying cause as has been pointed out by Burrows[354] is in equitable wrongs, in the present context, related to a breach situation (e.g. breach of confidence, in which case parallels between equitable damages and (say) an account of profits would be the injunction-supplementing alternatives they were in *Peter Pan Manufacturing Corporation* v. *Corsets Silhouette Limited*),[355] but with respect this may serve analysis well but may confound a scenario already laden with far-reaching choices requiring to be made. It can be all to easy in the most practical terms to confuse substitutional awards as well as the best cause of action upon which to base them. A better example of a cause of action for which equitable damages may be available is where the claimant asks the forum to formally rescind the contract in breach but is refused (e.g. because of laches as in *Leaf* v. *International Galleries*,[356] third party rights, affirmative action,[357] or the impossibility of compensation for losses). Section 2(2) of the *Misrepresentation Act 1967* specifically provides for damages where rescission is based on a misrepresentation.

[348] Cf. generally, P. Loughlan, "No Right to the Remedy?: An Analysis of Judicial Discretion in the Imposition of Equitable Remedies" (1989) 17 *Melb Univ L Rev* 132. At 132–133: "The inquiry into the decision-making process whereby equitable relief is granted or withheld also has a practical bent. The aim is to allay, at least in part, the anxieties raised by the increasing presence of [uncertain and unpredictable] equitable principles and remedies in commercial life".

[349] [1980] Ch 52. [350] Above, at n. 50.

[351] The *Malhotra* case above, n. 349; i.e., including e.g. the mitigation rules.

[352] This does not imply that past loss is excluded from the range of heads of equitable damages: see the Canadian decision in *Elsley* v. J.G. *Collins* (1978) 83 DLR (3d) 1.

[353] First raised above (n. 320) in the context of restitution.

[354] *Op. cit.*, at 246. [355] [1963] RPC 45. [356] [1950] 2 KB 86.

[357] *Peyman* v. *Lanjani* [1985] Ch 457.

The crucial factor demonstrated in *Whittaker* v. *Campbell*[358] by Robert Goff L.J. is the association of rescission with proprietary (i.e. restitutionary) rather than contractual interests mainly because the voidability of a vitiated contract by which the defendant would otherwise be unjustifiedly enriched lies in equity. The amplification of the issues is best done in the fuller context of general restitutionary remedies and is left until then. The unmistakably familiar point arising for this writer is the same one made earlier regarding the preferability of unification of the array of restitutionary measures. It is submitted that the harmony that exists as to the substance of these equitable remedies in money makes for the suggested ends. In making a worthwhile connexion between the remedy of equitable damages and the next, it may be observed that where damage cannot be proved as against the defendant, the English forum awards nominal damages as in *The Albazero*.[359] Compensatory damages would clearly not be the right relief to choose because nothing will have been established to justify them. It is to nominal damages to which consideration now turns.

NOMINAL AND CONTEMPTUOUS DAMAGES

These do no more than recognize the infringement of established contractual rights which indeed are actionable but for which there is no legal protection—i.e. there will have been no proof of damage—in the eyes of the forum. They therefore qualify as an exceptional measure of damages even though in reality it would be a very odd or an ill-advised claimant who sues for the trivial award (usually about two pounds sterling) whether on its own or as a fall-back from a claim for a larger compensatory sum on the basis of the main cause of action. They are therefore superfluous even though they are in principle available for every breach of contract. They are less effectual than an award of the discretionary costs of litigation because it is far from a matter of course that an awardee of nominal damages is, after *Anglo-Cyprian Trade Agencies* v. *Paphos Wine Industries Limited*,[360] to be taken to be successful as to costs. Nor are nominal damages much use in the assertion of any right while a choice of action for a declaratory judgment gathers dust. As a matter of fact and in a manner clearly removed from the sense in which restitutionary damages are looked at, the question begged is whether nominal damages are damages at all. It is worth remembering that the claimant in *D'Almeida* was awarded forty shillings, the same quantum as would have been awarded had action been instituted today.

Deserving of less attention are so-called contemptuous damages, usually a penny given by a jury in defamation cases. Either of these damages is forthcoming in contract and in tort.

[358] [1984] QB 318, at 327. [359] [1977] AC 774. [360] [1951] 1 All ER 873.

AGGRAVATED DAMAGES

Aggravated damages are compensatory, and the truth about them being a type of damages goes only as far as the fact that they are really a head of damage for injured feelings or mental distress which amounts to a breach of contract. They are rightly discussed by Treitel as belonging to the methods of limiting damages.[361] It is thus immediately clear that in a conflicts case in which they are pleaded and in which the lex causae is non-forum law, they would have to be available under the governing law of the contract in breach. A fundamental point of some difficulty is that while they are available for breach of contract, exemplary damages are not.[362] Yet there is a recognizable substantial intersection between their respective policies which are aimed more directly against the manner of the defendant's breach: the former goes to the claimant's proven sentiments and the latter aims to adjust the defendant's particularly reprehensible conduct. The categorical distinction was supplied in the classic case of *Rookes* v. *Barnard*.[363]

Nevertheless, and perhaps as a direct result of their shared policy basis, these types of damages are ambulatory and their respective sizes tend identically toward reflecting the awarding forum's aim of extracting a sum of money from the defendant for the common justifications in reproof. They are in fact frequently used practically interchangeably, for example in *Saunders* v. *Edwards*[364] and in *Archer* v. *Brown*[365] which involved aggravation from a fraudulent misrepresentation. Good examples are where a sum of money is awarded in breach of contract (e.g. a hotel room reservation which is denied at the point of the intending guest's wish to take up the room, or a new car which breaks down upon its being collected, as in *Bernstein* v. *Pamson Motors (Golders Green) Limited*)[366] in circumstances where a basis in inconvenience generated by the breach will overlap with the manner of breach.

The same type of aggravated circumstances are recognized in the civil law, e.g. in Article 266 of the French *Code civil* in recognition of non-pecuniary loss or *dommage moral* or *préjudice moral* such as when a passenger suffered mental distress from lateness in a travel schedule.[367] Article 1149 provides for injury and not to money loss per se. More or less the same interest is protected by *Scmerzgeld* in Paragraph 253 of the German *BGB*, and in Austria in Paragraph 1325 of the Civil Code.

In English law, consistent moderation is the guiding light in the assessment of these damages. The same may not be said of the substantial US courts' awards in line with the different economic levels between the systems.

[361] *Op. cit.*, at 194 *et seq*.

[362] Above, texts carrying nn. 25–29 (i.e. what exemplary damages protect is not the cause nor the consequence of breach). It may also be recalled that Civil Law systems do not award exemplary damages.

[363] [1964] AC 1129.

[364] [1987] 2 All ER 651.

[365] [1985] 1 QB 401.

[366] [1978] 2 All ER 220, at 231.

[367] Casscomet fin 7 Oct. 1953, GazPal 1953.2. Somm 19.

The closing remarks in present respects must be owed to the thorough-going Law Commission Consultation Paper already extensively referred to above. The kernel of the recommendations is that the weak differentiation between these and exemplary damages, arising from "the exceptional conduct requirement", might justify abolition of this type of relief, that it should be subsumed with compensatory awards where it naturally belongs.[368]

EXEMPLARY OR PUNITIVE DAMAGES

These damages punish the defendant for a wrongful breach of civil obligation in tort. They are controversial in the tradition of the Common Law because their deployment may appear to contradict the non-punitive aims of civil litigation. When they are granted, they put a tort victim in a better position than if the tort had not been committed. This expression of the basis for these awards must therefore significantly countermand the argument that they encroach upon the realm of criminal law. The law is contained first in *Rookes* v. *Barnard*[369] in which, mindful of doctrinal considerations of the applicability of these awards, Lord Devlin restricted their availability to instances of heavy-handedness of Crown officials[370] including the police, statutory provision for the purpose,[371] of a defendant profiteering beyond the compensatory measure[372] as in *Cassell & Company Limited* v. *Broome* [1972] A.C. 1027 in which a jury awarded a sum in reflection of a libellous publisher's profits.

There are substantial overlaps between these awards and so-called restitutionary damages in tort. For the reasons given, a conflicts claimant is very well advised to steer clear of the latter.

Exemplary awards were also discussed in the ubiquitous Law Commission Consultation Paper.[373] The Commission considered that the personal wrongs of defamation, trespass and malicious prosecution, as well as private nuisance and intimidation and other torts, were prime examples of the cause of action which, if proved by the claimant, would lead to an award. Conversely, as would breach of contract, the torts of discrimination, public nuisance, negligence in general and personal injury in particular, deceit and equitable wrongs would not. The Commission recommended that the law be put on a principled basis which would not rule out the possibility of their being renamed.[374] McGregor[375] has opined that the *Rookes* categories affirmed in *Broome* are not derived from

[368] *Op. cit.*, Para. 6.54. [369] [1964] AC 1129.

[370] *Rookes*, at 1226. It is noteworthy that this group of actions is not necessarily an actively used basis for these awards.

[371] Ibid., at 1133.

[372] Ibid., at 1226; it is irrelevant that the profit arises in the course of business or that the plaintiff cynically worked out that profit as being in excess of the compensation that might be payable.

[373] Paras. 3.33 to 3.112. See also Burrows (*op. cit.*, *Remedies . . .*), at 270–285.

[374] Paras. 8.4 to 8.13.

[375] *Op. cit.*, Para. 455; see also L.J. Anderson, "An Exemplary Case for Reform" (1992) 11 *CivJQ* 233, at 237–246.

principle and may well have had a greater effect on judicial practice than is proper. At any rate, they have availed unlawfully evicted tenants or trespass victims generally, so that the paucity of claims for this relief in the conflict of laws is a little surprizing and perhaps deserves encouragement especially, for example, in place, it is respectfully submitted, of damages in restitution.

Quantum is moderate and discretionary, and is made in consideration of the wrong-doing defendant's means,[376] of whether there has been criminal compensation as in *Archer* v. *Brown*,[377] of an underlying compensatory award of which the exemplary award is an itemizable part of the lump sum. There seems to be no need for aggravating circumstances, although lack of negligence will reduce the likelihood of an award.[378] Criticisms about the indeterminacy of the size of award, e.g. in jury trials, are in reality much the same as with compensatory awards and for this reason it might be more telling if caution were rather exercised as to their tenability, e.g. in the face of the availability of compensation for non-monetary harm.[379] It is to be emphasized that punitive or exemplary damages serve a considerable vindicative role, not to be belittled, particularly when other money relief is not to be had. Problems associated with class actions are in fact not as insurmountable as they are occasionally given to be once the number of claimants or of defendants sharing the entitlement or the liability is appreciated.

With particular reference to the conflict of laws, there is much to commend the view in the Australian decision in *Waterhouse* v. *Australian Broadcasting Corporation*[380] that exemplary awards are punitive and for the lex delicti. Similar authority is to be found in *Australian Consolidated Press* v. *Uren*,[381] and in the New Zealand case of *Taylor* v. *Beere*.[382] This is so because the underlying liability will have been determined by that law. The conflicts quantum will, it is to be expected, not necessarily conform to the likely award were the case heard before the forum of the lex delicti, for reasons of system specificity. Although the Civil Law does not generally recognize punitive awards as a separate item, Stoll[383] has set out the analogues which in real terms may be seen to amount to deterrence awards. A most interesting illustration is to be found in the South African law of damages which in general terms has been described as derived "in the case of delict from the civil law and in the case of contract from the common law",[384] with the result that punitive sums are available neither in tort nor in contract.

The caveat to be entered is that although exemplary damages do not ostensibly protect contractual interests in English law, a claimant who suffers loss and

[376] Cf. *Manson* v. *Associated Newspapers Ltd.* [1965] 1 WLR 1038, at 1045–1046.

[377] [1985] 1 QB 401, at 423.

[378] *A.B.* v. *South West Water Services Ltd.* [1992] 4 All ER 574, at 584–585.

[379] Law Comm. Paper, para. 5.8.

[380] [1989] 86 ACTR 1, at 19.

[381] [1969] 1 AC 590.

[382] [1982] 1 NZLR 81.

[383] "Penal Purposes in the Law of Tort" (1970) 18 *AmJCL* 3.

[384] P.J. Visser and J.M. Potgieter, *Law of Damages* (Cape Town, Juta; 1993), at 14–15, citing H.J. Erasmus; and at 156–157: "It is no longer possible to recover or award an amount to punish someone by means of an action for damages".

is minded as to an extra sum in fullsome but nevertheless limited relief—for example as a result of fraudulent misrepresentation, following Lord Denning's decision in *Doyle* v. *Olby (Ironmongers) Limited*[385]—is well-advised to claim damages in the tort of deceit or fraud for all losses, pursuant to the difference in the basis of assessment of the type of claim from the basis in contract damages: the remoteness test of reasonable forseeability does not apply (thus the expectation interest is different), and where property has been lost the recoverable measure is the property value and not the cost of its replacement.[386]

This alternative cause of action is to be recommended because, inevitably, a legal system that, as a matter of policy, amorally and pragmatically neither encourages nor deters simple contractual breach (and rates compensatory relief highest), can reasonably be expected to relocate its remedial policy in the circumstances in a way that protects the injured party as far as is legitimately permissible.

It is thus well in order that public policy will play an important part in a conflicts forum's decision whether to make an award. For example, the California Insurance (Paragraph 533) and Civil (Paragraph 1668) Codes respectively comply with the public policy there of not permitting a defendant's liability insurance to cover deterrence or punitive awards. It is not likely that a forum that will have applied Californian law of tort as the lex delicti will necessarily found an exemplary award exclusively on Californian public policy in this way. The basis for this is that, even disregarding the typically larger award that a Californian court seised of the facts will have made, the reason for the Californian rules may not necessarily be suitable for export in terms that will be acceptable to the conflicts forum. Punitive awards are of course generally taxable.

To conclude, and on a different note, the characteristic awards in the US are subject to statutory bans at both the federal and state levels.[387]

DAMAGES UNDER EUROPEAN UNION LAW

The law of the European Union, by which is meant the rules and principles applied in the courts of England and other jurisdictions of the Member States of the European Communities, involves damages awards on the basis of the application of state obligations enshrined in that law by virtue of the *Treaty of Rome 1957 Establishing the European Economic Community*. In the United Kingdom as a whole, the relevant rights and obligations are imported by Section 2 of the *European Communities Act 1972*. Thus, the feature which distinguishes the damages available under EU law, and which damages are awardable in the

[385] [1969] 2 QB 158, especially at 166.

[386] *Smith Kline and French Laboratories* v. *Long* [1988] 3 All ER 887. For obvious reasons, the same applies to damages under S. 2(1) *Misrepresentation Act 1967*: *Andre et Cie* v. *Michel Blanc* [1977] 2 LlRep 166.

[387] See the Law Comm. Paper, at 179–180.

normal procedures of any forum within the EU, is to do with the parties to the typical action: the claimant is an individual legal person, the defendant is the Member State (including its legislative, executive or judicial organ as may be the case)[388] which has failed to comply with clear directly effective Communities law.

The actions in view must comply with the forum's normal rules of process, e.g. a writ of summons or Order 53 *R.S.C.*; in proceedings directly against the Crown, Order 77 *R.S.C.* applies as may Section 17 of the *Crown Proceedings Act 1947* the first subsection of which requires the Attorney-General to publish all government departments and suable representatives; Subsection (3) of the same Section identifies the Attorney-General as the proper defendant in cases involving breaches of legislative duty, as arise under Article 5 of the *Treaty of Rome*, to effectively protect Community law rights. More is presently said of these in describing the actionable obligations in the national courts.

It is useful first to look at the description of these actions as being against private parties as some writers would seem to have done.[389] Innocuous and indeed, by and large, correct as this view is, its basis is in the broad grounds upon which these essentially tort-based actions (including those in breach of Community competition rules)[390] can be brought in furtherance of Community law, viz.: (i) breaches of statutory duty or, "Eurotorts" as Henry J. called them in *Barretts and Baird (Wholesale)* v. *I.P.C.S.*;[391] (ii) economic torts such as civil conspiracy to fix prices amounting to unlawful interference with trade or business as in *Lonhro plc* v. *Fayed*;[392] and (iii) so-called innominate torts arising exclusively by reason of EC law, and which Lord Diplock would not brook in the important decision in *Garden Cottage Foods Limited* v. *Milk Marketing Board*.[393] Much the same grounds are to be found in domestic cases involving the Crown or its servants or organizations. Perhaps the most useful observation, and one which makes convenient the other relevant considerations in this new area of the conflict of laws, is that the same criteria (e.g. the roles of policy, remoteness[394]

[388] R v. *Secretary of State for Transport, ex parte Factortame (No. 4)* [1996] 2 WLR 506 is authority that any of these organs may be liable for losses directly resulting from a serious breach of any individual right-conferring Community law provision, and that it is for national courts to create a new head of liability if necessary, e.g. to remove statutory exclusions of liability for pure economic loss or for fault-based liability which exceeds a serious breach of Community law in point. See also R v. *H.M. Treasury, ex parte British Telecommunications plc* [1996] 3 WLR 203.

[389] M. Brealy and M. Hoskins, *Remedies in E.C. Law* (London, Longmans; 1994), at 62–72. R. D'Sa, *Law and Civil Remedies in England and Wales* (London, Sweet and Maxwell; 1994) also contains a good exposé between its paras. 10–009 and 10–017, and does not make the same reference as to the nature of the defendants in these actions.

[390] See C. Kessedjian, "Competition" in McLachlan and Nygh (eds.), *op. cit.*, Chapter Ten, 171 *et seq.*, especially at 187 on there being "no need to open other courts with limited jurisdiction for damages to the plaintiff" and, previously, at 172–175 on the general issues of characterization and the types of interest involved. (i.e. "the economic interests of states, which it may be difficult for a foreign court to apply": 175).

[391] [1987] 1 IRLR 3, at 5. This is a useful reminder that these wrongs are indeed statutory.

[392] [1990] 2 QB 479, identified at 488.

[393] [1984] 1 AC 130, at 144.

[394] Indeed the European Court of Justice applies a remoteness test in cases involving Communi-

and reasonableness in the area of recoverability) can be imported from "normal" tort conflicts not involving the state.

However, the difference is to be observed in the view taken of the exact place and force of application or adaptability of Communities law in the national system. There is perhaps no better example of the extremes than Lord Wilberforce's dissent in the House of Lords' decision in the *Garden Cottage Foods* case. His Lordship held, with respect, with great compulsion, that *Treaty* rights, such as the Article 86 right concerning a state or public authority abusing its dominant position, are neither transformed nor enlarged into domestic rights capable of enforcement through a damages action, and that the proper relief in the particular circumstances was either an order to desist (Article 3), fines (Article 15) or a Court of Justice review (Article 177). The majority view, which included the position that new causes of action were not needed, has since been followed in a number of other cases including *Plessey Company plc* v. *General Electric Company plc & Siemens*,[395] and in *Bourgoin SA* v. *Ministry of Agriculture, Fisheries and Food*.[396]

Much in the nature of the trends in the law in the general area can be garnered from the decisions of the European Court of Justice and the English and other courts. In *Cases 5-7, 13-24 and 30/66, Kampffmeyer* v. *The Commission*,[397] recovery was held to be permissible of losses arising from the cancellation of the particular transactions involved in that case, because the losses were a consequence of the unlawful refusal of importation licences. However, in *Cases 67-85/75 Lesieur* v. *The Commission*,[398] there would be no recovery of loss of inexpensive supplies and of anticipated profits flowing from the abolition of the Community's monetary compensation amount scheme, since the remoteness-derived policy behind those amounts was to protect traders' legitimate expectations rather than to secure their revenues. In any case, no loss was proved. The circumstances in *Case 49/79 Pool* v. *The Council*,[399] of cattle breeders' compensation claims following the fixing of sterling exchange rates specifically for the agricultural sector, were held to be too speculative and unrealistic.

A graphic recent illustration is the joined *Cases C-6/90 and C-9/90 Francovich and Bonidaci* v. *Republic of Italy*,[400] concerning the Italian government

ties institutions under Article 215 of the *Treaty*. Cf Advocate-General Van Gerven in *Case C-128/92 H.J. Banks and Co. Ltd.* v. *British Coal Corporation*, 27th October 1993, concerning a breach of competition rules under the *European Coal and Steel Community Treaty*. The source of the obligation in the case serves as a reminder that Communities law includes the treaties so far identified as well as the *EURATOM Treaty*.

[395] [1990] ECC 384, at 393 and 394, concerning the Article 85 right to fair competition; similar provisions are carried, e.g., in the French *Ordinance No. 86-1243 Dec. 1 1986* and *Law of Jan. 29 1993* and the US *Clayton and Sherman Acts*.

[396] [1986] 1 QB 716, at 787 (per Parker L.J.) and at 790 (per Nourse L.J.) See also Neil J. in *An Bord Bainne Co-operative Ltd.* v *Milk Marketing Board* [1984] 1 CMLR 519, at 528: in this case, damages were refused for a minister's erroneously inferred failure to guarantee compliance with Community law.

[397] [1967] ECR 262. [398] [1976] ECR 391. [399] [1980] ECR 569.

[400] [1991] ECR I-5357. It may be noted that the British government opposed such state liability (at I-5368) before its own national courts, especially when English (or British) law itself did not impose it.

and a directive protecting employees' salaries. The plaintiffs had lost about a year's salary because of their employers' liquidation, the very circumstances which the directive at issue was designed to prevent. It was held that all individual-empowering provisions of Community law can form the basis for a similar damages award as long as the particular empowerment was sufficiently clear and as long as the Member State's breach was the cause of the loss or damage. A further facilitating (but difficult) requirement is that where Community law is inchoate, national law of liability is applicable to the respective measures of damage and of damages. The concept of "Member State" includes statal organizations like taxation authorities,[401] health authorities,[402] and public utilities corporations.[403] The European dimension, including in particular its unifying provisions on otherwise standard issues like product liability,[404] may yet produce the so-called private law, present and in the making, of Europe, having consequential ramifications as far-reaching as environmental issues, the type of recoverable loss at least at its own level and areas of application. Indeed, as Article 215 of the *Treaty* provides in terms of a "common law of Member States", it appears to be a mere matter of time that the differences of responsiveness among the countries will fade in the light of formal interpretations of their common obligations.[405]

A clear point which transpires in relation to the future scope of Community law-derived actions for damages is that the finiteness of possible actions (outwith the need for inventing new causes, per Lord Diplock in *Garden Cottage Foods*)[406]—i.e. new torts to attract an award of damages—may well arise by reason of the still evolving Community law, such as public officers' mis-feasance.[407] Indeed, it may well begin the re-thinking of the traditional exclusion of matters of public law from general conflict of laws jurisprudence, a matter which has been recognized in the field of administrative law both in the courts and in the academic literature.[408] Outside the Community, there is acknowledgment of the same, e.g. in the Commonwealth, in decisions like

401 Cf. *Fratelli Costanzo* v. *Comune di Milano* [1989] ECR 1839.

402 *Marshall* v. *Southampton Health Authority* [1986] 1 QB 401.

403 *Foster* v. *British Gas plc* [1990] ECR 3313.

404 E.g. Council Directive 85/374/EEC:L 210/29 of July 25th 1985 is Part I of the UK *Consumer Protection Act 1987*.

405 For an optimistic yet unquixotic view of harmonization and convergence theory, see B.S. Markesinis, "Learning From and Learning in Europe", Chapter Nine of his *Foreign Law and Comparative Methodology* (Oxford, Hart; 1997), especially at 181–193.

406 Above. The same disposition will be seen in relation to other EU-derived remedies actions.

407 E.g. as identified by Mann J. in *Bougoin* above, at 740, and followed in the Court of Appeal in the same case, at p. 777 (per Oliver L.J.) The same decision refers to further nascent torts, so to speak, of public officials either failing to abolish or affirming governmental acts which are contrary to Community law, or the same officials negligently or consciously failing to implement correct directives. It may be noted that there has to be a clear connexion between awards in these types of situation an exemplary awards under Lord Devlin's classification in *Rookes* v. *Bernard*, above, at note 370.

408 Cf. Sir W. Wade and C. Forsyth, *Administrative Law* (Oxford, Clarendon; 1994), Chapter 20 generally, as well as discussion, inter alia, of damages for "administrative torts" (580–581) and non-feasance (p. 792).

Miscota SA v. *Shetland Islands Council*.[409] In the area of English administrative law, the sometimes seemingly casuistic refusal in the courts to apply damages to what is typically regarded as falling outside the remit of private law has also been questioned.[410] Regional law as an integral part of the global process thus reduces to a workable level the conceptual boundaries which make legal process possible, and which, it is to be hoped, might point the way beyond similar territorial boundaries.

To return to the more familiar strictures of the conflict of laws, among the exciting propects would be the possibility, at some point in the future, of these actions being brought not in the fora of the State of infringement, but in those of a different Member State, or the likelihood of these integrated regional structures being efficaciously adopted beyond. In closing, it may be added that the relevance and the applicability of the usual issues of types of cause, quantum, policy and heads of loss as have been identified in the ordinary conflicts cases discussed earlier extends to issues of mitigation, and of the interest[411] to be added to these awards in the normal manner.

RESTITUTIONARY DAMAGES FOR BREACH OF CONTRACT AND THE ROME CONTRACTS CONVENTION

It is now settled that the judicial remedy of restitutionary damages is claimable in civil litigation in England. In the Master of the Rolls' leading judgment in *Attorney-General* v. *Blake*,[412] the court stated that the remedy can exceptionally be awarded either: (a) where the defendant is paid for contractual services he has not performed; or (b) he has profited from doing the very thing he contracted not to do. These dicta address long-standing issues of whether a claimant should, in such circumstances, seek restitution rather than damages or vice versa[413] and, indeed, whether there is not a conceptual misapprehension in the very nomenclature of "restitutionary damages".[414] Lord Woolf's judgment vindicates the pro-restitutionary damages argument predominantly led by Burrows.[415] Perhaps not entirely to be ignored, at least for the sake of

[409] 1986 SLT 193 (Supreme Court of Victoria).

[410] See P. Cane, *An Introduction to Administrative Law* (3rd ed., Oxford, Clarendon; 1994), at 73–74, and 76–80 on the irresistible tide of Community law and its bearing on English law in these respects including, in particular, the shifts toward strict or no-fault State liability as against individuals, and the worthwhile application of the so-called "risk theory" therein by which State liability may swiftly and effectively be contained.

[411] Cf. Case C-271/91 MK *Marshall* v. *Southampton Health Authority* [1993] 3 CMLR 293.

[412] [1998] 2 WLR 805 (CA) from 818.

[413] *Cf* Durand, "Restitution or Damages: National Court or European Court" (1975–6) 1 ELR 431–443, in which the question of the correct forum in which the elected remedy is to be sought in circumstances governed by European law is discussed

[414] *Cf* Master McGregor, "*Attorney-General* v. *Blake*: Restitution or Damages", *The Inner Temple Yearbook 1998/99*, p. 36–40.

[415] Eg., in "Aggravated, Exemplary and Restitutionary Damages: A Consultation Paper," No 132, 1993, especially at 155 *et seq*.)

completeness, is a difficult, less-vaunted, contrary view that general restitution law itself is a misconstruction of enduring Common Law principles, which adds nothing which has not always been catered for in its expansive remedial armoury.

Closer to the present article's subject are altogether different but important issues arising in connection with the construction and application of Article 10(1)(c) and (e) of the *Rome Convention on the Law Applicable to Contractual Obligations (1980)*. In light of the finding, these sub-provisions now require practical analysis. These cited portions of the Treaty respectively provide for the application of the proper law of a contract, first, to the quantification of damages and, second, to the consequences of nullity of the contract. The latter provision is not applicable in the United Kingdom because of legislative reservation thereto[416] because of a distinction between unjust enrichment and breach of contract which should result in restitutionary relief.[417]

According to the *Convention*, the law applicable to a transnational contract or to any part of it depends—all other things (e.g., existence and validity of contract and consensus) being settled—on either the parties' express or tacit autonomous agreement on the point (Article 3), or on the law of the objectively "most closely connected" country (Article 4). There are special rules to govern the scope of mandatory rules of an applicable non-forum law of a contract (Article 3(3)). There is also a set of presumptions to assist the ascertainment of the applicable or proper law.

Consequently, were the right circumstances subject to the *Convention* to arise in the English forum in which a successful claim for restitutionary damages is made, governed by the substantive contract law of another Member State, then the quantification of the profit to be reversed by the remedy would have to be subject to the non-forum law to be applied under the *Convention*.

As to sub-provision (e), a null contract definitionally cannot be breached and, therefore, it cannot be redressed in damages even though other monetary restitutionary relief might well be forthcoming in appropiate circumstances. Further, that the sub-provision is not applicable in the UK signifies that restitutionary damages for breach of a null transnational agreement—whatever be its applicable law, local or otherwise—would not be allowed. Thus, a claimant would be advised to seek other mistake/nullity-based relief in a jurisdictionally-relevant forum of another Member State subscribing to the sub-provision, or to seek some other non-damages resitutionary remedy in money in a UK forum without necessitating recourse to the Article.

The clarification affored by *A-G* v. *Blake* is certainly welcome as it takes the law in this area forward at the very least at the local-action level. It would therefore be an inestimable bonus of conceptual consolidation were facts to arise

[416] *Cf* Hansard (1989) 513 HL Debates, cols 1257–1273.

[417] See the present writer's "About a Proper Law of a (Restitutionary) Remedy", [1998] *Denning Law Journal* 85–110.

about which not only is the remedy in view actually awarded for breach of transnational contract to which the Article is applicable, but also the rationalization of which facts would define the fuller terms and scope of the remedy in situations of breach of other kinds of transnational obligation, such as torts and delicts. Further developments in this area are to be welcomed.

8

Injunctions and interim relief

ESSENCE AND VARIETY OF INJUNCTIVE RELIEF

INJUNCTIVE RELIEF RESTRAINS or compels a defendant against whom it is ordered, depending on the type of injunction involved and the circumstances of its being sought. It is as varied in its specific forms as it is versatile in its civil (including matrimonial) and commercial applications, perhaps less than could be deduced from Section 37 of the *Supreme Court Act 1981* which, tritely, is the primary source of the injunctive jurisdiction of the English forum. It provides:

> "(1) The High Court may by order (whether interlocutory or final) grant an injunction or appoint a receiver in all cases in which it appears to the Court to do so. (2) Any such order may be made either conditionally or on such terms or conditions as the Court thinks fit. (3) The power of the High Court under subsection (1) to grant an interlocutory injunction restraining a party to any proceedings from removing from the jurisdiction of the High Court, or otherwise dealing with, assets located within that jurisdiction shall be exercisable in cases where that party is, as well as in cases where he is not, domiciled resident or present within that jurisdiction."

Injunctions are not generally available as of right,[1] rather like orders for specific performance of contracts. Being discretionary or equitable, an injunction can serve to redress a wide range of breach of civil obligation, be it in tort or in contract: to protect propery rights; to enforce contracts; to restrain breach of confidence; in company law; in marital disputes. It can also be granted with other relief appropriate to the particular claim. It is available to coerce the defendant to perform or to observe a particular civil obligation as may be necessary in the circumstances, and there is probably not a more diversified form of judicial relief. Indeed to refer to it thus monolithically is bound to somewhat generalize its diversified nature. There is but the appearance of oversimplification in Lord Nicholls' dicta in *Mercedes Benz AG* v. *Leiduck*[2] that "[a]s circumstances in the

[1] Legal injunctions, i.e., those available automatically, can be granted under statutory authority, e.g., under S. 79 *Common Law Procedure Act 1854* (to augment a claim founded in "breach of contract or other injury"). See *Redland Bricks* v. *Morris* [1970] AC 652, per Lord Upjohn; I.C.F. Spry *Equitable Remedies* (5th ed., Sydney, Law Book Co.; 1997), at 323–328. The relevant Rules of Court are to be found in *RSC* Order 29. In the County Court, injunctions are similarly provided for in S. 38 *County Court Act 1984*.

[2] [1996] AC 284, at 308.

world change, so must the situations in which the courts may properly exercise their jurisdiction to grant injunctions".

The importance of the conflicts aspects of injunctive applications in general is a direct consequence of the divergences of approach as between Common Law and Civil Law countries respectively, e.g., as was pointed out in the particular context of the declining of jurisdiction by Fawcett.[3] What is also clear is that there seems to be a great deal more to be said about transnational injunctions, particularly the interlocutory, than there may be in the context of their domestic counterparts from which they may be said to have fundamentally been derived. The over-riding factor continues to be whether the one forum's order is to be accepted and enforced by the other; in different terms, how jurisdiction and conflicts are to be resolved.

In English law, the classifications and sub-classifications of injunction are serial, with a common theme in equitable principle. Lord Hoffmann has extra-judicially considered that there is juridical foundation for an even broader range of injunctive instruments in civil litigation.[4] His Lordship identified the scope for specialized (interlocutory) orders, e.g., to protect the privacy of intellectual property,[5] and to interrogate third parties about stolen money.[6] As is to be discussed in this Chapter, transnational circumstances have in fact brought about further development and ostensible expansion of the law on injunctions generally. A prime example is the so-called worldwide Mareva injunction, now known as the freezing order. Another is the antisuit injunction which is also available worldwide, for example, as it was recently applied in *Airbus Industrie G.I.E.* v. *Patel and Others*.[7] The availability of final injunctions especially in intellectual property cases is a further example of the way in which the remedy responds to new factual developments. More on these in due course. First, the functional and the formal classifications.

Classifying injunctions

As was mentioned above, an injunction can in essence either prohibit (or negative) or compel particular conduct, on the overall balance of convenience surrounding the order being made. The latter can also be restorative in its substantive content or effect, such as where the defendant is required to undo what he previously ought to have undone but did not—little, it might be said, to

[3] *Declining Jurisdiction in Private International Law* (Oxford, Clarendon; 1995), at 2. Apart from the difference in terms of how the respective legal systems determine the pre-requirement of forum jurisdiction in alternative forum situations, the critical dissimilarity is of course that the Civil Law in principle applies injunctions as primary relief ahead of damages, although fairly normal civilian practice is often to prioritize compensation.

[4] In "*Changing Perspectives of Civil Litigation*" (1993) 53 *MLR* 297.

[5] The "Norwich Pharmacal order", after *Norwich Pharmacal* v. *Commissioners for Customs and Excise* [1974] AC 133.

[6] The "Bankers Trust jurisdiction", after *Bankers Trust* Co. v. *Shapira* [1980] 1 WLR 1274.

[7] [1998] 2 WLR 686 (H.L.) Lord Goff of Chieveley's leading speech also emphasizes the underlying comparativist perspectives as between the Common Law and the Civil Law, especially on the point that the difference is not inapt to produce unwelcome practical results in realizing the streamlining objectives of the *Brussels Convention*.

differentiate restorative injunctive sub-forms from orders for specific performance. Apart from the substantive (in contradistinction to formal) basic mandatory/prohibitory categorization thus described, an injunction is also classifiable according to the stage at which it can be sought in an action: it may be interlocutory in the sense of being ancillary to process, or final in the sense of dispositively resolving the causa. The former, technically speaking to be distinguished from interim injunctions enforceable until before trial begins, avails a claimant until trial on the merits—it can of course also be ancillary to a final judgment—and, if the circumstances require, may be granted before notification to the defendant as is presently clarified in the correct portion of the Chapter. It is said that the most important, but mostly overlooked, categorization of injunctions is between the legal and the equitable.[8] In practical terms, the claim for legal injunction as final relief in a conflicts case must of course mean that the applicable substantive law indicates that this remedy is apposite to the claim.[9] It is likewise a matter of settled course that in order for the English forum to grant an injunction in a conflicts case, the merits resolved by reference to a foreign governing law must be resolvable by the given relief as it obtains according to internal forum law.[10] As was settled in the old case of *Martin* v. *Nutkin*,[11] future breach of negative contractual stipulations can be restrained through a prohibitory legal injunction,[12] even if no loss to the claimant is proved. For the purpose of this subsection, it remains to indicate the spectrum of final injunctive relief about which a useful function-based scheme is provided by Burrows as follows:[13] a mandatory enforcing injunction to compel performance of positive obligations; a prohibitory injunction to prevent wrongful acts; a mandatory restorative injunction to compel the undoing of a wrong. This is utilized in the discussion that follows that of interlocutory injunctions. It should be pointed out that interlocutory relief in view perforce includes staying actions, and antisuit (and so-called counter-antisuit) injunctions. The type of civil obligation to be redressed by injunction is also necessarily to be observed where necessary. By way of further general introductory interest, it should be pointed out that much of what is said of the remedy of specific performance applies mutatis mutandis to claims for injunction to indirectly enforce positive obligations.[14] These equitable principles need not be rehearsed at this stage in the Chapter.

[8] Cf. Spry, *op. cit.*, n. 1.

[9] See L. Collins *et al* (ed.). *Dicey and Morris on the Conflict of Laws* (12th ed., London, Sweet & Maxwell; 1993), 171.

[10] See, e.g., *Warner Brothers Pictures Incorporated* v. *Nelson* [1937] 1 KB 209.

[11] 2 P Wms 266 (1724). Should the contractual stipulation be in breach already, a mandatory injunction to undo the breach would be appropriate, complete with "balance of convenience" considerations: *Reed* v. *Madon* [1989] Ch 408.

[12] A.G. Guest *et al* (eds.), *Chitty on Contracts* (28th ed., London, Sweet & Maxwell; 1999), generalizes that all injunctions are, even in these circumstances, discretionary: para. 28–055.

[13] *Remedies for Torts and Breach of Contract* (2nd ed., London, Butterworths; 1994), at 8. In Chapter Nine of the same book (387 *et seq.*), the discussion is of final prohibitory injunctions, final mandatory injunctions, final *quia timet* injunctions, and interlocutory injunctions.

[14] Cf. *Lumley* v. *Gye* [1852] 1 De GM & G 604, especially at 619 (per Lord St. Leonards L.C.), concerning a contract of personal service (entertainment).

INTERLOCUTORY INJUNCTIONS

The general characteristic of these orders, distinct as they are from interim relief, is that they do not apply beyond the conclusion of trial on the merits. An interlocutory order may be either mandatory, prohibitory or in anticipation of consequential breach, and can be said to be in its element in the enforcement of positive obligations such as those obtaining under a contract. This section distils into three types of injunction (antisuit, the old Mareva jurisdiction, and the staying of forum actions), plus further kinds of interim (Anton Piller, and disclosure) order. There could hardly be a more interesting array of types of order responding to the same basic description. For the present writer, the material described and discussed in this section almost single-handedly makes transnational litigation and the conflict of laws the dynamic and exciting subjects they are and are to be observed to further develop into. The inherent trans-jurisdictionalism of these subjects is brought to life in arguably the best light.

ANTISUIT INJUNCTIONS

The Common Law: *Airbus Industrie G.I.E.* v. *Patel and Others*.

The leading speech of the Lord Goff in *Airbus Industrie G.I.E.* v. *Patel*[15] (hereafter, *Airbus*) must represent, as do his judgments generally,[16] a statement of the law in this area as it stands today, complete with the bonus of a giving set of transnational facts. Although his Lordship distinguished the "alternative forum"—i.e., as distinct from "single forum"—circumstances therein, his clarification of the law, as was acceded to by the other members of the House, seems set to stand foreseeably. In no way is the structure of the following analysis intended to undervalue prior survey of the principles governing the particular remedy.[17] It is simply in the nature of the issues that they are arguably more usefully presented in the form of a factual up-to-the-minute account[18] which,

[15] [1998] 2 WLR 686 (H.L.) For a debate based on the Court of Appeal decision as to whether, and to what extent, an underlying substantive right predicates entitlement to an antisuit injunction, see A. Briggs, "The Unrestrained Reach of an Anti-suit Injunction: A Pause for Thought" [1997] *LMCLQ* 90 and J. Harris, "Anti-suit Injunctions – A Home Comfort" [1997] *LMCLQ* 413. The former argues that there is an ignored choice-of-law issue which should attract a proper law approach in the case of equitable rights, the latter favours internal law of the forum in all cases which has always applied given that the necessary right "is simply not to have vexatious or oppressive proceedings brought against him overseas" (416).

[16] Cf. His Lordship's decisions on cognate questions in *Spiliada Maritime Corporation* v. *Cansulex Ltd*. [1987] AC 460 and *Societe Nationale Industrielle Aerospatiale* v. *Lee Kui Jak* [1987] AC 871.

[17] The Opinion in *Airbus* sets out the principles, at 692–694. These are discussed to close the subsection.

[18] It is of considerable interest that Lowenfeld, for example (in *International Litigation and the Quest for Reasonableness: Essays in Private International Law* (Oxford, Clarendon; 1996), 9–10)), finds it intellectually appealing that "all anti-suit injunctions are wrong, especially injunctions

true to its source, is succinct in mapping out the selfsame principles. Antisuit injunctions do not expressly fall under the scheme of the *Brussels Convention*, as was made clear by the European Court of Justice in *Overseas Union Insurance* v. *New Hampshire Insurance*.[19] Nor are they entirely free from being regarded as exceptional.[20] They involve some measure of interference with the relevant foreign jurisdiction(s).

The *Airbus* facts and their chronology were these. An air crash happened in Bangalore (India) in which the British claimants were severely injured or (and) bereaved of relatives. The cause of the crash was established as airline pilot error, with the result that damages were recovered against the Indian Airlines Corporation but not against the airport authority concerned since the injuries and deaths could not be said to have been caused by its employees' negligence. At the time of having begun the Indian claim, the claimants also started an action for damages in Texas mainly against Airbus, the Toulousian designers and builders of the aircraft (the defendants in the subsequent English claim) who happened to have been subject to the jurisdiction there by reason of their having transacted business with a Texan company in the past.[21] To counteract the Texan proceedings, Airbus successfully sued in India to have the Texan, and any other non-Indian, proceedings discontinued. However, the injunction obtained in India had little extraterritorial consequence.

Therefore, Airbus sued in England to enforce the Indian injunction because, among other reasons advanced on their behalf, it would be vexatious or oppressive for the Texan action to persist. At first instance, Colman J. declined to enforce the Indian injunction or to grant an English one to restrain Texan suit, respectively because the former was not a money judgment in personam[22] as is required under the *Administration of Justice Act 1920* or the *Foreign Judgments (Reciprocal Enforcement) Act 1933*, nor was the injunction to be granted since England was not forum conveniens (in the sense of being the most appropriate forum). This latter finding was reversed by the Court of Appeal (led by Hobhouse L.J.) in the interests of justice between parties properly subject to forum jurisdiction. The injured parties then appealed to the House of Lords on

issued in one state designed to restrain proceedings in another state", especially in view of the fact that restraining foreign suit could in effect deny the restrained party from remedy without the merits ever having been heard. The all-important primary issue of proper jurisdiction thus overshadows all other matters, at least in principle. Whether this should found the overall legal aspect can admit of no easy answer.

[19] Case C-351/89: [1991] ECR I-3317, at 3350, para. 23; but see the subsequent Court of Appeal decision in *Continental Bank NA* v. *Aeakos Compania Naviera SA* [1994] 1 WLR 588, concerning parallel proceedings in England and Greece about which an injunction based on vexation and oppression was in fact granted.

[20] Cf. *Tracomin* v. *Sudan Oil Seeds Co. Ltd. (No.2)* [1983] 1 WLR 1026; but see *Continental Bank NA* v. *Aeakos Compania Naviera SA* [1994] 1 WLR 588, at 598.

[21] That this jurisdictional basis was subject to observer criticism (see e.g., E. Peel, "Antisuit Injunctions—The House of Lords Refuses to Act as International Policeman" (1998) 114 *LQR* 543) and was subsequently reformed in Texas itself is simultaneously important and of little consequence to a presentation of the facts.

[22] See, e.g., *Beatty* v. *Beatty* [1924] 1 KB 807; *Sadler* v. *Robins* 1 [1808] Camp 253, at 256.

the point that, even if England was non conveniens as to the merits (India was), the English forum was nevertheless jurisdictionally competent to intervene between the respective other fora by restraining the Texan claim in order to enable realization, via recognition and enforcement, of the Indian orders.

Lord Goff's Opinion may be said to have run thus:

—Texan proceedings, *inter alia* for substantial punitive damages coupled with a contingency fees' arrangement, in product liability and negligent training of the pilots: on appeal to the Texas Court of Appeals from the Texas State District Court, Airbus had unsuccessfully sought to resist the jurisdiction of the Texan courts in that it (Airbus) was predominantly government-owned and therefore protected under the United States' *Foreign Sovereign Immunity Act 1976*, and was looking to make further appeal to the Texas Supreme Court at the time of their Lordships' adjudication in England. The doctrine of forum non conveniens was not accepted in Texas[23] at the time of the case but it has now been incorporated, the effect of this being that original jurisdiction had been acquired in Texas on the mere basis, that Airbus had transacted business there in the past, of strict liability. This would not have affected subsequent recognition and enforcement in England but, much in the vein of a trial on the merits at the interlocutory stage, Hobhouse L.J. had held that the claim would likely have been deemed to be without sufficient justification had it been pursued in a fault liability jurisdiction like England.

—The English High Court's "balance of convenience" reasons for declining jurisdiction: inter alia, with the significant result that conflicting decisions could arise if an English injunction was granted, Airbus would, if it was liable, need to have the matter of its liability in India reopened in Texas in order to recover contributions from the airline and the airport authority in Texas, even though the Indian proceedings would probably have continued (no injunction was sought by the claimants in Texas). Airbus had not proved that Texan proceedings were vexatious or oppressive, as would justify an English injunction to restrain.

—Hobhouse L.J.'s principal judgment as to (a) forum interest or interventionism outwith the preservation of its own process and (b) the availability of an injunction for the purpose: applying the Privy Council's finding in *S.N.I.A.*,[24] that the protection of own process does justify forum interventionism, his Lordship discountenanced Colman J.'s finding that clear oppression alone could found the type of injunction sought. Further, with India as the natural forum

[23] For recognition of the doctrine in United States law, see the *Restatement of the Law Second: Conflict of Laws* (American Law Institute Publishers, St. Paul, Minnesota; 1980), Vol. 1, para. 84; *Gulf Oil Corp.* v. *Gilbert* [1947] 330 US 501; *Piper Aircraft Co.* v. *Reyno* [1981] 454 US 235.

[24] Cf. n. 16 above. It is to be noted that Texas also featured as a competing jurisdiction in *SNIA*, complete with the same factors of the absence of a doctrine of forum non conveniens and the search for penal damages as in *Airbus*. A helicopter crash in Brunei had led to widow claims in Brunei and Texas against the manufacturers and the operators, the jurisdictional basis having been precisely the same as that applied in *Airbus*. Trial in Brunei rather than in Texas was countenanced by the Judicial Committee of the Privy Council.

and France as another appropriate forum, Texan suit was ostensibly oppressive because it was clearly inappropriate, as well as potentially and impossibly prejudicial.

—Common law principles governing the grant of an antisuit injunction (*S.N.I.A.*, the resolution of clashes between jurisdictions,[25] and the scope for comparativism): these are derived from jurisdiction over the defendant subject to the practical but undeniably imperfect principle of *forum non conveniens*. In sum, the natural forum for a dispute justifies the remission of trial thereto, because to do otherwise would be unjust to the defendant and would not further the equities of the claim. Further, the independence of self-restraining jurisdictions together with the principles of comity were to be observed; in other words, were England a contestable forum in a particular claim, an antisuit injunction would be available if the English forum was the natural forum according to its own law.[26]

—Comity: referring to the contest of and for antisuit injunctions as between the English and the District of Columbia jurisdictions surrounding *British Airways Board* v. *Laker Airways Limited*,[27] in which the House of Lords held that no antisuit injunction ought to have been granted by the Court of Appeal,[28] Lord Goff makes clear that the protection of forum interest is to be combined with the observance of forum public policy as was emphasized by Judge Wilkey in the District of Columbia Court of Appeals in *Laker Airways Limited* v. *Sabena Belgian World Airlines*.[29] In particular, he stated that "[a]s a general rule, before an anti-suit injunction can properly be granted by an English court to restrain a person from pursuing proceedings in a foreign jurisdiction in [alternative forum cases], comity requires that the English forum should have a sufficient interest in, or connection with, the matter in question to justify the indirect interference with the foreign court which an anti-suit injunction entails."[30] The judgment is much a state-of-the-art elucidation of the law on

[25] Cf. n. 7, above, and the main text it complements. His Lordship variously referred to *Spiliada* and the acceptance of its principles in New Zealand (cf. *Club Mediterranee NZ* v. *Wendell* [1989] 1 NZLR 216), Canada (cf. *Amchem Products Inc. et al.* v. *Workers' Compensation Ltd.* (1993) 102 DLR (4th) 96, especially at 118–121), India (the *Airbus* case itself), apparently in Japan (cf. E. Hayes, "Forum non Conveniens and the Allocation of Jurisdiction in Transnational Litigation" (1992) 26 *UBCLaw Rev 41*, at 112), and adaptively in Australia (cf. *Voth* v. *Manildra Flour Mills Pty. Ltd.*(1990) 65 *ALJR* 83 , *CSR Ltd.* v. *Cigna Insurance Australia Ltd. and others* (1997) 146 ALR 402: as to the consequence of forum non conveniens, especially at 437–438).

[26] *SNIA*, at 896.

[27] [1985] AC 58.

[28] Cf. *Midland Bank Plc* v. *Laker Airways Ltd.* [1986] QB 689, in which the "overwhelmingly English" character of the litigation, which was missing from the litigation in hand, was held to justify the grant of an antisuit injunction. For a general survey of the Laker litigations, see L. Collins, "*Provisional and Protective Measures in International Litigation*" in Essays in *International Litigation and the Conflict of Laws* (Oxford, Clarendon; 1994), 107–117.

[29] (1984) 731 F2d 909, at 926–927. See also L. Collins, *Current Legal Issues in International Commercial Litigation* (Singapore, N.U.S.; 1997) 3, 6–8, on the "stricter" and "laxer" standards to be found in different Circuits, the former based on considerations of comity deriving from Judge Wilkey's decision.

[30] *Airbus*, at 698–699 (cf. *Amchem Products* (Sopinka J., at 119)).

this type of injunction. Implicitly, the role of comity in "single-forum cases" is much reduced in considering the grant of these injunctions, that "any limiting principle requiring respect for comity cannot simply be expressed by reference to the question whether the English court may be the natural forum for the dispute."[31] It is unlikely that the law on antisuit injunctions can foreseeably be radically different from *Airbus*. Nor will much be lost in not further considering the other relevant authorities already referred to.

All the same it is in place to consider some remaining jurisdictional issues which run with a broader view of the decision:

a There is the unavoidable basic requirement that properly exercizable jurisdiction, and with it issues of forum conveniens, be had before an antisuit injunction can be issued. The English forum could effectively query the exorbitant exercise—based on a tenuous link with Airbus (France)—of Texan jurisdiction and consequently refuse to recognize the decision of that forum. To do otherwise, even on the back of considerations of comity, must go, first, to the quality of the view taken of the Indian decision which could itself not prevent the Texan proceedings and, second, to the doing of substantial justice as between the parties.

b In so far as both Airbus and the British claimants were parties domiciled within the territorial reach of the *Brussels Convention*, even though the place in which the tragic mishap occurred was well beyond, an unanswerable view of the question of the proper forum would, in compliance with the defendant protecting policy contained in Article 2 of the *Brussels Convention*, be that France is the only place in which the litigation should ever have taken place in Europe.

c It is ripe for fuller consideration that non-money judgments in personam be recognizable and enforceable between jurisdictions, after the *Brussels Convention* and status judgments respectively, not least because (a) what is to be enforced is distinctly res judicata in every decision that succeeds, jurisdictionally speaking, according to the law of the forum in which recognition and enforcement is sought and, perhaps less rigorously, (b) it is increasingly the case either that the quality of applicable law in most jurisdictions (in *Airbus*, it was India) is reasonably consistent or at least visibly more so than it is as between the Member States of the European Union wherein system difference is so pronounced (at least between England and the Civil Law jurisdictions) and yet of ostensibly little consequence to harmonization through cross-enforceability under the permissive, rather than authorizing, Articles 24 and 25 of the *Convention*. It is to be noted that the use of these provisions by Member States' fora is cautious, so as not to undermine the harmonizing system of the Convention as a whole, e.g., by imposing common, instead of national, interpretation on the terms, as in the French case of *Menegatti* v. *Société Mettalurgica Nava Stefano e*

[31] *Airbus*, at 698.

Giuseppina.[32] In that case, the Paris Court of Appeal appears to have held that interim measures sought in respect of a cause concerning the termination of an exclusive commercial agency agreement, containing an Italian exclusive jurisdiction clause, between a French resident Italian plaintiff and an Italian company, were measures best applied by the courts of the exclusive jurisdiction.

d The globalization of civil justice, which only appears to be less urgent than its regionalization, must require universal acceptance of the bases upon which any forum acquires or must decline jurisdiction.[33] Legal culture, however defined, is not really always the delimiting issue it is sometimes represented to be.[34]

e That a forum which is insufficiently interested in a given cause can nevertheless take jurisdiction thereon and apply the law of the natural forum on restraint of foreign suit might be commendable but is premature and, indeed, much less defensible than the basis described under the next point below.

f It is necessary to individuate the comparable law under the *Brussels Convention* as briefly as is necessitated by the fact that antisuit injunctions are not part of its express scheme for the acquisition and declination of jurisdiction. The difficulties and consequences of a divergence of approach between English law and the Civil Law-generated *Brussels Convention*—in particular the possibility of injustice from the rigidity of the defined conflict-avoiding jurisdictional rules of the latter which ostensibly eschew the flexible and practical doctrine of *forum non conveniens*—was broached by Lord Goff in the *Airbus* case.[35] A basic theme of the *Brussels Convention* is that the the jurisdictions concerned are inter-dependent rather than emphatically autonomous,[36] such that resolution of jurisdictional conflicts arising in connexion with concurrent litigation in the fora of more than one Member State is dependent on the fact of which court was first seised of the given matter rather than on substantive considerations of which forum is most appropriate to the cause. The common theme of forum restraint via, e.g., the declining of jurisdiction, is taken further in discussing the staying of actions.

g The importance of encouraging the parties in transnational litigation to be able to accurately predetermine the forum whose jurisdictional compe-

[32] Paris, 17.11.1987, 1989 *Clunet* 96, note Huet.

[33] See the present writer's "Proper Jurisdiction and the *Pakistan National Shipping* case" [1999] 14 *Amicus Curiae* 13.

[34] *Cf. International Litigation News*, July 1998, at 17.

[35] Ibid., at 692.

[36] Ibid., at 697–698 and in his Lordship's Postscript at p. 701; cf. Articles 21–23 of the *Convention*, respectively dealing with "proceedings involving the same cause of action and between the same parties", "related actions . . . so closely connected that it is expedient to hear and determine them together to avoid the risk of irreconciliable judgments resulting from separate proceedings", and conflicts of exclusive jurisdiction.

> tence is to be prayed in aid of disputes arising between them cannot be understated. This facilitates settlement of the primary question of original jurisdiction which is favourable to the different but no less consequential matter of the practical effectiveness to be accorded to the exercise of competence elsewhere as may subsequently become necessary.

A different composite of facts yet to arise could vary the foregoing analysis from *Airbus*. However, it seems unlikely that further deliberation, of jurisdictional autonomy and of acceptably final resolution of a transnational dispute in any forum, can justify a radically different approach. Whatever else might need to be said must be in the nature of more general transnational judicial jurisdiction, as this has been discussed in Part B of this book.

FREEZING ORDERS (THE MAREVA JURISDICTION)

In *Mareva Compania Naviera S.A.* v. *International Bulk Carriers S.A., The Mareva*,[37] the decision from which the present jurisdiction took its name, the defendant voyage charterers did not pay hire charges due to the claimant shipowners despite having received funds from the subcharterers. So as to prevent the disposal of these funds and (or) other assets before trial of the compelling case against the defendant, the Court of Appeal circumvented earlier authority (by which a defendant cannot be made to give security before judgment)[38] by granting a prohibitory injunction. The discretionary[39] jurisdiction now so familiar is statutorily provided for in Section 37(3) of the *Supreme Court Act 1981*. It is important to note that although a freezing order is nominally interlocutory, the standard flexible guiding principles on interlocutory injunctions as these are espoused in *American Cyanamid Company* v. *Ethicon*,[40] are not quite applicable,[41] albeit that the shared characteristics are that the success

[37] [1975] 2 Ll Rep. 509 (C.A.) *CPR* 25.1(1)(f) According to the *County Court Remedies Regulations 1991*, a Mareva is generally unavailable in a county court, except where as these *Regulations* were amended on 1st February 1995, the proceedings are brought before the Central London County Court Business List and the freezing application is made to a circuit judge nominated by the senior presiding judge. The wealth of thorough literature on the subject includes, e.g., R. Ough and W. Flenley, *The Mareva Injunction and Anton Piller Order* (2nd ed., London, Butterworths; 1993); S. Gee, *Mareva Injunctions and Anton Piller Relief* (3rd ed., London, F.T. Law and Tax; 1994); C. McLachlan, "Transnational Application of Mareva Injunctions and Anton Piller Orders" (1987) 36 *ICLQ* 669. See also the Inns of Court School of Law, *Civil Litigation & Remedies* (London, Blackstone Press; 1989), 101–106. According to *Channel Tunnell Group Ltd.* v. *Balfour Beatty Construction Ltd.* [1995] 2 WLR 762, the jurisdiction avails foreign arbitration.

[38] E.g., *Lister & Co.* v. *Stubbs* 45 Ch D 1 (C.A.); cf. A. Zuckerman, "Mareva Injunctions and Security for Judgment in a Framework of Interlocutory Remedies" 109 *LQR* 432 (1993).

[39] Cf. *Rasu Maritima* v. *Perusahaan Pertambangan* [1978] QB 644 (C.A.), concerning an admiralty claim for damages for breach of charterparty, in respect of which the value of the assets to be frozen was negligible in comparison with the claim being made. Needless to say Lord Denning M.R. refused to grant the order sought.

[40] [1975] AC 396 (per Lord Diplock): mainly that there be a serious question to be tried, and whether the balance of convenience favours the grant of the injunction (including whether damages can be regarded as adequate).

of either application depends on the equities as between the parties. It cannot be over-emphasized that the jurisdiction applies to practically every type of transnational litigation in respect of which the restraint of the party against whom the order is sought is deemed necessary.

In order for this injunction to be granted in its basic form, there has to be a justiciable cause of action in respect of which the defendant has assets within the jurisdiction,[42] which assets are at genuine risk (e.g., because the defendant is resident outside the jurisdiction and (or) has no substantial links with England) of being disposed of before judgment is reached. Justiciability depends on the defendant being properly served with process,[43] and on the claimant's affidavit being indicative of a good arguable substantive case.[44] Freezable assets[45] include money, bank accounts,[46] land[47] and chattels owned by the defendant. According to *Montecchi* v. *Shimco Limited*,[48] as to the issue of foreign enforceability, it is conducive that there be reciprocal enforcement arrangements in place with the relevant foreign jurisdiction.

A freezing order will not run if the essential pre-requirements are unfulfilled, if the defendant provides security against judgment (e.g., in the form of a charge over his property or payment into court or into a bank account for the purpose), or if the claimant maliciously withholds relevant information (e.g., a defendant's counterclaim based on either party's financial situation,[49] or a change in circumstances after the grant of the order).[50] An order can of course be appealed from, partly because it is open to a defendant to point out fundamental defects in the claimant's application. Most Mareva applications are likely to settle out of court.[51]

[41] Cf. *Polly Peck International plc* v. *Nadir (No.2)* [1992] 4 All ER 769 (C.A.), at 785.

[42] Exceptionally, according to *Derby* v. *Weldon (No.2)* [1989] 1 All ER 1002 (C.A.), assets abroad are freezable where there are no, or no sufficient, local assets. In the circumstances, interested third parties are to be provisionally unaffected except by local enforcement there: *Babanaft International Co. SA* v. *Bassatne* [1990] Ch 13 (C.A.) cf. *CPR* PD 25, Annex. See also D. Capper, "Worldwide Mareva Injunctions" (1991) 54 *MLR* 329.

[43] *Siskina (Cargo Owners)* v. *Distos Compania Naviera* [1979] AC 210 (H.L.)) Section 25 of the *Civil Jurisdiction and Judgments Act 1982* avails a claimant in *Brussels Convention* cases in which same party proceedings are pending in another *Convention State* (cf. L. Collins, "Provisional Measures, the Conflict of Laws and the Brussels Convention" (1989) 105 *LQR* 262. Service out may be authorized under *RSC* Order 11 r. 1(1) or r. 2(2) where necessary. For arbitrations, see Order 73, r. 8.

[44] *The Niedersachsen* [1983] 1 WLR 1412.

[45] *CBS* v. *Lambert* [1983] Ch. 37, at 42; Lawton LJ gives a liberal definition which covers choses in action. Freezables also include goodwill (cf. *Darashah* v. *UFAC (UK) Ltd.* 1982 CAT 349) as well as a local judgment debt but not likely an insured's rights under an insurance policy.

[46] *SFC Finance* v *Masri* [1985] 1 WLR 876: concerning a jointly held bank account.

[47] In the case of land, the fact of freezing does not amount to a registrable charge: s. 6(1) *Land Charges Act 1972*.

[48] [1979] 1 WLR 1180 (C.A.); see also P. Kaye, "Extraterritorial Mareva Orders and the Relevance of Enforceability" (1990) 9 *CJQ* 12.

[49] *Practice Direction* [1983] 1 All ER 1119; *Third Chandris Shipping Corporation* v. *Unimarine SA* [1979] QB 645, at 688.

[50] *Commercial Bank of the Near East* v. *P* (1989) 139 NLJ 645.

[51] Cf. L.Collins *Recueil des Cours*, [1992-III] 234 9, at 14, referring to *Fellowes & Son* v. *Fisher* [1976] QB 122, at 133 (C.A., Lord Denning M.R.).

Generally speaking, the main formal aspects are that the claimant is to give the typical undertaking as to damages at the time of the application, which application can be made at any stage of the proceedings (including in the course of trial or to assist execution of final judgment, as was the case in *Deutsche Schactbau-und-Tiefbohrgesellschaft mbh* v. *Shell International Petroleum Company Limited*)[52] without notice to the defendant. Thus, a freezing application is not, strictly speaking, interlocutory in the sense of having exclusively to be made before trial. Once the clear and specific order is granted, the defendant is immediately to be notified (as are any third parties affected,[53] e.g. banks) complete with the claim form, the order application and the sworn statement in support. What is frozen must not exceed the value of the claim, and if there are insufficient assets to meet the claim, there need not be any indication of a maximum asset value, as was stated in *Z Limited* v. *AA-ZZ Limited*.[54] Continuation of the order beyond the specified date, e.g., until judgment or further event is specified, requires further application with notice to the defendant.

A question which can arise in transnational litigation involving proceedings abroad concerns the likelihood of a stay of English proceedings, in which the order has been granted, in favour of another forum. Subsequent to the stay, it would appear that an order would nevertheless avail an applicant who is apprehensive of English assets being dissipated before the foreign proceedings are concluded;[55] this would uphold considerations of comity, and it would facilitate subsequent recognition and enforcement of the judgment anticipated of the foreign jurisdiction. Indeed, it ought in this regard to be recalled that all that is really required is that personal jurisdiction over the defendant be had in order for the relief to be grantable, as is confirmed by the Court of Appeal decision in *Republic of Haiti* v. *Duvalier*.[56] Similarly, the defendant in English litigation is able to seek to freeze the claimant's assets as against costs or a substantive counterclaim, with any necessary ancillary conditionalities (e.g., cross-undertakings as to damages) applying. Identical practice is observable in Civil Law countries, e.g., in the French case of *Société Intrabank* v. *Beidas*,[57] or under Article 4(3) of the Italian Code of Civil Procedure as it was applied, e.g., in *Gagliardi* v. *Larocca*.[58]

[52] [1988] 2 Ll Rep. 293.

[53] See generally P. Devonshire, "Mareva Injunctions and Third Parties: Exposing the Subtext" (1999) 62 *MLR* 539.

[54] [1982] 1 QB 558, at 576 (per Lord Denning M.R.) *CPR* PD 25, Annex. If further assets are subsequently acquired by the defendant, the order will cover them: *TDK* v. *Video Choice Ltd.* [1986] 1 WLR 141, at 145 (per Skinner J.).

[55] Cf. M. Hoyle, *The Mareva Injunction and Related Orders* (3rd ed., London, LLP; 1997), at 142.

[56] [1990] 1 QB 202, at 217; see also X v. Y [1990] 1 QB 220, and *Alltrans Inc.* v. *Interdom Holdings Ltd.* [1991] 4 All ER 458 (C.A.). These decisions involved resort to the *Brussels Convention*, Arts. 24 and 25, thus were not necessarily templates for non-*Convention* disputes.

[57] Trib.gr.inst., Paris, 14.1.1970, 1970 *Rev.crit.* 714, note P.L.; also, *Lafitte* v. *Soc. Les Transitaires Reunis et Ortoli*, Paris, 8.10.1964, 1965, Clunet 901.

[58] 8.6.1985, No. 3464, *Riv.dir.int.proc.*, 1987, at 79.

Thus, there are comparable types of order in other jurisdictions.[59] Consider that in France, the *saisie conservatoire* is provided for in Article 48 of the French Code of Civil Procedure (*ancien*),[60] to the effect that a supposed debtor's movables can be attached by court order so as to prevent the frustration of a judgment against that party. There are equal, or more stringent, requirements made of the creditor, such as that an action be commenced reasonably promptly or that the creditor's solvency in the event of his claim being refused be established. The difference between this procedure and the English equivalent is that the former gives the creditor proprietorial rights by which security for the debt can be enforced. What is less clear is whether, as is the case in English law, this procedure excludes the successful claimant from the defendant's other creditors in the event of insolvency. Because the French order is properly restricted to the particular claim, it appears that the substantive effect is identical to the English remedy.

The jurisdictions of the United States have long recognized a plaintiff's proprietary[61] (not personal) entitlement to foreign attachment of property held overseas by fleeing debtors or non-nationals, by which the taking of jurisdiction by the incumbent forum state is emphasized to be a central characteristic of the procedure. It is therefore a different asset-preserving pre-judgment procedure from the Mareva, even though it has the identical feature that it is sometimes not recognized in other forum states.[62] For applications on all fours with the English procedure, one needs to look to the Anglo-Commonwealth.[63] It transpires that

[59] See L. Collins, "Provisional and Protective Measures in International Litigation" in Essays in International Litigation and the Conflict of Laws, (Oxford, Clarendon; 1994), 10–15.

[60] There are also the saisie-arret under Art. 557 Code of Civil Procedure (*ancien*) for attachment of a third party debt to the defendant, the *saisie-revendication, saisie-maritime* (arrest of a ship). See also S. 916 of the German *Zivilprocessordnung* (30th January 1877), Art. 1298 of the Belgian Civil Code, and Article 670 of the Italian Code of Procedure. The forum states of the Arab Gulf and environs, including Egypt and the Middle East, are known to apply legal provisions similar to those of the Civil Law system. For more on EU practice, see Collins, *op. cit.*, at 22–26.

[61] Cf. *In re Chemical Separations Corp.* 29 Bankr 240 (Bankr ED Tenn 1983). A lien is created to let the plaintiff execute judgment against the asset. According to D. Laycock, *Modern American Remedies* (Boston, Little Brown and Co. 1985), at 735–736, "[u]sage varies from state to state . . . Some states make attachment very easy; others make it very difficult." It certainly operates in the context of priority in the event of insolvency: 11 USC para. 547 (1982).

[62] Cf. the Supreme Court decision in *Pennoyer* v. *Neff* (1877) 95 US 714; for further discussion of the US practice, see Collins, *op. cit.*, at 18–22. In examining the comparison between this practice and the English (29–34), he finds problematic the position by which the Mareva is classified by forum law as falling exclusively within personal jurisdiction, the result being—as in *The Siskina*—that it becomes necessary for the forum to have such effective jurisdiction over the absent defendant as well as the cause, especially where the assets (property) are within the forum state's territory. Where this jurisdiction is not to be had, there appears to be a shortfall in effective competence to freeze, which inadequacy is catered for in both civilian (e.g., in *Air Zaire* v. *Gauthier* (1984) 77 Int'l LR 510)and US practice, as well as in Ireland: *Serge Caudron* v. *Air Zaire* [1986] 6 ILRM 10. As between *Brussels Convention* states, the remedy is ostensibly furnished by S. 25 *Civil Jurisdiction and Judgments Act 1982*, as amended, which effectuates Art. 24 of the *Convention*.

[63] E.g., in Australia and New Zealand (e.g., *Ballabil Holdings Pty. Ltd.* v. *Hospital Products Ltd.* [1985] 1 NSWLR 155), Bermuda (e.g., *Locabil International Finance Ltd.* v. *Dimitrios Manios and Transways (Chartering) SA*, Civil Appeal 1988 No. 4; in *Bank of Bermuda Ltd.* v. *Arnold J. Todd*, Civil Appeal No. 13 of 1992, it was held that sustaining a Mareva is a matter for the party who had

the importance of the English procedure has been variably embraced and about which Schlosser enthused in his report concerning accession to the *Brussels Convention*.[64] Disclosure orders are presently seen to do what freezing orders are under-equipped to do.

STAYING FORUM ACTIONS AND THE DECLINATION OF JURISDICTION

The English forum may, as the circumstances require, be asked either to suspend (with the possibility of recommencement should proceedings elsewhere end)[65] or to decline to exercise its otherwise properly had jurisdictional competence in any type of civil[66] or commercial litigation. In such situations, the basic principle applicable to antisuit injunctions is but a denominator, the difference being that it is the forum's own jurisdictional rules that are being disapplied in favour of directing the litigants to pursue their claims in the correct forum. The incorrect view rendered in *Castanho* v. *Brown & Root (U.K.) Limited*,[67] that precisely the same discretionary principles apply to antisuit injunctions and the staying of forum actions, has since been departed from.

The applicable jurisdictional rules will either be the Common Law rules on forum non conveniens or the more exhaustively rendered pending litigation rules contained in Articles 21 to 23 of the *Brussels Convention*, depending on the rules to which the facts arising are subject.

The *Brussels Convention*

As has already been mentioned elsewhere in this Chapter, the relevant *Convention* provisions emphasize the importance of leaving jurisdiction with the court in which proceedings will have started between the same parties on the same cause. These mandatory requirements make for the avoidance of the undesirable effects of conflicting decisions being reached in different Member States' courts, as long as the matter is not the recognition and enforcement of judgments, this being catered for by a different set of provisions (Articles 25-49, Title III). In *Overseas Union*, the European Court of Justice held that the provisions relating

claimed it), Canada (e.g., *Elesguro* v. *Ssangyong Shipping Co. Ltd.* 117 DLR (3d) 105), Cyprus (e.g., in *Metro Shipping & Travel Ltd.* v. *Global Cruises SA* (Admiralty Action No. 199/88) [1989] 1 CLR 182; it is of interest that its basis in Cyprus is to be found in a statute of 1960, S. 32(1) *Courts of Justice Law 1960*), Malaysia (e.g., in *Aspatra Sdn Bhd and others* v. *Bank Bumiputra Malaysia Bhd and another* [1988] 1 MLJ 97), Singapore (e.g., in *Pek Seng Co. Pte. & others* v. *Low Tin Kee and others* [1990] 1 MLJ 75).

[64] O.J. 1979, C59, para. 183.

[65] Cf. *Internationale Nederlanden Aviation Lease BV* v. *Civil Aviation Authority* [1997] 1 Ll Rep 80.

[66] Family law litigation is largely, but not entirely, excluded: see *De Dampierre* v. *De Dampierre* [1988] 1 AC 92.

[67] [1981] AC 557.

to the parties' domicile (Article 2) and the jurisdictional scheme by which the proceedings are founded are immaterial in these regards, so that, as in *Owens Bank Limited* v. *Bracco (No. 2)*,[68] a non-domiciliary claim and counterclaim respectively in Member States' fora against a non-domiciliary defendant attracts the application of these Articles. According to *Zelger* v. *Salinitri (No. 2)*,[69] it is for national law to determine when a national court is in fact seised. In English law, this question is typically resolved by service of process: *Dresser U.K. Limited* v. *Falcongate Freight Management Limited*.[70] In amplifying the staying of actions and the declination of jurisdiction under the *Convention*, there are separate situations which are now to be described in turn:

(i)Article 21 (lis pendens): In *Gubisch Maschinenfabrik KG* v. *Palumbo*,[71] the European Court of Justice held that a *Convention* meaning—that the given matter must have the same subject matter or aim, cause of action, and parties—is to be ascribed to Article 21 dealing with parallel proceedings. In that case, an action had been commenced in Germany to enforce a doubtful agreement about which the defendant there had sued in Italy for a negative declaration as to not being bound by it. Needless to say, the Italian court was found to be the proper forum. In *Pearce* v. *Ove Arup Partnership Limited and Others*,[72] the English courts had no difficulty in finding that joinder (under Article 6(1)) of defendants not domiciled within the jurisdiction in a local action was within the scheme of the *Convention* even though it did not prevent the other parties from being subject to a continuing action in another *Convention* forum, viz. the Netherlands. If the substance of parallel proceedings differs as to being *in rem* in the one forum and being *in personam* in another, *The Nordglimt*[73] says that the correct provision to apply is Article 22 on related actions, the difference of detail still being caught by the similarity of result in favour of the exercise of jurisdiction by the forum first seised.

(ii)Article 22 (related actions): The decisive factor this Article provides for is the expediency of the one forum trying claims which are inextricably linked but which, as was said in closing the discussion of Article 21 above, are not fully provided for by the preceding Article. Actions are related if the ultimate result of allowing them to continue does not exclude the likelihood of different decisions being reached. Sub-article (1) refers to a discretion (ostensibly not akin to the forum non conveniens type of discretion, but to a carefulness to avoid discrepant decisions at all cost) to stay its own proceedings or decline its own jurisdiction rather than to an obligation to do so, more so where the law of the forum first seised permits consolidation of the actions. The Jenard Report[74] explains the first response of the court second seised in terms that it should

[68] Case C-129/92 [1994] ECR I-117. [69] [1984] ECR 2397. [70] [1992] QB 502.

[71] Case 144/86 [1987] ECR 4861. See also *Owners of the Cargo Lately Laden on Board the Ship Tatry* v. *Owners of the Ship Maciej Rataj* Case C-406/92 [1994] ECR I-5439.

[72] *Times Law Report*, 17th March 1997; see also *The Tatry*, above.

[73] [1988] 1 QB 183. [74] O.J. 1979 C59/41.

decline jurisdiction, mindful that the Article is not a jurisdiction-conferring provision.

(iii) Article 17 (where the parties' choice of jurisdiction is England): The agreement as to jurisdiction is required to meet the requirements of Article 17,[75] viz. that it be written or "in a form which accords with practices which the parties have established between themselves" or a form of international usage in the particular type of transaction. Should neither party be a Member State domiciliary, the exclusive jurisdiction of the selected forum state is beyond question. Much the same policy of sustaining the parties' objective expectations as to the forum for adjudication applies to other circumstances in which exclusive jurisdiction is had by a particular forum.

Internal law

Section 49(3) of the *Supreme Court Act 1981* (and Section 38 *County Courts Act 1984*) preserves the inherent discretionary jurisdiction to stay own proceedings out of necessity or expediency in the circumstances, either on own motion or at the application (by motion or summons to the Master of the Chancery Division) of a party or sometimes a non-party to the proceedings. The wording of Section 49 is in the nature of avoiding frivolity or vexation or an abuse of process. A good example for the context of the present work arises when the defendant raises forum non conveniens when s/he is served outside the jurisdiction. Another fine illustration arises when a different forum has exclusive jurisdiction (e.g., under the relevant Articles of the *Brussels Convention*), or where there is a pre-existing arbitration agreement as between the parties in relation to the facts in issue, although stays are not granted where the issue is the validity of such an agreement. It seems to be pie in the sky that a local action can ever be stayed where there is an agreed jurisdiction clause in favour of the forum: *The Standard Steamship Owners' Protection and Indemnity Association (Bermuda)* v. *Gann.*[76] Further examples of the application of stays arise under *R.S.C.* Order 22 rule 3 (where a claimant accepts a payment into court), and Order 42 rule 5A(2)(b) (as part of a consent judgment at the parties' mutual application). It is important to reiterate the difference between stays on the one hand and on the other the striking out, dismissal or discontinuance of claims, none of which preserves the continuity of the particular case. Additional conditions may be imposed as may be necessary. It is of course the case that a stay can be suspended if it is proper to do so.[77]

The general guidelines on the staying of forum actions are to be found in the well developed law of the natural forum, or forum (non) conveniens, as it is authoritatively set out in the leading judgment of Lord Goff in *Spiliada*

[75] Special provisions are made regarding trusts and trust instruments (sub-arts. (2)–(4)), and individual employment contracts (sub-art. (5)).

[76] [1992] 2 LlR 528; see also *British Aerospace plc* v. *Dee Howard Co.*[1993] 1 LlR 368.

[77] *Cooper* v. *Williams* [1963] 2 QB 567; cf. n. 65 and the main text it accompanies.

Maritime Corporation v. *Cansulex*,[78] albeit that the cause was to do with service out under *R.S.C.* Order 11 rule 1(1) and not an application for a stay. Either, however, is governed by the same set of principles, the main issue being upon which party the burden of proof lies; in the former, it is on the claimant while it naturally lies on the stay-seeking defendant in the latter. The old position, following decisions like *The Atlantic Star*[79] which hinged almost exclusively on vexation and oppression to the defendant in English proceedings subject to an application for a stay, is now no longer applied. The current much-discussed framework runs thus, requiring affirmative response to each inquiry:

— is there another available jurisdictionally competent court which prima facie is that with which the claim is most really and substantially connected having regard to factors such as the applicable substantive law, convenience or expense, e.g., in procuring witnesses?
— can the defendant persuade the forum that this other court avails the parties' interests and the justice of the case over and above the English forum?
— can the plaintiff reverse the persuasion, e.g., by proving that justice would not be forthcoming in the other forum? In this regard, the claimant's advantage must not be at any cost to the defendant.

This wholly discretionary approach to identifying the suitability of the place for trial and of the centre of gravity of the dispute has been adopted in most of the Anglo-Commonwealth save in Australia.[80] The methodology discourages appeals in the particular type of case it concerns. It also runs well with lis pendens jurisdiction, such as in *E.I. Pont de Nemours* v. *Agnew*.[81] In the case, a stay of recovery proceedings in favour of Illinois jurisdiction was refused in respect of a product liability claim for which punitive damages had been granted there. An English indemnity claim for the recovery of the award on the relevant insurance policy—governed by English law in the absence of express choice-of-law—had been met by an Illinois action for a declaration of non-liability to pay, based on public policy of that forum state opposed to punitive damages. In *Re Harrods (Buenos Aires) Limited*[82] concerning a corporate shareholder buy-out petition relating to an English company administered in Argentina and in respect of which there was no pending litigation, the existence of a natural forum (Argentina) from which justice was forthcoming was held to

[78] [1987] AC 460 (H.L.) The formal acceptance of the doctrine was in *The Abidin Daver* [1984] AC 398 (H.L.) after a long and fairly convoluted history in English law, at least, beginning in *St. Pierre* v. *South American Stores Ltd.* [1936] 1 KB 382 (C.A.).

[79] [1974] QB 364, at 382.

[80] Cf. *Voth* v. *Maniladra Flour Mills Pty. Ltd.* [1990] 171 CLR 536, following *Ocean Sun-Line Special Shipping Co. Inc.* v. *Fay* (1988) 165 CLR 197.

[81] [1987] 2 LlRep 585 (C.A.); see also *Banco Atlantico* v. *British Bank of the Middle East* [1990] 2 LlRep 504 (C.A.), in which a stay was also refused because no strong grounds for declining jurisdiction over an English company trading in England were adduced.

[82] [1992] Ch 72 (C.A.). See also *De Dampierre* v. *De Dampierre* [1988] AC 92 (H.L.), a divorce case with proceedings in England and France.

be sufficient to justify a stay, even though the relief available in that forum differed from the English remedy, and despite the possibility of English jurisdiction being had under the *Brussels Convention.* Mindful of the pro-English forum ethos of the rules laid down in *The Spiliada,*[83] extraterritorial jurisdictional competence necessarily requires prior settlement of the appropriateness of England as the forum from which the jurisdiction is exercized.[84]

FURTHER INTERIM ORDERS

Apart from the main types of interlocutory judicial order described above, the English forum is, generally speaking, further equipped to grant other types of provisional order to preserve the situation between the parties, whether or not the merits of the given dispute are to be resolved by the forum. The respective sets of enforcement jurisdiction rules are, as usual, the Common Law and Article 24 of the *Brussels Convention.* The main types of order to be discussed in turn are search orders (the Anton Piller relief) and disclosure orders.

Search orders (the Anton Piller Jurisdiction)

This so-called draconian in personam measure initially took its name from *Anton Piller K.G.* v. *Manufacturing Processes Limited*[85] in which the plaintiff company, a German firm of electrical engineers and manufacturers, sued its United Kingdom agents in copyright and passing off. The Court of Appeal felt it necessary to invent an ex parte order by which the defendant permits the claimant and his solicitor[86] to enter into defendant's premises for the purpose of inspecting and preserving evidence, often but not only in intellectual property disputes, which the defendant is likely to obliterate before open trial. It is obviously akin to the Mareva jurisdiction in that the object of either exercise is to enable fair and effective trial. Furthermore, these orders are characterized by secrecy[87] from and surprise to the defendant who is necessarily and formally to be notified only after they may have been made. As with the freezing order, it is also not unusual for further orders to be added on in the interests of overall

[83] In the sense that a stay will not be granted either if England is forum conveniens or justice in the supposed alternative forum is doubtful: cf. *Carvalho* v. *Hull, Blyth (Angola) Ltd.* [1979] 1 WLR 1228, contra *The Pioneer Container* [1994] 2 AC 324 (that the English forum will not avail a plaintiff who has been late in suing within an agreed forum's limitation period).

[84] Cf. *Société Generale de Paris* v. *Dreyfus Bros* [1985] 29 Ch D 239. A good discussion of the law in this area is provided in *Dicey & Morris op. cit.* (12th ed.), at 408–417.

[85] [1976] Ch 55; see also C. McLachlan, "Transnational Applications of Mareva Injunctions and Anton Piller Orders" (1987) 36 *ICLQ* 669, especially between pp. 678–679, and other works referred to in connexion with freezing orders. Statutory authority:5.7 Civil Proceedure Act 1997; subs (1) limits the jurisdiction to premises in forum state territory only.

[86] Not the claimant's representatives: *Manor Electronics Ltd.* v. *Dickson* [1988] RPC 618.

[87] It should be noted that an application, for the delivery up of goods, on notice to the defendant is provided for in RSC Order 29 r. 2; see also S. 4(2) and (3) *Torts (Interference with Goods) Act 1977.*

jurisdictional efficacy. Indeed, *Anton Piller* itself involved further injunctive restraint of copyright and of use of confidential information. This type of order also extends to all manner of civil and commercial proceeding, including marital causes in the Family Division, as in *Emanuel* v. *Emanuel*.[88]

The basic principles are that there be a convincing prima facie case for resolution, that the addressee's activities must be actually or potentially harmful to the interests of the claimant, and that damning material likely to be destroyed exists on the premises.[89] The claimant must undertake the sanctity of the application, its proper service and explanation to the defendant, to meet any requirements as to damages for the purpose, the preservation and return of all material in particular for the sole purpose for which it is taken. The reality is that, on the authority of *Home Office* v. *Harman*,[90] the search order is in fact a discovery order ahead of pleadings even though there are previous contrary decisions such as *Sony Corporation and Another* v. *Anand and Others; Seiko Time (U.K.) Limited* v. *Domicrest (Fancy Goods) Limited and Others*.[91]

The adaptability of the relief in transnational circumstances is well illustrated in *Cook Industries* v. *Galliher*.[92] The facts were that a third party had allegedly dispersed his expensive fine art collection to the defendant in Paris before a New York judgment could be enforced against the third party. Third party and defendant were United States citizens, although the defendant was frequently present within the forum's jurisdiction. The plaintiffs sued in England and obtained a freezing order as well as a search and seizure order because the English forum was jurisdicitionally competent over the cause and the immovable property and its contents. It was not an issue either that the claimants had effectively applied the English jurisdiction to the enforcement of their foreign judgment as against extraterritorial property not necessarily belonging to the judgment debtor or that if the orders made in France were to have been deployed in England without an English authorization the holders of the foreign order would have been in contempt of court.[93] As Goulding J stated

[88] [1982] 1 WLR 669, per Wood J; see also *K* v. *K* [1982] 13 Fam Law 46.

[89] Cf. Ormrod LJ in *Anton Piller*, at 62. The Staughton Committee Report—"Anton Piller Orders—A Consultation Paper"—of the Lord Chancellor's Department (London, HMSO; November 1992), Para. 2.8 adds that "[t]he harm likely to be caused by the execution of the Anton Piller order to the respondent and his business affairs must not be excessive or out of proportion to the legitimate object of the order." Thus, the civil liberties aspects are taken into account. Further, on this score, S. 14(1) *Civil Evidence Act 1968* upholds the privilege against self and/or spousal incrimination; *Rank Film Distributors Ltd.* v. *Video Information Centre* [1982] AC 380, at 443, and *IBM* v. *Prima Data International* [1994] 1 WLR 719.

[90] [1983] 1 AC 280 (H.L.)

[91] [1981] FSR 398. It concerned the use of Anton Piller evidence in civil or criminal proceedings against third parties outside the jurisdiction, per Browne-Wilkinson J.; cf. *Norwich Pharmacal Co.* v. *Customs and Excise Commissioners* [1974] AC 133.

[92] [1979] 1 Ch D 439. The decision also appears to go some way toward a stance opposed to so-called "worldwide status" for search orders, in contradistinction with freezing orders or roving/class injunctions (based on sufficient identity of interest, the latter being provided for in *RSC* Order 15 r 12(2) and *EMI Records Ltd* v. *Khudhail* [1985] FSR 36 (C.A.))

[93] For a reasonably detailed discussion of the contempt aspects, see S. Gee, *op. cit.*, at 219–220, 226–229, 231–232.

in *Protector Alarms* v. *Maxim Alarms*,[94] even as between England and Scotland, it is "not consistent with the comity prevailing between the courts of the several parts of the United Kingdom for the English court to make an *Anton Piller* order in respect of premises in Scotland."

Execution of the order itself requires efficiency and planning on the applicant's part right from the stage at which service is to be effected. The circumstances of *Columbia Picture Industries Incorporated* v. *Robinson and Others*[95] are instructive in that the applicants did not fully and frankly disclose all relevant facts in their application nor did they return items seized or take only those specified. Compensatory and aggravated damages were awarded to the plaintiff for loss of legitimate business. The search order also avails judgment execution, as in either of *Distributori Automatici Italia SpA* v. *Holford General Trading Company Limited*[96] or *Orwell Steel (Erection and Fabrication) Limited*.[97]

In general terms, as these are rendered in *Dicey and Morris*,[98] "[t]he power to grant interim relief where the English court has no jurisdicition over the substance may be extended by Order in Council . . . But no Order in Council has yet been made" in non-*Convention* disputes. However, the *Civil Jurisdiction and Judgments Act 1982 (Interim Relief) Order 1997*[99] empowers the English forum to make interim orders to assist proceedings in other Member States in respect of Section 25(3) of the *Civil Jurisdiction and Judgments Act 1982* as amended (taking further Article 24 of the *Brussels Convention*). Yet there is marked reluctance to grant interim relief in support of forieign litigation as is derivable from *Mercedes Benz A.G.* v. *Leiduck*.[100] Mercedes Benz had sought a Hong Kong High Court injunction, to trading in shares held by the defendant (Mr Leiduck) in a local company there, in furtherance of a Monaco attachment of his assets. He had no connexion with Hong Kong as would justify the grant of interim relief. Lord Mustill's leading speech was to the effect that no injunctive jurisdiction was therefore to be had. Much the same rationales apply to other types of interlocutory order.

Disclosure orders

Using the factual circumstances of the recent decision of the Privy Council in *Brannigan and Others* v. *Davison*,[101] McLachlan[102] has extensively discussed the scope for this type of order albeit in the particular asset-tracing context of fraud in the international banking system, his central argument being:

[94] [1978] FSR 442, at 446. See also *Altertext* v. *Advanced Data* [1985] 1 WLR 457 in which lack of personal jurisdicition over a Belgian defendant prevented the making of the order sought.

[95] [1987] 1 Ch 38, at 76–77. [96] [1985] 1 WLR 1066. [97] [1984] 1 WLR 1097.

[98] *Op. cit.*, at 196.

[99] S.I. 1997 No.302, *Rules of the Supreme Court (Amendment) 1997* (S.I. 1997 No.415 (L2)).

[100] [1996] 1 AC 241 (P.C.)

[101] [1997] AC 238 (P.C.) English jurisdiction is provided for in *RSC* Order 48.

[102] "The Jurisdictional Limits of Disclosure Orders in Transnational Fraud Litigation" (1998) 47 *ICLQ* 3.

> "Once the courts step outside generally accepted bounds of enforcement jurisdiction, they are led inexorably to irreconciliable conflict with the courts of other countries . . . [that] the only ultimate solution which may be presented is one which develops remedies specially tailored to deal with the transnational nature of the problem . . . [and that] it is only by carefully delineating [between the conflict of laws and the entirely different question of the privilege against self-incrimination] that a more fundamental distinction in the proper scope of enforcement jurisdiction between parties to civil litigation and third party witnesses may be appreciated."[103]

For fuller context, and one which shows the homogeneous nature of transnational relief in general, it is pointed out, for example, that "effective tracing requires effective information in order to trace."[104] The general basis for the equitable jurisdiction to order disclosure is recounted by Robert Goff J. in *A* v. *C*,[105] as being in proprietary rather than personal claims. It extends to judicial assistance in respect of foreign proceedings.

Discovery of documents consists in disclosure by the one party to all the others of all the relevant documents in his possession, custody or power, and in the inspection by those others of the same documents as are not privileged: *R.S.C.* Order 24. Its aim is to put the parties in a position in which they and indeed the court are as aware as is possible of the relative strengths and weaknesses of their case before trial. It is automatic procedure as long as the case is not in the nature of third party proceedings and should take place within a fortnight of pleadings closing. Its central role, as secondary evidence, in ensuring a fair ethical trial cannot be over-emphasized, and failure to give discovery is met by written request to comply, e.g., in the form of a verifying affidavit. It is trite that discovery can be required of a non-party in personal injury or fatality litigation. Order 29 regulates the retention (or detention), preservation and inspection of property, and Order 26 covers the use of interrogatories, such as in seeking to locate foreign beneficially owned assets as in *Re a Company*.[106] The summons for directions stage, governed by Order 25, is the last step in pre-trial procedure, their object being to enable the court to consider the preparations for trial of the claim in question.

With regard to the context of the *Brussels Convention*, it is doubtful that cross-enforceability under Section 25 of the *Civil Jurisdiction and Judgments Act 1982* (as amended) can extend to the initiation of disclosure litigation against a non-resident defendant because Order 11 rule 1(2) is not susceptible to a contrary non-*Convention* interpretation that could make this possible: an identical order in a wholly domestic case would likewise probably not be forthcoming. Indeed, the *Convention* excludes evidential matters from its

[103] *Loc. cit.*, at 4.

[104] [1981] QB 956. Further, "the potential for conflicting obligations in the tracing of assets context is particularly acute, because of the way in which the world's major banks are organised on a unitary basis: the same entity operating in many countries."

[105] [1980] 2 All ER 347.

[106] [1985] BCLC 333, at 338; also *Mercantile Group (Europe) A.G.* v. *Aiyela* [1993] 3 WLR 1116. In *Bayer A.G* v. *Winter (No.2)* [1986] FSR 357, an order requiring responses from the defendant's agents (a bank) abroad was granted.

ambit.[107] In *Credit Suisse Fides Trust S.A.* v. *Cuoghi*,[108] in which the claimant sought an English worldwide freezing order as a means to ancillary disclosure of the location of the defendant's assets, Millett L.J. looked to the defendant's English domicile as the basis for what would otherwise have been an exorbitant exercise of forum jurisdictional competence in relation to Swiss substantive proceedings. Therefore, it makes sense that disclosure orders having extraterritorial effect should be forthcoming if they are aimed at locating assets and if the grant of the order is from the forum in which the substantive trial is to take place. As with search orders, the privilege against self-incrimination operates.[109]

The position of third party witnesses is significantly defined by these territorial considerations. The third party is often a bank, e.g., in *MacKinnon* v. *Donaldson Lufkin & Jenrette Securities Corporation*,[110] in circumstances in which it was necessary for it to be clarified that "[i]t does not follow from the fact that a person is within the jurisdicition and liable to be served with process there that there is no territorial limit to the matters upon which the court may properly apply its own rules or the things which it can order such a person to do." Disclosure orders from abroad (most frequently from United States' jurisdictions)[111] are viewed by the English forum in much the same light as local jurisdiction. Put differently, it is not usually the case that jurisdictional conflicts (either personal or subject matter) will be identified when a foreign order arises for enforcement in England,[112] although it ought to be questioned whether (a) issues of foreign criminal law would thereby accrue (b) to a much less incidental extent, the competence of the foreign court in making the order is sound.

FINAL INJUNCTIONS

The types of perpetual injunction identified to close the introduction to the present Chapter will now be discussed compendiously. That the particular injunction is mandatory (i.e., either to compel the performance of positive

[107] The Schlosser Report, O.J. C59/71 (1979), paras. 184–187; *Reichert* v. *Dresdner Bank (No. 2)* [1997] ILPr 404. It may be argued that disclosure properly belongs within the scheme of Section 25 if its object is expressed as being to trace and preserve assets, but even then it would have to be an order from the proper forum for the substantive dispute.

[108] [1997] 3 All ER 724. The judgment differs from earlier decisions such as *Republic of Haiti* v. *Duvalier* [1990] 1 QB 202 in that, in such cases, the only connexion with England was the location of the documents.

[109] *Sociedade Nacional de Combustiveis de Angola UEE ("Sonongol") and Others* v. *Lundqvist and Others* [1991] 2 QB 310.

[110] [1986] Ch 482, at 493 (per Hoffmann J.).

[111] See, e.g., *Société Internationale* v. *Rogers* 357 US 197 (1958), *Alfadda* v. *Fenn* 149 F.R.D. 28 (SDNY, 1993) (on the significance of interest analysis in US courts' practice in this area), and Ss. 442(1) and (2) *Restatement (Second) of Foreign Relations Law* (A.L.I. Publishers, St. Paul, Minn.; 1965).

[112] Cf. *Bank of Tokyo Ltd.* v. *Karoon* [1987] AC 45; see also *South Carolina Insurance Co.* v. *Assurantie Maatschappij De Zeven Provincien NV* [1986] 3 WLR 398.

obligations or to coerce the undoing of a wrong) or prohibitory will be shown to be inconsequential as a practical issue in these respects. As with the other remedies discussed in this Chapter, final injunctions may be granted in any type of civil litigation. An example is the local matrimonial action in *Nanda* v. *Nanda*[113] in which the issue concerned the jurisdiction to grant an injunction pursuant to a decree ordering restitution of conjugal rights under Section 45(1) of the *Supreme Court of Judicature (Consolidation) Act 1925*. Rather than ventilate the general principles of internal law on the topic,[114] it is proposed instead to attend to the transnational context in which they could become relevant. The existing scope for final injunctions in the conflict of laws is perhaps the classic case in which the localizing character of the rules and principles governing the allocation of jurisdiction and general forum competence (e.g., as in Article 16(4) of the *Brussels Convention*) rule the roost and do so in the interests of practical efficacy. Nor is it particularly gainful to the present purpose to seek to extrapolate from the law on injunctions in public law, discretionary as these also are. An uncommonly answerable reason for the restricted and pronounced recourse to perpetual injunctions as transnational relief is that they subsist in personam but are more often than not to be sought in connexion with property-based disputes.

As is said elsewhere in this Chapter and book, the final injunction can, in its mandatory form, have little to differentiate it from an order for the specific performance of contract terms. *Warner Brothers Pictures Incorporated* v. *Nelson*,[115] on the non-compellability of performance of express negative promises in a personal service contract, need not be rehearsed in the present Chapter. However, because the remedy also avails a victim of a tort—in the sense that an injunction in these circumstances is essentially restorative[116]—it deserves separate discussion where the contract analogues discussed in the appropriate Chapter of this book need not be repeated. A similar reluctance is to be identified to subsist on the part of the courts as to the grant of either order in respect of positive obligations. It is also inescapable that the vast bulk of injunctive relief is sought, not as part of the forum's final dispositive jurisdiction but, at the pre-trial or post-judgment (execution) stage, often with the complement of other relief, typically damages, even in situations in which restraint would appear at first sight to be the essence of the claimant's cause, e.g., in intellectual property disputes, or in employment contract circumstances

113 [1968] 2 WLR 404.

114 See generally F.H. Lawson, *Remedies of English Law* (2nd ed., London, Butterworths; 1980), 198–202.

115 [1937] 1 KB 209 (on judicial unwillingness to indirectly specifically enforce a contract—not normally remediable that way—by granting an injunction to restrain breach of a negative covenant contained in the contract). See also *Sky Petroleum* v. *VIP Petroleum Ltd.* [1974] 1 WLR 576; *Scandinavian Tanker Trading Co. AB* v. *Florta Petrolera Ecuatoriana (The Scraptrade)* [1985] AC 698, especially at 701.

116 See, e.g., *News of the World Ltd.* v. *Allen Fairhead and Sons Ltd.* [1931] 2 Ch 402 and *Allen and Another* v. *Greenwood and Another* [1980] Ch 119, concerning unsuccessful claims for injunctions to suppress nuisance from obstructing an unusually large amount of ancient light.

where an injunction to enforce negative obligations could in fact bring about indirect compliance with positive obligations without necessarily compelling the employee to directly meet the given obligation. However one looks at the current private international law and applications of final injunctive relief, the justificatory as well as the practical scope for the general remedy in the conflict of laws and in transnational litigation seems, almost scandalously, narrow.

To refresh,[117] this injunction is discretionary, and the circumstances in which it may be granted must exclude any uncertainty be it in relation to the obligation at issue, to what equitable restorative action is to be required of the defendant should the claim succeed, or indeed as to whether the claimant has mitigated his loss. The adequacy of damages in place of a coercive order often means that the latter will not be the remedy forthcoming. No hardship to the defendant must be caused by the mandatory order, nor can the tort at issue be trivial. Any need to continuously supervize also militates against the granting of the order. This last criterion of itself must, as long as it remains a characteristic aspect of the availability of discretionary relief in general, explain the limited recourse to final injunctive relief in transnational circumstances in which the order is to be enforced extraterritorially. Without a co-ordinated international jurisdictional arrangement, such as that subsisting in the scheme of Article 24 of the *Brussels Convention*, the position by which money judgments or judgment debts are the only cross-enforceable forms of judicial relief will continue to ensure that final inunctions have little or no transnational application.

An aspect of earnest interest arises in connexion with choice-of-law about which there must be merit at least in distinguishing (a) the possibility of applying the given relief because an applicable lex delicti specifies it and (b) the situation in which the remedy might be grantable on the basis that the inherent jurisdiction of the forum indicates this as a cogent or realistic solution to a dispute or to some aspect of it.[118] Either scenario must naturally involve the right originating in non-forum law being classified by the forum in terms that co-ordinate the relief with that right, that the wrong in question must be substantively identical to the English cause of action. Neither need necessarily require that what the defendant be judicially compelled to do in compliance be something that can only be done within the jurisdiction. That the relief is in personam means that non-compliance would bring the addressee in contempt of court.

It is in this context that the present writer would argue that the rational justification for the extraterritoriality which may underscore interim or interlocu-

[117] Cf. *Redland Bricks* v. *Morris* [1970] AC 652 (per Lord Upjohn).

[118] For example, a generalized negative injunction may be severable with a view to enforcing the severed part by injunction, as long as doing so is not inequitable in all the circumstances. In the context of shipping law, an injunction avails a charterer to stop a shipowner from using the chartered ship contrary to the charterparty: *Associated Portland Shipping Manufacturers Ltd.* v. *Teigland Shipping A/S (The Oakworth)* [1975] 1 LlRep 581. In the mercantile context, *Decro-Wall Internationala SA* v. *Practitioners in Marketing Ltd.* [1971] 1 WLR 361. In either instance, the injunctions were found not to be indirect specific performance.

tory injunctions ought in principle to be applicable to final injunctions in transnational litigation, subject only to the entreated original forum being assured as to the jurisdictional propriety of taking up the litigation and as to the effectiveness of such an order being made.

Practical considerations naturally limit the necessity for taking this argument further. First and foremost, it is a matter of course that the type of obligational situation in which injunctive relief is sought is one which readily explains the virtually exclusive incidence of the relief in interlocutory circumstances—the claimant will typically be seeking to prevent the defendant from continuing with particular conduct which infringes the claimant's legal entitlements, or be seeking to have the defendant coerced to undo something which the defendant should have done in recognition of the claimant's rights—with a view to a cause of action based on the same facts and about which the claimant may be seeking to be compensated and/or to have the terms of the interlocutory order made permanent,[119] once the rights at issue have been dispositively settled in his favour. Secondly, it is trite that because the most effective contemporary jurisdictional arrangements are but those which permit the making of orders for enforcement elsewhere, rather than those which require compliance between or among jurisdictions, even the best intentions on the part of a forum which grants a final injunction will not ensure the effectiveness of such an order. Whether the "Article 10(1)" gloss to be identified in the Chapter of this book on the remedy of specific performance can be correctly interpreted to specify a basis for the grant of a final injunction because a lex causae so stipulates remains to be seen. Some matters of consequence both to this issue and to a complete descriptive analysis deserve to be brought up.

Especially in the area of transnational torts in a global framework, there is force of contention in a view partly deriving from the extraterritorial dimension which enables and characteristically runs with interlocutory relief rationales already discussed in this Chapter. To begin with, an injunction is the best relief to ensure the discontinuation of a repeatable or recurrent tort. Such torts are often exclusively subject to local-action laws. They include defamation and infringements of intellectual property[120] which, by definition, are perhaps under-recognizedly integral to globalized civil or commercial activity. Typically, the latter include the torts of passing off[121] and breach of confidence. It is in the nature of the jurisdictional (including the interim remedial) issues that are currently being addressed and resolved in intellectual property disputes,[122] that

[119] Cf. *Jobson* v. *Record and Another* [1998] 9 EG 148, 75 P & CL 375 (C.A.)

[120] Cf. *Erven Warnink BV* v. *J Townend & Sons (Hull) Ltd.* [1979] 2 All ER 927, a passing off case. An identical law topic particularly potentially amenable to injunctive and not to compensatory relief must be environmental law. But there must be a defensible public interest argument in favour of localization in such cases.

[121] As in the above case; cf. *Pearce* v. *Ove Arup Partnership and Others*, above, n. 72: it included claims for injunction and monetary relief.

[122] See, e.g., P. Trooboff, "Intellectual Property" in C. McLachlan and P. Nygh (eds.), *Transnational Tort Litigation: Jurisdictional Principles* (Oxford, Clarendon; 1996), 128–134; J. Fawcett and P. Torremans, *Intellectual Property and Private International Law* (Oxford, Clarendon; 1997).

the better solutions are those which incorporate a re-evaluation of the issues of causa and relief in terms which are not as localized as the existing rules markedly appear to make them out to be. That damages are likely to be less effective relief in every type of case is clear,[123] given that they would only compensate for injury or loss already suffered.[124] *In Delta Crompton Cable Limited* v. *Copper Cable Company Limited*,[125] the Patents Court held that an action based on intellectual property rights to enforce monopoly rights is best furthered by it being construed as an action for injunction, not merely because the particular relief is claimed but because including a damages claim would not make the action one for damages. It should make no difference to the type of intellectual property at issue, nor should transnational circumstances markedly alter the approach the forum takes, at least as far as the issue is substantive rationalization of the causa.

It seems perfectible sensible that perpetual injunctions be granted, for example, to prohibit trespass to foreign land. Without necessarily relapsing into the erroneous conflation of the situs rule on immovables with choice-of-law in intellectual property, operational rationales can be distilled by analogy. For example, in the Danish case of *Egmont Films A/S and Others* v. *Laserdisken and Others*,[126] a final injunction had been granted to restrain the renting out of films contrary to manufacturers' and distributors' rights. It was also the central relief sought in *Ford Dodge Animal Health Limited and Others* v. *Akzo Nobel NV (patent licensed to Internet International BV)*.[127] Indeed, the characteristic of finality is consonant with the basis in property rights or interests which frequently typify the exercise of the jurisdiction to make the remedy available. Strictly speaking, there are no countermanding public policy arguments in these regards of which the writer is aware, and such arguments must be separately considered from the original notion that the localism of intellectual property rights derives from local public policy (*Coin Controls Limited* v. *Suzo International (U.K.) Limited and Others*)[128] and those, such as the registration of protectable interests, which derive from statutory requirements for public authority action.

Much the same pro-injunction argument is supported by the view that a prohibitory injunction is the best way to prevent the breach of a negative obligation under a contract even where the breach is only anticipatory, as long as the

[123] An eloquent examination of the arguments for and against damages in place of injunctions in the definitive local-action setting is provided by Burrows, *op. cit.*, 399–403.

[124] Cf. *Allen* v. *Gulf Oil Refining Ltd.* [1979] 3 All ER 1008, at 1016, where Lord Denning M.R. awarded damages for past or future loss in place of an injunction. The quantification of this type of award, which does not ostensibly go to protecting a discernible (restitutionary) interest, must border on the impossible.

[125] [1997] FSR 850.

[126] [1999] All ER (E.C.) 366 (Case C-61/97).

[127] Court of Appeal, 27th October 1997.

[128] [1999] Ch 33. *Silhouette International Schmied GmbH & Co. KG* v. *Hartlauer Handelsgesellschaft mbH (Case C-355/96)* [1998] 3 WLR 1218 demonstrates how Art. 43 of the German *ABGB* allows a prohibitory injunction claim where a person's right to use his name is in dispute or where the person is adversely affected by unauthorized use of his name or pseudonym.

claimant has neither been unconscionable nor suffered questionable harm. The reason of practical policy why insistence on greater application of the transnational final injunction might be misplaced is that the need for the remedy might be over-ridden by the judicial rationalization of other substantial relief (typically damages), by the necessity for upholding comity and by the difficulties of enforcement or execution in the other relevant jurisdiction(s). Useful parallels can be drawn from decisions of the United States Supreme Court, primarily *Vanity Fair Mills* v. *T. Eaton Company*,[129] in which an injunction was refused against a foreign (Canadian) defendant supposedly acting in breach of the claimant's United States trademark rights. The alleged breach was limited to the United States because the defendant actually had legitimate rights in Canada. The test applied is comprised of the defendant's position under forum law, the effect of the alleged breach on forum state commerce, and the likelihood of conflict with rights under a relevant foreign law.

With respect, given the territorialized shape of things, the way forward is properly to be identified in the legal environment of choice-of-jurisdiction and choice-of-law and, further, in mutual arrangements for cross-border enforceability of the type of injunction.

[129] 234 F 2d 633 (2d Cir., 1956).

9

Remedial performance of contracts

SPECIFIC PERFORMANCE IN DOMESTIC, CONFLICTS AND COMPARATIVE LAW

A PARTY WHO breaks or will break a contract may, at the wronged party's application, be subject to a coercive forum order for specific performance of the positive terms which define the contract, or be ordered to perform any contract terms if doing so redresses the breach. The post-trial contract remedy of specific performance safeguards a claimant's expectation interest, and is seminally defined as "a decree of the court which compels the defendant personally to do what he promised to do".[1] It has been eloquently given to subsist in the truism that "t]here are some wrongs that law cannot undo and some aspects of life into which law should not intrude. The bond-destruction that results from breach of contract is a wrong that law cannot cure and the bond-creation that results from the completion of a contract is an area of life into which law should not intrude",[2] and that "the law's reluctance to award specific performance and to punish breach of contract is best understood as a response to general concerns about the proper limits of legal interference in private life".[3]

In general terms, the circumstances in which specific performance is ordered are those in which the leading substitute remedy of an award of compensatory damages, discussed in Chapter Seven of this book, are considered by the forum to be inadequate. It is trite that specific performance is discretionary or exceptional in that it does not automatically accrue to a claimant.[4] But Sir Edward Fry once opined somewhat contrariwise that "[i]f the contract has been entered into by a contract party and is unobjectionable in its nature and circumstances,

[1] G. Jones and W. Goodhart, *Specific Performance* (2nd ed., London, Butterworths; 1996), at 1.

[2] S.A. Smith, "Performance, Punishment and the Nature of Contractual Obligations" (1997) 60 MLR 360), at 377, discussing *inter alia* "the intangible harm of breach" (so-called at 367). A typically relevant standpoint is represented in R. Posner, *Economic Analysis of Law* (4th ed., Boston, Little Brown; 1992), especially at 117–126, on the so-called theory of efficient breach, and the sufficiency of damages. Economic analysis generally supports party stipulation of specific performance: American Law Institute *Restatement Second of the Law of Contracts* (St. Paul, A.L.I.; 1981), para. 588.

[3] Smith, *loc. cit.*, at 365.

[4] Relatively recent authority on the point is *Jobson* v. *Johnson* [1989] 1 All ER 621 (a penalties case). See also the decision of Goulding J. in *Patel* v. *Ali* [1984] 2 WLR 960, at 965; an earlier illustration is *Lamare* v. *Dixon* (1873) LR6 HL 414, at 423.

specific performance is as much a matter of course and therefore of right as are damages".[5] As does an order for compensatory damages, it operates ad personam, is punishable by contempt proceedings being brought against a defaulting defendant.[6] But, unlike damages, its origins are in the equitable jurisdiction of the Chancery courts in which it still subsists in part. Section 49(1) of the *Supreme Court Act 1981* empowers the High Court generally with the necessary jurisdiction, although Section 61(1) of the statute provides that contracts relating to land will be heard only in Chancery.

The decree takes one or other of a variety of forms depending on the particular circumstances. For example, Section 39 of the *Supreme Court Act 1981* empowers the court to secure the execution of a contract if the contractual party who is obligated to make the execution does not do so at or after the time that that party should have done so. Quite apart from the requirement that there must be an enforceable executed contract (written or not), or one which may be but executory,[7] the judicial exercise of the discretion to award specific performance is emphatically based on durable underlying principles which presently are to be adumbrated in the Chapter.

The incidence of the remedy in the conflict of laws brings about a great many points of practical interest, and just as much of a variety of elucidating fact-permutations in the transnational context. Consider the defining limits of forum jurisdictional competence regarding, for example, orders affecting title or to compel the transfer of title pursuant to a contract for the sale of foreign land. The principle stated by Lord Herschell L.C. in *British South Africa* v. *Companhia de Moçambique* that "[n]o nation can execute its judgments whether against persons or moveables or real property in the country of another"[8] was purposively but flexibly applied as settled law. Contemporary reality strongly suggests that justifiable recourse to and the potential of specific performance in the conflict of laws is as marked as it is in its domestic setting. Indeed the court procedures and governing principles in the latter defining setting are pragmatically (i.e., adaptively) applied to the conflicts setting whenever the courts are presented with an action for the relief in transnational cases. Because the conflict of laws issues arising are by definition contractual, it is reasonable that proper law considerations, especially those relating to the United Kingdom's *Contracts (Applicable Law) Act 1990* Schedule 1 of which incorporates the *Rome Convention on the Law Applicable to Contractual Obligations 1980*, feature prominently.

[5] *A Treatise on the Specific Performance of Contracts*, 2nd. ed. (1881), at 12, as it is reproduced in the 6th edition (London, Sweet & Maxwell/Ashford Press; 1985).

[6] E.g., in *Enfield LBC* v. *Mahoney* [1983] 1 WLR 749.

[7] Cf. Spry, *The Principles of Equitable Remedies* (4th ed., London, Sweet & Maxwell; 1990), at 51–55; Jones and Goodhart, *op. cit.*, at 9 *et seq.*

[8] [1893] AC 602, at 625. For a realist argument *inter alia* that "[a]t least under traditional common law rules, the question of jurisdiction should be according to whether the remedy sought is *in personam* or *in rem*", see generally S. Lee, "Jurisdiction over Foreign Land: A Reappraisal" [1997] 26 *Anglo-Am L Rev* 273.

The forum's general transnational jurisdiction, e.g., under the *Civil Jurisdiction and Judgments Acts 1982* and *1991* (these incorporate the *Brussels* and *Lugano Conventions*; particularly, in the present context, Article 16(1)(a) of the former Convention) includes provision for circumstances to except Lord Herschell's principle as does the much older Common Law doctrine founded on a similar basis. Statute and doctrine stipulate exclusive jurisdiction for the courts of the situs in cases of rights in rem in immovable property. But an action for specific performance would fall outside the statutory provision, unless it be established that the right at issue subsists in personam. However, the remedy avails a conflicts plaintiff suing even under *CPR* 24. for summary judgment when a defendant has no defence to a good claim for the relief, as well as in cases where the defendant and (or) the subject matter of a contract to be specifically performed is not located within the jurisdiction, as will presently be seen from the leading decisions.

Not all types of contract nor terms or circumstances of a contract are specifically enforceable: e.g., personal service contracts; voluntary promises; uncertain, discharged, or void(able) contracts; contracts having readily replaceable subject matter; contractual penalties; unperformable whole contracts; or contracts wanting as to mutuality between the parties. Articles 5 and 6 of the *Rome Convention*, providing respectively for consumer and individual employment contracts, are given separate treatment in the discussion of the relevant remedial standards and principles applicable to contracts not specifically performable. Particular contractual subject-matter—e.g., land, special movables, shares, intellectual property—typifies the relief, while other subject matter (e.g., that which is easily compensable) is characteristically excluded from its scope unless specified equitable conditions are met.[9]

Being non-contractual, trusts and equitable charges—the latter to be distinguished from mortgages—are also not specifically performable even though their enforcement may be the result of a coercing judicial order. With regard to contracts the subject matter of which are choses in action or future interests, specific performance is hardly ever necessary because the contract itself sufficiently and equitably allocates its subject matter, and is in writing as is required by Section 53(1)(c) *Law of Property Act 1925*.[10]

The House of Lords' decision in *Beswick* v. *Beswick*[11] shows that the courts will award specific performance if it is clear that it is the proper remedy in all the circumstances. But it has been stated on considerable authority that there is

[9] For an overview, see *Halsbury's Laws of England* (4th ed. Reissue, London, Butterworths; 1996), Vol. 44(1), paras. 830–839.

[10] On the last point (the requirements of written form), see also *Oughtred* v. *IRC* [1960] AC 206.

[11] [1968] AC 58 (in which an "adequate" damages award would, however, have been but nominal rather than compensatory). See also Lord Diplock's statement *obiter* in *Sudbrook Trading Estate Ltd.* v. *Eggleton* [1983] 1 AC 444, at 478; Millett L.J.'s dissentient views in *Co-operative Insurance Society Ltd.* v. *Argyll Stores (Holdings) Ltd.* [1996] 9 EG 128, at 133–134 (that the court "is entitled and bound to reexamine its practice to see whether it accords with modern conditions"); the New Zealand case, *Butler* v. *Countrywide Finance Ltd.* [1993] 3 NZLR 623, mainly at 631.

"strong resistance [in Australia] to the exposure of commercial transactions to equitable remedies",[12] significantly because of the discretionary characteristic of the underlying jurisdiction. However, judicial and advisory recourse to the Common Law ethic thus described via reference to the defining equitable principles remains primed.

Remedial competence having the coefficient of coercion in the conflict of laws was well illustrated by the Privy Council, on appeal from the Hong Kong High Court and Court of Appeal, in *Union Eagle Ltd.* v. *Golden Achievement Limited*,[13] dismissing an action for specific performance of a contract for the sale of landed property in Hong Kong. The contract contained a term which stipulated the essence of time to perform. The tardy purchasers sought the remedy as against a further stipulation that a pre-paid ten per cent deposit by them as well as the purchasers' interest in the transaction were to be retained by the rescinding vendors, as liquidated damages rather than as a penalty. Specific performance was withheld by the courts on the principle that the vendors had unexceptionally neither waived nor been estopped from having equitably asserted their right to forfeiture as they had done.

Likewise, the decision of the Court of Appeal in *Wahda Bank* v. *Arab Bank Plc.*[14] concerning choice of law in international contract financing provides further illustration of the nature of forum coercive competence, particularly as to contractual clauses which stipulate performance bonds or payment guarantees therein. These issues can be subject to non-forum law that affords variable or differing protection, from that which forum law would make available to the parties. It is of course the case, following the decision in *South Wales Railway Company* v. *Wythes*,[15] that the enforceability of performance bonds—to be distinguished from their being specifically performable strictly speaking, because they exclusively do not define the contract—have rightly always been taken to depend in the general case on the enforceability of the main contract, that these bonds are characteristically ancillary.[16]

Thus, the present Chapter further covers the judicial enforceability of liquidated contractual compensation or similar sums as well as contractual penalties and deposits, equitable relief from forfeiture of proprietorial rights over the subject matter of a contract, contractual security rights over property which are exercizable in the event of breach and, significantly, agreed jurisdiction clauses be such clauses in favour either of a particular forum and (or) law

[12] Sir Anthony Mason, "Themes and Prospects" in P.D. Finn (ed.), *Essays in Equity* (Sydney, Law Book Co.; 1985), at 243; see also P. Loughlan, "No Right to the Remedy?: An Analysis of Judicial Discretion in the Imposition of Equitable Remedies" (1989) 17 Melb UL Rev 132, especially at 138.

[13] [1997] 2 All ER 215 (Lord Hoffmann).

[14] [1996] 1 LlRep 470.

[15] [1854] 5 De GM & G 880.

[16] Cf. C. Procter, *International Payment Obligations: A Legal Perspective* (London, Butterworths; 1997), at 57–60, and H.N. Bennett, "Performance Bonds and the Principle of Autonomy" [1994] *JBL* 574. From 581, the latter article discusses the possibility of separate enforcement of these clauses, e.g., where international obligations have been breached, or where there is fraud, or when the parties have expressly derogated from dependence on the main contract's enforceability.

or, e.g., arbitration.[17] As a matter of principle, none of the foregoing other enforced relief is specifically performable but, for example, the actual payment or execution of arbitration awards may be judicially ordered, subject to any equitable defences being overcome. They are to be respectively examined in the Chapter,[18] with due notice of the fact that they are generically distinguished from specific performance strictly speaking. They are not necessarily available as exceptional breach-of-contract relief as is specific performance.[19]

For perspectives from Civil Law and comparativism, it is worth continuous recall that the doctrine of Civil Law systems generally regards performance and not compensation as the primary remedy for contract breach,[20] so that in discussing the *Draft International Sales of Goods Act* almost fifty years ago, Rabel commented in these respects that "the contrast between common law and civil law [is] too deeply rooted to be eradicated".[21] There is no Common Law type of pre-requirement in the Civil Law that the (in)adequacy of damages be settled as part of a decision to grant specific relief. It is a bonus from comparativism, however, that much the same types of contract qualify for specific performance in most legal systems.[22] Indeed most aggrieved parties frequently do not sue other than for compensation. Ultimately and practically, much of course depends on claimants' preferred relief, as has been observed to be decisive, for example, in the French and German systems in which performance is, so to speak, the superior relief.[23]

Although this book is not quite the medium for extensive deliberation of arguments for or against the exceptional characteristic of the remedy in English courts,[24] they appear in the rationalizations towards the end of the Chapter. And for initial description of the purview of the remedies discussed in the Chapter, analogues in other (different) remedies which also involve judicial enforcement of post-breach performance such as mandatory injunctions which likewise bring about or result in the performance of agreements,[25] are to be differentiated and dealt with in a separate eponymous chapter, as respectively are (specific) restitution and remedies in rem. An order for specific performance may in the right circumstances of course be complemented with other relief including an award of damages or an injunction. Perhaps of greater conceptual

[17] Cf. *Medov Lines SpA* v. *Traelandsfos A/S* [1969] 2 Ll Rep 225.

[18] For an inexhaustive preview, see generally H. Collins, "Fairness in Agreed Remedies" in C. Willett (ed.), *Aspects of Fairness in Contract* (London, Blackstone; 1996), at 97–121. Specific restitutionary relief is discussed in the Chapter on restitutionary remedies.

[19] Cf. A. Ogus, "Remedies 1: English Report" in D. Harris and D. Tallon (eds.), *Contract Law Today* (Oxford, Clarendon; 1989), at para. 20 (251).

[20] See G.H. Treitel, *Remedies For Breach of Contract: A Comparative Account* (Oxford, Clarendon; 1987), 43–74; also, Jones and Goodhart, *op. cit.*, at 2 *et seq.*

[21] E. Rabel, "The Hague Conference on the Unification of Sales Law" 1 *AJCL* 59 (1952), at 65.

[22] Cf. Ogus, *loc. cit.*, para. 1 (247).

[23] Cf. J.P. Dawson, "Specific Performance in France and Germany", (1959) 57 *Mich LR* 495, especially at 530.

[24] Cf. Ogus, *loc. cit.*, paras. 32–43 (at 257–262), for a good concise account.

[25] *Warner Brothers Pictures Inc.* v. *Nelson* [1937] 1 KB 209.

and practical consequence is that they must all be considered in their general "procedural" characterization.

AVAILABILITY OF AND SCOPE FOR SPECIFIC PERFORMANCE IN CONFLICTS CASES

English law generally

The typical conflicts action involving a claim for specific performance begins by securing the forum's permission (leave) to serve a defendant outside the territory under Order 11 rule 1(i)(d)(iii) *R.S.C.*, or without the need to do so under the other contract provisions of sub-rule (1), e.g., (d) or (h). English law will expressly or by implication often be the governing law of the contract. The usual principles of or grounds for the remedy will apply. *Dicey and Morris* elucidates thus:

> "If the plaintiff is by the *lex causae* only entitled to damages but is by English law entitled to specific relief, the latter type of remedy is available in England. Conversely, an English court will not grant specific relief where to do so is contrary to the principles of English law . . . [A] remedy which is discretionary according to English law cannot be demanded as of right in an English court merely because this is possible according to the *lex causae*".[26]

The principle is that the essence or availability of a remedy depends on the legal system the procedure of which is prayed in aid. In *Warner Brothers Pictures Incorporated* v. *Nelson*,[27] performance of a film-making contract subject to Californian law was not ordered by the English forum, because the English remedy did not avail a party in the circumstances. The general effect of the exclusivity of forum law is described as follows in *Halsbury's Laws of England*: "This may mean that a remedy unknown to the proper law of the contract is available...[and] this may necessarily cause a claim, good by its proper law, to fail".[28]

Alongside this account of the law is to be placed its codified updating gloss by way of a general import of the *Rome Convention*-based *Contracts (Applicable Law) Act 1990*: that the identification of the proper law of a particular contract may now involve the direct presumption that rules in point (if any) of the proper law, or legal system, are to be exclusively applied to the question of determining the appropriate relief available in the event of breach: Article 10(1)(b) on the performance (outwith breach) of contractual obligations, sub-articles (c) on the consequences of breach in general, and (d) on the methods of bringing contractual obligations to a close, so provide, albeit that only (c) expressly relates to the judicial remedy of damages.

[26] L. Collins *et al.* (eds.), *Dicey and Morris The Conflict of Laws* (12th ed., London, Sweet & Maxwell; 1993), at 171.

[27] Above, at n. 25.

[28] *Op. cit.*, Vol. 8(1), para. 886.

Dicey and Morris[29] furthermore states and clarifies the gloss in terms that "[w]hether the availability of a[n]... order for specific performance will depend on the *lex fori* or (at least in part) on the *lex contractus* turns upon whether it is to be regarded as part of 'the consequences of breach'". It is suggested, with some hesitation, that it is to be regarded as a matter for the *lex contractus*. Consequently, if an injunction or specific performance would be available under the *lex contractus* it should be available in principle in England, subject to "the limits of the powers conferred on the court by its procedural law"...Conversely, if such a remedy were not available under the *lex contractus* it should not be available in England", as would appear naturally to flow from the exceptional nature of the relief.

Article 10(1) extends the scope of application of the proper law beyond what the dicta in *Warner Brothers* may otherwise reasonably infer, with the overall result that although at least one remedy (damages) continues nominally to be regulated by procedural law, it may not quite need to be exclusively determined in accordance with the internal lex fori. The closing paragraphs of the foregoing general description of the English conflicts general rule argue that this has always been the case with regard to specific performance, that it might have been a bonus if the *Convention* had included an identical and updated codification more specifically for the particular remedy as well. These arguments are further amplified in due course, in connexion with the law as to a defendant or contractual subject matter outside forum territorial jurisdiction. It is of course the case that the *Rome Convention* applies only to contracts made after April 1 1991 and, therefore, that contracts made before then are governed by the Common Law should they survive lex contractus limitation or prescription. Whether similar rationales can be raised in contracts regulated by the Common Law must depend on whether the courts apply or have applied the proper law of such a contract to the issue of enforcement of the fundamental promises exchanged in the contract, in the way that the proper law applies to the same basic issue in *Rome Convention* contracts in general.

Performance of an (unbroken) contract has always been taken to go to the substance of the contract in question.[30] The law of the place of performance, rather than the proper law, naturally governs the method of performance, such as whether there are days of grace between when a debt falls due and when it is forecloseable, as it did in *Rouquette* v. *Overmann and Schou*,[31] what "usual business hours" may be for the purpose of effecting contractual delivery, or what the currency of payment is (distinguished from the lex monetae or the national law in which a financial obligation is to be expressed), as in *Mount*

[29] *Op. cit.*, at 1264 (both passages sub-quoted are from the wording of Article 10(1)).

[30] Cf. *Jacobs* v. *Crédit Lyonnais* (1884) 12 QBD 589; *Bonython* v. *Commonwealth of Australia* [1951] AC 201 (Privy Council). The latter case disposes of the possible inference that performance is wholly referrable to the lex loci solutionis, e.g., as in *Adelaide Electric Supply Co. Ltd.* v. *Prudential Assurance Co. Ltd.* [1934] AC 122, at 151.

[31] [1875] LR 10 QB 525, at 535–536.

Albert Borough Council v *Australian Temperance and General Mutual Life Assurance Society Limited*.[32]

Thus when the "Article 10(1) gloss" does apply, it ought indifferently to be understood in terms that non-forum law on the remedy can, as is the substantive law, be conveniently characterized and applied, indeed, localized by the forum. This application (or localization) is facilitated by the fact that the substance of the performance stipulated in an award of specific performance will over-ride, and need not precisely replicate, the contractual performance, but nevertheless that "the order of the court is not independent of the contract".[33] Insofar as a breach of contract remedy is construed to be a consequence of breach, such a remedy is to be subjected to the contractual proper law in the broad manner envisaged, and provided for, in the Article.

These general statements are amplified by considering the governing principles. The precision of the statements depends on the parameters for their interpretation being taken to be those of procedural law. The procedures or forms of action, discussed after the jurisdictional principles, by which a conflicts litigant can sue for specific performance are necessarily the procedures which avail a claimant in a domestic action for the remedy. Without due care, these undifferentiated procedures are apt erroneously to justify a possible conclusion that the principles which determine the availability of the remedy in domestic cases are mechanistically alike to be applied to conflicts cases in which the relief is sought.

THE RELEVANT PRINCIPLES, FROM JURISDICTION

The principles[34] distil into broad self-explanatory categories. Specific performance of a contract tritely depends on whether compensatory damages can be awarded instead. Consideration of the remedy of performance requires that there be a valid enforceable contractual obligation which falls within the forum's personal and subject-matter jurisdiction, and this principle is to be discussed first. The assumption, which admittedly is not always necessarily sustained,[35] in the present discussion is that the subject matter relates to a contract as for example is pre-required by Article 5(1) of the *Brussels Convention*.

Article 4(2) of the *Rome Convention*'s provision that the "most closely connected" law, in the absence of the parties' express choice of law (under Article 3), is that of the habitual residence of the party whose performance is "characteristic" of, or characterizes, the contract. This provision can indirectly

[32] [1938] AC 224, at 240–241.

[33] *Singh* v. *Nazeer* [1979] Ch 474, at 480–481 (per Megarry V.-C.)

[34] Cf. *Halsbury's Laws*, *op. cit.*, paras. 805 et seq; Jones and Goodhart, *op. cit.*, Chapters Two and Three; and Order 11 rule 1(i)(d)(iii) cited at the beginning of the present Section.

[35] See, e.g., *Atlas Shipping Agency (UK) Ltd.* v. *Suisse Atlantique Société d'Armament Maritime SA* [1995] 2 Ll Rep 188, about a shipping broker's entitlement to sue a buyer as trustee of commission money, so as to enable the former to sue in the forum solutionis qua the place of payment.

determine whether England is indeed the place to sue (as the place of performance of the characteristic obligation in question), within the Article 5(1) *Brussels Convention* exception to the basic Article 2 requirement that a defendant be sued in forum domicilii; in typical effect, the lex loci actus. It is the characteristic obligation which may be specifically enforceable.

Several E.U. Member States' courts have applied an individual case approach to the issue of characteristic obligation. In the Dutch cases of *Machinale Glasfabriek de Maas BV* v. *Embaillerie Alsacienne*[36]concerning the sale of goods, sale and delivery were taken to be characteristic performance of the whole contract, as was an agent's act in the agency case of *Bata* v. *Beugro*.[37] Similarly, the Paris Tribunal de Grande Instance in *S.* v. *K and Others*[38] held that the actual provision of lawyers' services characterized a contract for the services.

Unclearly, however, and somewhat in retrograde mode, the Court of Appeal in *Mercury Publicity Ltd.* v. *Wolfgang Loerke GmbH*[39] affirmed the declining of jurisdiction by the court below in favour of German courts by conveniently, but it is submitted erroneously, applying mere evidence rather than proof[40] of a good arguable case as the sole precondition to the plaintiffs' establishment of forum jurisdiction. *Mercury* has not been overruled.

A possible problem of unpredictability of proper forum, which might have a distorting effect on the relatively cohesive and unifying Conventions[41] in that the applicable substantive law might need to be resolved before jurisdiction can be settled, flows from the fact restated by the European Court of Justice in *Custom Made Commercial Ltd.* v. *Stawa Metallbau GmbH*, involving a contractual payment obligation, that "the place of performance of the obligation...is to be determined pursuant to the substantive law governing the obligation in dispute under the conflicts rules of the court seised".[42] The easy solution is for the parties to specify contractually what is to constitute the definitive performance, alert that if, for example, the contract relates to a banker/customer relationship then the matter of characteristic performance does not arise as was so held in *Royal Bank of Scotland* v. *Cassa di Risparmio delle Provincie Lombardi*.[43] The action begun, the basis on which the forum assumes jurisdiction, whether it be domicile or habitual residence, is generally of no consequence, although it can influence the claimant's choice of remedy if the chosen forum does not award performance relief in particular circumstances.

36 [1984] ECC 123. 37 N.J. 1984 No. 745, at 2663. 38 3 Feb. 1982, D. 1983 J. 146.

39 [1993] ILPr 142, at 152 (Purchas L.J.).

40 See the ECJ's stricter, and more accurate, burden in *Effer* v. *Kantner* [1982] ECR 825, at para. 7.

41 Cf. The *Tizzano Report on the Protocols on the Interpretation of the Law Applicable to Contractual Obligations*, para. 22: that the *Rome Convention* logically complements the *Brussels Convention*.

42 Case C-288/92 [1994] ECR I-2913, at 2958 (paras. 27–29) (following *Tessili* v. *Dunlop* Case 12/76 [1976] ECR 1473 and *De Bloos* v. *Bouyer* Case 14/76 [1976] ECR 1497). The substantive obligation could easily be different from simple payment: see generally C. Forsyth and P. Moser, "The Impact of the Applicable Law of Contract on the Law of Jurisdiction under the European Conventions" (1996) 45 *ICLQ* 190.

43 [1991] ILPr 411; on the basis that the English rule is that a debtor must seek out a creditor's residence or place of business.

Choice of forum itself is influenced by the relief available under the lex contractus or proper law.

The principles to be discussed also effectively operate as bars or defences to the relief in English courts.

(i) The species of contracts not specifically performable

(a) Gratuitous and voluntary contracts, i.e. those which do not meet the pre-requirements for legal enforceability, as may be stipulated by the proper law[44]

Article 9 of the *Rome Convention* provides for a facultative approach by which the formal validity of a contract is to be determined either by the governing law (real or putative) of the contract, by the law of the place where the contract is concluded or, where the parties are in different countries, by the law of either of those countries. Older authorities—which, incidentally, involve the difficult presumption for all cases (i.e., even in the absence of an exclusive jurisdiction clause) that the lex fori is known at the time of contracting—point to the lex loci contractus as the law that governs the formalities.[45] Modern contract practice and authoritative comment affirm the importance of the proper law of the contract in these respects even if, in theory, the proper law is to be construed as but alternative to the lex loci.

Thus, gratuitous or voluntary contracts are not enforceable by an order for specific performance. The same applies to unilateral promises and other types of obligation which, according to forum law, are not capable of being legally binding either because they are simply not contracts or because there is no formal means of sustaining them applying the lex fori. If a foreign lex causae is inconclusive about the agreement in question being gratuitous, voluntary, or otherwise, it would appear to be more likely than not that the English forum will apply its own rules in point in determining how to categorize the contract an order for the performance of which is sought by the claimant.

In *Penn* v. *Lord Baltimore*,[46] the making of orders settling the physical boundaries of land situated outside the territorial jurisdiction was held to fall within forum international competence, to the extent that jurisdiction as to title or real (as contrasted with personal) rights over the land in question was not involved. A domestic case illustration is to be found in *Cannon* v. *Hartley*,[47] where the principle that equity will not avail a volunteer was the basis for having refused the relief for similar land. Yet in *Mountford* v. *Scott*,[48] an option to buy land for nominal (i.e., practically with no contractual consideration) value only was found to be enforceable. But imprecise contractual obligations, particularly those which cannot generate even an impliable accuracy as to the agreed terms, will not be specifically enforceable but can attract damages.[49]

[44] Cf. art. 9 *Rome Convention*.
[45] E.g., *Leroux* v. *Brown* (1852) 12 CB 801.
[46] [1750] 1 Ves Sen 444, at 450.
[47] [1949] Ch 213.
[48] [1975] Ch 258.
[49] *Sudbrook Trading Estate Ltd.* v. *Eggleton* [1983] 1 AC 444.

(b) Trusts

Although trusts are not enforceable contracts, a beneficiary can get specific performance of the terms of a trust settlement if one of the parties to the settlement had ostensibly contracted as the beneficiary's trustee. The awardee need not have been the settlor who will have provided the pre-requisite contractual consideration in furthering the settlement in accordance with the lex causae of the trust. It was so held on similar facts in *Re Cook's Settlement Trusts, Royal Exchange Assurance* v. *Cook.*[50] It is the equitable remedy of specific performance which is available to secure the execution of a formally defective mortgage or charge for which mortgage or charge there has been the transfer of value by or on behalf of the party seeking its enforcement.

The *Recognition of Trusts Act 1987* incorporates the *Convention on the Law Applicable to Trusts and on Their Recognition 1985*. Articles 6 and 7 respectively provide for the governing law (to exclude conflicts rules thereof: Article 17) of the validity, construction, effects and administration of such voluntary written trusts: in terms of the settlor's express or implied choice, or the law most closely related (on the bases of the settlor's designated place of administration, of the situs of the trust assets, of the trustee's place of residence or business, of the objects and place of fulfilment of the trust) to the trust where the settlor's choice carries no law in point. Central to the present discussion is the detail in Article 8 of the items so governed, all of which must necessarily be presumed to be subject to a judicial order where appropriate.[51] Articles 9 and 10 deal with administrative severability and, in particular, the validating law being the law to determine the law to govern the severable part.

Generally, the *Convention* makes it possible for the forum to construct its orders to cater for the property registration rules of a relevant legal system other than its own (Article 12), for the mandatory rules of such a relevant law (Article 15) as well as its own (Article 16). Article 18 makes public policy override the convention's provisions. Article 22 extends the scope for the *Convention* to any trust, wherever or whenever created.

(c) Wholly or substantially personal contracts, e.g., consumer and individual employment contracts

These are not specifically performable at the instance of either the employee or the employer,[52] whatever may be the substance of the contract. For example, the principle extends to ship time charters other than by demise, as long as the issue is the use of the ship by the shipowner's own servants: *Scandinavian Trading Tanker Co. AB* v *Flota Petrolera Ecuatoriana, The Scaptrade.*[53] However,

[50] [1965] Ch 902, at 915; also *Vandepitte* v. *Preferred Accident Insurance Corporation of New York* [1933] AC 70.

[51] Cf. the paragraph carrying n. 10, above. See *Dicey and Morris*, *op. cit*, Rule 28(6), at 367–368.

[52] E.g., in *McGhee* v. *Midlands British Road Services Ltd.* [1985] ICR 503, at 508; this is so despite some old authorities to the contrary, such as *Ball* v. *Coggs* 1 Bro Parl Cas 140 (1710). For a sound comparative common law account, see Jones and Goodhart, *op. cit.*, 169–176.

[53] [1983] 2 AC 694.

C.H. Giles & Company Limited v. *Morris*[54] is authority that the execution, rather than the performance, of these contracts may be ordered by the court, thus underscoring the rationale of the limits of judicial interventionism from which the principle derives. Indirect enforcement of personal contracts may nevertheless be secured through actions for injunction as has been mentioned earlier, so that, for example, a contractual power to nominate or appoint a company director may not be restrained, nor may a reasonably objectionable nominee be forced upon a company.[55]

Articles 5 and 6 of the *Rome Convention* contain special rules for selecting the governing law of certain consumer contracts and individual employment contracts, because the typical consumer and employee is considered to be in a weak bargaining position and, consequently, "that special protection be provided for that party by rules which apply irrespective of any inconsistent rules apparently agreed in the contract itself".[56] The gloss in Article 10(1) makes it necessary and worthwhile to examine these substantive law provisions in the discussion of remedial considerations, attentively of the following important but partly extraneous considerations:

— few problems from the transnational aspects of these types of contract have arisen in the courts. Therefore, national and "labour law" approaches respectively may better indicate the courses to follow for judicial enforcement in those breach situations that arise;[57]

— the provisions primarily aim to restrict the consequences of the parties' choice of law, rather than to resolve the remedial considerations that can arise if litigation were begun;

— the preservation of mandatory protective forum rules in point (be they consumer or employee legislation) and the pervading relevance of national protective law (e.g., the United Kingdom's *Unfair Contract Terms Act 1977*, *Employment Protection (Consolidation) Act 1978*, or *Consumer Protection Act 1987*; in particular, the distinguishing national provisions therein) as likely being the applicable law means that one would strain to identify a policy justification for applying the remedial rules, under Articles 5 or 6, of an invalidating habitual law of the consumer or the employee who is seeking to enforce the contract where the parties' choice of law rather validates the contract. In point of fact, as regards Article 6, if the "characteristic performance" exception in Article 5(1) *Brussels Convention* were applied,

[54] [1972] 1 All ER 960.

[55] Cf. *British Murac Syndicate Ltd.* v. *Alperton Rubber Co. Ltd.* [1915] 2 Ch 186.

[56] C.G.J. Morse, "Consumer Contracts, Employment Contracts and the Rome Convention" (1992) 41 *ICLQ* 1, at 1; also, *Report on the Rome Convention by Giuliano and Lagarde* (1980) OJ C282/1.

[57] Morse, *loc. cit.*, at 10–11 and 21; see also, P.M. North, "'Reform, but not Revolution', General Course on Private International Law" [1990] I Hag Rec, at 184. Such an approach is discernible from S. 236 of the UK's *Trade Union and Labour Relations (Consolidation) Act 1992* which restrains a court from ordering an employee to perform a contract of employment. But see, generally, *Dicey & Morris*, *op. cit.*, 359–360.

then the obligation in question would be the doing of the work and the invalidating habitual law of the locus actus would have to apply;[58] and

— in the case of individual employment contracts, especially those which specifically provide for the remedy of reinstatement of a terminated employee,[59] there is much to commend the application of the law (including the remedial rules thereof) which most favours the employee, unless doing so would result in affording double protection under both the applicable law and the "habitual" law where these are autonomous of one another and stipulate divergent relief (e.g., compensation, not reinstatement) for the aggrieved employee.

A certain inference that needs to be drawn in either type of contract is that the minimum protection available under the law of habitual residence (Article 5(2)) or of habitual performance (Article 6(2)), respectively, would be upheld by the forum once the issue of liability has been positively resolved in the claimants favour. It is to be noted that Article 10(1) does not necessarily differentiate as between how the governing law of a contract is to be ascertained, be it by the parties' choice or by implication (under Article 3(1)) but that the law of habitual residence or habitual performance, as may be the case, is necessarily important. Nor do Articles 5 or 6 differentiably feature in the scheme of Article 10.

Finally, what would appear to be the denominator in either type of contract is the jurisdictional provision that forum law makes or, in other words, whether likely disputes are indeed to be subject to a generalized, rather than a specified jurisdiction-based, régime applicable in the forum by virtue of the nature of the cause of action, including in particular any applicable remedial law such as is inferrable from the *Convention*. This attenuates the need for harmony between *Convention*-defined applicable law and national law, which need is self-evidently otherwise reasonably justified and warranted.[60]

(d) Court-supervized contracts, e.g. building contracts:

The general rule, by which these contracts fall outside the scope of specific performance, has important exceptions especially when the express or implied contractual definition of the subject matter is clear, and when the usual requirements, e.g., that the defendant be in possession of the land in question, are met.[61] According to *Gyllenhammar and Partners International Limited.* v. *Sour Brodogrovedna Industrija*,[62] the exception obtains if the court is thereby enabled to specify a decree against the defendant. Thus, the carrying on of a

[58] Cf. *Ivenel* v. *Schwab* Case 133/81 [1982] ECR 1891; *Shenavai* v. *Kreischer* Case 266/85 [1987] ECR 239; *Mercury Publicity Ltd.* v. *Wolfgang Loerke GmbH*, above, n. 39.

[59] E.g., under S. 89 *Merchant Shipping Act 1970* and, limited to an industrial tribunal's powers of recommendation only, also S. 16 *Trade Union and Labour Relations Act 1974*.

[60] Cf. *Dicey and Morris, op. cit.*, at 1301–1303.

[61] See, e.g., *Hounslow London BC* v. *Twickenham Garden Developments Ltd.* [1971] Ch 233, at 251; also *Chitty on Contracts* (26th ed., London, Sweet & Maxwell; 1989), at 1213.

[62] [1989] 2 LlRep 403, and also *Tustian* v. *Johnston* [1993] 2 All ER 673 as to the adequacy of damages.

business[63] is not so enforceable, but a landlord's covenant to repair a dwelling house is.[64]

(e) Contracts and mutuality:

Buckley L.J. in *Price* v. *Strange*[65] stated the principle that the obligation of the defendant may, at the court's discretion, be enforceable only if any obligation of the claimant is also to be specifically enforced. This is the requirement of mutuality, and the lack of it is really a waivable[66] defence to the grant of the type of order being considered, and its incidence depends on the full circumstances at the date of the trial. If, for example, the defendant has already done some of the contracted work, then the cost can be set-off against costs, rather than be required to be re-performed along with outstanding obligations as would be covered by the order for performance. To sum up, if an agreement be non-contractual, void, voidable or prescribed, its being specifically performable is, as the general rule, to be ruled out.

(ii) The (in)adequacy of compensatory, or liquidated, sums[67]

Judicial intervention to compel the actual performance of contractual obligations is withheld where substitute relief in damages is appropriate. Mutuality applying, some types of goods are characteristically replaceable, while others are not. *C.N. Marine Incorporated* v. *Stena Line A.B.*[68] holds that it is for the claimant to establish the inadequacy of damages.

Restricted shares in a company,[69] unascertained but irreplaceable personal property[70] (e.g., under Section 52 *Sale of Goods Act 1979*), unique[71] or special goods[72] (including land[73]) or goods the procurement of which could damage

[63] As in *F.W. Woolworth Plc* v. *Charwood Alliance Properties Ltd.* [1987] 1 EGLR 53.

[64] S. 17 *Landlord and Tenant Act 1985*.

[65] [1978] Ch 337, at 367; see also 359 and 370.

[66] Ibid., at 356 (e.g., by the defendant allowing the claimant to expend time and money in meeting obligations).

[67] *Anders Utlikens Rederi A/S* v *O/Y Lovisa Stevedoring Co. A/B, The Golfstraum* [1985] 2 All ER 669, at 673, is authority that the principle might extend to penalties or liquidated sums.

[68] [1982] 2 LlRep 336.

[69] E.g., *Re Schwabacher, Stern* v. *Schwabacher, Koritschoner's Claim* [1907] 98 LT 127; *Langen and Wind Ltd.* v. *Bell* [1972] Ch 685; regarding debentures, see S. 195 *Companies Act 1985*.

[70] *Dominion Coal Co. Ltd.* v. *Dominion Iron and Steel Co. Ltd. and National Trust Co. Ltd.* [1909] AC 293 (involving a contract to supply coal over a number of years); but where the delivery or supply of chattels forms but part of an otherwise enforceable contract, delivery may be enforced: *Marsh* v. *Milligan* [1857] 3 Jur NS 979. See also *Astro Exito Navegacion SA* v. *Southland Enterprise Co. Ltd. (The Messianiki Tolmi)* [1981] 2 Ll Rep 595 (Court of Appeal), on the remedy at the seller's suit for the price, outwith s. 49 *Sale of Goods Act 1979*.

[71] E.g., contracts for the sale or lease of ships or aircraft having exceptional value to the plaintiff: *Astro Exito Navegacion SA* v. *Southland Enterprise Co. Ltd (No. 2) (Chase Manhattan Bank NA intervening), The Messianiki Tolmi* [1982] QB 1248; *Bristol Airport Plc* v. *Powdrill* [1990] Ch 744, at 759 (per Browne-Wilkinson V.-C.)

[72] E.g., an ornamental door, as in *Phillips* v. *Lamdin* [1949] 2 KB 33; an undivided half of mineral property, as in *Hexter* v. *Pearce* [1900] 1 Ch 341; there is the analogous remedy of specific delivery of chattels.

[73] I.e., having special value to the buyer, as in the *Sudbrook Trading* case, above.

other property,[74] patent sales,[75] or contracts for which a damages judgment might not be satisfied,[76] have all been held to be specifically enforceable. The decision in *Verrall* v. *Great Yarmouth B.C.*[77] concerned the grant of specific performance of an agreement to award a licence to use an assembly hall because inter alia to do so would promote the civil liberty of freedom of speech and assembly in a way in which compensatory damages would be insufficient.

Concerning corporate securities, according to Section 127 of the *Insolvency Act 1986*, share transfers subsequent to winding up are void without a court order to this effect (as was held in *Re London, Hamburg and Continental Exchange Bank, Emmerson's Case*).[78] In the absence of such an order (and it is rarely made), the transferor can be indemnified for calls on the shares even if specific performance will not be awarded.

Conversely, the sale of government stock,[79] replaceable goods albeit that the replacement may involve distended procurement,[80] and covenants affecting demised premises,[81] have attracted damages awards. In relation to the sale of government stock, however, an important underlying conflicts principle that foreign fiscal law is definitionally inapplicable appears to have been placed on one side in a number of old decisions, such as *Doloret* v. *Rothschild*[82] about the sale of Neapolitan stock, and *Gardener* v. *Pullen*[83] on the sale of East India stock. These cases involved the respective contracts, as well as the proceedings, having been deemed to be wholly local and therefore subject exclusively to English law wherein the defendant's entitlement to revoke or dissolve the contract must have contributed significantly to the awards of specific performance in either case. The defendant in either case was a forum domiciliary. Therefore, the relief would realistically have been neither without value nor a waste of resources.[84] Equity, it must be remembered, does nothing in vain, and it is these equitable principles which permeate the availability of specific performance, so that were these contracts (and, indeed, other types of investment contract generally) to be construed in transnational cast[85] today, to form the

[74] *Record* v. *Bell* [1991] 4 All ER 471, concerning the sale of a house with chattels and furnishings *in situ*.

[75] *Cogent* v. *Gibson* [1864] 33 Beav 557; see generally C. Wadlow. *Enforcement of Intellectual Property in European and International Law* (London, Sweet & Maxwell; 1998), paras. 5–22 to 5–25 (264–266) for a discussion of territorialized Community law.

[76] *Evans Marshall & Co. Ltd.* v. *Bertola SA* [1973] 1 All ER 992, at 1006 (per Sachs L.J.).

[77] [1981] QB 202; see also *AMEC Properties Ltd.* v. *Planning Research and Systems plc* [1992] BCLC 1149 in which the circumstances of the defendant's insolvency did not disavail the claimant of the relief.

[78] 1 Ch App 433 (1866).

[79] E.g., in *Nutbrown* v. *Thornton* [1804] 10 Ves 159, at 161.

[80] *Société des Industries Metallurgieques SA* v. *Bronx Engineering Co. Ltd.* [1975] 1 LlRep 465 (industrial machinery constructed to order).

[81] *Posner* v. *Scott-Lewis* [1987] Ch 25.

[82] [1824] 1 Sim & St 590.

[83] [1700] 2 Vern 394.

[84] *Tito* v. *Waddell (No. 2)* [1977] Ch 106, at 326; *Udall* v. *Capri Lighting Ltd. (in liquidation)* [1988] QB 907.

[85] These circumstances (i.e., in which the government concerned does not waive its public international law-derived immunity from suit in these regards) would involve the careful treatment of the particular government organ's jurisdictional amenability and its contractual obligations in the

basis for judicial pronouncements as to their being specifically performable, their being subjected to a non-forum lex causae ought in principle and in few words to thereafter result in the Article 10(1) *Rome Convention*-type methodology previously discussed above.

Curiously perhaps, the considerations and attending principles generically labelled "equitable" could probably bring about an appealing convergence of approach between the Common and Civil Law systems to which reference has already been made and which, to an extent, has been begun by Article 10(1) of the *Rome Convention*. This is so in the sense that the discretionary withholding of specific performance in the sufficiency of compensatory damages in the Common Law is rooted in the notion of breach of promise (tacitly, a lesser instance of breach) rather than of contractual obligation, or at least more so than the withholding is rooted in the notion of breach of the former (i.e., contractual obligation) strictly speaking. The award of damages to restore losses incurred on the basis of the former notion is perhaps not necessarily irrefutably inflexible, as is clear from such grants in the doctrine of the Civil Law. Thus, the broader remedial function of Civil Law damages is, in this sense, limited by the terms of the primacy it is judicially accorded in the Common Law and by litigants' preferred practice in the Civil Law. Significantly, if the issues of hierarchy were to a greater or lesser extent to be pragmatically and unifyingly rationalized, to do so could at least well produce a more harmonious private international obligations and remedies law.

What has just been said must of course be understood in light of other limitations imposed by the sufficiency of damages. These include the avoidance of inordinate hardship or cost to the non-performing defendant, as in *Tito* v. *Waddell (No. 2)*,[86] the avoidance of the element of surprise upon a defendant which would accompany the making of the order such as where a defendant is hurried into leasing land to the claimant soon after the land was bought and with little knowledge that the land had greater value because it carried mineral ores, as was found in *Walters* v *Morgan*.[87] Likewise, in *Wroth* v. *Tyler*,[88] the required performance, viz. an action against a third party, namely the defendant's wife, was refused because it would have been apt to divide that family. But a defendant's "pecuniary difficulties", however, are not enough to disavail a claimant, as in *Patel* v. *Ali*,[89] although want of adequate contractual consideration (a matter no doubt for the lex causae) or the claimant's unfair conduct in furtherance of the contract[90] will properly militate against a grant of the remedy.

context of private international law and adjudication (cf., generally and referentially, R.R. Drury, "The Regulation and Recognition of Foreign Corporations: Responses to the 'Delaware Syndrome'" [1998] 57 CLJ 166).

86 [1977] Ch 106, at 326; see also, [1984] Ch 238, at 288.

87 [1861] 3 DF & J 718; see also *Quadrant Visual Communications* v. *Hutchison Telecommunications (U.K.) Ltd.* [1993] BCLC 442.

88 [1974] Ch 30.

89 [1984] Ch 238, at 288.

90 E.g., "commercially disreputable" behaviour, as was found in *Wilton Group* v. *Abrams* [1990] BCC 310, at 317.

It would appear that the matter of the sufficiency of compensatory damages is to be interpreted by the forum of adjudication, because referring the question to the lex causae will likely involve more than the letter of that law if indeed an hierarchical choice of relief is expressly provided for or applied therein. There is a lack of commentary on the point in transnational circumstances, nor perhaps should there be such commentary, because there is little by way of a discernible pre-existing unified practice in point among relevant fora.

(iii) The feasibility of performance, e.g., where the contract has been varied, rescinded or discharged, or if the subject matter is defective

Watts v, *Spence*[91] confirms that a decree will be withheld if its substance can neither lawfully nor factually be fulfilled, with the latter condition (i.e., the objective and indisputable facts of a given breach situation) emphasized. This principle is an extension of the broader pre-requirement that the contract to be specifically performed be live and enforceable, and its fuller implications are to be observed in the other principles on which the remedy depends.

(iv) A defendant or contractual subject matter not subject to forum jurisdiction

The mere fact that the subject matter is physically outside the territory of the forum does not of itself preclude the award of the relief. What is required by the personal nature of the jurisdiction on which the remedy is founded is that the defendant be (made) amenable to forum jurisdiction. Illustrations include the early cases of *Archer* v. *Preston*[92] and *Penn* v. *Lord Baltimore*,[93] and latterly *Richard West & Partners (Inverness) Limited.* v. *Dick*,[94] *Webb* v. *Webb*,[95] and *Mackinnon* v. *Donald Lufkin & Jenrette Securities Limited*,[96] in which the defendants were within the jurisdiction in order for service to have been duly effected (in *Duder* v. *Amsterdamsch Trustees Kantoor*[97] service out of the jurisdiction was permitted). In *Mercantile Investment and General Trust Co.* v. *River Plate Trust Loan and Agency Company*,[98] Mexican land bought by an English company was held to be subject to an enforceable pre-existing equitable charge in England even though the charge was void by the lex situs.

Megarry J. made clear in *Richard West & Partners*[99] that there is no distinction to be made in these regards between foreign jurisdictions that are civilian rather than Common Law. Conversely, having regard to the particular issue of equitable discretion, it is held on sound authority[100] that if situs jurisdiction, as

[91] [1976] Ch 165; see also *Newman* v. *Dorrington Developments Ltd.* [1975] 3 All ER 928.

[92] Cited in *Earl of Arglasse* v. *Muschamp* [1682] 1 Vern 76.

[93] Above, n. 46. [94] [1969] 1 All ER 943. [95] [1992] 1 All ER 17.

[96] [1986] 1 All ER 653. [97] [1902] 2 Ch 132.

[98] [1892] 2 Ch 303; see also *Ex parte Pollard* [1840] Mont & Ch 239 (per Lord Cottenham L.C., at 250: although the lex situs did not deem a deposit of title deeds to suffice to create a mortgage or charge, but forum law did, the depositor-mortgagee under forum law was given priority over other secured creditors).

[99] Above, n. 94. [100] Jones and Goodhart, *op. cit.*, at 141.

"the ultimate arbiter of questions relating to the title and possession of land within its jurisdiction", is civilian this may well generate an "embarrassing conflict between an English court and a court of the *situs*". Reciprocity applying, by which English courts reject a foreign court's jurisdiction over English land and immovables, the Canadian precedent, in the absence of English authority on the point, in *Duke* v. *Andler*[101]—that a foreign (equitable) decree relating to English land will not be recognized—appears to confirm the principle to be applied in England in these respects.

The range of enforceable contractual subject matter is wide. It includes, as has been mentioned, contracts for the sale of foreign land, foreclosure of foreign land mortgages,[102] orders for the inspection of foreign premises thought to contain improperly acquired valuable works of art,[103] the enforcement of foreign landed trusts held by deed by a creditor,[104] and the recovery of rents due under a lease of foreign land.[105] The law of mortgages and charges is replete with case illustrations of the judicial disposition towards the relief in conflicts cases and these are eminently discussed by Jones and Goodhart,[106] the denominators being, first, that proper jurisdiction in personam is had by the forum, and secondly, that the object of the order sought is not to enforce titular or possessory rights to foreign immovables.

However, if the lex situs does not recognize the defendant's contractual capacity[107] or the contractual interest at issue,[108] then the forum will not make an order. At least one commentator[109] has sought to argue persuasively that, practically speaking:

> "[A]t the level of direct jurisdiction, the courts should adjudicate title to foreign land irrespective of the nature of the right sought to be vindicated, as long as the court is asked to award *in personam* relief, that is a money award or an order compelling the defendant to do or refrain from doing some other act in relation to the land. Similarly, at the level of indirect jurisdiction, non-*situs in personam* land decrees should be regarded (in the absence of a statutory scheme for registration) as creating an obligation or an interest in the land enforceable by separate proceedings at the *situs*" and that "[o]n such a view, the title rule is simply subsumed into the rule (applicable to movables, as well as immovables) that there is only jurisdiction over actions *in rem* if the property the subject of the action is situate within the territory of the court".

Subscription to these views must depend to a greater or lesser extent on whether the particular circumstances and, more importantly, the forum would so permit, e.g., via the pleadings of the party seeking the results described.[110]

101 (1932) 4 DLR 529.

102 *Toller* v. *Cartaret* [1705] 2 Vern 494.

103 *Cook Industries Inc.* v. *Galliher* [1979] Ch 439.

104 *Jenney* v. *Mackintosh* [1886] 33 Ch D. 595.

105 *St. Pierre* v. *South American Stores (Gath and Chaves) Ltd.* [1936] 1 KB 382.

106 *Op. cit.*, at 139–141.

107 *Bank of Africa Ltd.* v. *Cohen* [1909] 2 Ch 129.

108 *Hicks* v. *Powell* [1869] 4 Ch App 741.

109 Lee, *loc. cit.* (n. 8), at 328–329.

110 Cf. Chapter Six of this book; in particular, *Henderson* v. *Henderson* [1843] 3 Hare 100, that courts of equity require proof that a foreign court will cooperate before an order requiring execution there will be made.

These predominantly procedural considerations—in the sense of remedial judgment enforcement subsisting between (pre-ascertained) fora such as under Article 34 of the *Brussels and Lugano Conventions*—appear well enough to conform with the *Rome Convention*, at least to the extent that the lex situs, qua lex causae, is applied to the substance if not directly to the relief in the way that the governing principles are typically rendered in domestic cases. The Conventions do not, of course, express the founding of jurisdiction on the issue of effective remedy nor should they, especially in consideration of the fact that the issue is not the exercise of jurisdiction simpliciter but rather of remedial jurisdiction. Thus, the pragmatic analogy may be permitted in these respects by which due regard is to be given to the equities as between the parties; that is, their respective legal positions in the eyes of the jurisdiction of actual enforcement should perhaps always necessarily be a determining factor in the eyes of the forum from which the award is sought, indeed as always was the case in the decisions referred to above.

On the transnational enforcement of contractual interests in securities and, more particularly, on the conflicts issues of the provision and structure of collateral in securities markets, it has commendably been observed[111] that the proprietorial rights delivery aspects (as are separable from the contract formation aspects) may involve discrete specifically enforceable obligation(s) to perfect a transferee's security interest, to enforce the security interest; if the formal and the material validity issues have been favourably determined. The proprietorial interest is governed by the lex situs, sometimes with the necessity for a facilitating legal fiction as was applied in *Macmillan Incorporated* v *Bishopsgate Investment Trust plc (No. 3)*,[112] in which intangible movables (viz., shares) were deemed to be located at the physical point of regulation of the practical aspects of enforcing the proprietorial interest.

(v) Contrariness to public policy, e.g. illegal contracts, contracts contravening relevant statutory requirements; contracts with the Crown or any other legal person who is immune from civil jurisdiction[113]

Section 13(3) *State Immunity Act 1978* provides that in actions brought against the Crown, where an order for specific performance would otherwise run, the appropriate relief is a declaratory judgment.[114] The Crown can be awarded specific performance according to the same provision. Where a foreign state is a

[111] J. Benjamin, "Conflicts of Law and Collateral in International Securities Markets" in B. Rider et al. (eds.), *Amicus Curiae* (Issue 9, London, CCH; 1998), at 19-21.

[112] [1995] 1 All ER 747; see also, *Dicey and Morris*, *op. cit.*, 931 (Rule 114), and ss. 8–11 and 9–103 of the New York *Revised Uniform Commercial Code* and the decision in *Fidelity Partners* v. *First Trust Company of New York* 97 Civ 5184 (SHS) (SDNY December 1, 1997).

[113] The *State Immunity Act 1978*, S. 13(3) (cf. *Maclaine Watson & Co. Ltd.* v. *Department of Trade and Industry, Maclaine Watson & Co. Ltd.* v. *International Tin Council* [1989] 3 All ER 523); s. 2(1) *Diplomatic Privileges Act 1964*. It is of course the case that the proper parties will have contested or been the parties to the suit in hand (Jones and Goodhart, *op. cit.*, Chapter five).

[114] Cf. Order 77 rule 7(2) *RSC*. The same result is reached where there is an application for summary judgment.

defendant, the state must have given written consent such as by treaty (Section 17(2), but not by mere submission to the jurisdiction) in order for the remedy to run against it. A contract by which a claimant would be enabled to evict a family will not be specifically enforced,[115] nor will a publishing contract by which the contractual author did not in fact do the writing, as in *Post* v. *Marsh*.[116]

There are several other more particularized rules, principles and considerations which run with the availability of the relief, but little would be added to the description of its nature and scope beyond what has thus far been discussed.[117] The over-arching concern is with the proper limits of the scope for the foregoing principles of English law to be applied in transnational circumstances, mindful that the in personam nature of the particular remedial jurisdiction renders its flexible or adaptive exercise as a central function of that scope of relevance. The particular facts of a case will of course determine the importance of (dis)applying a given principle, as will the basis upon which English law arises, whether as lex contractus or (and) as lex fori, as will whether the particular fact(s) subject to decision subsist(s) within forum competence. The nature and scope of specific performance thus clarified, the formats by which it may be made available will now be discussed.

THE PROCEDURAL ASPECTS: THE ACTION FOR SPECIFIC PERFORMANCE[118]

The present section concerns the formal aspects of litigation for specific performance, viz.: the commencement of actions (including those for summary judgment) for the remedy in the High Court or in the county courts; the formal aspects of a judgment in a case involving the remedy; post-judgment enforcement of the award; the matter of pleadings (or, "statements of cause", as they must now be called under the *Civil Procedure Rules*); the parties to these actions. What now follows is a statement of English law in point, and it is extremely unlikely that any other law can or should be applicable in the present scheme of things. It transpires that contracts involving interests in land persist to provide much of the illustrations, that the incidence of non-forum law in these respects is almost confined to issues of the detail of the court order itself and of the matter of propriety of litigants.

[115] *Wroth* v. *Tyler* above, n. 88. [116] (1880) 16 ChD 395.

[117] For the detail of these, see, e.g., *Halsbury's Laws*, *op. cit.*, or Jones and Goodhart, *op. cit.*, Chapters Four, Five and Seven.

[118] See generally, *Halsbury's Laws*, *op. cit.*, paras. 907 *et seq*; Jones and Goodhart, *op. cit.*, Chapter Six.

The courts: choosing to sue in England

Depending on the subject matter of the contract at issue, the requisite jurisdiction is had by the types of court referred to directly above.[119] For the purposes of initiating High Court proceedings for the relief (typically by the issuance of a writ, otherwise by originating summons if summary judgment is sought by the claimant: Order 86, rule 1(1) *R.S.C.*), there are three broad categories of agreement under the *Supreme Court Act 1981*:

— land (to be heard in the Chancery Division of the High Court: Section 61(1), and Schedule 1 paragraph 1(a));
— carriage of goods by, or other use or hire of, a ship (in the Admiralty Court (Queen's Bench Division): Sections 20(1)(a) and (2)(h), 62(2) and Schedule 1 paragraph 2(c));[120] and
— under Section 64, at the claimant's option, any other types of subject matter may found an action in any Division of the High Court, but subject to transfer among the Divisions, as may be necessary after further clarification, or to a county court[121] if the value of the subject matter is within the county court limit[122] or if the parties had autonomously specified a particular county court, under Section 24 *County Courts Act 1984*.

Section 49 *Law of Property Act 1925*, dealing with landed interest-holder's rights be the holder a vendor or purchaser, requires special attention. The holder of an interest in land may summarily apply to the court by means of an originating "vendor and purchaser summons" on any contractual issues arising other than the existence or validity of the particular contract, whether or not the opposing party admitted that existence or validity:[123] Section 49(1). This procedure is given to be "a relatively cheap and quick alternative to a full specific performance action, particularly where a specific objection to title is raised and the parties accept that the contract must stand or fall by the validity of that objection".[124] Therefore, it is not apposite to resolving disputed facts as to which, if they did arise in the course of hearing the application, the court, according to Order 28 rule 8 *R.S.C.*, proceeds as though the relief had been claimed by writ. Section 49(4) describes the procedure as it applies in the county courts, with the contract value limit of £30,000 applying.

119 Also, cf. the second and third paragraphs this Chapter, above. Unless a contract providing for arbitration stipulates otherwise, arbitrators' remedial competence is equal to the High Court's: S. 15 *Arbitration Act 1950*.

120 See also *Petrofina SA* v. *AOT Ltd., The Maersk Nimrod* [1991] 3 All ER 161.

121 S. 41 *County Courts Act 1984* (as amended by s. 46(1), Sched. 1 para. 30 *Matrimonial and Family Proceedings Act 1984*; by S. 2(2) *Courts and Legal Services Act 1990*); and Order 16 Part III rules 9 to 11 of the *County Court Rules* (CCR). The principal enabling statutory provision is Ord. 4 r. 2 of the CCR. Part I of Order 16 of these rules provides for transfers between county courts.

122 S. 23(d) *County Courts Act 1984* (also, Ss. 145, 147(1); the current limit is set at £30,000, by the County Courts Jurisdiction Order 1981, SI 1981/1123, Art. 2, Table (as amended by SI 1991/724)).

123 Cf. *Re Hughes and Ashley's Contract* [1900] 2 Ch 595 (Court of Appeal).

124 *Halsbury's Laws*, *op. cit.*, para. 910 (at 531).

Perhaps the main metaphorical spectre that looms in the general procedure to follow in seeking a transnational specific performance award, especially one that is sought under summary jurisdiction, concerns the recognizability and enforceability of the award in (an)other jurisdiction(s). Non-forum rules which might characterize the action differently from the forum can decidedly not be relevant to the ascertainment of these issues. But the attractions of international codes to regulate these procedural issues cannot be undervalued or usefully ignored.

The formal grant of specific performance[125]

This begins with a judicial statement that the agreement at issue should be specifically performed. The statement then literally details consequent references or directions to suit the given case, such as a reference for an enquiry concerning title (typically at the purchaser's application in a vendor's action, so that an award will not be futile), an award of compensatory damages (e.g., to offset delays in completing the underlying contract),[126] the judicial imposition of a lien, or (and) the incidence of interest etc., as may be necessary and within the discretionary jurisdiction of the court. Interestingly, in *Seven Seas Properties Limited* v. *Al-Essa*,[127] specific performance was combined with a Mareva in the making of an order for the retention of the purchase price while a damages enquiry was yet to be resolved.

The scope for a title reference, procured on either an interlocutory motion or a vendor and purchaser summons,[128] is limited to the requirements of the ordered performance, and may include restrictions upon the purchaser's rights of objection or further enquiry as to the vendor's title. The reference will not be ordered if the purchaser has waived the right to it, but the waiver would need to have been pleaded. As always, the remedy is to be appreciated in its equitable character, so that, for example, prejudice to third parties' rights, the purchaser's prior knowledge of the vendor's incapacity to transfer the property in the goods sold, etc. will operate negatively.

Specific performance, subject to compensatory damages

This relief may avail a claimant, on that party's fulfilment of, or without, conditionalities imposed by the contract and thus by the court. The remedy arises mostly in connexion with representations surrounding a particular contract, and it is necessary to separately treat the respective litigants' reliance-based entitlements in the capacity of claimant, because their respective rights are construed on different bases.

[125] Cf. Vol. 37 *Court Forms* (2nd ed., London, Sweet & Maxwell; 1995) at102 *et seq*., Forms 64 *et seq*.

[126] Cf. *Oakacre Ltd.* v. *Claire (Cleaners (Holdings) Ltd.* [1981] 3 All ER 667, in which a conveyance of land to claimants, after they had issued a writ, caused the main action for specific performance to flounder.

[127] [1989] 1 All ER 164.

[128] Cf. *Re Scott and Alvarez's Contract, Scott* v. *Alvarez* [1895] 2 Ch 603 (Court of Appeal).

A condition which attracts the conditionality of compensation would be that of terms of sale which are interpreted against the seller, so that the purchaser obtains neither more nor less than the expectation interest in the bargain. Accordingly, a contract for the sale of land in *Price* v. *Macaulay*,[129] substantially misdescribing the proprietorial interest as copyhold rather than freehold, was held to be specifically performable but with compensation to the purchaser for material inconvenience arising therefrom. Section 2 of the *Misrepresentation Act 1967* allows only an award of damages for a non-contractual misrepresentation; no specific performance of such a representation is ever ordered. Section 3, however, imposes requirements of reasonableness on any contractual terms purporting to disclaim liability for this type of misrepresentation.

A purchaser may be awarded performance with compensation, but subject only to the normal rules by which contract terms are to be construed, so that a vendor's defective title does not amount to a mistake or misrepresentation in the details of the sale,[130] more so when the purchaser was aware of the defective description as in *Cobbett* v. *Locke-King*.[131] A representation needs however to have raised a reasonable purchaser's attraction to the contractual subject matter in which case the purchaser may be required, as he was in *Re Hare and O'Moore's Contract*,[132] to elect between rescission and simple completion of the contract. Other bars to purchaser compensation have included a contractual condition by which the vendor may rescind[133] and the impossibility, rather than the difficulty, of quantifying the compensation.[134]

Where there are no conditionalities, a vendor's entitlement to specific performance on the payment of compensation respectively depends on whether the purchaser's expectation interest evidenced in the bargain would thereby be secured and, secondly, on the facility with which the effect on the value of the subject matter can be quantified.[135] Otherwise, the applicable rules (e.g., as to waiver; representations; extra-contractual representation; titular defects vis-à-vis non-encumbrances; disclaimers; the exactitude of quantum of compensation) are much the same as those discussed above in relation to conditional awards.

A purchaser will obtain performance with compensation in circumstances which attract Slade L.J.s "doctrine of partial performance", set out in *Thames Guaranty Limited* v. *Campbell*.[136] The circumstances will be that the vendor cannot deliver the letter of the bargain, and that the difference in value between

[129] [1852] 2 De GM & G 339.

[130] *Debenham* v. *Sawbridge* [1901] 2 Ch 98.

[131] [1900] 16 TLR 379.

[132] [1901] 1 Ch 93.

[133] Cf. *Williams* v. *Edwards* [1827] 2 Sim 78, where the contract was to be consensually avoided in the absence of good title.

[134] Cf. *White* v. *Cuddon* [1842] 8 Cl & Fin 766 (H.L.)

[135] Cf. *SB Property Co. Ltd.* v. *Chelsea Football and Athletic Co. Ltd.* 64 P & CR 440 (1992) (Court of Appeal).

[136] [1984] 2 All ER 585, at 595 (see also *Rignall Developments Ltd.* v. *Halil* [1987] 3 All ER 170, where land charges register expenses were deducted from the specific performance of payment of the contract price), to be differentiated from the repealed doctrine of part-performance previously carried in S. 40 *Law of Property Act 1940*.

the subject matter sold and that agreed upon will not only be quantifiable but is deductable from the contract price. A vendor will likely not usually be coerced to indemnify a purchaser, and vice versa, against contingent defects or losses, unless the parties had so anticipated and contracted. And if a contract specifically provides for compensation for contractual representations, the particular clause or term is enforceable only before the contract will have been completed.

It makes sense to consider next the issue of post-judgment enforcement relief, because it is the form of judgment just described that is registrable by the awardee for the purpose of its execution or literal enforcement.

Post-judgment enforcement of the remedy

The instrument to transfer property in the contractual subject matter will need to be prepared and served inter partes if previously it has not. This is dealt with in Order 44 rule 3(1)(c), on Masters' directions.[137] If this does not resolve the issues, the judge then gives the appropriate directions, according to Order 31 rules 5 to 8 *R.S.C.*[138] Once this is done, the contractual price is adjusted by the master (subject to appeal) for any interest, profits, compensation, damages, costs accruing, property deterioration or any other outgoings.[139]

Thereafter, a defendant's failure to perform means that the claimant must obtain yet another executing order with a time limit on the defendant to complete the required performance: Order 42 rule 2 *R.S.C.* Further non-compliance will lead to the procurement, under Order 45 rules 5 and 7 *R.S.C.* respectively, of a writ of sequestration or a committal order against the defaulting defendant.

Order 45 rule 1 *R.S.C.* does however enable a vendor's order to be enforced as a money judgment and, similarly for a purchaser of a landed interest, Sections 48 and 50 of the *Trustee Act 1925* provide to the same effect by means of a court declaration that the vendor is trustee of the proprietorial interest at issue and that the purchaser be invested with, or have conveyed to them, the interest.[140] It is not intended in this discussion to exhaust the variety of other post-judgment rules of court that can be prayed in aid.[141] It is sufficient to add that directions may be forthcoming from the court as to the quantum of damages for delayed compliance, as they were in *Easton* v. *Brown*.[142] Similar provisions to Order 44 *R.S.C.* obtain in county courts.[143]

[137] Masters' jurisdiction is dealt with in Order 32 rule 14 *RSC*; see also *Supreme Court Practice-Practice Directions (Chancery Division) Vol. 2* (London, Sweet & Maxwell; 1996), para. 854.

[138] Cf. *Charalambous* v. *Ktori* [1972] 3 All ER 701.

[139] Ord. 44 rr. 11 and 12 *RSC*.

[140] Cf. the second paragraph of the Introduction, above.

[141] See, e.g., Ord. 45 r. 4(1) (on the writ of specific delivery of goods); Ord. 45 r. 8 (on the appointment of some other performer, at cost to the non-complying defendant); the unpaid vendor's lien.

[142] [1981] 3 All ER 278.

[143] Ord. 23 r. 2(1)-(4), 29 r. 1 (committal) *CCR*.

A thwarted claimant, and indeed an identical defendant, must obtain formal just discharge of the contract even if performance is either no longer required or has become impossible, and the justness of the discharge may depend on the imposition of supplemental conditions such as or including an award of damages separately pursued.[144]

In closing, it should be remembered that Title III *Brussels Convention* regulates the inter-State recognition and enforcement of these orders whose definition falls within the description of "judgment" in the preceding Article 25. Special recognition procedures are rendered irrelevant but possible, e.g. where recognition is the main issue, in Article 26. Article 27 sets out the bases for withholding recognition of any judgment, viz.:

— its contrariness to the public policy of the recognizing State;
— its having been awarded in default of the defendant's appearance for not having been duly served with initiating process;
— its irreconciliability with a recognizing State's court's judgment as to the same parties;
— its inapposition to the recognizing State's private international law rules on preliminary questions of any of natural persons' legal status/capacity, matrimonial property rights, testacy or succession;
— its irreconciliability with a non-Member State's previous recognizable judgment on the same cause.

These grounds are supplemented in Article 28 by further bases, as follows:

— incompatibility with the jurisdiction-acquisition provisions of Articles 3 (which excludes jurisdiction founded on the defendant's presence or ownership of assets in the territory of the forum State), 4 (which gives jurisdiction over a non-domiciliary defendant to the law of the State), 5 (on jurisdiction - in contract, maintenance, tort, civil claims for criminal causes, agency, trusts, and marine salvage - founded on further specified and differentiated bases) or 59 (on forum Member States' recognition obligations to third party States).

The enforcement aspects and dimensions are discussed in better detail and context in Chapters Five and Six.

The issue of statements of cause (pleadings)[145]

These (now known as statements of cause) are contained in the claim form and statement of claim, and must indicate any supplemental or alternative relief[146] such as damages, rescission, return or forfeiture (as may be the case depending on whether the claimant is the vendor or the purchaser) of a deposit and

[144] Cf. *Johnson* v. *Agnew* [1980] AC 367, generally, and especially at 399.

[145] The actual process precedents appear in Vol. 37 *Court Forms*, *op. cit.*, at 47–54 and 65–76, Forms 1–12 and 23–24.

assertion of a lien for its repayment, an injunction, rectification, accounts and enquiries and (or) a trust vesting order. There is practically no authority which suggests that any rules but the normal forum rules of the form and content of pleadings can be applicable. But it would often appear that the bonus to a conflicts litigant, that normal pleading rules apply in conflicts cases, is often under-utilized in the sense that there is little in the rules in question which precludes the pleading and adduction of evidence of non-forum law as would avail the given party in transnational litigation, or as could give a better account of the real scope of specific performance in the conflict of laws; and this really is a separate matter from the fact that the remedy is relatively commonly sought in international litigation as the cases thus far discussed in connexion with explaining the governing principles will have shown.

Chapter Six of this book and the "Article 10(1) gloss" have expressed some of the limitations—over-localization—which can stem from almost exclusively identifying the lex fori with the governing substantive principles for the availability of the remedy. These need not be reiterated except to indicate that there will be cases where the inferred irrelevance of non-forum principles and rules in point will beggar belief. For example, the rule subsists that where there is judgment for the claimant in default of defence, no previously unclaimed relief on the claim form will be recoverable;[147] the claimant must draft and file a precise form of the order sought,[148] to accompany the application (by summons to a master, or by motion in Chancery).

In land cases, a vendor's title is to be pleaded only if the purchaser has not questioned it[149] or if the vendor wishes to dispense with the need to prove title, e.g., by insisting that the purchaser had waived any objections to title.[150] However, the purchaser is entitled to plead the vendor's defective title, to secure a dismissal at the trial of the latter's action for specific performance, as in *Lucas* v. *James*,[151] but must deploy the vendor and purchaser summons if defective title is the sole defence to the relief. At any rate, want of the defendant-purchaser's pleading of the vendor-plaintiff's title will prevent the court from dismissing the action, where necessary with compensation which likewise need not have been pleaded, if trial evidence does subsequently indicate defective title.[152]

The importance of accurate pleading, being a matter for the lex fori, is arguably not clearer than in reference to a party entitled to rescind, who has

[146] Cf. *Halsbury's Laws*, *op. cit.*, paras. 92 *et seq.* (540 *et seq.*).

[147] Cf., e.g., *Palmer* v. *Lark* [1945] Ch 182, where judgment interest at the contractual rate was withheld because the claimant had not pleaded the relevant contract term that would have been enforceable. Even for summary judgments, the claimant must, according to Ord. 13 r. 6(1) *RSC*, file and serve a statement of claim. See also Ord. 18 rr. 7(4) and 8(4) *RSC*, and *Ward* v. *Chief Constable for Avon and Somerset* (1985) 129 Sol J 606.

[148] *De Jongh* v. *Newman* [1887] 56 SLT 180.

[149] Ss. 1–13 *Law of Property (Miscellaneous Provisions) Act 1994*.

[150] Cf. *Phipps* v. *Child* [1857] 3 Drew 709.

[151] [1849] 7 Hare 410, at 425.

[152] *Wilson* v. *Williams* [1857] 3 Jur NS 810.

directly or constructively affirmed a contract, and is alternatively seeking judicial rescission. Such a party may well have obtained the opposing party's acceptance of rescission, which would release both parties from fulfilling any remaining contractual obligations. But the contract is not thus avoided ab initio, and damages may accrue to the aggrieved party (subject to the election of that relief in lieu of specific performance, because affirmation and rescission would otherwise be inconsistent) on the basis that suing for specific performance goes to affirm the contract.[153]

The matter of proper parties

Procedural as these considerations of propriety of litigants are, the issue is ultimately one that may depend on the forum's interpretation—complete with its own public policy—of relevant non-forum rules on the right or the locus to sue in the particular circumstances, as was held in the different setting of the scope (and proof) of foreign law generally, in *Bumper Development Corporation* v. *Commisssioner of Police*[154] in which a temple's right to sue according to Indian law was upheld. All the same, the clear rationale for the non-derogable nature of the forum rules that are applicable is that the forum's complementing formalized post-judgment enforcement procedures in personam are also for the internal lex fori.

On the authority of Lord Parker C.J. in *Howard* v. *Miller*,[155] "[t]here is no equitable principle by virtue of which land can be taken away from the true owner under colour of specific performance of a contract to which he was not a party and which he did not authorise to be made on his behalf". Accordingly, the contractual parties—or their legal successors, agents or assignees—are the only proper parties to an action for specific performance. The various law subject areas' rules on vicarious responsibility will indicate the propriety of suing either the contractual party or that party's successor, agent etc. In *Gewa Chartering BV* v. *Remco Shipping Lines Ltd., The Remco*,[156] a third party's agent who had actually but unprejudicially acted for himself was held to be capable of personally enforcing the particular contract as against the other contractual party.

The law will sometimes operate to assign or to convey the benefit of a contract in circumstances where the general rule against unnovated assignments[157] to third parties would otherwise disallow the assignment or transfer. The result is that, in such cases, the contract is enforceable either by or against a third party assignee or transferee, such as by or against a personal representative following the death or bankruptcy of a contractual party or, more directly,

153 *Johnson* v. *Agnew* (above, n. 144), at 393 (per Lord Wilberforce).

154 [1991] 1 WLR 1362.

155 [1915] AC 318, at 323 (Privy Council).

156 [1984] 2 Ll Rep 205.

157 Cf. *Tollhurst* v. *Associated Portland Cement Manufacturers (1900) Ltd.; Tollhurst* v. *Associated Portland Cement Manufacturers (1900) Ltd. and Imperial Portland Cement Co. Ltd.* [1902] 2 KB 660, at 668 (per Collins M.R.)

where a trustee had contracted for the third party as in *Les Affrétours Réunis SA* v. *Leopold Walford (London) Limited*.[158] What is required is proof of the fiduciary capacity in which the original contractual party had contracted.[159] A third party may also be a party to specific performance proceedings if the third party has or asserts an interest in the matter.

In the case of enforcement of a contract by an assignee, not only will the assignee need to be able to perform the assignor's contractual obligations, the obligations will also not be of a personal (e.g., skilled) nature or be illegal or contrary to public policy. Therefore, there is no reason on the barest of facts to join the assignor in an action for specific performance at the assignee's instance.[160] If however the assignment is equitable and is of a legal chose in action, the action must be brought in the assignor's name or if the assignor does not consent then s/he will need to be joined as co-defendant, so as to ensure full compliance with the order.[161]

A transferee of property compares well with the assignor in the paragraph directly above in that the holder(s) of legal rights may obtain specific performance against the transferee. This was the view of the Privy Council, in *Meng Leong Development Company Pte Limited* v. *Jip Hong Trading Company Pte Limited*[162] in which the claimant successfully sought specific performance against a vendor's transferee. In *Jones* v. *Lipman*,[163] a vendor and the company to which he had sold the subject matter were co-defendants in an action for specific performance of the original contract.

A contracting party's bankruptcy can support an order for specific performance, perhaps with conditionalities, in favour of or against the bankrupt in relation to trust property held by the bankrupt for others. However, the trustee in bankruptcy is vested with the bankrupt's own estate: Section 311(4) *Insolvency Act 1986*. Bankruptcy neither terminates the contract at issue nor, according to Section 283(3)(a) of the same statute, causes the bankrupt's holdings of property on trust to vest in a trustee in bankruptcy. The rules in these regards are detailed in *Halsbury's Laws of England*[164] and in the *Insolvency Act 1986*.

It is noteworthy that Section 315 (as amended by Section 117(4) *Housing Act 1988*) of the *1986 Act* precludes post-bankruptcy specific performance of an unprofitable agreement which a trustee in bankruptcy had disclaimed, thus leaving the aggrieved party's recovery for losses to the outcome of the latter's submission of a proof in the bankruptcy. If the equitable interest has not yet passed to the purchaser, then a disclaimer of the contract is not permissible and the trustee in bankruptcy may be compelled to conclude the contract of sale,

[158] [1919] AC 801 (H.L.) [159] *Beswick* v. *Beswick*, above, at n. 11.

[160] Cf. Vol. 37 *Court Forms*, *op. cit.*, at 67, Form 25.

[161] *Crouch* v. *Crédit Foncier of England* [1873] LR8 QB 374, at 380 (per Blackburn J.).

[162] [1985] AC 511. See also Vol. 37 *Court Forms*, *op. cit.*, at 68, Form 26.

[163] [1962] 1 All ER 442. For the position of a company promoter's personal liability for specific performance, see S. 36C(1) *Companies Act 1985*, as amended by s. 130(4) *Companies Act 1989*.

[164] *Op. cit.*, Vol. 3(2) Reissue, paras. 407 *et seq*.

mutuality of obligations permitting.[165] But, by reason of section 164(1) *Companies Act 1985*, Section 315 does not extend to market contracts[166] or contracts collateral thereto.

Unavoidable differences from function exist in the case of an insolvent company in the hands of a liquidator. The similarities are explainable on the basis that specific performance in either circumstance improperly prioritizes the plaintiff over other creditors. The first difference is that company property remains vested in the company, but the liquidator can disclaim onerous property within Section 178(2) and (3) of the *1986 Act*, with the exceptions as to market or collateral contracts also applying as it does to a trustee-in-bankruptcy's disclaimer of similar contracts. Where a company is being wound up by court order, Section 127 of the *1986 Act* makes dispositions of company property void if they are not made pursuant to a court order, or are neither market nor collateral contracts (Section 164(3)–(6)). The performance of bona fide contracts by which equitable title has passed from the company to the purchaser before the commencement of winding-up will be specifically ordered, on the authority of *Re Coregrange*;[167] a stay of specific performance proceedings in these circumstances will normally not be granted. In *Freevale Limited* v. *Metrostore (Holdings) Limited*,[168] a company contract to sell land in receivership prior to completion sufficed in an award of specific performance to the purchaser.

The developing law on the transnational infringement of intellectual property rights is often accompanied by incidents of standing to sue.[169] Be the subject matter generically considered or individuated according to the particular type of right, the registered proprietor of the right invariably appears to be the party best placed to sue. Given the yet territorial nature of these rights and the current law, the matter of proper parties appears more than ever to be a matter for the lex fori, as national law, which may allow licensees to sue, mindful that "any increase in the number of possible plaintiffs correspondingly increases the number of choices of forum against defendants outside the Community".[170] The closing remarks in these regards, culled from context of the EU, could not be better expressed than they were in the following way:

> "[T]here is . . . no implication that a court seized of an action on a Community intellectual property right can entertain related actions under domestic or foreign law unless it can independently derive jurisdiction over every such cause of action from the Brussels Convention or national law. Given the differences between the Brussels

[165] Cf. *Freevale Ltd.* v. *Metrostore (Holdings) Ltd.* [1984] 1 All ER 495, at 501.

[166] These are defined in S. 155 of the *1989 Act*, as amended by the *Financial Markets and Insolvency Regulations 1991*, SI 1991/880, Regulation 3.

[167] [1984] BCLC 453. [168] Above, n. 165.

[169] Cf. Wadlow, *op. cit.* (n. 75, above), paras. 5–94 to 5–106 (292–296), discussing the EC *Luxembourg Patent Convention 1975* (Arts. 15, 35, 39, 42, 43, 45, 46, 47), the Community *Trade Mark Regulation 40/94* (O.J. L11/1; on the significance of the bearer of a contractual licence under Art. 22 thereof).

[170] Wadlow, *op. cit.*, para. 5–94 (at 292).

> Convention and the Protocol on Litigation or the Community Trade Mark Regulation, especially against defendants domiciled outside the Community, this will not always be the case".[171]

It is as well to add the useful practical simplification of matters remedial, in Article 35(1) of the *Protocol to the Community Patent Convention on Litigation* as well as in Article 98(1) of the *Council Regulation on the Community Trade Mark*, that for the infringement of either type of right normally attracts a mandatory final injunction, excepting that in English law that availing remedy in its final form is equally subject to the territorial principle.

COMPARATIVIST PERSPECTIVES

The diammetric opposition between the Common and the Civil Law traditions concerning remedial performance of contracts generally is at root a consequence of the fact that, terminologically if not functionally, worthwhile comparable analogues in the latter type of legal system either involve a difference of emphasis or are misnomers as to their effect if not their substance or organic (intra-systemic) nature and function.[172] By and large, in civilian systems, there is little that is in principle extraordinary, subsidiary or exceptional about an aggrieved bona fide contractual claimant's entitlement to have a contractual obligation unequivocally enforced provided that execution of the required enforcement is actually possible. However, the reality of court practice may differ.

In *Tibaldi* v. *Société des fondeurs de métaux prétaux précieux*,[173] for example, a defendant who had borrowed gold was held to have obligated himself to return the quantity and quality he had borrowed, rather than pay compensatory damages as is permissible under Paragraph 1184(2) of the French Civil Code, even though there was a governmental rationing of gold. The particular provision gives the aggrieved party the option between coercive and substitutional relief, as likewise is presupposed in Paragraphs 97(1) and 107(2) of the Swiss *Obligationenrecht* and, much less concessionally, in Paragraph 241 of the German *Bürgeliches Gesetzbüch*.[174] In any of these legal systems, the basic principle for performance is never unequivocal, but it remains but a superficial enquiry in which one would be engaged if the complex co-ordination of the remedial rules of the respective systems is not better amplified than the English law focus of this book will allow.

Suffice it perhaps to look only as far as the Scots case of *Stewart* v. *Kennedy* in which the equivalent, specific implement, was so eloquently described by Lord Watson in terms that the aggrieved party "cannot be compelled to resort to the

[171] Wadlow, *op. cit.*, para. 5–106 (at 296).

[172] Cf. C. Szladits, "The Concept of Specific Performance in Civil Law" (1955) 4 AJCL 208, at 212.

[173] Paris, July 17 1946 (1948) Dalloz, 169, note Weil.

[174] Cf. A. von Tuhr, "Naturalherstellung und Gelderstaz" (1904) 46 Iherings Jahrbücher 39.

alternative action of damages unless implement is shown to be impossible, in which case, *loco facti imprestabilis subit damnum et interesse*. Even where implement is possible, I do not doubt that the Court of Session has inherent power to refuse legal remedy upon equitable grounds, although I know of no instance in which it has done so".[175]

Of greater practical and theoretical value, to the issue—previously encountered in discussing equitable orders intended for enforcement in Civil Law jurisdictions—of the likelihood of systems' rights/remedies-distorting procedural disparities, is consideration of the unifying trends of and from the EC Conventions, about which Kerameus has made pointed observations, especially that "procedural unification may serve practical ends, both where several states are connected through international commerce, as well as where they have reached an advanced stage of integration. Where the achievement of such ends is not paramount in individual states the ideal of improving the quality of rules may be achieved through moves towards unification".[176]

The crux of his harmonization matrix[177] is concerned with "supplying the technical tools that are necessary for the operation of the body of substantive law", with "instances where procedural rules are specifically designed to meet specific needs of substantive norms", and with "making policy decisions in crucial areas of adjudication". In other words, procedural unification without substantive harmony is difficult and doomed to fail. And this is all quite apart from a further consideration that "European procedural harmonization, regardless of how limited subject-matterwise it may be, should encompass all litigation in the national courts of the Member States, purely domestic and transnational alike".[178]

Wide-ranging and utopian these views must seem if taken out of the festschrift context in which they were rendered. But they are, with next to no doubt in this writer's view, the shape of things to be, by adaptation in emerging or evolving regional structures on the subject as it obtains and can better be provided for elsewhere.

A RECAPITULATION

That specific performance of a contract is discretionary has little distinguishing impact on its conflict of laws' range of applications. Perhaps it should because it can. It is materially different from other performance relief to be discussed next. In order for specific performance to avail a conflicts litigant, it must, first, be relief forthcoming under the lex fori. Particular types of agreement have shown themselves to prominently feature in the conflicts cast of the remedy, as they do in the internal law case.

The remedy is presented in the literature as being no less important as the

175 (1890) 15 App Cas 75, at 102.

176 "Procedural Harmonization in Europe" (1995) 43 *AJCL* 401, at 403.

177 *Loc. cit.*, at 404–405.

178 Ibid., at 412.

supposedly normal[179] remedy of compensatory damages, as well sometimes as being arguably more relevant.[180] These divergences of opinion are of little consequence if a claimant prefers to sue for substitutional relief in money as often is the case.

Indeed, contemporaneously with Birks's statement, albeit in the completely different setting of remedial restitution law, that the hegemony of compensation for loss is more often than not illusory,[181] there subsists the sometimes strongly held—but, with respect and as the wealth of cases cited earlier in the discussion must show, somewhat misdirected—supposedly commercialist view that the Common Law's remedy of specific performance is really rather redundant in the overall remedial structure of any modern legal system.

Discussing *Beswick*, Mann[182] poignantly expressed the view:

> "[i]n the realm of monetary obligations there is very little left of the distinction between debt, damages, and specific performance...[A]t the present stage of legal development there is no justification at all for retaining all the verbiage which has grown around equitable remedies and their discretionary character. Why, in the name of rational law, should a judge not award to the plaintiff what he has contracted to receive, what he is, therefore, entitled to and what the defendant has failed to pay? Why should conceptions, words, history continue to have precedence over the demands of justice?".

And Article 28 of the United Nations *Vienna Convention on Contracts for the International Sale of Goods 1980* "subjects the availability of the remedy of "specific performance" to any limitations that may be imposed on it by the domestic rules of the forum. [Equitable] "specific performance" seems here to include the [legal] action for the price".[183]

Indeed, one might as well seek to maintain that the restrictive scope of the remedy is a basis for doing away with it. To do so would, however, be derisory of an (albeit narrow ethical) enduring justification for it be the particular facts commercial or non-commercial. Ogus's is an exceptionally lucid balanced account of extra-legal but no less objectivist purposes served by the remedy.[184]

Consequently, it is difficult to attempt meaningfully to prognosticate that remedially enforced performance somehow will come to be seen to inhibit the crystallizing schemes for proper and efficient administration of transnational civil justice, or even that there exists a really legitimate foundation for any of the perceptions of a general reluctance to submit the redress of commercial contracts in breach to the particular remedy.

179 See, e.g., P.S. Atiyah, *Essays on Contract* (Oxford, Clarendon; 1986), at 177: "[S]pecific performance today plays a fairly minor role in contract law", the larger context of this statement being to refute a defence of the remedy by S.J. Waddams in, "The Modern Role of Contract Law" (1983–1984) 8 *Can Bus LJ* 2.

180 E.g., A. Burrows, "Specific Performance at the Crossroads" (1984) 4 *Leg Stud* 102.

181 *Restitution—The Future* (London, Butterworths; 1992), e.g., at 25.

182 See, e.g., F.A. Mann, "Specific Performance of Foreign Money Obligations?" (1968) 31 *MLR* 342, at 344–345.

183 Treitel. *op. cit.*, at 181.

184 *Loc. cit.*, at 256–262.

The contractual allocation of the risks which accompany due completion of agreed obligations would be distortingly rendered as a fortuitously artificial, or as an unnecessary extra-contractual, judicial imposition upon the parties and in fact on the legal system. Nor is the protection of substantial or legitimate (not less) expectations afforded by the exceptional availability of specific performance to be contemned, bearing in mind especially that the remedy will have been carefully granted by the forum, to reiterate, applying durable principles and only when performance is in fact possible.

These principles are concisely delineated in *Chitty on Contracts*,[185] albeit tentatively in the context of the remedy in favour of third parties:

> "[A]s a general principle, it is submitted that the promisee should be able to obtain specific performance in favour of a third party whenever that is the most appropriate method of enforcing the contract which was actually made. But it should be open to the defendant to resist specific enforcement by showing that this remedy would lead to one of the undesirable results against which the established limitations on the scope of the remedy are meant to provide protection".[186]

Effective remediability must count for a great deal more or, at least, be reckoned with much differently in the transnational context because forum control of process becomes more of an issue in the particular context, and specific performance—with its attendant considerations discussed in preceding sections of the present Chapter—will foreseeably continue to be available to the right claimant in the right circumstances, in much the same way as doctrines of repudiation and anticipatory breach secure a promisee's expectations.

Attention must now turn to stipulations the post-breach enforced performance of which is naturally remedial in their respective consequences.

OTHER PERFORMANCE RELIEF: JUDICIAL ENFORCEMENT OF CONTRACTUALLY STIPULATED REMEDIES[187]

Judicial relief in view in this section covers the enforcement, following an action begun by claim form under the Civil Procedure Rules, primarily of the expectation interest contained in the following types of contractual clause in particular:

— forum or jurisdiction clauses generally;
— payments clauses, viz. liquidated or agreed sums, penalties, deposits/part-payments;

[185] *Op. cit.*, paras. 27–034–27–036 (1304–1307).

[186] Para. 27–034 (at 1304–1305); see also the examples from services, share transfer, and future interests contracts where want of privity is not exceptable in para. 27–035 (at 1305 *et seq.*).

[187] E.g., R.J. Sharpe, *Injunctions and Specific Performance* (Toronto, Canada Law Book Co.; 1983), paras. 587–605 (at 302–309, especially at 302 ff. 118).

— equitable relief from forfeiture clauses;
— delivery clauses and proprietary interests, e.g., title, contracted goods, security rights.

The usual jurisdictional rules, e.g. the *Brussels and Lugano Conventions* rules on "civil or commercial matters" or the traditional rules such as those to govern service out under Order 11 *R.S.C.* where necessary, apply to set the proceedings in motion. The primary sense of "judicial remedy" in respect of the actual enforcement of contract provisions is a matter for injunctive relief, e.g., stays and antisuit injunctions, as is discussed in Chapter Eight. That these agreed, rather than strictly judicial, remedies may or may not be judicially enforceable (or, better, controlled or pragmatically restrained, for reasons, e.g., the sense of fairness between the parties as is conveyed by the particular contract interpreted in its entirety, of parties' fides, of the sufficiency of contractual consideration, of an inequality of parties' bargaining positions; conscionability or other defect in the bargain) is really the basis on which they fittingly are to be identified with the scope of this work.

These clauses are of course subject to the lex contractus because they go to the substance of the contract of which they are a part, but their enforcement must also depend on forum public interest in their conscionability as non-punitive arrangements. The categories of clause are substantially but not exclusively legal. They are "equitable" in the sense that they inevitably are derived from the public interest or "the morality of promise-keeping",[188] albeit that disobeying a judicial order for their performance cannot attract contempt proceedings.[189] The procedural forms of post-trial and post-judgment enforcement of the clauses in view are the same as with orders for specific performance, previously discussed in this book.

The common characteristic is that the issue of enforcement is normally occasioned by breach of a contract term for which, as with an order for specific performance, the inadequacy of a grant of damages must be proved by the claimant; for example, whether default as to an enforceable contractual obligation to pay should be regarded as waiver of the aggrieved's otherwise counter-enforceable contractual entitlement to forfeiture.

The succeeding discussion is typified by the courts' response to the parties' autonomously determined contractual relationship, as the relationship is affected by the given clause. The complete diversified genre of other enforced relief has been eminently discussed in a pervading context of "the justifications for judicial control over [them]",[190] the moderately concomitant sub-contexts being those of their procedural (i.e., judicial enforcement) (un)fairness, and of their substantive content (i.e., their validity and enforce-

[188] A. Burrows, *op. cit.*, at 315, discussing liquidated damages.
[189] Cf. Treitel, *op. cit.*, at 45 (ff. 12).
[190] H. Collins, *loc. cit.*, n. 18, above.

ability),[191] primarily in the straight-forward domestic law case from which forum practice is derived.

An important presumption in what now follows in the separate discussion of these remedial terms is either that forum law in point is applicable or that the lex contractus contains particularized, thus relevant and applicable, rules in point. The presumption is expanded in the course of discussion as may be necessary. These perspectives support the present conflicts discussion because, to a greater or lesser extent, they can be construed to be part of applicable forum law that includes, e.g., the *Unfair Contract Terms Act 1977*.[192]

Partly perhaps because of the explicable absence of a satisfactory general English rule or principle that is generically applicable to these remedies (the very different question of whether there should be one is, with respect, for a different discussion), issues of equities between the parties, particularly in the various forms of "substantive (distributive) fairness", coupled with any "good [corrective] reasons for objecting to agreed remedies which effectively compel performance of contracts",[193] are the justificatory denominators in the matter of judicial enforcement practice on the point.

Using the contrasting backcloth of liquidated damages presently to be discussed, because these are contract issues sufficiently but not wholly contextualized by remedial performance, the key issue of substitutional relief in money also features as an important criterion in rationalizing agreed relief with the actual loss from the breach, as is the case with specific performance. Judicial practice in these regards is arguably as rational and balanced as it could be in any area of the law, so that the quest for unifying principle such as more or less founds the articulate commentaries cited above will in practical terms probably add but a sublime refinement to the resolution of the dominant issues of validity and effect which surround much of the consideration of the topic of enforced performance of consensual relief. To reiterate, coerced performance of these clauses is but secondary judicial intervention, and not judicial relief in the ordinary sense of an award of damages, specific performance or injunction in their purer forms. General comparisons with some of the aspects of other jurisdictions' judicial practices feature to make discussion of the individual classes of clause more complete.

[191] Ibid., especially at 100–102; see also, generally, S.A. Smith, "In Defence of Substantive Fairness" (1996) 112 *LQR* 138.

[192] Cf. F.A. Mann, "Unfair Contract Terms Act 1977 and the Conflict of Laws" (1978) 27 *ICLQ* 661, discussing S. 27, for the present especially subs. (2), of the statute which deals with non-forum leges causae, in contracts for the international supply of goods, selected "for the purpose of enabling the party imposing it to evade the operation of [the] Act".

[193] Collins, *loc. cit.*, 111. Such reasons would presumably include public policy but not, e.g., "unjust enrichment" (his 111–113), the "reduction of social cost" (113–114), "wealth maximization" (114–116), "risk averaging" (116–119).

Forum-selecting clauses in English law

Background, and the general law[194]

As is suggested by their description, these clauses (thus, they must have some written form) provide for the forum in which one or either of the parties to an agreement may sue on the agreement. Their practical enforcement and effectiveness is therefore self-evidently significant, and it has been accorded considerable attention in the literature, sui generis[195] or as it features in broader considerations of international contract law.[196] The practice of the English courts, including the foundations thereof, has been put through thorough-going criticism complete with suggestions for improvement along these lines with attention to the public interest in the effect to be accorded to them.[197]

Enforcement of this type of clause by an English forum is akin to the position in arbitration practice and law[198] in that it of course depends first on their validity, and then their scope (i.e., respectively, their enforceability and effect), applying the governing law of the contract[199] or mandatory forum law. The general principle as was espoused by Brandon J. in *The Eleftheria*[200] will presently be discussed below, and it can be noted that these clauses are often enforced rather than disapplied, even historically.[201] A clause of the type in consideration can either nominate an exclusive forum or give otherwise absent jurisdiction to a forum without aiming to bar process in other competent fora. In either case, it makes not much difference that the clause stands alone or is part of a contract.

[194] Cf. Orders 10 r. 3, 11 r. 1(1)(d)(iv) *RSC*; art. 17 *Brussels Convention*; see generally, *Dicey and Morris*, *op. cit.*, at 419 *et seq.* (Rule 32).

[195] A selection of leading commentary includes the following: L. Collins *et al.* (eds.), *op. cit.*, 421; O. Kahn-Freund, "Jurisdiction Agreements: Some Reflections" (1977) 26 *ICLQ* 825; A. Briggs, "Jurisdiction Clauses and Judicial Attitudes" (1993) 109 *LQR* 382; A.S. Bell, "Jurisdiction and Arbitration Agreements in Transnational Contracts" (1996) 10 *JCL* 97. Further afield, see, e.g., J.M. Perillo, "Selected Forum Agreements in Western Europe" (1964) 13 *AJCL* 162; Z. Cowen and D. Mendes da Costa, "The Contractual Forum: A Comparative Study" (1965) 43 *Can Bar Rev* 453; A. Bissett-Johnson, "The Efficacy of Choice of Jurisdiction Clauses in International Contracts in English and Australian Law" (1970) 19 *ICLQ* 541; M. Pryles, "Comparative Aspects of Prorogation and Arbitration Agreements" (1976) 25 *ICLQ* 543, and M.F. Sturley, "*Strengthening the Presumption of Validity for Choice of Forum Clauses*" (1992) 23 *JMLC* 131.

[196] E.g., F.A. Mann, "Statutes and the Conflict of Laws" (1972–1973) 46 *BYBIL* 117; A.J.E. Jaffey, "Offer and Acceptance and Related Questions in the English Conflict of Laws" (1975) 24 *ICLQ* 603; A. Briggs, "The Formation of International Contracts" [1990] *LMCLQ*. 192.

[197] E.g., E. Peel, "Exclusive Jurisdiction Agreements: Purity and Pragmatism in the Conflict of Laws" [1998] *LMCLQ* 182. At 270, he adopts the distinction between procedural and substantive fairness (deprecated by Atiyah in *Essays*, *op. cit.*, at 329) simply "as a convenient way of considering the possible application of a general doctrine of unconscionability to foreign jurisdiction clauses" (compaere Collins on fairness, above). Public interest mainly features at 221–224.

[198] Cf. *Dicey & Morris*, *op. cit.*, Rule 57 (at 573 *et seq.*). Arbitration clauses are discussed below.

[199] Cf. Kahn-Freund, *loc. cit.*, at 827–836.

[200] [1970] P. 94, at 99–100.

[201] Cf. *Gienar* v. *Meyer* [1796] 2 H Bl 603; *Austrian Lloyd S.S. Co.* v. *Gresham Life Assurance Society Ltd.* [1903] 1 KB 249.

In *Continental Bank N.A.* v. *Aekos Companhia Naviera S.A.*, the classical English legal position was stated in broad terms that "it would be a surrender to formalism to require the jurisdiction clause to provide in express terms that the chosen court is to be the exclusive forum".[202] In *Baghlaf Al Safer Factory Co.* v. *Pakistan National Shipping Company*, a moderately characteristic want of ethical transparency in jurisdiction disputes was identified but distinguished from "a reason for depriving a party of a negotiating advantage which accrues...as a result of a contractual agreement as to jurisdiction".[203]

Jurisdiction clauses in transnational contract-making can either choose the English forum or a different forum. Aware that it matters little that an exclusive clause might effectively oust an otherwise competent forum's jurisdiction,[204] one is unlikely to find a better measure of the position which English law applies to these clauses than as it is rendered in the foregoing dicta. One might add that "a level of sanctity of obligation which is singularly lacking in applications for a stay"[205] etc. further characterizes English jurisdiction.

The importance of these clauses is further underlined by the inter-connectedness of choice of forum and choice of law, the one more often than not following the other.[206] And the incidence of other contract-derived factors (e.g., canons of construction; exemption clauses; parties' intentions and consequently their legitimate expectations; particular clause-enforcing relief such as automatic or discretionary stays) is likewise to be underscored. About foreign jurisdiction clauses in particular, it is said that "by far the most interesting dimension...is the need to balance the purity of contract theory, under which the parties should be held to their agreement, with the pragmatism of international litigation, which acknowledges that the exercise of the civil courts' jurisdiction does not represent a purely private interest to be left to the redistributive will of the parties";[207] i.e., whether and how parties' autonomy in relation to and as is manifest in these clauses is controlled by the forum.

Brussels and *Lugano Conventions* cases, i.e. where at least one party is domiciled in a Member State

Choice of forum problems in EU cases have of course been largely settled by the *Brussels Convention* (as amended and supplemented) which need not be surveyed in any detail in the present discussion, except to emphasize Article 17 as being in point, and to draw attention to the relative structural, if not the commensurably substantive, fluidity of cross-border enforcement in these

[202] [1994] 2 All ER 540, at 544 (per Steyn L.J.); the commentary of J.G. Collier (*All England Reports 1994 Annual Review* (London, Butterworths; 1995), 83–87), principally to the effect that the case was wrongly decided along with many other English cases, deserves to be recorded.

[203] *The Times Law Reports*, December 17th, 1997 (per Phillips L.J.); see the present writer's, "Proper Jurisdiction and the *Pakistan National Shipping* Case" (1999) Vol. 14 *Amicus Curiae* 13–15.

[204] Cf. *Compagnie des Messageries Maritimes* v. *Wilson* [1954] 94 CLR 577, 587–588 (Fullagar J.)

[205] Peel, *loc. cit.*, at 200.

[206] *The Komninos S* [1991] 1 Ll Rep 370.

[207] Peel, *loc. cit.*, at 182 (in his abstract).

cases. Article 17(1) provides that there is neither a discretionary nor a mandatory[208] basis—other than jurisdiction conferred by Articles 16 or 18—for the seised forum to decline jurisdiction if the parties have agreed to sue only in the named forum. The general effect of Article 17 is that these clauses are enforceable if post-breach reliance on them is by a party who ought reasonably to be allowed the reliance, such as an employee under an employment contract.[209]

In non-Convention cases,[210] the localizing principles discussed immediately below apply in English courts.

National law — The *Eleftheria*-type Principles

These are, put briefly, to do with the discretionary nature of the enforcement of a jurisdiction clause by means of an injunctive stay of proceedings, the discretion not to award a stay being exercized only where there is a compelling reason not to do so in consideration of all things, and with the burden being on the claimant. Apart from the fundamental conceptual and functional difference, which does account for the extent of separation in the considerations to determine the availability of these clauses on the one hand and whether the forum is conveniens on the other respectively, there is little that is otherwise apparent to distinguish these principles thus condensed from those applied, for example by Lord Goff in the House of Lords in *Spiliada Maritime Corporation* v. *Cansulex Limited*[211] in finding as to the latter. As was stated by his Lordship, of the typical variably weighted (i.e. depending on the particular facts) relevant factors, some of the most important are these:

- — the location of evidence;[212]
- — the applicable substantive law;[213]
- — the respective parties' forum affiliations,[214] intentions,[215] and entitlements[216] in relation to the clause;
- — incidental provisions of the competing fora (e.g., the incidence of time bars[217]); the likelihood of multiple proceedings;[218]
- — fair trial.[219]

208 Cf. *Sanicentral* v. *Collin* [1979] ECR 3423.

209 Cf. R. Kidner, "Jurisdiction in European Contracts of Employment" (1998) 27 Industrial LJ 103, at 117–118; and para. 60 of the Jenard-Möller and para. 27 of the Cruz-Real Jenard Reports respectively at O.J. 1990 C-189/77 and O.J. 1990 C-189/47.

210 Cf. the Schlosser Report on the *Brussels Convention* [1990] O.J. C59, 124, para. 176.

211 [1987] AC 460, at 476.

212 E.g., in *The Adolf Warski* [1976] 2 Ll Rep 241. (concerning loss assessment surveys).

213 Ibid.; cf. Art. 3(1) *Rome Convention.*

214 See, generally, *Akai Pty.* v. *People's Insurance Co. Ltd.* [1997] CLC 1508 (regarding choice of a neutral (English) venue as being indicative of the irrelevance of this factor); compare *The Fehmarn* [1958] 1 WLR 159, and *DSV Silo und Verwattungsgesellschaft mbH* v. *Sennar (The Sennar)* [1985] 2 All ER 104.

215 E.g., in *Trendtex Trading Corporation* v. *Crédit Suisse* [1980] 3 All ER 721, at 735 (per Goff J.)

216 Cf. *The Havhelt* [1993] 1 Ll Rep 523, at 524–525.

217 The *Pakistan National Shipping* case, above, at n. 203.

218 E.g., in *The El Amria* [1981] 2 Ll Rep 119, at 128.

219 Cf. Brandon LJ in *The El Amria* [1981] 2 Ll Rep 119, at 126.

And as was the case with the doctrine of forum non conveniens, foreign jurisdiction clauses, rather than forum jurisdiction clauses wherein absent a defendant's objection "the submission of the defendant through his appearance is in itself a sufficient basis of jurisdiction",[220] had previously been the main source of intractableness for the English forum. That difficulty stemmed from the differences of effect between prorogation and derogation, on the one hand, and on the other, between forum and foreign court selection; not so much so in non-exclusive clauses or those which exclude an otherwise competent forum.[221]

A brief note about arbitration agreements before the courts

Under Section 1 *Arbitration Act 1996* which repeals all previous statutes on arbitration—save Part 11 of the eponymous Act of 1950 dealing with "*Enforcement of Certain Foreign Awards*"—the courts are required, regardless of any apparently sufficing discretionary inclinations and in the absence of restricted appeal to them from an arbitration, to stay proceedings in favour of a valid arbitration clause or agreement, "subject only to such safeguards as are necessary in the public interest" as is recognized in the same Section of the Act. Similarly now removed is the old flexibility by which the courts can stay numerous related arbitrations in favour of joined or consolidated court actions. In any case, the issues are of how the particular clause is to be interpreted as to its scope—a matter governed by the lex contractus[222] subject to mandatory forum rules and public policy in point—and its effects in general which appear convincingly in the absence of precise authority to be settled by reference to the lex fori.

Agreed payments clauses

Liquidated sums other than penalty clauses (*or agreed measures of true contractual compensation pursuant to breach, e.g., unpaid but due amounts*).

In English law, these are awarded in an action for an agreed sum, like the different actions for price provided for in Part IV of the *Sale of Goods Act 1979* against a buyer either to whom property in goods has passed pursuant to a contract of sale but who has either not timeously paid for the goods or in cases where payment for rather than delivery of the (unappropriated) goods is essential. *Judicial Statistics (Annual Report) 1991*[223] confirms that the action for price is the most widely-brought claim in English courts. Order 6 rule 2(1)(b) *R.S.C.* classifies the formats for the recovery of a contractually stipulated amount as being either a debt or a liquidated claim and, according to dicta in

[220] Kahn-Freund, *loc. cit.*, at 826. [221] Kahn-Freund, *loc. cit.*, 827 (ff. 12).

[222] *Hoerter* v. *Hanover Caoutchouc, Gutta Percha & Telegraph Works* [1893] 10 TLR 103; *Egon Oldendorff* v *Libera Corporation* [1996] 1 Ll Rep 380. The latter illustrates the same choice of law in choice-of-arbitration agreements; cf. S. 9 *1996 Act*.

[223] Cmnd. Paper No. 1990.

Beswick,[224] these formats might instead of an unliquidated claim avail a promisee acting in a third party's beneficial interest. Quite apart from an unpaid price for goods is the action on a debt owed. Either depends on the lex contractus for the determination of the obligation to pay.

For the purpose of just and effective enforcement of the obligation, the forum's fictional ascription of a situs to a debt or other chose in action[225] (usually the debtor's residence[226] "with or without the extra criterion of the place of enforcement or payment")[227]—after the fashion of a concrete ascription of the same to tangibles—has been strenuously argued to be illogical, unnecessary and misleading.[228]

Commentary runs that even though the situs rule is likewise variably applied to speciality debts (as in *R* v. *Williams*)[229], to bearer securities and to letters of credit (as in *Power Curber* v. *National Bank of Kuwait*),[230] its derivation from internal law—where choice of law does not arise—is faulty; that in conflicts cases in which the situs operates as the connecting factor in the choice-of-law rule,[231] it needs be noted that a situs moves with the debtor, that the situs does not reflect the incidence and function of the proper law of the debt obligation and, consequently, that that proper law is to be preferred to the situs law because the former is equally commercially certain, is the law to govern the debtor's contractual obligations and is consistent with internationally widely accepted principles. Surely the simple solution is neither to go so far as an extremely unlikely but attractively dubbed "proper law of a debt" nor to seek to differentiate debts so as to assail the use of the lex situs. The solution is to differentiate the law of the place of payment from the generally applicable lex contractus, because the actual payment aspects of international obligations are of themselves unavoidably subject to the law of the place of payment rather than to the proper law or lex contractus.

Mann's phrase, an "illustration of a form of action ruling an important problem of modern commercial law from its grave",[232] in a related context, could

[224] At 58, 81, 88, and 97 (please refer to the appropriate portions of the Civil Procedure Rules) . But see *Cleaver* v. *Mutual Reserve Fund Life Association* [1892] 1 QB 147.

[225] See, e.g., *Kwok* v. *Estate Duty Commissioners* [1988] 1 WLR 1035 (Privy Council); *D.S.T.* v. *Shell International Petroleum Co. Ltd.* [1990] AC 295.

[226] E.g., as in *New York Life Insurance Co.* v. *Public Trustee* [1924] 2 Ch 101; *Deutsche Bank und Disconto Gesellschaft* v. *Banque des Marchands de Moscou*, unreported Court of Appeal decision (Romer L.J.), December 14th 1931 (cited in *Re Banque des Marchands de Moscou (Koupetschesky) (No. 2)* [1954] 1 WLR 1108, at 1115–1116).

[227] P.J. Rogerson, "The Situs of Debts in the Conflict of Laws- Illogical, Unnecessary and Misleading" (1990) 49 *CLJ* 441, at 457.

[228] Ibid., in particular at 453–460.

[229] [1942] AC 541, at 555–556 (that by having a certain tangibility from its documented nature, such a debt is deemed situated where the document is found).

[230] [1981] 1 WLR 1233; cf. n. 16, above (Bennett) and, in relation to the principle of autonomy, *Edward Owen Engineering Ltd.* v. *Barclays Bank International Ltd.* [1978] QB 159, at 171 (per Lord Denning MR, in reference to analogy between letters of credit and performance bonds stipulating payment).

[231] Cf. Ord. 49 *RSC* (garnishment of debts), *Interpool Ltd.* v. *Galani* [1988] KB 738 and *D.S.T.* v. *Shell International Petroleum Co. Ltd.* [1990] AC 295, at 343.

[232] "Specific Performance of Foreign Money Obligations" (1968) 31 *MLR* 342.

not be more incisive of the present topic. There are two inter-related main types of issue that can arise the solutions of which are not necessarily to be regarded as inflexibly clear either from the decisions or from cases involving a non-forum lex causae which provides rather differently from the internal law: the first is whether or how to differentiate the action for an agreed sum from liquidated damages and, perhaps more consequentially, from penalty clauses which "normally be considerably in excess of the loss actually suffered";[233] the second is the enforceability of an agreed sum where a duty to mitigate runs with a defendant's almost invariably anticipatory rescission of the underlying contract.[234]

In the contexts of foreign (and comparative) law, matters of conceptualization are not necessarily helped by the fact that the term "penalty clause" in its varied forms[235] is applicable to the particular English law actions, as well as to a clause properly so-called in English law as is separately discussed below. The difficulty is greater where the clause in question is imprecise as to the breach situation(s) it covers, as to whether (and how far) "a performance other than the payment of a sum of money is intended to be included".[236] The fact that they require the performance of the contractual obligation to pay, that they are contractually provided for, explains much of the current law.

In the leading domestic law case of *White and Carter (Councils) Ltd.* v. *McGregor*,[237] the House of Lords narrowly sustained the parties' agreement on price, in consideration of the claimants' prompt rejection of the defendants' repudiation, interestingly as was held in reverse in the much-earlier New York Court of Appeals decision in *Clark* v. *Marsiglia*[238] in which a repudiation-rejecting claimant could conscionably get compensation and not price only because he had acted with the defendant to complete his contracted obligation to restore the latter's valuable painting.[239]

The case is to be distinguished from situations in which a claimant has unreasonably rejected repudiation and wrongly discountenanced compensatory damages, has acted wholly independently of the other contractual party. Such were the differing circumstances in the demise charterparty case of *Attica Sea Carriers* v. *Ferrostaal*[240] where the charterers' repudiation was not met with the owners' acceptance of the former's repair and redelivery of the vessel. Needless to say, the owners thereby disentitled themselves to keeping the contract live, and therefore to the agreed sums from hire. One commentator has had the

233 Treitel, *op. cit.*, at 229 (see also p. 180 for the difference between them).

234 See Burrows, *op. cit.*, at 317–331, generally, a part-comparativist critique.

235 Cf. Treitel. *op. cit.*, at 208 *et seq*.

236 Treitel, *op. cit.*, 209.

237 [1962] AC 413; followed in *Anglo-African Shipping Co. of New York* v. *J. Mortner Ltd.* [1962] 1 Ll Rep 81, and by Kerr J. in *The Odenfeld* [1978] 2 Ll Rep 357.

238 1 Denio 317 (1845).

239 See Treitel, *op. cit.*, at 127.

240 [1976] 1 Ll Rep 250; see also *Clea Shipping Corporation* v. *Bulk Oil International Ltd.* [1984] 1 All ER 129 (a High Court (Lloyd J.) appeal from arbitration) which emphasizes the point at which repudiation ought to, rather than could, be accepted by the claimant.

perspicacity, rightly, it is submitted, to profile the doctrine of election of the relief properly claimable in these circumstances where repudiation must be taken into account.[241]

For the sake of precision, it is just as well to differentiate as to the class of clause which, in order to draw comparisons and contrasts between systems, Treitel loosely referred to as "a stipulation providing for the payment of a fixed amount of money by the debtor in the event of his default".[242] Put differently, what is or is not an enforceable agreed sum?

Consider agreed sums which fall due pursuant to the contract, without breach: e.g., reimbursement provisions; insurance policy payments; a conditional sale or hire purchase payment. The reality is that non-payment or non-performance is usually treated as the material breach that it is. The practical effect of this is that the issue of enforceability depends, as it does with liquidated damages clauses, on those principles applicable to the estimation of a claimant's consequential loss, lest equity "grant[s] relief to a man who breaks his contract but will penalise the man who keeps it".[243] The deprecable penalizing attribute, which would bring about unenforceability of such clauses, is displaced or refuted by the relevance of loss liquidation as the criterion for judicial enforcement. If a clause at issue is valid as a liquidated damages clause, then and only then is it enforceable: *Export Credits Guarantee Department* v. *Universal Oil Products Company*.[244]

Accordingly, clauses limiting or accelerating[245] liability, penal bonds, post-default provisions (even though they may be construed as part of the original contract or agreement), and forfeiture clauses and the like set out below, being judicially unmodifiable liquidated sums clauses, are different from unenforceable penalty clauses.[246] This is in part because they do not let contract parties oppressively punish one another, are not contrary to public policy, nor are they illegal or illegitimate stipulations even though they are likely to form a separate secondary (remedial) obligation to a valid breach-based primary fault. In *Clydebank Engineering Co.* v. *Don Jose Ramos Yzquierdo y Castaneda*,[247] a builder's excessive promise to pay £1 million if he did not perform a task valued at only £50 was held to be too unreasonable, in the huge discrepancy between loss and compensation, to be enforced.

[241] E. Tabachnik, "Anticipatory Breach of Contract" [1972] CLP 149 (e.g., at 159, 162, 164–172); see also A.L. Goodhart, "Measure of Damages When a Contract is Repudiated" (1962) 78 *LQR* 263, *inter alia* on the control which a contract party must be taken to unilaterally exercize over performance and relief.

[242] *Op. cit.*, at 208.

[243] Lord Denning in the domestic case of *Bridge* v. *Campbell Discount Co. Ltd.* [1962] AC 600, at 629; see also the Law Commission Working Paper No. 61, "Penalty Clauses and Forfeiture of Monies Paid" (1975), para. 26 (reform proposals).

[244] [1983] 2 All ER 205 (H.L.)

[245] Cf. *Wadham Stringer Finance Ltd.* v. *Meaney* [1981] 1 WLR 39, at 48.

[246] Cf. Treitel, *op. cit.*, 228–223.

[247] [1906] AC 6; see also, *Dunlop Pneumatic Tyre Co. Ltd.* v. *New Garage and Motor Co. Ltd.* [1915] AC 79, at 86–88 (the facts involved payments due on speculative loss, so that the clause was not construable as a genuine pre-estimate of loss that would arise from breach).

Treitel summed up the quality of the Common Law on these clauses, presumably as they fare in hard cases, in terms that the rules manifest in the foregoing discussion:

> "[a]chieve neither the certainty of the principle of literal enforcement, since there is always some doubt as to the category into which the clause will fall, nor the flexibility of the principle of enforcement subject to reduction, since there is no judicial power of reduction . . . The chief danger is to "home-made" clauses which may be invalidated even though they are not intrinsically unfair".[248]

His cautionary note will now be explained by scrutinizing penalty clauses properly so-called, forfeiture clauses, and terms which consensually limit one or the other party's liability for losses incurred mostly in the event of breach.

Unenforceable penalty clauses

The status of punishment in the private law of remedies, national or transnational, was first encountered in Chapter Seven of this book. Two fairly recent noteworthy cases on agreed sums clauses shed light on the current position.

The first is the Privy Council decision (Lord Woolf M.R. presiding) in *Philips Hong Kong Limited* v. *Attorney-General of Hong Kong*,[249] in which the drafting requirements of a complex road-building contract—complex inter alia because of difficulty of realistically meeting the enforcement requirement that all conceivable losses be higher than or equal to the agreed sum—turned out significantly to be normal validatory factors, more so when the actual loss was marginally greater than the contracted sum. A few years earlier, in *Jobson* v. *Johnson*,[250] and in respect therein of a football club share acquisition contract clause stipulating the retransfer of shares at an over-rated premium in the event of default of instalmental payments, Dillon L.J. elucidated the principle that "a transaction must be as objectionable and unconscionable in the eyes of equity if it requires a transfer of property by way of penalty on default in paying money as if it requires a payment of an extra, or excessive, sum of money".[251] Because the vendors' assignee, the claimant, sought specific performance of the agreement rather than allowed the defaulting defendant to retain the shares and meet the actual losses incurred by the vendors, the court's solution was to have him elect between the remedy sought plus due compensation on the one hand and, on the other, the sale of the shares by court order with necessary deductions for losses.

The thorny problems arising then are whether penalty clauses deserve to be upheld in those unusual cases where, for example:

— the loss ends up exceeding the agreed penalty sum such as in *Wall* v. *Rederiaktiebolaget Luggude*[252] where by-passing the lower limit of a penalty

[248] *Op. cit.*, at 233. [249] [1993] 61 BLR 41, especially at 59.

[250] First cited at n. 4, above. [251] Ibid., at 628.

[252] [1915] 3 KB 66; in neither domestic case of *Cellulose Acetate Silk Co. Ltd.* v. *Widnes Foundry Ltd.* ([1933] AC 20) nor *Robophone Facilities Ltd.* v. *Blank* ([1966] 1 WLR 1428, at 1446) was the

clause so as to claim the larger true loss was permitted; or

— the losses recovered by way of the clause included mitigated loss;[253] or

— the clause is a downward limitation of liability and thus construable really as an underestimated liquidated damages clause, like the demurrage clause in *Société d'Armament Maritime SA* v. *Rotterdamsche Kolen Centrale NV*.[254]

These issues firmly embedded in doctrinaire laissez faire[255] are far from easy to resolve, especially in conflicts cases where the lex causae is favourable to the penalty[256] but the lex fori policy is not. Best advice would be that a claimant sues in the courts of the proper law of the agreement, not simply because the law is familiar to the forum but also because, by analogy from present limited application of "the Article 10(1) gloss", that law will likely apply exclusively for reasons of convenience and forum (public) policy.

Deposit and part-payment forfeiture clauses[257]

Deposits are different from part payments in that the former, being "a guarantee that the contract shall be performed",[258] is repayable in the event of payee default unless the contract provides contrariwise or retention would be in the nature of a penalty. The latter, however, may serve as payment for part performance so that if it has been promised but not been paid (and the payor has not terminated the contract)[259] the payee is entitled to it as the best way of being restored to the pre-contract position. Treitel maintained though that "[t]he distinction between claiming a penalty and suing for a deposit which has not been paid is one that is wholly lacking in substance".[260] In either type of clause, the payee's non-performance or breach must of course attract liability in damages, to include any such sums already handed over. In all cases, the forum

question of enforcement of the penalty clause categorically dismissed respectively by the House of Lords or by Diplock L.J. The Canadian Supreme Court decision of *Elsley* v. *JG Collins Insurance Agencies Ltd.* [1978] 83 DLR (3d) 1 went one better, at 14–15, to uphold the penalty clause in those circumstances, because it was adjudged substantively and procedurally fair to have done so.

[253] Cf. *Robophone Facilities*, above.

[254] [1967] 1 AC 361, at 421 (per Lord Upjohn).

[255] Cf. T. Downes, "Rethinking Penalty Clauses" in P. Birks (ed.), *Wrongs and Remedies in the Twenty-First Century* (Oxford, Clarendon; 1996), 249–269, especially at 262–265. Also, at 271–299 of the same edition, see M. Chen-Wishart, "Controlling the Power to Agree Damages", especially between 282–298.

[256] Examples are rife. A small selection includes, e.g., German *Bürgerliches Gesetzbüch* Paras. 339, 340, 342 (but not 344, where the primary fault is null) and *HGB* Para. 348 (cf. BGH March 24th 1954, NJW 1954, 998); the French *astreinte* (cf. J. Carbonnier, *Code civil* (10th ed., Dalloz (1979)), Vol. IV (*Les obligations*), at 291), *Code Commerciale* Arts. 1227 and 1230 (the *mise en demeure*), 1152 (the penalty as a species of damages) and 1231 (making mandatory penalties non-derogable, thus over-riding Cass. civ. 4 June 1860, D.P. 1860.1.257); provided that the defendant is liable, e.g., Cour d'appel Paris 1 Feb. 1936, DH 1936, 242.

[257] For a good study, see J.W. Bridge, *Breach of Contract* (2nd ed., Sydney, Law Book Co.; 1991), paras. 1059 *et seq.*

[258] *Howe* v. *Smith* [1884] 27 ChD 89, at 95.

[259] *McDonald* v. *Denys Lascelles Ltd.* [1933] 48 CLR 457; approved in *Johnson* v. *Agnew* (396).

[260] *Op. cit.*, at 242.

must of course have jurisdiction, whether it be statutorily (e.g., under Section 146(2) *Law of Property Act 1925* in cases of forfeiture in accordance with a lease contract rather than because of non-payment of rent;[261] or Sections 90, 92 and 132 *Consumer Credit Act 1974*) or inherently (i.e., in equity) conferred.

In *Pye* v. *British Automobile Commercial Syndicate Limited*,[262] a deposit forfeiture clause was upheld on the basis that the payor's default was not readily pre-determinable. But it is to be noted that a vendor (not a service provider to be paid pro rata) may be entitled to enforce forfeiture clauses if the buyer defaults. Thus, what would otherwise be a penalty clause is in fact enforceable. Indeed, invalidating principles in the case of penalties are applied to forfeiture clauses, for example, in India,[263] the rationale in either case being the undue pressure exercized on the defaulter.

In both Common and Civil Law systems, the basis on which a part payment or deposit is made is central to the question of whether the payee's right to forfeiture is to be countenanced by the courts. The bases vary from evidencing the conclusion of or giving security for the given agreement—Paragraph 357 (2) of the American Law Institute's *Restatement of the Law of Contracts 1932* calls it "earnest money"[264]—to reserving the right of withdrawal by forfeiture. But, having surmounted the defining issue of the reason for payment when clarity and precision in the parties' terms make it possible to do so, the solutions of the consequences sometimes greatly differ, especially in connexion with deposits. In some leges causae, the deposit gives the payor a somewhat stronger, but hardly commercially viable, position which is withheld in others. In other systems, rules on deposits are sometimes complicated enough to be virtually indistinguishable from those applicable to penalties. Therefore, if the *lex* contractus' rules applied in an English case do not of themselves assist the resolution of the enforceability of such a clause, it is not unlikely that forum law will be given effect.

A certain amount of expansionism in the courts' attitude towards relief against forfeiture clauses, away from land contract cases where they typically feature, was discerned and tested in a relatively recent academic paper.[265] Starting from penalty clauses and their enforceable alternatives, e.g., extended periods for payment or the reinstatement of the contractual subject matter, its commentator later identified the relevant judicial policies[266] as to these clauses:

[261] Cf. *Ladup Ltd.* v. *Williams and Glyn's Bank Plc.* [1985] 1 WLR 851; *Official Custodian for Charities* v. *Parway Estates Developments Ltd.* [1985] Ch 151.

[262] [1906] 1 KB 425.

[263] *Fateh Chand* v. *Balkistan Dass* AIR 1963 SC 1405.

[264] Cf. The French *Code Civile* Art. 1590 (*arrhes*, which founds an alternative contract obligation).

[265] M. Pawlowski, "The Scope of Equity's Jurisdiction to Relieve against Forfeiture of Interests in Property other than Land" [1994] *JBL* 372.

[266] Ibid., at 375–376; as was stated, e.g., in *AS Awilco of Oslo* v. *Fulvia SpA Di Navigazione of Cagliari, The Chikuma* [1981] 1 WLR 314, at 321–322 and, previously, in *China National Foreign Transportation Corporation* v. *Eulogia Shipping Co SA, The Mihalis Xilas* [1978] 2 Ll Rep 397, at 409.

the respective parties' mutually stipulated self-protection, and certainty of transaction. Having reviewed inter alia Lord Simon's apparent pro-expansion dicta in *Mardorf Peach & Company Limited* v. *Attica Sea Carriers Corporation of Liberia, The Laconia*,[267] concerning the scope of a time charterparty forfeiture clause to secure payment of contract sums and his Lordship's scepticism about disapplying the equitable jurisdiction to grant relief against forfeiture, and those of Lloyd J. in *Afovos Shipping Company SA* v. *R. Pagnan & F.lli, The Afovos*,[268] the commentator settled for the House of Lords in *Scandinavian Trading Tanker Co. AB* v. *Flota Petrolera Ecuatoriana, The Scraptrade*:[269] that the enduring legal position is that because, e.g., a time charterparty is a contract for services (i.e., neither a commercial nor a proprietary contract), it is neither autonomously derogable from by the parties nor, consequently, capable of being specifically enforceable.

In the end, the equitable intervention to relieve against forfeiture in the event of breach boils down to a reasonably finite set of factors, viz.:

— Lord Wilberforce's "special heads" of fraud, accident, surprise or mistake, in *Shiloh Spinners Limited* v. *Harding*,[270] whenever the contract aims for a performable effective obligation through enforcement of the forfeiture clause;
— the conscionable party seeking the relief must be adequately (i.e., protectably) interested, not so much in the forfeiture but, in the contractual subject matter: e.g., risk loss of a restorable proprietary or possessory interest rather than a personal (or service) one[271] such as is had in equity by a purchaser of land;
— the agreement can be a commercial contract involving, e.g., the assignment of (proprietary) patent rights as in *B.I.C.C. Plc.* v. *Burndy Corporation*,[272] land contracts,[273] or any agreement in which aggrieved party cannot be compensated for the other party's default, and in which the aggrieved's right to terminate or discharge performance of the agreement has not been exercized;
— the practicability of the jurisdiction to relieve.

Delivery clauses

A contract can tacitly provide, for example, that the basic promises exchanged between the parties is premised on certain other perfectionary requirements of

[267] [1977] 1 All ER 545 (H.L.), at 554.

[268] [1980] 2 Ll Rep 469.

[269] [1983] 2 All ER 763; followed in *Sport International Bussum BV* v. *Inter-Footwear Ltd.* [1984] 2 All ER 321 (regarding an accelerated performance clause), and in the dicta of Dillon LJ in *BICC Ltd.* v. *Burndy Corporation and Another* [1985] 1 All ER 417, at 427.

[270] [1973] AC 691, at 723.

[271] Cf. the *Scandinavian Trading Tanker Co.* case, above, nn. 53 and 269.

[272] Above, n. 269.

[273] See, e.g., the Privy Council decision in *Kilmer* v. *British Columbia Orchard Lands Ltd.* [1913] AC 319 and, latterly, in *Union Eagle* (n. 13, above).

one or the other party. A good example is in a contract for the sale of land, which implicitly requires the vendor to convey both land and title thereto. Another is an international loan transaction wherein the financing aspects involve the securitization or collateralization of the subject matter, the loan. Some of the performance relief aspects of this type of transaction were previously encountered in explaining forum jurisdictional competence in cases where the defendant or (and) the subject matter are outside its territorial range.

If, for instance, the provider of security is allowed to retain and to register a proprietorial interest pending discharge of the taker's secured contractual obligation (e.g., an equity of redemption in the case of a mortgage or charge), the taker's default absent an outright transfer may cause the taker to seek enforcement of its security interest, e.g., by means of a sale of the securities by court order. The default does not negate the formation ceteris paribus of a valid contract which gives the parties (in particular the taker) rights in personam[274]—particularly as to the clause at issue—which are enforceable as between the parties or as against third parties.

It makes good sense that the issue of delivery of an encumbrance-free personal interest is subject to the law of the place where delivery is formally to be effected. However, it seems clear enough from the cases that the complexity and fluidity of these cross-border transactions have not necessarily always been commensurately responded to in the conflict of laws especially on the issue of how the matters arising are characterized by the forum or by a cognate jurisdiction: e.g., the jurisdiction of the situs of enforcement of the collateral or of the registered interest;[275] the jurisdiction of insolvency (as an important eventuality); the jurisdiction of the lex contractus.

The object of course is to facilitate a sufficiently clear, precise and serviceable forum order for performance of the clause. The task can be enormous, for example, in the case of transactions involving registered securities mostly where the characterization of the question which arises for the forum is different from that of its enforcement mechanism obtaining in the other jurisdiction.[276]

The exercise is palpably lighter in less complicated transactions, like those which are clear enough to require a party to simply deliver goods as agreed. It is noteworthy that in contracts for the disposition of a landed interest, bar undue delay in making a claim, the normal relief is specific enforcement of the conveyance. As with the less palmate situations just discussed, the lex contractus determines the issue of obligation to deliver in accordance with the clause in breach, while the law of enforcement resolves the actual fulfilment of the coerced obligation. Because enforced performance is almost certain to take place later than it should have done if the contract or clause had not been breached, it may be necessary for the forum to supplement its order, e.g., with further directions as can where necessary accompany a wider order for specific performance.

[274] The present Chapter is of course concerned not with proprietary relief.

[275] Benjamin, *loc. cit.*, at 20.

[276] Cf. *Dicey & Morris*, *op. cit.*, at 931 (Rule 114(5)).

A little colour is added to the foregoing by the concept of substitute performance which, in the Civil Law (e.g., Article 1142 French *Code Civile*), applies to contracts for generic goods or, in the Common Law, to contracts which inter alia, e.g., require the repair of premises. Other situations include the delivery up of possession of an expired tenancy or of sold property however described. The circumstances of course determine the possibilities of a precisely tailored order which is typically followed by a post-judgment writ of delivery under Order 45 rules 4, 5 and 12 *R.S.C.* which authorizes the sheriff to distrain the defendant's real and personal property until delivery of the subject matter, or the less commonplace writ of assistance to put the successful claimant in possession of the goods.

CONCLUSION

There are quite a few unresolved imponderables, primarily but not exclusively arising from courts' practices. They stem from the general legal policy and method from which the theory of foreign suit derives, from the differences of scope of jurisdiction and merits, or a lacuna in the law to be identified in the conceptualization of the roles of the lex contractus and the lex fori respectively in the availability of specific performance of transnational contracts.[277] Leges causae can provide differently from forum law, may or may not be compatible with forum forms or rationalizations and post-judgment enforcement of awards of enforced performance relief. The question is whether applicable remedial law depends more on the lex causae than it is to be governed by forum law, and it is often a blurred line between entrenched forum attitudes on the one hand, e.g. toward penalty clauses, derived from internal law and, on the other, public policy or interest in the enforcement of like obligations. Litigants frequently and not unwisely play safe by avoiding inordinate or unprecedented innovation in the interpretation and representation of their legal interests before the courts.

Yet it is quintessential private international law that forum and applied substantive laws need not be sourced in the same legal system so that, in a difficult case, conflicts doctrine and practice would revert to the usual pragmatic solution: that litigational dispute resolution be pursued in competent courts which have the procedures to deliver the parties' precise legitimate expectations. The so-called "Article 10(1) gloss" from the *Rome Convention* appears more often than not to promise what respective national courts seem, for whatever reasons, reluctant to deliver: co-ordination of substance with procedure, where necessary and possible, in parties' interests-optimizing terms, terms which are neither so abstract as to suggest that the promise in the gloss is impracticable (in the sense of not being easily implemented) nor untenable especially in light of the existing cross-border facility afforded by transnational Conventions.

The contemporary progression from choice-of-law conflicts to choice-of-

[277] Cf., nn. 26 and 29, above.

jurisdiction ones therefore seems, in the present context at least, to be a little inequable in the sense that, consequently, the harmonizing provision of exceptions to express or implied governing law in choice-of-law conflicts is taken to satisfactorily dispose of substantive law issues as well as provide a sufficient basis thence for focusing on the inferrably less wieldy jurisdictional aspects. While this of itself does not mean that these jurisdiction aspects cannot meaningfully be contended with in much the same breadth as is substantivist harmony (itself eminently different from unification), it does mean that an uninhibited study of international legal obligations and remedies resounds in the pre-eminence of jurisdiction and procedure or, further significantly, in the very real limitations (over-localization) that can arise therefrom. There is no quick fix, nor perhaps should there necessarily be one. There is a long way to go for the dedicated harmonizationist, and recourse to the lawyer's art of the comparativist and the analogue is not more relevant.

If the present Chapter has clearly described the "hows" and the "whethers" of securing performance relief in the English forum in conflicts cases, then it should, it is respectfully submitted, have done as much as may be expected of it by having indicated areas requiring renewed deep concept-broadening or redefining consideration, or the real limits of conflicts law and legal process. Simple solutions to conflicts problems arising in the quest for enforced performance relief have presented themselves as being responsive to a conceptual constant which makes accessible the legal data or criteria which indicate the scope and the conditions for it in English courts.

It cannot be gainsaid that remedial (correctivist or redistributive) performance of transnational contracts can exert considerable pressure on the analytical parameters provided by internal law on the particular remedy sought and by the transnational circumstances themselves. Indeed, a subscriber to question-begging economic analysis of law and to the theory of efficient breach—for whom (agreed) performance relief is for several compelling reasons (e.g., so-called parties' voluntary "bilateral monopolies") nearly always to be preferred to substitutional relief—might add that whenever the cross-border legal relationship or transaction costs between the parties (e.g., to terminate a contract; to compensate the aggrieved party; to make alternative arrangements) are low enough to make damages insufficient (and when performance is possible), then performance should be ordered. That argument is strengthened by the fact, as expressed by Fuller and Purdue in explaining compensatory damages and the range of contractual interests,[278] that the legally protectable expectation interest flows from, rather than causes, legal intervention and, as such, the protection is at once curative and preventive of breach-of-contract expectation losses and that, economically speaking, it encourages and systemically furthers principled reliance on commercial agreements without the requirement that such reliance be proved or otherwise made topical to the context.

[278] "The Reliance Interest in Contract Damages" [1936] 46 *Yale LJ* 52, at 57 *et seq*.

10

Remedial restitution

FORUM PERSPECTIVES ON LOCALIZING RESTITUTION

RESTITUTION REFERS TO the way(s) in which the law brings about the redirection of the one party's indefensible gains accruing from either that party's wrongdoing or from another party's expense, where the yielding up is in fact possible. According to this broad principle which is opposed mostly to unjustifiable enrichment,[1] an action for restitution is restrictively aimed to undo and (or) reverse enrichment which, as a legal matter, should not be allowed to remain where it has fallen. Strictly speaking, the private law of restitution is corrective, neither punitive nor operating in anticipation of enrichment as criminal, property or tort laws may do in appropriate circumstances. As will be discussed in this present Chapter, it comprises personal as well as proprietary relief, and it can be properly granted with other different remedies where necessary. In discussing so-called restitutionary damages in Chapter Seven of this book, some elements of the prevailing twinned concepts of enrichment and restitution were broached, as was the terminological coincidence of literal restitution, in the broad sense of legal restoration, e.g. in the law of compensatory damages, in emphasizing claimant loss which is central to those but not to the present[2] remedies.

This background section of the present Chapter consists in discussion of the late-comer terms of restitution law in England wherein the topic undergoes principled and effective conceptualization, analysis and accommodation in the legal system. Remedial restitution in its substantive and formal contexts is a matter best approached in the terms of "restitutionary right" and co-ordinate "recovery". In view of the potential relevance and applicability of non-forum restitution law to a given enrichment-based action, comparativist viewpoints of the function of remedial formalism in enrichment cases constitute further themes which assist the exposition of the topic. The remaining main sections of the

[1] See, e.g., Lord Goff of Chieveley and G. Jones, *The Law of Restitution* (5th ed., London, Sweet & Maxwell; 1998), at 3–5; American Law Institute, *Restatement of the Law of Restitution* (St. Paul, Minnesota, A.L.I. Publ.; 1937), para. 1; *Bürgerliches Gesetzbuch* (*BGB*), e.g., at Para. 812. The term, "unjustifiable enrichment", in place of "unjust enrichment", after F.H. Lawson, *Remedies of English Law* (2nd ed. (with H. Teff), London, Butterworths; 1980), at 139, is deployed in this Chapter whenever feasible.

[2] Cf., e.g., Slade J. in *English* v. *Dedham Vale Properties Ltd.* [1978] 1 WLR 93, at 112; see also M. McInnes, "At the Plaintiff's Expense: Quantifying Restitutionary Relief" [1998] *CLJ* 472, especially at 473–477.

Chapter then take up the actual restitutionary remedies, having had regard to the procedural requirements especially from jurisdiction and characterization.

In general terms, it is clear from contemporary decisions and scholarly literature in point that there are limits to the settled cogency of the subject in action, which limits arise from its relative inchoacy particularly as it obtains in the conflict of laws. The Chapter elaborates the essential characteristics and ramifications of the subject matter with a view to presenting the reader with a diet of the topic's contemporary theoretical and practical aspects. The main contribution of what follows lies in its emphasis on claimants' accessibility to the relief in transnational situations. It is in the nature of contemporary legally characterized human discourse that restitution is increasingly one of the most availing but less conclusively rationalized types of judicial relief especially in private international law.[3] Needless to say, what follows in the nature of English law rules on restitution directly applies especially where the lex causae is forum law or where a foreign forum's conflicts rules may require that forum to apply English law. Significant public law aspects of restitution, such as were acknowledged by the European Court of Justice in *Amministrazione delle Finanze dello Stato* v. *San Giorgio*,[4] necessarily do not quite belong in this book.

The importance and development of remedial restitution law.

The relatively late development of restitution law in English (conflicts) law[5] can be explained as the result of factors the general bearing of which is summarized in the present subsection, aware that "[r]estitution [if not 'unjust enrichment'] has always been part of the common law."[6] Until late on in the present century, the topic of this Chapter was taken to form part of the law of quasi- or implied contract. In *Sinclair* v. *Brougham*,[7] ultra vires borrowing by a company in liquidation was held to be inappropriate to found a claim for restitutionary recovery of the sums because the loan contract was void. The reality is of course that quasi-contract is but part, albeit a substantial one, of the scope of restitution as has since been recognized in the leading authoritative texts[8] on the internal law dimensions. However, the relevant chapter in the leading classical treatise on

[3] See F.D. Rose (ed.), *Restitution and the Conflict of Laws* (Oxford, Mansfield; 1995), at viii.

[4] Case 199/82 [1983] ECR 3595 (Part V), e.g., at 3627, for Advocate-General Mancini's Opinion (referred to in *Woolwich Equitable Building Society* v. *Inland Revenue Commissioners* [1991) 2 AC 548).

[5] Cf. T.W. Bennett, "Choice of Law Rules in Claims of Unjust Enrichment" (1990) 39 *ICLQ* 136, at 137 (ff. 12, 13).

[6] S. Hedley, "Unjust Enrichment" [1995] CLJ 578. The insertion in the above rendition of Hedley's opening sentence is in keeping with the general tenor of his argument: that theoretical conceptions of "unjust enrichment" have "gone too far", "have so far proved detrimental", "fail[ed] the test [of solving] the problems it addresses", that "the judiciary have so far shown little awareness of it" (at 578–579), indeed that the future of "unjust enrichment theorists...looks grim" (at 599).

[7] [1914] AC 398. See also, Goff and Jones, *op. cit.*, at 5 *et seq.*; P. Birks, *Introduction to the Law of Restitution* (Rev. repr., Oxford, Clarendon; 1994), at pp. 29-39; Bennett, loc. cit., at 140–141; S.J. Stoljar, *The Law of Quasi-Contract* (Sydney, Law Book Co.; 1964), at 1.

[8] Cf. Goff and Jones, *op. cit.*, at 4–5; Birks, *op. cit.*, e.g., at 263.

English conflict of laws, which cannot be criticized for its incisive treatment of the substantive subject, retains the title "Restitution or Quasi-Contract."[9]

Quasi-contract theory was set aside by the House of Lords in *Fibrosa Spolka Akcyjna* v. *Fairbairn Lawson Combe Barbour*,[10] concerning a transnational contract, frustrated by war conditions, which was subject to forum law on the basis that relevant and arguably applicable Polish law was not pleaded. In securing the recovery of the price paid under the contract, it was adjudged to be unnecessary to imply the continued existence of the contract. In much more recent conflicts litigation in *Westdeutsche Landesbank* v. *Islington London Borough Council*,[11] Lord Browne-Wilkinson reiterated that *Sinclair* v. *Brougham* was over-ruled on the point of justification being based on implied contract theory. However, it is very much the notable case that early derivations from the theory produced some of the most enduring remedial forms: recovery based on a quantum meruit or on a quantum valebat, mostly in actions based on the claimant's provision of goods or services which have not been paid for. These forms are an important part of the Chapter's focus.

As Lawson had observed, "particular [restitutionary] rights and wrongs and their attendant remedies are so intertwined that the remedies cannot be understood or described without substantive law."[12] Consequently, it obtains on eminent and persisting text-book authority that "until a generalised right of restitution is firmly recognized, attention [is] concentrated on the substantive grounds of recovery."[13] Substantive restitution clarifyingly pervades the rationalization of the topic in English law in and outside the courts[14] and continues to do so, but at some cost to remedial restitution.[15]

From several points of view, this comparably less attention paid to the remedies themselves has further been due to "history, linguistic preconception, or exaggerated concern about the effect which a remedial emphasis is liable to have upon the integrity and discipline of judicial reasoning."[16] The positive upshot is that it is bound to become less heretical that restitution can properly be considered without the need for the "remedial" prefix which, for a ready example, accompanies the title of the present Chapter. It might be said that the pervasive terminology is all that justifies the title of the Chapter in keeping with

[9] L. Collins *et al.* (eds.), *Dicey and Morris on the Conflict of Laws* (12th ed., London, Sweet & Maxwell; 1993), Chapter thirty-four, at 1471 *et seq.*

[10] [1943] AC 32; but see *Guinness plc* v. *Saunders* [1990] 2 WLR 324, at 331 (per Lord Templeman).

[11] [1996] AC 669, at 710.

[12] *Op. cit.*, at 139.

[13] Goff and Jones, *op. cit* (3rd ed; 1986), at 57. The fourth edition of the work (1993), at 70, expresses much the same view thus: "[F]or reasons [of importunity of a remedy-based classification of restitutionary claims] already explained, attention must still be concentrated on the substantive grounds for recovery".

[14] See, generally, Rose (ed.), *op. cit.*; cf. the present writer's "Global Law and Policy: A Review Article" [1998] 10 *AJICL* 390, at 391–392.

[15] Cf. P. Birks, *Restitution- The Future* (London, Federation Press; 1992), at 1, 25.

[16] K. Barker "Rescuing Remedialism in Unjust Enrichment Law: Why Remedies are Right" [1998] *CLJ* 301, at 303.

the familiar vein in which its content is typically dealt with in the literature, that restitution and the enrichment which generally founds it coexist as perhaps a contractual relationship, or a tort situation, is necessarily cognate to an award of, say, compensatory damages.[17]

Substantially unaddressed but, it is submitted, elemental considerations like the foregoing have produced accurate comment that "the subject [of unjustifiable enrichment] was officially born in 1991"[18] in England when the House of Lords adjudicated on the justifiability of enrichment in the particularized terms of the substantive defence therein of bona fide change of position as to money had and received in the wholly domestic law case of *Lipkin Gorman (a Firm)* v. *Karpnale Limited*.[19] Applying *Fibrosa* so as to overcome implied contract rationalizations, their Lordships held that money stolen from its true owner, a firm of solicitors, which total sum was fairly and honestly received by a gambling club, was recoverable in equity by the true owner, albeit not as equity's darling since honour only, rather than valuable consideration, had moved from the thus enriched gambling club. The respondent club's position had altered to such an extent as would make an order for full disgorgement unfair, because of the risk involved in computing the recoverable sum in view of the accretion from other bets in the hands of the recipient.[20] In other words, it was not factually possible to sustain such an order to reverse as against the club. An action for compensatory damages for conversion would be the correct relief.

The foregoing is self-evidently insufficient to suggest that enrichment (or any other apposite cause) and restitution are so disparate that the one can be usefully discussed without the other. The idea would be futile or simply not conducive, because of the way in which current law is preponderantly substantive. All the same, the sharp-set significance of the respective concepts is a matter of considerable practical attraction as, for example, is accentuated by the conceptual and remedial varices, e.g. in dealing with monies erroneously paid, in the better resolved law of obligations comprising contract and tort.

[17] The present writer's "Law in the Global Village" [1996] 8 *AJICL* 1031, at 1034. See also G. Virgo, "What is the Law of Restitution About?", Chapter twenty of W. Cornish, R. Nolan, J. O'Sullivan and G. Virgo (eds.), *Restitution- Past, Present & Future: Essays in Honour of G. Jones* (Oxford, Hart; 1998) 305, at 307:

> "If we are asked what the law of restitution is actually about there is only one matter of which we can be certain, namely that the law of restitution concerns the award of restitutionary remedies...More technically, the essence of the law of restitution is that in enables a plaintiff to be restored to the position which he or she occupied before the occurrence of a particular event...[W]hat these events are...is a matter for other areas of the law...Since the law of restitution is only about remedies, the analysis of the subject needs to focus on two particular issues, namely the type of restitutionary remedy which is available and the function of these remedies."

[18] Barker, *loc. cit.*, at 311.

[19] [1991] 2 AC 548, especially at 577–583 (per Lord Goff). See A. Burrows, "Restitution: Where Do We Go From Here?" in M.D.A. Freeman (ed.), *Law and Opinion at the End of the Twentieth Century (Volume 50, Current Legal Problems)* (Oxford, Clarendon; 1997) 95, at 111.

[20] *Loc. cit.*, above, Lord Goff; see also, P. Birks, "The English Recognition of Unjust Enrichment" [1991] *LMCLQ* 473, at 487–490.

Restitution is apt to be attractive alternative relief in the right conditions, as it already often is.

Its conceptual autonomy, from as early on as *Moses* v. *Macferlan*,[21] and its differentiated supplementary, rectifying or correctivist functions in the structure of the private law of obligations and remedies are increasingly recognized as being central to its practical scope. This reconceptualization perhaps began in the wake of Lord Diplock's refutation of any general restitutional doctrine of English law in *Orakpo* v. *Manson Investments Limited*,[22] a good few decades after the older cases which were derived the common law action of indebitatus assumpsit (literally, an undertaking arising from indebtedness) were first overruled by their Lordships in *Fibrosa*.

All the same, courts' practice and academic literature go some way to affirm that a relief-dedicated pragmatistic emphasis, analysis and orientation is worthwhile, even in a book about conflicts remedies wherein the particular relief can, at its present developing best, be but assumed. The benchmark for its proper exposition must go beyond indicating the application of the basic forms of relief in private international fact-situations, mindful that "the law on this topic is both fragmentary and uncertain."[23] Further conflicts-specific limits are imposed by these and other equally fundamental questions, such as those of jurisdiction and characterization in claims originating, for example, from non-forum substantive law. An encouraging measure of reassurance—this is all it can be in further consideration of conceptual overlaps with, e.g., property law[24] where, for example, corporate securities are the subject matter—is forthcoming from the deterministic accommodation provided by the forum's localizing matrix. As the case law will demonstrate in due course of this Chapter, it is increasingly the case that these and other uncertainties are being favourably resolved.

The remainder of the Chapter makes clear that although remedial restitution, especially in the conflict of laws, must necessarily proceed step by step, there is much to anticipate in the development and rationalization of this very important area of the law of remedies. An operable basic presumption of similarity in the comparative law,[25] at least insofar as the different legal systems in view are

[21] [1760] 2 Burr 1005; see also *Exall* v. *Partridge* [1799] 8 TR 308 (1799), on the action for the recovery of money paid, which is widely used today, e.g., in *Kleinwort Benson Ltd.* v. *Glasgow City Council* [1997] 4 All ER 641. At the time of *Moses* v *Macferlan*, the causal aspects derived from implied promise or quasi-contract provided little technical support for an exercise in identifying its rational and justificatory basis.

[22] [1978] AC 95.

[23] Lawson, *op. cit.*, at 139.

[24] See, e.g., J. Bird, "Restitution's Uncertain Progress- Macmillan *v.* Bishopsgate" [1995] *LMCLQ* 308, on intersections with the law of property that can arise; see also, Virgo, *loc. cit.*, at 312–318.

[25] See, e.g., generally and respectively, J. Blaikie, "Unjust Enrichment in the Conflict of Laws" [1984] *JR* 112; Bennett, *loc. cit.*, n. 5, above; B. Dickson, "Unjust Enrichment Claims: A Comparative Overview" [1995] 54 *CLJ* 100. Important less contemporary writing includes H. Gutteridge and K. Lipstein, "Conflicts of Law in Matters of Unjustifiable Enrichment" [1941] 7 *CLJ* 80, and A. Ehrenzweig, "Restitution in the Conflict of Laws" [1961] 36 *NYULR* 1298. The volume of commentary is a good deal more substantial.

all to a greater or lesser degree derived from the old Roman law *condictiones* (or actions for the recovery of debt) for property and money claims, will assist the process of rationalizing or harmonizing recognizedly disparate laws for transnational adjudication. Indeed, it is a matter of modest remedialist interest perhaps that the old *condictiones* involved no deterministic consideration of underlying substantivist causae.[26] Comparativist perspectives are themselves discussed in the course of the Chapter.

The pre-requirements for localization: jurisdiction, characterization and procedure.

It was previously stated that restitution and contract share historical pedigree and antecedents so much so that not only do the questions arising continue to do so in concurrent liability terms, which made it necessary in *Westdeutsche Landesbank* to over-rule *Sinclair* anew, they are still rationally linked in such cases.[27] Actions for restitution continue to arise, though not at all exclusively, from contract situations. Substantive law considerations of the "proper law" type have a telling role in restoring wealth transferred under void or ineffective contracts, in distinguishing contractual restitutionary interests with or without the incidence of breach.[28] Choice of law does not necessarily point to the solution of questions of jurisdiction other than by reference to the mutuality of practical convenience that often but not always subsists between the respective—choice-of-law and jurisdiction—concepts, the latter necessarily to be had in order for claims to be remedially or otherwise determined.

So it was that on the important fundamental issue of proper jurisdiction, the House of Lords held, in *Kleinwort Benson Limited* v. *Glasgow City Council*,[29] that a restitution claim, for money paid under a void contract, is ordinarily outside the narrower "contract" or "tort" scopes of Article 5(1) and 5(3) of the *Brussels Convention*'s exceptions to the defendant's forum *domicilii* rule contained in Article 2. It is noteworthy that Lord Goff was reluctant to exclude restitution claims altogether from the scope of Article 5, thus allowing for the application of the Article's provisions in restitutionary circumstances, e.g., involving concurrent liability under a valid and enforceable contract for which the promisee's consideration has totally failed[30] (under Article 5(1)) or from a tort (Article 5(3)), and in which the forum is conveniens.

[26] Cf. R. Zimmermann, "A Road Through the Enrichment-Forest? Experiences with a General Enrichment Action" (1985) 18 *Comp & Intl L of SA* 1, at 4–6.

[27] See, e.g., P. Brereton, "Restitution and Contract" in Rose (ed.), *op. cit.*, at 142–179 (especially between 143–148).

[28] For compelling explanations directly in point, see J. Bird, "Choice of Law and Restitution of Benefits Conferred Under A Void Contract: Baring Brothers & Co. Ltd. *v.* Cunninghame District Council" [1997] *LMCLQ* 182.

[29] Above, n. 21: Lord Goff (at 644–654), Lords Clyde and Hutton; Lords Mustill and Nicholls dissenting. See A. Burrows, *The Law of Restitution* (London, Butterworths; 1993), 487–490, M. Hales, (1999) 19 *Amicus Curiae* 15.

[30] See, e.g., P. Key, "Restitution, Void Contracts and Jurisdiction under Article 5 of the Brussels Convention" in the International Bar Association's *International Litigation News* (London, July 1998 ed.) 38, at 40.

Furthermore, it is important to the present point that Britain entered reservation to the scope of application of Article 10(1)(e) of the *Rome Convention on the Law Applicable to Contractual Obligations 1980*, because it was considered preferable to relate the consequences of nullification of a contract to restitution, and not to contract in the way that the particular provision does. This importantly implies that an applicable non-forum law of enrichment might conceivably not be directly relevant to the matter of restitutionary relief available in the English forum; that is, remedial restitution is perfectly capable of being independently considered away from the characteristically substantive vein in which it features in the bulk of contemporary literature.

In furtherance of these jurisdictional considerations, it is important to note that caution, which is material to the subject matter of the present Chapter, has been convincingly sounded in a number of works on enrichment conflicts, on the importunity of avoiding a misconceptualization of the law in this area in terms that preponderantly relate its content to "procedure".[31] If this is not heeded, further errors of treating restitution conflicts as though they were wholly local are bound to arise. Some of these errors were identified by Briggs[32] in noting the decision in *Arab Monetary Fund* v. *Hashim*,[33] in which the substantive issues with which this Chapter is not primarily concerned, were wholly referred to local law at some cost to the requirements of applying relevant, pleaded and argued, non-forum law. Thus, by analogy from avoiding over-localization more generally, the forum's treatment of the remedial issues which concern book and Chapter, as was brought to the fore in *Baring Brothers & Company Limited* v. *Cunninghame District Council*[34] in which the term "proper law of a restitutionary remedy" was used,[35] it is the case that a via media between these respective terminologically polar points of view—the one emphasizing internal law, the other heavily relying on the lex causae which may not be forum law—is to be preferred, mindful that it is in the nature of contemporary English restitution conflicts law that commentative speculation is fleeter in the offing given the relative sparsity of cases on the issues.

On the different issue of characterization, for example, of restitution of payments mistakenly made under a foreign lex causae, the Law Commission had recommended[36] inter alia the reformatory substantive policy that proof

[31] See, e.g., C.M.V. Clarkson and J. Hill, *Jaffey on the Conflict of Laws* (London, Butterworths; 1997), 275–276; Bennett, *loc. cit.*, 144, that by characterizing these issues as procedural, the lex fori would improperly thus be exclusively applicable.

[32] A. Briggs, "The International Dimension to Claims for Contribution" [1995] *LMCLQ* 437.

[33] [1994] TLR 502.

[34] [1996] TLR 538.

[35] Thus suggesting the correctness of applying choice-of-law technique to matters of forum relief. See the present writer's, "*About a 'Proper Law of a (Restitutionary) Remedy'*" [1998] *Denning LJ* 85, and Chapters Five and Six of this book.

[36] *Restitution of Payments Made Under A Mistake of Law*, Consultation Paper No. 120 (London, HMSO; 1991), para. 2.16 (see also paras. 3.5. and, especially, 5.2); see also Lord Goff, "The Search for Principle" [1983] 59 *Proc Br Acad* 169, at176–177. In the domestic case *Kleinwort Benson Ltd.* v. *Lincoln City Council* (*The Independent* newspaper, November 4th, 1998), the House of Lords (Lords Browne-Wilkinson, Goff, Lloyd, Hoffmann, and Hope) repealed the rule by which money paid under a mistake of law was irrecoverable in restitution.

of the relevant law, as fact and according to which law the restitutionary right is to be established, ought not to suffice to allow recovery which would be withheld if similar circumstances wholly governed by internal law arose. It therefore appears that characterization is at present apt to be ampler in such cases in its unreformed favourability to a party relying on non-forum law. This is not necessarily typical English conflict of laws in several respects, not least in the sense that it inordinately appears to predispose the forum to claims arising in the globalized shape of things personal and (or) commercial. The so-called homeward trend in the more general conflicts approach of the English forum is thereby presented in a relatively unprecedented, liberalized, light. However, it is not necessarily clear whether, for example, forum policies (e.g., as to public interest-dictated defences) are to be brought to bear on claims otherwise regulated by non-forum law as a matter of course in the localization of such claims.

In the absence of decided authority, it is submitted that an individual case approach which rests on the type and strength of connexion with the forum (thus, a matter of jurisdictional propriety) will contend to be the underlying theme, imbued with the levelling consideration that parties before an English forum will more likely seek to rely on properly adapted internal enrichment and restitution law, for reasons of practical convenience. More is presently said of cognate issues and probable scenarios in succeeding subsections, particularly in considering issues from enrichment and ensuing rights on the one hand and, on the other, restitutionary recovery, with much to emphasize the good influence of comparativism in closing the present general survey of dimensions of localization, and introducing succeeding discussion of restitutionary claims and orders.

Some further features of consequence to restitutional process deserve beforehand to be identified and, to a limited extent, discussed. In the first place, a direct function of what is to be the governing law of the substantive claim is to be found in the parties' statements of cause (pleadings). In other words, if forum substantive law is intended or likely to apply, as more often than not will be the case if the present jurisdictional rules are to be adhered to or are to remain unrecast, then the existing under-utilization of internal procedural law rules on pleading, coupled with the all-important matter of foreign law as fact, about which Fentiman[37] has queryingly advanced several general telling practical and theoretical points of criticism, would need to be complied with. Alike, Bennett identified the narrower but extremely relevant point that "[w]here enrichment remedies are supplementary in nature it is also quite likely that the possibility of pleading them is overlooked or ignored",[38] as they must be in the current shape of things.

[37] *Foreign Law in English Courts: Pleading, Proof and Choice of Law* (Oxford, Clarendon; 1998), at 6–11; see also Virgo, *loc. cit.*, at 319.

[38] *Loc. cit.*, at 139; cf. P. Hay, "Unjust Enrichment in the Conflict of Laws: A Comparative Overview of German Law and the American Restatement 2d" 2 (1978) 6 *AmJCompL* 3, at 41.

A point also partly dealt with in parties' initial representations concerns the necessary demarcation between those mainly proprietary (in the sense of their interlocutory operation ad rem: e.g., tracing orders at law or in equity as may be necessary) judicial orders to assist the identification and location of what is to be disgorged, by whom and how, thereby facilitating, where necessary, the existing variety of dispositive restitution. In order to avoid repeating what has been discussed elsewhere in this book, it is sufficient to say that the formal commencement of in personam proceedings for restitutionary relief is not different from the procedures to be complied with in cases of breach of contract or tort, applying the *Civil Procedure Rules*. To these points of procedure might be added the incidence of substantive (following the *Foreign Limitation Periods Act 1984*) considerations of limitation. Some of these were mentioned in Dickson's commentary[39] in the context of comparative law and, more directly, by Burrows.[40] The crucial substantive issue of there being an enforceable right to restitution could thus not be better crystallized to take the present description to the next Section.

In closing the present subsection, it is useful to outline some of the most frequently advanced bases of claims for restitutionary relief. They lie in claims in the wake of a failed, discharged, frustrated or illegal contract, as was stated earlier in discussing the progress of an independent jurisdictional foundation for restitution actions. They can also arise from actions for breach of trust, from tort actions in which the right to sue for compensation is waived, from subrogated claims, from criminal gains, and even from unsolicited gains. For the sake of the Chapter's focus on the remedial aspects of restitution law, it is by and large to be assumed that defences[41] to these claims, such as a change of parties' position, bona fide purchase, illegality, estoppel, incapacity, the doctrines of election and res judicata, and the incidence of prescription rules, can respectively operate to deny entitlement to the relief. Considerations deriving from these and other points of substance, for example, policy or (and) public interest, invariably turn up in the course of the next section.

[39] "Unjust Enrichment Claims: A Comparative Overview" [1995] *CLJ* 100, at 101. See also H.M. McLean, "Limitation of Actions in Restitution" [1989] *CLJ* 472, in which it is said that a comprehensive limitation policy is required in English restitution law, that the issue be regulated by the public interest in protecting the security of defendants from stale litigation, especially in proceedings which depend on neither the date of receipt of the value transferred nor on the date on which the restitutionary factor is known to the claimant.

[40] (1993) 143 NLJ 480, at 481.

[41] Cf. P. Birks, *Introduction to the Law of Restitution* (Rev. repr., Oxford, Clarendon; 1994), Chapter XII generally; also W. Swadling (ed.), *The Limits of Restitutionary Claims: A Comparative Analysis* (London, BIICL/UKNCCL; 1997) as to these defences, and payments made under mistake of law, as the interpretive limits to the accretion of the fundamental right to restitution; also, Dickson, *loc. cit.*, at 105–108. For a superb rejection of a possible defence of passing on by the claimant in restitution law, see F.D. Rose, "Passing On" in P. Birks (ed.), *Laundering and Tracing* (Oxford, Clarendon; 1995), Chapter ten, at 261–287. Virgo, *loc. cit.* (320–326) defends his remedy (as opposed to enrichment) by a justified appraisal of change of position, the enrichment being the correct basis for bona fide purchase and limitation.

The active "restitutionary interest" or "right to recover"

Although it is persuasively argued that comparative internal and conflicts laws widely diverge[42] as to their aims, their scopes and levels of operation and development, and as to their underlying policies, it is the present writer's view that the divergence is not quite as unforgiving of pragmatistic rationalization as one might thus be otherwise inclined to think. Indeed, attractive as a black letter statement of the applicable choice of law rule in these cases might be, as may be found in German law for example,[43] to do so would nevertheless not necessarily lie beyond worthwhile analysis in terms that can make possible a useful differentiation of the remedial aspects which themselves flow from the forum's ascertainment of an enforceable right to restitution. Ascertaining the right itself is of the essence of the localizing or characterizing design of the forum's policy of entertaining cross-border actions of this, or indeed of any other, type of legal liability.

Not only are the comparativist differences neither necessarily always present nor insuperably pronounced, they also often have significant points of jurisprudential interest and of the facility of dispute resolution in their wake. The much-recognized head-start which Civil Law systems are considered to have, from their longer standing familiarity with and use of analogous enrichment and restitution law, can be taken to provide the needed reflexive emphases on enrichment and formal restitution, albeit that the Common Law's institutional rationalization of the topic is not formalized in terms identical to these, nor need it necessarily be.

Consider the example of restitution of gains on the basis of the general public interest to grant trustees remuneration for substantial (past) services which, were it to be withheld, would enrich the beneficiaries at some cost to the trustees. This was precisely the case in the domestic case of *Foster* v. *Spencer*.[44] It is not essentially different from, e.g., the German law ***abstraktionprinzip*** or principle of abstraction by which proprietary title and ownership can pass and, therefore, be reversable without reference to a contractual cause of action.

Similarly, restitution may be ordered on the back of the policy of encouraging the preservation of the property of others, as in *Re Berkeley Applegate (Investment Consultants) Limited*[45] in which confluence of a voluntarily liquidating

[42] Seminal comparativist discussions of contemporary relevance are to be found in works previously referred to in the Chapter, notably by Bennett and Dickson. Of some relevance to the broader practical policy framework is the comment of W.H. Reinicke in *Global Public Policy* (Washington DC, Brookings Institution; 1998), at 86: "[I]t will be necessary to demonstrate that the operational aspects of international sovereignty can indeed be decoupled from territoriality, its formal legal counterpart. One central challenge is the fact that what is and what is not in the collective or public interest differs across countries. Hence, for global public policy to be successful, not only would participating societies have to show a willingness to cooperate in the establishment of internal sovereignty; in practice they would have to recognize and accept others' definition of the public good."

[43] Bennett, *loc. cit.*, at 159–166.

[44] [1996] 2 All ER 672. See also, *Ministry of Health* v. *Simpson* [1951] AC 251; *Gray* v. *Richards Butler*, *The Times*, 23rd July 1996; *Hardoon* v. *Belilios* [1901] AC 118.

[45] [1988] 3 All ER 71.

trustee company's assets with those of the beneficiaries was held to be insufficient to deny the extraction of the liquidator's fees from the former. The practical effect of this finding is very similar to the conflicts forum acknowledging a Roman/Civil Law *negotiorum gestio*, or gain freely given,[46] as a basis for awarding restitution as is done, for example, in German conflict of laws.[47]

Substantial differences of doctrine must unavoidably persist in the face of possible parallels of functional[48] and dispositive similarity thus drawn. These facilitating conceptual similarities are strengthened by the fact that claims arising from non-forum law, as in *Batthyany* v. *Walford*,[49] are characterized by the forum's reference to the lex causae. In that case, an English tort-based claim for permissive waste of land in Austria and Hungary—thus the situs of enforcement of the decision reached—was brought by an English fiduciary of the deceased tenant for life. The forum's characterization in accordance with the then prevalent justificatory basis in implied contract, rather than in tort as was pleaded by the executor, was the best approach necessitated by the forum's justiciability of the cause. Therefore, it appears that the absence of a fixed rule is in fact a boon to equitable adjudication that must be responsive to widely varying fact situations that can arise in which proven extraterritorial enrichment is to be reversed by order of the English forum.

It has been succinctly rendered that the preferable general orientation for the law's progress is one which prioritizes "[t]he broad question *when* the law intervenes in private entitlements and *how* it intervenes",[50] on the basis that "[u]nderstanding the principles which regulate the choice of restitutionary forms plays a vital part in our understanding of the *nature* of restitutionary rights themselves".[51] The causes of action recognized in English law of restitution do not quite reflect, as perhaps they should, the criteria which the courts use to determine a claimant's entitlement, e.g., to proprietary as opposed to personal restitutionary relief.[52]

Perhaps the most frequently overlooked point of consequence in present respects is that unjustifiable enrichment does not exclusively provide the basis

[46] Cf. P. Birks and W. Swadling, "Restitution" in the *All England Law Reports Annual Review 1996* (London, Butterworths; 1997), at 385; also L. Collins *et al.*, (eds.), *op. cit.*, at 1473 and 1477.

[47] Cf. Bennett, *loc. cit.*, at 165–166.

[48] See M. Bogdan, *Comparative Law* (Tano, Kluwer Norstedt Juridik; 1994), 60: "[T]he compared legal rules and institutes must be comparable to each other *functionally*: they must be intended to deal with the same problem...[and] [i]t is not necessary that they also are intended to achieve the same goals", indeed that the pragmatistic comparison does "consequently not start out with the names of the legal rules and legal institutes."

[49] [1887] 36 Ch D 269.

[50] Barker, *loc. cit.*, at 323 (the inquiring emphases are from the article). Parallels are drawn at the same place with causes of action and appropriate relief in other areas of the law of obligations; e.g., culpability and compensation in tort law, injustice (or unjustifiability) and restitution in enrichment law.

[51] Ibid. (the emphasis is from Barker's work).

[52] Ibid., at 322, and previously at 310–318, that subordinating procedure to merits unnecessarily overstates the formalistic preconception by which a given remedy subsists independently of its underlying cause.

for a right to recover in restitution cases, that in their typical form and scope of application "for the purposes of the conflict of laws at least, enrichment deserves no separate category of its own".[53] This would be relevant, for example, to the preparation of a separate head of jurisdiction under (say) the *Brussels Convention.*

Accordingly, it is necessary to look to authoritative accounts of the sources of accrual of the right in English law as, for example, is set out in *Goff and Jones*:[54]

(a) from the claimant's mistaken, compelled, necessitated, or void transaction;
(b) from a third party in circumstances which oblige the recipient-defendant to account to the plaintiff for any gains made by the third party;
(c) from the defendant's own wrongdoing.

Thus, common denominators for the spectrum of restitutionary relief are several. When a party is correctly attributed with a restitutionary right in any given circumstances, the attribution is, generally, the law's secondary response to the enriched party's gains. Birks opined that "the generic conception of the event which triggers restitution adds nothing to the existing law and effects no change except what comes from better understanding of what there is already."[55] In the transnational context, "what there is already" perforce includes the facilitating adjudicatory method by which choice of law does not quite apply to procedural issues, other than in the formal requirement that forum law must clearly accommodate substantive rights originating elsewhere if those rights are to be enforced by the forum.

In seeking restitution, by itself or in plural interest claims, a claimant's merits—the demerits being the incidence of defences—are in the defendant's sufficiently serious autonomous receipt of reversable enrichment. As was stated at the outset, the former's loss, strictly speaking, if any is wholly immaterial to restitution itself. Herein lies the isolation of the recoverable interest which the claimant tabulates as restitution in the initiating process by accordingly indorsing the claim form (writ).

A good illustration derives from a purchaser's claim for repayment of an agreed sum either because the seller has not made sound delivery or because the defendant contracted in the unilateral knowledge that required performance was in fact impossible or illegal, that the supposed contract was void for want of true consideration from him. It is therefore not necessarily always so clear whether the interest at stake—separate, alternative or conflated—lies in loss-free reliance or in restitution, especially where actual loss may have arisen but is neither separately pleaded nor proved.[56]

[53] Bennett, *loc. cit.*, at 167.

[54] *Op. cit.*, Part II. See also A. Tettenborn, *Law of Restitution in England and Ireland* (2nd ed., London, Cavendish; 1996), at 33–36.

[55] *Op. cit (Introduction...)*, at 27.

[56] Cf. G.H. Treitel, *Remedies for Breach of Contract—A Comparative Account* (Oxford, Clarendon; 1987), at 83–84; see also, McInnes, *loc. cit.*, n. 2, above.

In *Cargill International S.A. and Another* v. *Bangladesh Sugar & Food Industries Corporation*,[57] the appropriate action could as well have been for restitutionary relief, with or without pleas from other interests. In that case, the Court of Appeal affirmed the recoverability of moneys implicitly paid to a party who had suffered no loss under a contractual performance bond in the event of breach and in the absence of contractual terms forbidding such recovery. There was a bond forfeiture clause in the carriage contract, as there also were clauses stipulating the essence of time within which to perform, and providing for the accretion of liquidated damages or termination if there was any delay in performance.

English law regards an obligational interest as restitutionary mostly in circumstances where the defendant has not clearly been deceptive or otherwise reprehensible in conduct. The celebrated Australian case of *McRae* v. *Commonwealth Disposals Commission*[58] contains classic dicta that in such circumstances, and where there is no proof of any other type of interest, the claimant is thereby disentitled to a restitutionary award in excess of money paid in furtherance of the legal relationship in question, that there is to be a separate item for recoverable loss (as injurious reliance) if this is proved. It is primarily on this rationalization that obligation-rescinding restitution, strictly speaking, is differentiated from, rather than be unclaimable with, obligation-enforcing damages. If other interests are to be recoverable, there can of course be necessary offsets between the restitutionary and such other interests, as was held in *Millar's Machinery Company Limited* v. *David Way & Son*.[59] Paragraph 344 of the American Law Institute's *Restatement Second of the Law of Contract*[60] also refers to "one or more of" these recognized interests. The solution clearly lies in avoiding a plea for complete restitution with full compensation.

Scots law provides in identical terms, as was recently illustrated by the Lord Hope's leading judgment in the House of Lords in *Dollar Land (Cumbernauld) Limited* v. *C.I.N. Properties Limited*,[61] emphasizing the reverse situation in which enrichment is justified, nevertheless assisting the definition of the particular interest. A landlord had removed an irritant tenant from possession, had assumed the latter party's substantial sub-rental income because that party had not paid rents due. Not only was the landlord thereby found to have been justi-

[57] [1998] 1 WLR 461 (noted by H. Brewer in [1998] ITLQ 247–248).

[58] (1950) 84 CLR 377, especially at 411.

[59] (1934) 40 Com Cas 204; see also the US cases of *Balon* v. *Hotel and Restaurant Supplies Inc.* [1967] 433 P 2d 661, and *Blumrosen* v. *Silver Frame Industries* (1952) 54 NW2d 712. In the latter case, the plaintiff recovered money paid to the defendants use, reliance costs, and expectation costs, the last of these being distinctively non-restitutional.

[60] (St. Paul, Minnesota, ALI Publ.; 1979). See also, paras. 345, 371, and 373.

[61] The Times Scots Law Report, August 17th, 1988 (Lords Jauncey, Browne-Wilkinson, Nolan and Hoffmann concurring); see also D.M. Walker *Civil Remedies* (Edinburgh, W. Green; 1974), at 806. On the point concerning contractual stipulation for restitution in the event of breach (it arises in due course of the paragraph in the main text above), see H. Beale, "Exceptional Measures of Damages in Contract" in P. Birks (ed.), *Wrongs and Remedies in the Twenty-First Century* (Oxford, Clarendon; 1996), 217, 244–245. See also P. Birks, "Inconsistency Between Compensation and Restitution" [1996] 112 *LQR* 375.

fiably enriched—indeed there was no contractually stipulated response to an enrichment claim—as would disentitle the tenant to restitution, it was held that uniform development of the law would be impeded if the available remedy was described as compensatory in anything but its general illiteral form, more so where the order sought was for the return of movable property by way of payment of a sum representing the value of the benefit received by the defender. More to the point, the agreement actually entitled the landlord to the enrichment, and to the termination of all rights and entitlements otherwise accruing to the tenant, by its stipulation of forfeiture in the circumstances such as arose.

The short point of principle is that the establishment of the recoverable restitutionary interest is inseparable from the quality of the enrichment in the sense that it must have been at the expense of the party seeking restitution. The transnational facts of *Dimskal Shipping Company S.A.* v. *International Shipping Workers Federation, The Evia Luck*[62] make clear that the obligation to restore does not run with party autonomy. The obligation was, in the particular case, imposed by operation of English, rather than foreign (Swedish), substantive law as the law of the place of enrichment.

In the absence of direct judicial authority, *Dicey and Morris* may be paraphrased to provide the formal remedial kernel in these respects:

> "[The proper law of the obligation to restore provides] the precise legal concept by which the obligation to restore the benefit is secured..., at least to the extent that the concept which obtains in the proper law is properly characterized [as a matter for English law as *lex fori*] as substantive[*]...[having] regard to the function which the concept serves in the context of the foreign legal system", that "the characterization is arrived at by considerations of practical convenience rather than by a simplistic distinction between 'right' and 'remedy'".[63]

This is the quintessence of the localization of the right itself, without which restitutionary relief cannot be granted. With the central restitutionary "right-remedy" issue[64] at least in sight, discussion of restitutionary remedies in conflicts cases can be begun with a descriptive statement of their nature and scope.

FORMAL ASPECTS OF RESTITUTIONARY RECOVERY

Preliminaries

Restitution can take any of a fairly straight-forward array of individual remedial forms. It was convincingly argued by Lord Millett (or Millett J., as he then was)—in the context of an article dealing with legal and equitable trac-

[62] [1991] 4 All ER 871 (Lords Keith, Templeman, Ackner, Goff and Lowry).

[63] *Op. cit.*, 1477–1478, citing *Chase Manhattan Bank N.A.* v. *Israel-British Bank (London) Ltd.* [1981] Ch 105, at 124, at the place asterisked in the main text above.

[64] For an excellent concise preview of these issues albeit in the limited context of proprietary, as opposed to personal, restitution, see R. Goode, "Property and Unjust Enrichment" in A. Burrows (ed.), *Essays in the Law of Restitution* (Oxford, Clarendon; 1991), 215, at 222–225.

ing, rather than in a judgment—on the forms of relief presently individuated in the present section, that "[a] unified and comprehensive restitutionary remedy is capable of being developed by recourse to traditional equitable principles and terminology",[65] that it is the abundance of Common Law and equitable principles which causes problems of recoverability and of concurrent obligational liability. These distinguished arguments are likely to assist the subjection of the forms in view to a more relevant modern rationalization as often is required, particularly in conflicts cases. More is presently said of this issue.

Restitutionary claims, to be distinguished from restitutionary remedies, e.g., because the former require the application of a connecting factor in settling forum jurisdiction and choice of law, inevitably overlap with claims subsisting in the general law of obligations, in trusts law or (and) in property law. Consequently, the taxonomy of restitutionary relief largely reflects the legal system's overall remedial scheme and classifications:

- the personal, the proprietary, the specific;
- issues of and from election from among different restitutionary and (or) other remedies; and
- the widely used actions for the restitution of money, as well as discretionary restitution.

Indeed, the types of remedial problem—e.g., the evaluation or assessment of restorable enrichment—presented to the courts and to restitution law and policy makers are manifest from the classification, as are those irresolute issues for litigants and commentators alike. Then there are the material judicial orders or measures, like those which provided a template for Lord Millett's comments, e.g. an award of the right to trace proceeds of fraudulent enrichment, the cumulative forte of which lies in their enabling the forum's resolution of a restitutionary cause.

The sheer diversity and availing qualities of restitution laws in comparative contexts, internal and transnational, is to be well-noted. As has been observed,[66] "the litigant who has a choice of legal systems might be advised to avoid bringing an enrichment claim in English law, for example, to select West German law instead", on the basis that German law has always accorded a much-deployed space of its own in its legal system to enrichment cases. Paragraphs 812 and 813 *et seq.* of the *Bürgerliches Gesetzbuch* (the Code dealing with civil obligations) provides for a prominent unified general enrichment action which may be identical to Lord Millett's recommendation referred to in the preceding subsection above. Similarly, the United States *Restatement* provides for a general but less unified response in its first paragraph, in contrast to the existing variety in comparable English restitution law.

[65] In "Tracing the Proceeds of Fraud" [1991] 107 *LQR* 71, at 85.
[66] Bennett, *loc. cit.*, at 139–140.

On the relevant rules and principles of current English law and practice, Beatson[67] points out that "[t]he intellectual foundations for the recognition by the courts of a generalized right to restitution are now secure and the courts are becoming increasingly confident about deploying the new category although they have not yet recognized a generalized right to restitution". To unify restitutionary relief or claims must better rationalize the part-legal, part-equitable enrichment principle. In light of these and further reaching complexities and differences between legal systems, localizing recourse to internal law, especially for the purposes of resolving a claim originating from that law, cannot be so difficult to pragmatically or rationally justify in contemporary conflicts cases. Conceptualized as the (un)justifiability of enrichment and the identification of the proper victim and the proper relief where appropriate, restitution in transnational private law has immense potential and function which can be brought to fruition if the causal and the procedural principles are co-ordinated.

The clear advantage in such recourse, for the purpose of optimizing the remedial competence of the restitution forum having a strong predilection for forms and procedures in the localizing design of its laws, is that existing forms of relief about which there is much less difficulty of practical dispensation than there is in the resolution of the substantive right to restitution, can conceivably contribute in a far-reaching way to the development of remedial restitution conflicts law, subject to careful separation or "enrichment", not "restitution", from the ambit of the pervading considerations from "procedure".

Although there are several alternative possible approaches to the determination of the substantive issues, such as are stated and discussed in *Dicey and Morris*,[68] and by Hay,[69] the real question which is to be addressed is whether, having established a right to restitution under the applied approach, the forum is equipped to proceed to grant restitutionary relief.

In general terms, once restitutionary claims arising from a legal relationship (e.g., a contract, in which case the proper law of the relationship applies as it was held to do in *Chase Manhattan Bank* v. *Israel-British Bank*[70] where there was conveniently little material difference between forum substantive law and that of New York State on the entitlement to trace payments made by mistake, based on the imposition of a constructive trust, with a view to their being recovered) howsoever arising have been properly established to the forum's satisfaction, from the point of view of the grant of relief, the given claim and the remedy sought should reflect one another.[71]

[67] In *The Use and Abuse of Unjust Enrichment: Essays on the Law of Restitution* (Oxford, Clarendon; 1991), at 19.

[68] *Loc. cit.*, Rule 201, at 1471; see also Burrows, *op. cit.* (*The Law of Restitution*), at 490 *et seq.* (especially 491–494, for compelling critique of *Dicey and Morris*, e.g., for having emphasized (a) the place of enrichment even where the gains have subtractively accrued (as opposed to where they are acquired by the defendants wrong), (b) relied so much on a centre-of-gravity theory).

[69] *Loc. cit.*, at 6–9.

[70] [1981] Ch 105 (per Goulding J.).

[71] Bennett, *loc. cit.*, at 159.

Therefore, if the forum's preference for a proper law approach to the obligation to restore is to be taken to its conclusion—wherein the applied substantive law would go further and would indicate the nature and extent of appropriate relief, especially in cases involving immovable property in which the lex situs rules' applicability is strongest[72]—then the result vindicates the categorization of restitution claims separately from contractual actions, the "Article 10(1) gloss" or any analogy from it is hard to justify in enrichment cases, without internationally co-ordinated civil procedure rules.

Nor, incidentally, does this assertion necessarily assist the case for a unified restitutionary remedy. Indeed, the existing variety of forms of restitutionary relief can be described in terms that no type of legal obligation in breach, be it contract or tort, is capable of being suitably redressed by reference to a monolithic remedy in the way that unified restitution, e.g., under German law is often presented to be capable of doing. It is of the utmost importance that even though, to use the example of German internal and conflicts law previously deployed in this subsection, a possible single remedy based on a diversity of methods of solving questions of substance which can conceivably arise may be found, it is as one should expect not the case that the unified relief takes the same form or content for all cases.

Burrows[73] points out the position in English law that, for procedural reasons by which restitutionary "remedies are applicable to different situations of unjust enrichment", "a single label is inappropriate". However, it is important to recognize, as Tettenborn does, that a unified right can streamline existing variations in the forum's recognition of the right,[74] especially considering further that "there is in this [characterizing or localizing] respect, nothing unusual about enrichment claims."[75] Characterization is always for the conflicts rules, to be distinguished from the internal law, of the forum.

Before classifying and elaborating on the remedies themselves, it is useful to be briefly re-appraised of the general nature of a claim for restitution, particularly as it coexists with other types of recoverable interest, especially in contract-related situations, albeit, as Birks put it, that "[t]he remedial part of restitution is not concerned at all with defining causes of action...[that it] raises large questions for the substantive law of wrongs, challenging the hegemony of compensation for loss and the old habit of dividing common law and equitable wrongs."[76]

[72] Cf. the decision of the Supreme Court of Canada in *Pettkus* v. *Becker* [1980] 117 DLR (3d) 257.

[73] *Loc. cit.* (n. 68, above), at 29–30 where he refers (in ff. 9 and 10) to the existing variety of forms of causes of action, to Ord. 29 rr. 11–12 *RSC* on interim payments which differentiate between damages and other claims in money, to S. 29(5)(a) *Limitation Act 1980* on the difference between acknowledgement of debts or liquidated claims and other claims, and to Ord. 6 r. (1)(b) *RSC* on the indorsement on a writ; see also the doctrinal reasons (from adversarialism, the present positivistic shape of restitution law, the centrality of enrichment) he gives from 54 for persisting without a generalized right.

[74] *Law of Restitution in England and Ireland* (London, Cavendish; 1996), para. 1–05 (at 5).

[75] Bennett, *loc. cit.*, at 145.

[76] *Restitution—The Future* (London, Federation; 1992), 25.

The point is that *Goff and Jones*'s standard "instinctual"[77] classification of the ways in which the substantive restitutionary right can be established under forum law is not necessarily intended by the distinguished authors to meet all the preparatory requirements of litigants who have joined issue or who are at the stage at which their knowledge and application of forum process in point is crucial. Their tripartite classification does not necessarily relate to, let alone settle, the pre-requisite issues of claimant entitlement to disgorgement nor, indeed, disgorgement itself.

The description is as much a presentation of basic substantive enrichment law as a remedies-based classification presents basic remedial restitution law. They must cohere in a way in which a work devoted to the one rather than the other is a fortiori miscast to deliver. This much explains the consolidating practical approach, of book and chapter, which accentuates judicial relief in a qualitative way. English restitution law is sufficiently different in form as well as in comparison with other restitution laws, such that it properly may not respond to substantive rights originating elsewhere.

General

The most frequently sought dispositive restitutionary remedy takes the form of a (substitutional) pecuniary judgment in personam, complete with fiscal considerations like interest, appropriate deductions, commercial rates and like considerations. Extra-judicial relief in the form of recaption of goods and rescission do not necessarily require judicial intervention. As was mentioned earlier, restitution is substitutional more so when it is awarded in the form of money, although this does not do away with the general coercive attribute which generally defines judicial orders. It is trite that restitution may be personal or (and) proprietary, the former responding to the value received by the defendant rather than to whether that party retains the property at issue as does the latter which, in addition, aims to restore retained property and give priority in the event of defendant's insolvency.

It is said that "[t]he bulk of the law of restitution is concerned with personal remedies."[78] It is not clear whether this statement is empirical or purely doctrinal. As will be seen, proprietary facilitative restitutionary relief, e.g. tracing (including the equitable lien) and subrogation respectively, are widely resorted to and legally imposed be it in Common Law or in equity. It is the diversity of justifications for the variety of forms that explains in part the previously broached debate about a unified restitutionary claim/remedy, fuelled by the concurrency of legal and equitable rationalizations the inconclusiveness of which has been described as "one of the great unfinished tasks"[79] of restitution law. Much is owed to the work of Birks[80] and to Burrows[81] by the present writer in describing the remedies. They are illustrated in the next subsection,

[77] Above, at n. 54. [78] Burrows, *op. cit.*, at 29. [79] Beatson, *op. cit.*, at 245.
[80] In the chapter "Techniques and Measures", *op. cit.* (*Introduction*).
[81] *Op. cit.* (*The Law*...), at 28–45.

beginning with the personal forms which, as Burrows[82] put it, comprise "restitution of value received". Indebted as the present writer is, in deploying this description, for the reasons, of avoiding the damages rules altogether (e.g., rules on causation, remoteness, mitigation, penalties), given at the appropriate place of the chapter of this book dealing with damages and other awards of money in personam, he would beg to differ from its alternative representation by its author in terms of "restitutionary damages"; indeed, Burrows separately itemizes restitutionary damages from the personal remedies, viz. the Common Law remedies (comprising money had and received to the claimant's use; money paid to the defendant's use; quantum meruit for services rendered; quantum valebat for goods) and the equitable remedies (an account of profits made; contract rescission).

Before individual description of the remedies, the essential issues of measure, which precede the issue of deployable form(s) from those set out above, need to be dealt with first. The question "how much?" itself follows the establishment of an actionable restitutionary right. Any of the Common Law forms of relief may be either liquidated or requiring assessment. Commonly, the core is the basic often fiduciary obligation to pay in reversal of the enrichment. The point of practice is that these different remedies are alternative, thus not available where it is inconsistent with principle to grant them for the corresponding reasons on the same facts.

PERSONAL RESTITUTIONARY REMEDIES

It goes without saying that in the same way as damages, for example, can be forthcoming right across the spectrum of the law of obligations in breach, the remedies discussed herein are restitutionary in character only and, unless so stated as in the case of the remedy of account in connexion with proprietorial infringements, they do not especially run with any particular class of civil obligation. An important main consideration is to recognize the restitutionary function of the constructive trust, the equitable lien, the ancillary order to trace, contribution, and the award of rights in subrogation as deserving of attention whether or not one nominates any of them as a restitutionary remedy in the same way as the relief itemized above. It should be pointed out that tracing is more usefully considered in the context in which it most frequently arises, of proprietary claims, in the knowledge that it can also be sought in personal claims. These other types of judicial order are discussed after the main remedies in the lists above. But first the issue of extent of recovery.

Scope of restitutionary recoverability

Whatever be the form of recovery, it is given on eminent authority[83] that the question of scope depends, as it was held to do in *English* v. *Dedham Vale*

[82] Ibid., at 29. [83] Birks, *op. cit.* (*Introduction...*), at 74.

Properties Limited,[84] on the value received by the defendant. The relevant facts of the case were that profitable transactions by the defendants, to improve landed property on which the action for recovery was based and which transactions were completed after undisclosed planning permission in the claimants' names was granted to the defendants, entitled the claimants to fiduciary disclosure in the form of an account of profits by the defendants.

Exceptionally, as in *Sinclair* v. *Brougham*[85] in which depositors in a building society being wound up were held to be disentitled to recover moneys they had paid under an ultra vires contract, the measure of recovery is the value remaining with the defendant. In the normal case, value remaining, as opposed to value had, does not arise even where the claimant's position as to the nature of the claim to recover has changed; he is nearly always interested in events as far as the point of receipt or acceptance by the defendant. It is the question of extent which predominates the current law to the virtual exclusion of issues of remedial form. Nor is the question of antiquity of forms at all helpful.

A further aspect of scope of recovery is adaptable, for transnational situations, from a local law illustration by Birks.[86] Consider that non-forum restitution law precludes restitutionary recovery of mistaken payments if the moneys are subsequently applied to charity. Call it the defence of charitable donation. The original payor of the moneys seeks to recover the sum in England. Forum law does not permit the recovery because it falls outside the scope afforded by its own law. The defendant's gain is remote even though in more literal or less technical terms the money is nevertheless value received rather than value remaining. In other words, the enrichment at issue is not without legal justification.

Consequently, the law is that recoverability can vary with cause of enrichment, so that were the sum due in commercial and not charitable circumstances, its recoverability may be permissible as value received or transferred, limited as it must be by the deterministically remediable act of tainted acceptance by the defendant. It is often but not always necessary that effectiveness of these orders depends on those facilitating equitable techniques of identification of the money involved, to enable a proper evaluation of the recoverable sum.

It goes without saying that there are situations, particularly those in which the claimant has incurred losses consequent to breach of obligation,[87] in which the better claim is for compensatory damages. In contract cases, he can of course only claim restitutionary relief if the contract has already been terminated. This is because to do otherwise would be to seek net loss simultaneously with consequential loss.

[84] [1978] 1 All ER 382, per Slade J., especially between 393–394, 395 *et seq*., respectively citing *inter alia* (at 398–399) *Phipps* v. *Boardman* [1965] 1 All ER 849, *Selangor United Rubber Estates Ltd*. v. *Cradock (No. 3)* [1968] 2 All ER 1073, and *Re Coomber* [1911] 1 Ch 723, at 730 and 731.

[85] [1914] AC 398.

[86] *Op. cit*. (*Introduction...*), at 74 *et seq*.

[87] Cf. *Mason* v. *Burningham* [1949] 2 KB 545, in which stolen goods were transferred on hire-purchase terms.

RESTITUTION OF MONEY HAD AND RECEIVED, AND OF MONEY PAID.

Birks[88] pointedly differentiates between money had and received and money paid, mainly for the purpose of rationalizing the old cases from which these orders respectively survive, that "to go on using [the orders'] language is merely perverse."[89] Accordingly, to apply these orders' quasi-contract origins as a basis for their contemporary practical applications remains useful, as is to be seen from an early publication on the former topic[90] where the underlying moralistic principle was stated that "the money which ought to be refunded was received for the use of the party by whom it was paid, and that the person receiving it made a promise to pay it on request". The action is confined to money, albeit as property. The action subsists in mistaken payments, in agreements for which the contractual consideration has failed (in the sense of no gains having accrued from the performance agreed by the defendant), or from void contracts. Its pedigree is ancient as is clear from its formally intact survival since, e.g., *Moses* v. *Macferlan*.[91] Tettenborn has described the particular relief as "protean",[92] thus adaptable, as is apparent from its contemporary applications.

Kleinwort Benson was an action for the recovery of money paid under a void contract. The circumstances of the case substantiate the difference between the respective actions in that the money paid in the case was paid to the defendant's use for the claimant's benefit. The money had and received in *Moses* was paid by the plaintiff to his own use in the hands of the defendant. Given that the proper law of an obligation to make restitution on the basis of money paid is, according to *Re Jogia (a Bankrupt)*,[93] the law of the place of enrichment or of receipt, the real task with which a conflicts claimant is faced is that of satisfactorily establishing the existence of those facts which justify the grant of the order, having regard to the requirements of bona fides and of defences previously identified in the Chapter, as to which it may be useful to recall the discussion of *Lipkin Gorman*[94] which involved an action for money had and received.

The claim lies where, for a simple example, the claimant has made an advance payment for goods the delivery of which is, for whatever reason, not made (e.g., under the *Law Reform (Frustrated Contracts) Act 1943*). Where the defendant has performed part of the obligation, the aggrieved party can only get damages less the value of the performance. In the different circumstances of money paid under a contract which was void ab initio, recoverability ordinarily

[88] *Op. cit. (Introduction...)*, e.g., at 78–79.

[89] Ibid.

[90] Sir William Evans, "An Essay on the Action for Money Had and Received" (1802), reissued in [1998] *RLR* 3, at the opening page.

[91] [1760] 2 Burr 1005, at 1012.

[92] *Op. cit.*, *Law of Restitution in England and Ireland*, para. 2-05.

[93] [1988] 1 WLR 484; also, the American *Restatement*, *op. cit.*, comment (d) of para. 221.

[94] Above, in the paragraph which carries n. 19.

depends on whether there has been payment by the claimant. In some statutory circumstances, as well as where the contract is void for illegality or for incapacity to contract, recoverability may likely not be restitutionary.

RESTITUTION OF A QUANTUM MERUIT, OR OF A QUANTUM VALEBAT: REASONABLE RECOMPENSE.

These are respectively available to found claims on tacit obligations to pay reasonable value either for work done or for the property in goods transferred. It must be made clear from the outset that, in certain circumstances presently discussed, it would be overly expansionist to seek to bring enrichment claims within the scope of these orders. The orders' basis in the now defunct implied contract theory means that to persist in all cases with founding them in restitution is itself difficult to justify. The issue is whether given circumstances, particularly those surrounding the defendant's receiving of the value at issue, require the law to impose the supposed or pleaded obligation to pay; whether the transfer was gratuitous and therefore irretrievable, or for consideration and thus reversable. The basic rationale for disgorgement of value transferred under either type of order lies in the fact that the defendant ought not to be relieved of a risk which he took by acceptance[95] of the claimant's request, even though it turns out to work against the claimant. In other words, the defendant could have refused to accept.

It is noteworthy that the current *Court Forms*[96] do not at all refer to the latter type of order, perhaps because the quantum meruit is applied to the respective types of restitution of value transferred. The defendant's breach is usually the reason for the claimant not having completed the agreed performance, so that the contractual rate can be fairly applied to the question of scope of recovery.[97] It is not decisive that there may have been a stipulation that payment was to be effected only after performance may have been completed.

The charterers in *Société Franco Tunisienne D'Armament* v. *Sidermar*[98] were held to have freely accepted the risk involved in a carriage of goods by sea by a longer route, brought on by war conditions, than that which had been agreed. Although the decision was later overturned in *Ocean Tramp Tankers Corporation* v. *V/O Sovfracht*,[99] partly on the basis that the original carriage contract was held not to have been discharged, no further issue was taken on the trial judge's findings on whether recovery for the service rendered was reasonable.

[95] On the issue of risk, see Beatson, *op. cit.*, at 6–7. The contract if any will of course need to have become defunct: see J.W. Bridge, "Quantum Meruit and Building Contracts: Part II" (1990) 2 *JCL* 189, at 198–205.

[96] (London, Butterworths; 1989).

[97] Cf. Beatson, *op. cit.*, at 12–15.

[98] [1961] 2 QB 278.

[99] [1964] 2 QB 226.

Because these are Common Law remedies, a cautionary note deriving from the need that they be estimated, is to be sounded in their being sought with compensatory damages and (or) an agreed sum, rather than as an alternative to damages. It is a matter of course that a quantum meruit award does not go to protect an expectation interest, rather to the claimant's reliance. It is unwise to seek to explain the theory for the more apposite relief in terms of whether restitution or damages would provide a larger quantum, although in practical terms the choice is of course the claimant's.

In *Rover International Limited* v. *Cannon Film Sales Limited (No. 3)*,[100] a quantum meruit was claimed with an action for the recovery of money mistakenly paid under a contract which subsequently was invalidated because one of the parties had not been incorporated at the contractual commencement date as would confirm the capacity of that party. Partial performance of the contract was held to found recovery to the extent of the performance even though the money had been paid in ignorance of that party's lack of incorporation. The quantum meruit claim was for goods supplied by the defendant whose position had changed, so that consideration had not totally failed.

It is of particular importance that Kerr L.J. did not feel obliged in that case to estimate the award in accordance with the (ineffective) contract price, relying instead on the analogy of frustrated contract so, incidentally, that any expectation interests were more clearly excluded from the scope of recovery, that an innocent party who has done only little of the agreed performance is no better off than one who has done the bulk of it, nor is a void contract differently treated from an invalid one. It was perhaps never more clear that restitution does not avail a claimant in all so-called partial or total "failure of consideration" cases the remedies for which can be said to fall outside the scope of the more usual relief for breach of contract. Remedies for vitiated contracts depend on autonomous enrichment by subtraction, rather than on a breach of obligation or civil wrong.

RESTITUTION BY AN ACCOUNT OF PROFITS

The essence of this equitable ancillary order is that the defendant provides an accurate statement of otherwise indeterminate net profit or value received by the defendant's tort against the claimant, the sum to be obligatorily paid in restitution to the latter. The relevant rules of court are to be found in Order 44 *R.S.C.*, the immediately preceding Order 43 being applicable to undefended applications for the particular order. In either case, all sums due as between the parties are to be stated and (or) set off as may be necessary and must be accompanied by an application that the sums found due be paid over to the deprived party.

100 [1989] 1 WLR 912 (Kerr and Dillon LL.J.); noted by N.H. Andrews in [1990] CLJ 15.

Proof of breach of obligation is required, as was held by Warrington J. in *Re Wrightson, Wrightson* v. *Cooke*.[101] Otherwise, a wilful omission to act in which case a plea of the basis for the order, that the moneys would have been had but for the wilful default, must have been entered. A defence is available if the facts were that the parties had between themselves previously rendered accurate accounts which show a restitutionarily recoverable excess.

The typical circumstances were previously described in the present Chapter in discussing the case of *English* v. *Dedham Vale Properties Limited*.[102] Having pointed out that the relief is available only for the infringement of intellectual property rights,[103] or for breach of confidence or of fiduciary obligation[104] (with or without injunctive relief as these were discussed in the Chapter of this book dealing with injunctions), Burrows[105] identified the main aspects of contemporary application as those arising in connexion with (a) innocent wrong-doing, (b) the particular profits which are to be accounted for, (c) the problems of rendering account, and (d) the material overlaps between an account of profits and compensatory damages, arising from the respective incidental processes of estimation.

As was stated by Lord Parker in *Spalding & Brothers* v. *A.W. Gamage Limited*,[106] the gist of these issues is, first, that the defendant will not have acted dishonestly, e.g., in the way that he was held to have done in *Seager* v. *Copydex Limited*[107] by having, as a confidant, innocently exploited (i.e., profited unaware of his inadvertent betrayal of) another's trade secret, and accordingly was ordered to pay the secret's market value in damages based on analogy from the tort of conversion, rather than account for the gains made from having done so. Indeed, the injured party has a choice between these remedies. Discretionary requirements of bona fides are made of the confidant in these circumstances.

It is well settled that an account of profits cannot be awarded with damages,[108] because to do so would not only disregard the definitive trust or fiduciary situation the breach of which characterizes the former but not quite the latter, and amount to recovery which exceeds the restitutionary entitlement. An award of these remedies is made even less tenable because it could thereby mean that the infringement is to be condoned.[109] It is of consequence that, bearing in mind the limited types of cause in which an account is to be ordered, it is

[101] [1908] 1 Ch 789, at 799–800 (i.e., that the order is not designed to assist the proof of breach).

[102] Above, the paragraph carrying n. 84.

[103] E.g., in *My Kinda Town Ltd.* v. *Soll* [1982] FSR 147, particularly on the point of the account being aimed at a fair apportionment, so that neither party will have what justly belongs to the other (at 159, per Slade J.).

[104] *Peter Pan Manufacturing Corporation* v. *Corsets Silhouette Ltd.* [1963] RPC 45; *Attorney-General* v. *Guardian Newspapers Ltd. (No. 2)* [1990] 1 AC 109, the *Spycatcher* case. See G. Jones, "Restitution of Benefits Obtained in Breach of Another's Confidence" [1970] 86 *LQR* 463, at 486–488.

[105] *Remedies for Torts and Breach of Contract* (2nd. ed., London, Butterworths; 1994), at 301–305.

[106] (1915) 84 LJ Ch 449. [107] [1967] 2 All ER 415.

[108] See, e.g., *Neilson* v. *Betts* [1871] LR 5 HL 1.

[109] Ibid., at 22, per Lord Westbury L.C.

easier to analytically distinguish among the compound objectives of the respective relief in the types of cause in which the balance of convenience considerations which generally attend equitable awards typically apply.

For example, in the context of interlocutory injunctions, Spry[110] points out that "[i]f the keeping of an account is proposed, then 'the substantial question is whether the balance of convenience will be better served in the circumstances of the case by adopting that course or by adopting that course or by granting an injunction until the trial.'" In the Australian case of *Attorney-General of the United Kingdom* v. *Heinemann Publishers Australia Pty Limited*,[111] the lex fori applied to govern the respective claims *inter alia* for an account of profits and for injunction. The present writer submits that, all other factors being resolved, there is no reason of principle outside the forum's inherent general or exclusive jurisdiction why these explications ought not to apply in post-trial circumstances. An account can of course be interlocutorily ordered where the trial on the merits make it necessary to do so.

To return to the coincidence of damages referred to in the paragraph above, it is often the case that "the matters that would cause undue prejudice or hardship to the claimant if he were confined to damages serve also to render insufficient the taking of an account by the defendant",[112] that equitable avoidance of undue hardship is sometimes possible only through an order to account, that "the balance of justice is found to depend largely on the extent to which the respective businesses of the parties are established and on the effect on their respective goodwills of the various orders that it is open to the court to make",[113] especially in intellectual property disputes.

The US decision in *Maier Brewing Company* v. *Fleischmann Distilling Corporation*[114] about the recovery, under Section 35 of the Lanham Act, of profits accrued to the defendants from the sale of beer under the plaintiffs' registered trade name is comparable to, e.g., restitution via an account of profits under Section 61(2) of the British *Patents Act 1977*, that "[t]he court shall not, in respect of the same infringement, both award the proprietor of a patent damages and order that he shall be given an account of the profits."

It is clear that in transnational claims with an English centre of gravity, the foregoing applies with little difficulty, and likewise in *Brussels Convention* cases with the supplementary bonus of its Article 25, particularly as to the essential factors connecting the claim to the forum: locus of breach, applicable substantive law of the defendant's receipt or accretion of value, not so much the place in which the defendant is to be found and made to render account

[110] *The Principles of Equitable Remedies* (5th ed., London, Sweet & Maxwell; 1997), at 458–459, quoting from the Australian decision, *Beecham Group Ltd.* v. *Bristol Laboratories Pty. Ltd.* (1968) 118 CLR 618, at 625 in the passage in the main text above.

[111] (1987) 10 NSWLR 86, and on appeal at (1988) 165 CLR 30; see also *Thahir* v. *P.T. Pertambagan Minyak dan Gas Bumi Negara (Pertamina)* (1994) 3 SLR 257.

[112] Spry, *op. cit.*, at 476.

[113] Ibid., at 477–478, citing *inter alia American Cyanamid* Co. v. *Ethicon* [1975] AC 396.

[114] 390 F2d 117 (9th Circuit, 1968).

although the domicile of that party would determine forum jurisdiction according to Article 2, and their Lordships' finding in *Kleinwort Benson*. Indeed, international intellectual property conventions are flexible on the issue of jurisdiction based on domicile such that proceedings may be begun in the courts of either party or, better yet, at the (registered) situs of the infringed property.[115]

If a non-forum law of enrichment applies,[116] it is submitted that the relevant (remedial) provisions of that law need not provide for an equivalent of the English remedy of account in order for that relief to be granted in England, that the requirements of co-ordinability are sufficiently met by fulfilment of the jurisdiction acquisition rules' requirements. It is said that, in the final analysis, it is the forum court's obligation to:

> "Take whatever measures are appropriate under its national law to ensure that the order is complied with. Apart from the mandatory injunction, the Community patent or trade mark court is obliged to apply the law of the member state in which the acts of infringement or threatened infringement were committed, including its private international law...It follows, at least in principle, that an exercise in comparative law will be required whenever there has been infringement on a sufficiently large scale and in several countries."[117]

Reluctant as one realistically must be to accept the notion of a forum independently applying comparativist method as is suggested by the author of the above passage, it would appear that it is precisely the approach which may directly or otherwise best equip the legislator or the draftsman of anticipated modernization particularly of the jurisdictional rules in this important area of globalized commercial activity. This writer submits that, subject to yet undetermined possible modification particularly in light of talk of a unified action/remedy, this present remedy is foreseeably indispensable to monetary restitution.

RESTITUTIONARY RESCISSION OF VOIDABLE CONTRACTS

The equitable restitutionary remedy in view operates at the safe intersection, for jurisdictional purposes—e.g. under Article 5(1) *Brussels Convention*—of restitution and contract laws, subject to the obligation in question (which itself

[115] E.g., Art. 16(4) *Brussels Convention*, providing for exclusive jurisdiction not based on domicile.

[116] See, e.g., J. Bird, "Choice of Law" in Rose (ed.), *op. cit.*, especially at 92–136.

[117] C. Wadlow, *Enforcement of Intellectual Property in European and International Law* (London, Sweet & Maxwell; 1998), at 265. The reference to comparative method is one which might well be alien to the English forum, but one which in the developing nature of intellectual property conflicts would not necessarily be amiss especially if it is accepted that the real problems are mostly of administrability, rather than of consensus about the concepts and the consequences of infringement. Analogues from other areas of tort law may be drawn from B.S. Markesinis, *Foreign Law and Comparative Methodology- A Subject and a Thesis* (Oxford, Hart; 1997), at 235–240.

could be an implied term)[118] as well as the place in which it is to be performed being established. The restitutionary issue could not be more contract-based than it is in the present context. It needs to be made clear that the discretionary judicial, rather than a party's unilateral and perhaps uncontested, setting aside of the contract for whatever vitiating reason(s) (misrepresentation, mistake, undue influence) can itself be restitutionary, quite apart from the restoration of value or reliance loss which may already have passed and which forms the basis for rescission.

It is said that rescission is equity's equivalent of reliance damages, and it is to be distinguished from contract-breaking repudiation. Rescission is certainly not substitutional, strictly speaking; rather, it is to discard the contract, as though it was never made,[119] by the rescinding party's principled refusal to perform or otherwise to carry on with the contract. Rescission, it must be remembered, renders the contract void ab initio, even though the contract must be taken to have been valid until it was rescinded. Indeed, Treitel discusses rescission as a subdivision of failure of consideration, in the broader context of restitutionary recovery of money paid.[120]

Rescission of transnational contracts has been a prominent feature of contract law for a considerable time. Illustrations are as familiar as they are rife. These include the cause célèbre, *Hong Kong Fir Shipping Company Limited* v. *Kawasaki Kisen Kaisha Limited*.[121] There will necessarily have been a false representation of material fact, rather than mere non-disclosure where the contract does not require the utmost good faith. In seeking to avoid transnational reinsurance contracts for non-disclosure or innocent misrepresentation, the claimants in *Trade Indemnity plc* v. *Försäkrindsaktiebolaget Njord*[122] were required to prove that the supposedly avoiding circumstances were part of the performance, and not the formation, of the contracts, which they could not prove thereby mischaracterizing the cause of action as would make Article 5(1) inapplicable to provide the required jurisdictional foundation.

The key point is that in order for an order to be validly made, there has to have been partial performance that will have transferred some recoverable value under the contract. Rescission will however be withheld if restitution is impossible in the sense of the status quo ante being unrestorable, neither merely imprecise[123] nor involving breach of trust caused by undue influence.[124] There can of course be no restitutionary right to rescission where equity's darling,

[118] See *Raiffeisen Zentralbank Osterreich Aktiengesellschaft* v. *National Bank of Greece SA*, *The Times*, 25th September, 1998 (Tuckey J., Commercial Court, Q.B.D.), especialy for the purpose of a jurisdictional basis under Art. 5(1), where there was more than one obligation.

[119] Cf. Treitel, *op. cit.* (*Remedies*...), at 1–2.

[120] *The Law of Contract* (9th ed., London, Sweet & Maxwell; 1995), at 945–946.

[121] [1962] 2 QB 26, especially at 70 (per Diplock L.J., as he was then).

[122] [1995] 1 All ER 796.

[123] *Erlanger* v. *New Sombrero Phosphate Company* [1878] 3 App Cas 1218.

[124] Cf. *OSullivan* v. *Management Agency & Music Ltd.* [1985] QB 420.

rather than a volunteer or a defendant's trustee in bankruptcy, is involved before the rescissionary circumstances arise. Similarly, if a claimant otherwise entitled to rescind does in fact expressly or impliedly affirm the contract (e.g., by persisting with taking value thereunder, or by mere delay), there will be no basis for seeking rescission. Where rescission is forthcoming in misrepresentation cases, damages may be awarded instead, under Section 2(2) *Misrepresentation Act 1967*. Burrows[125] is of the worthwhile opinion that rescission for misrepresentation is "better viewed as within autonomous unjust enrichment, rather than by wrongdoing."

While it is clear that rescission can hardly be deemed to be a consequence of a contract, as would confirm the issue of inapplicability of a non-forum contractual lex causae, it is not necessarily clear that should such a proper law provide differently from forum law in point the forum would apply that law as a basis for ordering rescission. The questions are clearly substantive in nature. The writer submits that in those cases in which the respective laws are radically different, it makes sense to apply forum law on rescission where the facts are closer to the forum, and to apply the foreign law where the reverse is the case, for simple policy reasons of predictability of result (mindful of the proper scope of recovery in multiple relief claims), thus conveniently leaving the issue of foreign enforcement of the award, where this arises, to the jurisdiction of enforcement.

The basic principle of equity jurisdiction is that the claimant can rescind in substantial albeit inexact restitution if the subject matter of the contract is restorable even if it is altered (an allowance would of course need to be made for any deterioration), and if necessary with an account of any profits from user of the subject matter. As is borne out in *The Mikhail Lermontov*,[126] in which a holiday cruise was ruined by the vessel being shipwrecked, rescission with recovery may depend on whether value has been transferred to the claimant. Rescission can of course be proprietary in the sense of revesting the transferor's rights to property that may already have been transferred. This last point conveniently leads discussion on to the proprietary forms of restitution.

PROPRIETARY RESTITUTIONARY REMEDIES

Proprietary restitution ensues when a defendant has received property or (and) property already belonging to that party has been improved. In either case, the enrichment would need to have been at the claimant's expense, thereby accentuating the restitutionary interest therein, be the interest legal (e.g., where property is transferred in the mistaken belief that the transferee has capacity to receive it) or equitable (e.g., a trustee who has wrongfully appropriated trust property).

[125] *Op. cit.* (*Remedies...*), at 289.

[126] [1991] 2 Ll Rep 155.

The difference between restitutionary remedies properly so-called and doctrinal means of obtaining them is probably not better defined than it is in the case of proprietary restitution, which, as a definitional issue, is limited to assets or "value surviving".[127] As was pointed out earlier, proprietary restitution accords precedence (save as against equity's darling) where the defendant is insolvent, subject to general expenses of the insolvency. Proprietary claims can avail a claimant, complete with any increase in value of the property, in circumstances where a personal claim would be impossible. Only the judicially ordered relief of this present type are to be discussed in this section.

It is of course possible that, radically different as they are,[128] personal and proprietary restitution be conjunctively granted, such as where money is mistakenly paid into a bank account and the payor asserts a constructive trust over the sum as might have already been expended, e.g., on acquiring securities. A proprietary remedy per se is in general typically made with the following aims:[129]

— to reverse the proceeds of property of which the claimant as owner has been deprived (tracing);
— to reclaim value from a third party which value has been applied by that party to another in whose place the recovery is pursued (subrogation);
— to reverse gains made from a breach of fiduciary duty or from an error as to the facts of the relationship subsisting between the parties (respectively, a constructive trust or a lien); or (and)
— to revest the property in an avoided contract or other transfer (recovery, with or without rescission).

The general theme—the vindication of proprietary rights[130]—often subsists outwith unjustifiable enrichment, as seems to have been sufficiently illustrated in the Court of Appeal decision in *Macmillan Incorporated* v. *Bishopsgate Investment Trust plc. (No. 3)*.[131] The issue was the nature of the choice-of-law rule to govern the recovery of property (shares) transferred to the defendants by a third party acting in breach of fiduciary obligation. The prevailing eminently supportable view is that restitution and property laws are separate but significantly interrelated, so that the issue of enrichment therein, which may be said to found restitution, is not to be subjected to considerations of its justifiability.

These remedial devices, or rights accruing to a party entitled to restitution, with interest or not,[132] will now be individually discussed through the cases. By way of explanatory introduction, in commenting on the decision in *Westdeutsche* particularly as it analysed the coincidence of contract and property

[127] Birks, n. 86 above, and the paragraph which carries it.
[128] Cf. D. Hayton, "Equity's Identification Rules" in P. Birks (ed.), *Laundering and Tracing* (Oxford, Clarendon; 1995), Chapter I, at 1–3.
[129] Hayton narrows down the proprietary relief afforded by equity to the lien or charge, and the constructive trust: ibid., n. 128, above, at 4–6.
[130] Cf. Virgo, *loc. cit.*, at 312–318. [131] [1996] 1 WLR 387.
[132] Cf. the *Westdeutsche Landesbank Girozentrale* decision.

laws, Worthington[133] points out in a way which affirms the closing remarks of the last section above (on rescission) that "the [contractual] obligation to perform, or the obligation to undo, is postulated as the prime requirement for delivering proprietary consequences"[134] and that "the common law rarely, if ever, visits contractual failure with proprietary consequences. Instead, it relies upon personal remedies, whether contractual or restitutionary."[135]

More extensively, she concluded her study as follows:

> "[C]ontract failure is visited with proprietary consequences only when one party is obliged to act—whether to *perform* or to *undo* the contract—and the property which must thereby be dealt with is identifiable...[E]quity regards as done that which ought to be done. Such proprietary interests do not deliver undesirable and unacceptable commercial consequences: they merely ensure that an interrupted contract is neither performed nor reversed; they put the parties, and their general creditors, in either the pre-contractual or post-contractual position. They only do this with those contracts which equity sees the parties as compelled to perform or compelled to undo. In the scheme of things, this limitation means that very few contracts are affected: most contracts are not specifically enforceable or void or voidable. The commercial impact of this when insolvency intervenes is not to deliver a windfall to either party, or to the general creditors. It is simply to shift the risk time-frame to pre- or post-contractual performance." [136]

The remedial restitutionary aspects of *Westdeutsche* feature in what now follows.

TRACING ORDERS: LEGAL AND EQUITABLE.

Passing reference has already been made in the Chapter to the extra-judicial writing of Lord Millett in signposting the law of tracing.[137] More than anything, it is clear, as Burrows put it[138] that tracing is not quite a remedy. It "serves an evidential purpose. The cause of action is for money had and received. The remedy is an order for account and payment. Tracing at common law enables the defendant to be identified as the recipient of the plaintiff's money and the measure of his liability to be determined by the amount of the plaintiff's money he is shown to have received."[139] While there are real limits on tracing at Common Law (e.g., that there be a physical asset such as a cheque by which to trace funds), "Equity can follow the chose in

[133] In, "Proprietary Consequences of Contract Failure" in F.D. Rose (ed.), *Failure of Contracts: Contractual, Restitutionary and Proprietary Consequences* (Oxford, Hart; 1998), 67.

[134] Ibid. (*loc. cit.*), at 69.

[135] Ibid., at 69; underlying policies—e.g., of certainty, transparency, and fairness—are subsequently ventilated at 69–76.

[136] Ibid., at 89.

[137] See also, generally, L. Smith, *The Law of Tracing* (Oxford, Clarendon; 1997).

[138] *Op. cit.* (*The Law of Restitution*), Chapter two.

[139] Millett, *loc. cit.* (LQR), at 72; see also, C. Band, "The Development of Tracing Rules in Commercial Cases" [1997] LMCLQ 65, at 66–67.

action through its transmutation",[140] "[t]he only restriction [being] the requirement that there must be some breach of trust or other fiduciary obligation which permits the assistance of equity to be invoked."[141] This book is not necessarily the place to discuss the internal law rules on tracing at great length, although it is inevitable that whatever is to be said about the adaptive rules that are applicable in transnational litigation are commonly rooted with the same rules relied on in domestic cases.

His Lordship's succinct and compelling analysis of the personal claim at law against a recipient who has parted with the funds at issue, which claim "is at variance with both the juristic bases which have at different times been ascribed to the action",[142] shows that because "[t]he [proprietary] tracing claim in equity...[only] depends on the continued existence of the trust property in the hands of the defendant" (as was clarified to be the essential characteristic of the recipient in *Agip (Africa) Limited* v. *Jackson*)[143] and therefore that "[u]nless [the defendant] is a bona fide purchaser for value without notice, he holds the property on a resulting trust for the true owner and must restore it to him if he still has it".[144] Much the same approach is advocated by Birks.[145] It may be recalled that tracing relates to the latter measure of recovery ("value surviving") previously described in the appropriate subsection of this Chapter.

In transnational litigation, these issues were central to the facts in *Chase Manhattan Bank N.A.* v. *Israel-British Bank (London) Limited*,[146] especially as to the proper characterization of the judicial order as procedural or substantive. *Dicey and Morris*[147] carries submissions that whether the forum will grant the right to trace under its own law depends on whether the lex causae of the restitutionary obligation so permits as it did in *Chase Manhattan*,[148] subject of course to the practical facility or the co-ordination with which the forum can in fact apply such rules of another legal system. Consequently, the effect of the difficult law/equity divide which is predominant in the law of tracing is a direct function of the exclusivity with which forum law applies in a given case. If it applies as lex causae, then full recourse is to be had to the provisions of internal law since the case would be little different from a straight-forward domestic case.[149]

140 Ibid., at 74.

141 Ibid., at 75. At 76, he states: "[T]he requirement that the loss must have arisen from a breach of fiduciary duty is difficult to understand and impossible to defend."

142 Ibid., 77, those bases being *ex aequo et bono* (as in *Moses* v. *Macferlan*) or in implied contract (as in *Sinclair* v. *Brougham*).

143 [1990] Ch 265, at 290, i.e., that the receipt should have been for the recepient's own use and benefit.

144 Ibid., at 80.

145 *Op. cit.* (*Introduction*), Chapter XI, generally. However, it may be noted that he sets greater store by the defendant's moral quality (e.g., at 359) than does his Lordship.

146 [1981] Ch 105.

147 Collins *et al.* (eds.), *op. cit.*, at 1477.

148 At 124 of the decision.

149 Cf. Birks, *op. cit.* (*Introduction*), at 83–87, and on to 93, which discussion pretty much encompasses not only tracing but the other types of restitutionary device listed in the main text above; and in greater detail, at 358–375.

A significant point which requires equally less abstract analysis from substance and procedure is one that arises in the context of property law, in which a claimant's inability to be availed of tracing rules does not, as was held in *Space Investments Limited* v. *Canadian Imperial Bank of Commerce Trust Co. (Bahamas) Limited*,[150] operate to exclude the imposition of a restitutionary proprietary interest; the type of interest can in those circumstances be established without the separate necessity for its identification by recourse to tracing. There are four separate general questions to be resolved in any attempt to rely on the rules on tracing. There is evidence of the courts' increasing flexibility and pragmatism in responding to applications for resort to these rules:

— the first hurdle is to define the given claim as being either for a legal remedy (e.g., for money had and received) of for one in equity (e.g., the lien, the constructive trust), because the particular characterization determines, rightly or wrongly, which set of tracing rules are to apply;

— second, generally, either type of claim would be satisfied by proof of the defendant's identifiable receipt (not identifiable retention, as is material only to proprietary restitution and to the likelihood of a defence) of the property to be restored. For legal tracing rules to operate, the aim of the difficult and often unsuccessful exercise, especially where money that has been physically transferred to a recipient who thus acquires legal title is the subject matter, must be to follow the claimant's surviving legal (and possessory) title. Tracing in equity follows the claimant's enduring equitable title to the property held by another, having passed through a fiduciary as in *Chase Manhattan*, and beforehand in *Sinclair* v. *Brougham* and in *Re Diplock*;[151]

— third, the subject matter of the tracing exercise must be discrete and identifiable, especially where it forms a part of mixed funds or property. It is in this situation that the profound divergence of scope as between the legal and the equitable rules begins to be evident. While the legal rules refuse tracing into mixed funds or into subsequent exchanges on the basis that the right is limited to tracing property (rather than value),[152] the equitable

[150] [1986] 1 WLR 1072; see also *Barlow Clowes International Ltd.* v. *Vaughan* [1992] 4 All ER 22.

[151] [1948] Ch 465 (C.A.)

[152] After Lord Ellenborough's speech in *Taylor* v. *Plumer* [1814-1823] All ER Rep 167 (K.B.) But, see also Lord Millett, "The Law of Restitution: Taking Stock" (1999) Issue 14 *Amicus Curiae* 4, at 5–6: "The best way forward, in my opinion, is either to assert, with Lionel Smith, that there is nothing either legal or equitable about the tracing exercise, and that there is only one set of rules which is applicable both at common law and in equity; or to assert with Viscount Haldane LC in *Sinclair* v. *Brougham* [1914] AC 398 at 421 that the equitable tracing rules form part of equity's auxiliary jurisdiction and are available to support a common law claim. On either footing no further time need be wasted on trying to breathe life into the common law tracing rules, which can be left to fall into disuse, as the common law action for account did centuries ago. The way will be open to a unified law of restitution", and D. Hayton, *loc. cit.*, in Birks (ed.), *Laundering & Tracing*, at 32: "If tracing has different rules at law and in equity, that is because the rules were evolved to deal with different situations and still do so". But see P. Matthews in Birks (ed.), *Laundering & Tracing, op. cit.*, e.g., at 50, 56, and L. Smith, "Tracing in Taylor *v.* Plumer: Equity in the Court of King's Bench"[1995] *LMCLQ* 240, especially at 251, 263, and "Tracing into the Payment of a Debt"[1995] *CLJ* 290, at the opening page there and, subsequently, at 293, 294, 303.

rules allow tracing in either type of situation as long as there subsists an equitable proprietary basis such as was taken to have been established in *Sinclair* v. *Brougham* but not in either of *Westdeutsche Landesbank* in which the money to have been traced had in fact been paid under a void contract or in *Re Goldcorp Exchange Ltd.*,[153] in which property in mixed and unallocated bullion stored on behalf of several customers was held never to have been transferred to the customers as would justify their having a proprietary basis from which to seek the application of tracing rules;

— lastly, in order for equity's rules to operate there is authority, rather than practical principle,[154] that the subject matter should have been passed from the claimant to a fiduciary (*Chase Manhattan*, in which the payor's mistake did not cost him the right to trace) who need not be the defendant, as long as either a resulting or a constructive trust is to be inferred in the circumstances.

The rules have been usefully described as having "provided a technical code whose application to particular fact situations was not always straightforward or easy, and which often produced results which had no obviously logical justification."[155] In this regard, on a positive note, there are more recent context-specific flexible applications, e.g., payments into and out of bank accounts and the banks clearing system.[156] In *Trustees of the Property of F.C. Jones & Sons* v. *Jones*,[157] it was stated:

> "[T]here is no merit in having distinct and differing tracing rules at law and in equity, given that tracing is neither a right nor a remedy but merely the process by which the plaintiff establishes what has happened to his property and makes good his claim that the assets which he claims can properly be regarded as representing his property. The fact that there are different tracing rules at law and in equity is unfortunate though probably inevitable, but unnecessary differences should not be created where they are not required by the different nature of legal and equitable doctrines and remedies."

The minimum requirement, by analogy from the Court of Appeal's decision in *Jones*, is that the recipient be entitled to the credit and loss from the transaction and, in the case of mixed funds, that equitably recovering repayable trust

[153] [1995] 1 AC 74 (Privy Council).

[154] Cf. Millett J. in *Agip (Africa) Ltd.* v. *Jackson* [1990] Ch 265, at 290; Fox LJ in the Court of Appeal [1991] Ch 547, at 566.

[155] Band, *loc. cit.*, at 71.

[156] See, e.g., *El Ajou* v. *Dollar Land Holdings plc* [1993] 3 All ER 717 in which money electronically paid through clearing systems was held by Millett LJ (as he was then) to be untraceable at law because of the tracing pre-requirement that the property in the money needs to have been physically transferred (cf. Also *Bank Tejarat* v. *Hong Kong & Shanghai Banking Corp. (C.I.) Ltd.* [1995] 1 LlRep 239, per Tuckey J). For critique of this finding, see e.g. P. Birks [1989] 105 *LQR* 528, at 533, and also at [1995] 9 TruLl 91, at 92.

[157] [1996] 3 WLR 703, at 712 (per Millett LJ).

money from such a fund is all a claimant needs upon which to predicate his ability to trace his money.[158]

The restrictive technicality of the legal tracing rules may leave much to be desired from the points of view of practicality and even doctrine, not least, to reiterate, where money in the bank is involved. As long as it is worthwhile and, more to the point, correct to elide as between the actual claim for restitution and the invocation of tracing rules, then the perpetuation of the dichotomy between the legal and the equitable rules often appears to be less well-grounded, not least because want of elision can lead to treatment of a successful invocation of tracing as though it automatically meant the claimant's right to recover, and vice versa. Tracing is first, and indeed ultimately, mechanistically concerned with the identification and location of proprietary value, and with little else in the nature of the concomitant substantive considerations that may arise.

SUBROGATION

General

As with tracing,[159] subrogation is a means of access to restitutionary relief; subrogation profoundly differs of course in the sense that the asset at issue will not have been taken from the claimant who is usually an insurer seeking indemnification from an insured or from a lienholder. It consists of express or tacit voluntary transfer to a third person of the performance a creditor's secured and subsisting legal rights: the substitution of one creditor for another, with the substituted person succeeding to the legal rights and claims of the original claimant. It is applied to the recovery of any claims paid, e.g., by an insurer on behalf of the injured party, to enable the insurer to acquire that party's rights to sue on the payment. In English domestic law, the transferee of these rights must then sue in the name of the creditor—as in the case of insurance claims—so that the "restitutionary" attribute is arguably more preventive (rather than strictly corrective) of unjustifiable enrichment than it is squarely restitutionary.[160] Indeed, where a debt is paid by a third party without the

[158] Ibid., at 737; see also *Space Investments Ltd.* v. *Canadian Imperial Bank of Commerce Trust Co. (Bahamas) Ltd.* [1986] 1 WLR 1072 (Pricy Council, per Lord Templeman, at 1074): that beneficiaries can trace, and equitably recover, trust funds to all the insolvent trustee bank's assets. The old case of *Roscoe* v. *Winder* [1915] 1 Ch 62 is authority that only the lowest intermediate balance of funds in the receiving account is traceable, so that an overdrawn account is not subject to tracing at least if it was overdrawn between payment and claim: cf. *Space Investments*, at 221.

[159] See, e.g., *Boscawen* v. *Bajwa* [1996] 1 WLR 328 (per Millett LJ) for an instance of tracing and subrogation arising in the same factual context.

[160] Cf. R. Stevens, "The Choice of Law Rules of Restitutionary Obligations" in Rose (ed.), *op. cit.*, 180, at 206. He refers to the American Law Institute's *Restatement* (1937), at para. 162. *Goff and Jones* (5th ed., at 120–121) assert that subrogation "is in essence a remedy, fashioned to the particular facts, and designed to ensure 'a transfer of rights from one person to another...by operation of law,' in order to deprive B of a benefit gained at A's expense." The passage they quote is from Lord Diplock's speech in *Orakpo* v. *Manson Investments Ltd.* [1978] AC 95, at 104.

debtor's ratification of the debt, it remains undischarged, so that the creditor could easily be the party who thus becomes unjustifiably enriched.[161]

If a contractual relationship subsists between creditor and third party, it obviously is to be regulated by its proper law.[162] Should the debtor not be party to that contract, the proper law may be the place to look for answers to questions as between creditor and third party, but not as to the determination of whether the third party was legally bound to effect due discharge of the debt or whether the third party can properly claim from the enriched creditor. Neither party autonomy nor privity make reference to the proper law the rationally applicable law in relation to the debtor. Subrogation of the third party to the creditor's rights (as to the debtor's obligation to discharge the debt) must depend on whether the original contractual obligation to discharge indicates the possibility of subrogation. In most insurance contracts, the insurer's right to subrogation of the assured's rights is implied.[163] Article 13(1) of the *Rome Convention* provides that "the law which governs the third person's duty to satisfy the creditor shall determine whether the third person is entitled to exercise against the debtor the rights which the creditor had against the debtor under the law governing their relationship and, if so, whether he may do so in full or only to a limited extent." Unhelpfully, the travaux preparatoires[164] seem to confound the stated scope of the Article (i.e., the assignment of rights by the operation of law) by the references therein to the effect that the third party must have an (unclarified) "economic interest" recognized by law, and to the court's discretion whether to subrogate.

Banque Financière de la Cite v. *Parc (Battersea) Limited*[165] concerned the contractual and proprietary aspects of a failed contract under which the indigent party mistakenly believed that an obligation with the enriched party—by which the latter would refrain from enforcing a loan with a third party advised by the former—was being entered into. No contract ever existed between the party enriched and the party who claimed to have lost out. It fell to be determined whether restitution ought to leave the claimant better off than if the claim arose from a successful contract. In his speech, Lord Steyn found no reason why the facts could not give rise to subrogation.[166] It mattered little that the claimant was a large professional but negligent financial organization.[167]

[161] See, e.g., C. Mitchell, *The Law of Subrogation* (Oxford, Clarendon; 1994), Chapter Two generally.

[162] *Dicey & Morris*, *op. cit.*, at 1522 (on subrogation provided for in an insurance contract situation).

[163] See e.g. the speech of Lord Goff of Chieveley in *Lord Napier & Entick* v. *Hunter* [1993] AC 713 (H.L.); and S. 79 *Marine Insurance Act 1906*.

[164] 1980 OJ C282, at 35 (the Giuliano Lagarde Report); *Dicey and Morris*, *op. cit.*, at 219 (see also p. 1269) point out the limitedness of the Article's provision side by side with English conceptualizations of subrogation.

[165] [1998] 1 All ER 737 (H.L.)

[166] Ibid., at 742 (see also Lord Hoffmann at 749, and Lord Hutton at 752).

[167] For critiques of this decision, see M. Bridge, "Failed Contracts, Subrogation and Unjust Enrichment: Banque Financière de la Cite *v.*Parc (Battersea) Ltd. [1998] *JBL* 323 (for commentary on the Court of Appeal decision of 29th November 1996 (unreported) on the same case, see C. Mitchell, "Subrogation and Part Payments of Another's Debt" [1996] *LMCLQ* 14).

This case is presently returned to below in connexion with establishing entitlement to subrogation.

Tort-related subrogation would appear to be most conveniently governed by the law which applies to the debtor's obligation,[168] rather than that which applies as between the third party payor and the creditor, more so where the third person is not legally obligated to the creditor. Indeed, in *Red Sea Insurance Company Limited* v. *Bouygues SA and Others*,[169] a decision perhaps best known for having presaged the abolition of the dual actionability rule applicable to transnational torts in the Common Law, neither the law applicable to the tort nor forum law recognized the appellant insurers' claim to be subrogated prior to their having made insurance indemnity payments to the parties to whose rights they sought to be subrogated. On textbook authority, it is said that subrogation "gives insurers the right to have their cake and eat it" unless the exercise is aimed at reducing premiums,[170] that it enables the claimant to share or relocate litigation risks and expenses with the insurer.[171]

Establishing the right to subrogation, and its legal consequences

Goff and Jones[172] are unequivocal in emphasizing subrogation's origins in equity as is confirmed by ancient authorities discussed by their Lordships in *Lord Napier's Case*.[173] It is founded in natural justice and thus is equitable, but it is not exclusively discretionary. It arises independently of contract, mainly in one of the following broad scenarios: (a) as was stated in *Re Downer Enterprises Limited*,[174] it "applies in any case where there is a primary and secondary liability for the same debt", such as in a trust situation where it is necessary to prevent the trustee from personally taking the proceeds of creditors' trust property or, furthermore, in connection with suretyship, bills of exchange, and insurance; (b) where a loan of money has been applied by the borrower to discharge his liability to a third person, and the lender seeks subrogation to the third party's rights. As is normal, the claimant is required to prove the defendant's unjustifiable enrichment at the former's expense.

Looking to the circumstances of the *Banque Financière* case, it would appear that there are significant issues of policy that are yet to be resolved in precisely defining the bases for subrogation, especially in commercial cases. It is sufficiently clear, however, that one such basis lies in unjustifiable enrichment. While there is little doubt that subrogation has a cogent function in the law of restitution once it is established that the enrichment involved is without justifi-

[168] Cf. C.G.J. Morse, *Torts in Private International Law* (Amsterdam, North-Holland; 1978), at 148.

[169] [1995] 1 AC 190 (Privy Council).

[170] B. Markesinis and S. Deakin, *Tort Law* (4th ed., Oxford, Clarendon; 1999), 53.

[171] Ibid., at 120. At 790, it is pointed out that insurers do not typically seek to be subrogated to an employer's rights as against an employee.

[172] *Op. cit.*, at 121.

[173] Variously, e.g., at 741, 749.

[174] [1974] 1 WLR 1460, at 1468 (per Pennycuick V.-C.)

cation,[175] it is much less easy to avoid some confusion as to whether a stricter remedial scope for the topic could be practicable.

Subrogation may be contractually excluded or modified, as was held in *Banque Financiere*.[176] Relevant statute law, e.g. concerning value added tax and its recoupability in insolvency, may hinder the elucidation of rights of subrogation as was the case in the local law claim in *Re T.H. Knitwear (Wholesale) Limited*,[177] in which Sir Nicholas Browne-Wilkinson (as he was then)[178] set store by the fact that a creditor's contractual rights are privy as against the debtor who thus cannot be subrogated: where an insurer pays an assured, the latter's rights are not automatically extinguished as against a third party, rather the insurer must sue that third party for indemnity in the assured's name.

It is unlikely that subrogation will follow the making of a gift, because there is little upon which to found the accretion of enforceable rights,[179] nor will it be awarded if the underlying legal relationship does not confer legally enforceable rights. Equity does not avail a volunteer, as was reiterated in *The Esso Bernicia*.[180] Under a contract with tanker operators in that case, Esso had paid certain Scottish farmers for oil pollution damage and now sought—in its own name—to recover the moneys from the designers of the vessel which had caused the damage. As there was no indemnity contract between Esso and the farmers, the claim failed since it could not have discharged the vessel designers' liability to the farmers.

So far so good for orthodoxy from localism in these respects. The local design of English conflicts rules is ineluctable. Transnational circumstances may make separate demands of adjudication in the way that *Red Sea Insurance* demonstrates. Indeed, *The Esso Bernicia* was transnational in that it involved English and Scots laws. That subrogation is remedial, in a way that tracing for example is not, implies that the requirements of co-ordination as between the basis for subrogation and its availability are as cogent as they are in relation to any type of forum relief. In *Orakpo* v. *Manson Investments Limited*,[181] Lord Edmund-Davies pointed out the flexibility of the remedy. A conflicts claimant seeking subrogation would therefore be well advised to frame his claim in accordance with the local remedial law, be it in relation to sureties, to indorsed bills of exchange, or to insurance.[182]

The right to subrogation may be waived by its holder, subject to the extent of recovery and best where the waiver is mutually beneficial to the parties concerned.[183] This applies in most if not all of the Common Law world. The California Court of Appeal held, in *Firemen's Fund* v. *Maryland Casualty*,[184]

[175] Cf. *Goff and Jones*, *op. cit.*, at 122–126; that it goes beyond is taken further between 126 and 131.

[176] *Loc. cit.*, at 753 (per Lord Hutton).

[177] [1988] Ch 275.

[178] [1987] 1 WLR 371, at 376.

[179] Cf. Mitchell. *op. cit.*, at 22–23, 37–38.

[180] [1989] A.C. 643.

[181] [1978] AC 95, at 112.

[182] Cf. *Goff and Jones*, *op. cit.*, Chapter Three, generally.

[183] See http://www.lcgroup.com/resource/waiver.htm.

[184] Cf. http://news.propertyandcasualty.com/litigation-internat-reins/19980828-3154.html.

that where a plurality of insurers separately insure the same risk, the carrier who settles the loss or defends the assured's suit is entitled to equitable contribution from the other insurers.

In closing, on the matter of the insurance law applicable to subrogation arising contractually, *Dicey and Morris*'s Rules 186 *et seq.* make important points.[185] The location of the insured risk is properly taken to raise the prima facie presumption that the law of that place is to govern the rights arising under the contract because it manifests the requisite closest connexion with the contract. Local or internal law is to be applied to locating the risk. The choice of law rules stipulated in the European Community's Second Directive on Non-Life Insurance (22nd June 1988, O.J. L172/1) reflect this position. They are brought into operation in Section 94B and Schedule 3A Part 1 of the *Insurance Companies Act 1982*. All insurance contracts made prior to 1 July 1990 are governed by the common law rules founded on closeness of connexion, and those made after that date are regulated by the new rules. The new rules' policy—to facilitate Union-wide provision of insurance services—is however not as easily furthered by the complexity of the rules themselves, especially when party autonomy as to choice of law is factored. These are not issues of direct concern in the present work but it may be noted that much the same rationales obtain in the courts of the United States.[186]

Once entitlement to subrogation is established, i.e., the claimant is held out as legally competent to sue in another's name, it will be immaterial that the subrogated party was unaware of the extent of his position in relation to the party to whose rights they are thence subrogated, and the subrogated party receives the full measure of those rights as would reduce loss. The rights include those accruing in litigation against third parties, whether these may have been exercised by the original party or not, and the subrogating party is then accountable on trust to the subrogated party for any value obtained in loss reduction after the latter may have met the loss. The type of conflicts question yet to be directly addressed in litigation in this important area of transnational commerce is that of the propriety of parties, a matter which may be subject to non-forum law where necessary, by civil analogy from the decision in *Bumper Development Corporation* v. *Commissioner of Police of the Metropolis*,[187] particularly where the right to be enforced originates under the non-forum law to which recourse must be had in settling whether claimant and defendant are indeed the proper parties. It is unlikely that the public policy of the forum will, in general, prevent reference to the relevant non-forum law. Closer to the point is the House of Lords' decision in *Arab Monetary Fund* v. *Hashim (No. 3)*[188] in which the appellants' English claim for contribution was allowed on the basis that comity required United Kingdom courts to recognize a body corporate created under foreign law.

[185] *Op. cit.*, at 1338–1384, especially Rule 187(7) at 1350–1352; see also the *Insurance Companies Act 1982*, Schedule 3A, Part I, para. 2(4).

[186] See, e.g., D. Laycock, *Modern American Remedies* (Boston, Little Brown; 1985), at 568–574.

[187] [1991] 1 WLR 1362 (C.A.)

[188] [1991] 2 AC 114 (H.L.)

JUDICIAL IMPOSITION OF A CONSTRUCTIVE TRUST OR A LIEN

Reference has been made in this Chapter to the instructive extra-judicial writing of Lord Millett in the law of restitution. The remedy in view under the present heading has also been the subject of his commentary.[189] Taking into consideration the terminological problems associated with the concept "constructive trust", the starting point is that the constructive trust seems not likely to become an institutional remedy (in the sense of creating personal obligations beyond mere property rights)[190] in English and Australian courts in the way that it has done in the United States and Canada.[191] One could say that the English law makes further discussion not based on comparativist perspectives unnecessary in a book concerning judicial remedies particularly in transnational litigation. The American Law Institute's *Restatement of Restitution*[192] expressly refers to the constructive trust as a remedy imposed by the court in order to prevent unjust enrichment, without a fiduciary relation necessarily being involved as between the constructive trustee and the beneficiary. The undeniable fact that makes inclusion worthwhile is that in several instances the imposition of a constructive trust through the operation of law will, as it must, depend on a judicial finding and declaratory order, the latter nevertheless merely affirming the existence of enforceable rights and could lead of course to application of other restitutionary relief more narrowly so-called.

The description "remedial constructive trust" at least serves to differentiate other types of trust imposition, e.g., the resulting trust which is unhelpfully used sometimes when really the correct designation is the former,[193] or the express trust.[194] To be clear, a constructive trustee is anyone who must be regarded as bound by conscience to hold and to assert legal and (or) beneficial title without denying another's beneficial interest[195] or, where for example the context is of a contract for the sale of land, the constructive trust affirms the seller's specifically enforceable promise to convey in which circumstances full payment of the price renders the seller as full trustee for the buyer as well as

[189] "Restitution and Constructive Trusts" (1998) 114 *LQR* 399. See also his, "The Law of Restitution: Taking Stock", in (1999) 14 *Amicus Curiae* 4, especially at 6–7.

[190] *Re Montagu's Settlement Trusts, Duke of Manchester* v. *National Westminster Bank Ltd.* [1987] Ch 264, per Megarry V.-C. at 285. But see the dicta of Lord Browne-Wilkinson in the *Westdeutsche* case ([1996] AC 669, at 714–715): that the remedial constructive trust "is a judicial remedy giving rise to an enforceable equitable obligation: the extent to which it operates retrospectively to the prejudice of third parties lies in the discretion of the court." And at 716: "The court by way of remedy might impose a constructive trust on a defendant who knowingly retains property of which the plaintiff has been unjustly deprived. Since the remedy can be tailored to the circumstances of the particular case, innocent third parties would not be prejudiced and restitutionary defences, such as change of position, are capable of being given effect." See also n. 159, above.

[191] Lord Millett, *loc. cit.*, at 399. See also G. Elias, *Explaining Constructive Trusts* (Oxford, Clarendon; 1990), at 159–164.

[192] (A.L.I. Publishers, St. Paul, Minnesota; 1937), para. 160.

[193] See W. Swadling, "A New Role for Resulting Trusts" (1996) 16 *Leg Stud* 110.

[194] Cf. A.W. Scott, "Constructive Trusts" (1955) 71 *LQR* 39, at 39–40.

[195] Lord Millett, *loc. cit.*, at 400.

converts the trust to an implied one. Further, the constructive trust is but one equitable proprietary mechanism alongside, e.g., the equitable charge and proprietary subrogation.

Personal or fiduciary liability, it is said, is not generated by the trust, rather from its antecedents. This is illustrated by the constructive trust identified in *Attorney-General for Hong Kong* v. *Reid*;[196] in which the Privy Council held in effect that a fiduciary was a constructive trustee of a bribe from a third party, thus involving the bribe being regarded as restorable money paid under a void contract for the beneficiary as in Lord Browne-Wilkinson's finding in *Lord Napier and Ettrick* v. *Hunter*.[197] The short facts were that insurers, who had paid out settlement moneys as to facts which also founded a successful negligence claim of the payee assureds (Lloyd's names), were subrogated to the assureds' equitable proprietary right to the moneys—via an equitable lien—thus enabling them to recover the sums they had paid.

In the framework of restitution law, Lord Millett has written that "[t]he event to which the trust most commonly responds…is breach of fiduciary duty. This places it in the context of restitution for wrong."[198] Therefore, whether one regards the constructive trust as being remedial or strictly substantive as it is under English law, it is arguably not worthwhile to keep the substantive aspects so far from the remedial or those in which a constructive trust is judicially upheld. Elaborating the restitutionary incidents is not made any easier by the variety of remedial restitutionary responses.

What is sufficiently clear is that the constructive trust refers to "an equitable right and the proprietary remedy to which it gives rise," invariably in unjustifiable enrichment circumstances in which it will have been established that no defence avails the defendant and in which the claimant has a restitutionary remedy sounding in the property concerned.[199] At all times, the intersection between the constructive trust and the law of remedies is that the former may arise in equity to make a remedy available to the claimant to prevent the defendant's unjustifiable enrichment.The decisions indicate that a constructive trust is to be identified or imposed where:

— a fiduciary gains from that position without the beneficiary's authority;[200]
— a fiduciary acquires property because of information received in that capacity;[201]
— a third party facilitates fraud on trust property;[202]

196 [1994] AC 324. 197 [1993] AC 713.

198 *Loc. cit.*, at 400. The context of the passage is the contradistinction of constructive from resulting trust. In the latter type of trust, the transferor of legal title will not have intended to pass the sum of the beneficial interest to the transferee. For this reason, the resulting trust's want of dependence on unconscionable conduct or transferee's notice places it in the bounds of subtractive, and not wrong-based, restitution (Lord Millett, at 401n).

199 At 408.

200 *Keech* v. *Sandford* [1726] Sel Cas Ch 61.

201 *Boardman* v. *Phipps* [1967] 2 AC 46.

202 *Selangor United Rubber Estates Ltd.* v. *Craddock (No. 3)* [1968] 1 WLR 1555.

— specific property is subject to a fiduciary duty.[203]

Not to be included is, for example, the situation in which an agent (e.g., a solicitor) simply performs duties running with that function: *Williams-Ashman* v. *Price and Williams*.[204] There has to be identifiable property in order for the question of proprietary relief to arise on the back of a constructive trust.[205] This much has been mooted in the discussion of the *Westdeutsche Landesbank* decision in which a personal claim would have been better justified in the absence of a proprietorial substantive foundation. That foundation, which forms a substantial basis for the present discussion, is settled where the claimant proves a continuing beneficial interest in the particular property or an original transfer is revoked but replaced (in the event of monetary restitution being insufficient) by an order for the transfer to be remade.[206]

The constructive trust is not exclusively restitutionary by definition, let alone be independently classifiable with forms of judicial redress.[207] Consider the relevant circumstances in *Chase Manhattan Bank NA* v. *Israel-British Bank (London) Limited*.[208] Mistaken payments in the hands of an insolvent payee recipient became (traceable) trust property of the payor, quite apart from the personal restitution to which that party was entitled, as beneficiary, from the defendant. Goulding J.'s restitutionary trust imposition as well as the proprietorial right to trace were questions referred to the applicable substantive law, rather than have been consigned to forum procedure, had they been classified as remedial as the defendants had argued. As Bird has said, "[c]auses of action in unjust enrichment which lead to the imposition of proprietary remedies should be characterised by reference to the underlying cause of action, not the proprietary remedy"[209] and the constructive trust is "entirely dependent on the cause of action in unjust enrichment or equitable wrong being established."[210] Thus,

[203] *Tito* v. *Waddell (No.2)* [1977] Ch 106.
[204] [1942] Ch 219.

[205] Cf. *Goff and Jones*, *op. cit.* (1998), at 84–91.

[206] Lord Millett, *loc. cit.*, at 417. His closing submission (at 418) is that "we cannot afford to have contradictory rules for the passing of property in equity and the right to a proprietary restitutionary remedy."

[207] Elias, *op. cit.*, at n. 191. For a more liberal reading, on eminent authority, see R. Goode, "Property and Unjust Enrichment" in A. Burrows (ed.), *Essays on the Law of Restitution* (Oxford, Clarendon; 1991), 215, especially at 237–244 where, having reviewed comparative common law positions, he identifies four policy preconditions for its imposition, viz.: (i) the defendant must have been fiduciarily obligated in his possession of the particular assets; (ii) the assets must derive from breach of the fiduciary obligation; (iii) the interests of creditors (e.g., value; priority of claims; pari passu; transparency; representation; commercial stability) must be protected and; (iv) the claimant must have a sound basis for seeking proprietary restitution.

[208] [1981] Ch 105.

[209] In "Choice of Law" in Rose (ed.), *op. cit.*, at 82.

[210] Ibid., at 83. It is perhaps only right to point out that Bird subscribes to the view of the constructive trust as a judicial remedy. At the same page, e.g., "the particular law which causes the trust to arise is...the law of unjust enrichment, or equitable wrong, and the trust is clearly the remedy imposed to reverse the unjust enrichment." Earlier, on the constructive trust as a substantive, not a remedial, institution, she makes clear: "[I]t is not adopted in the United States, Canada and Australia [from where she writes] and the English courts may [on the authority of *Metall und Rohstoff AG* v. *Donaldson Lufkin and Jenrette Inc.* [1990] 1 QB 391, at 478–479] in fact be moving towards recognition of a remedial constructive trust, at least in the law of restitution."

constructive trusteeship may require, but is not quite, in the nature of formal remedial response. What thus far in the present section has been sauce for constructive trusts must needs also be sauce for liens and comparable equitable charges, as has been demonstrated in the course of reference to the circumstances of *Lord Napier and Ettrick* v. *Hunter*. Existence of a recognizable proprietary interest is the main requirement. Neither charges nor constructive trusts are commercially attractive. They can both be discharged by transfer of property in specie. The essential difference between an equitable charge and a constructive trust is to do with quantum. This book's scope does not justify discussion of what properly belongs to equity principles of property law, but some observations that are pertinent to the conflict of laws must be in order. One need only recall that *Penn* v. *Lord Baltimore*,[211] for example, involved personal accountability of the defendant as trustee in respect of foreign land. It is not difficult to envision English trusts law as the applicable substantive law of a conflicts case: attempts to vindicate equitable interests would often reveal that property law can prove the existence of a cause which attracts restitution without reference to the redirection of unjustifiable enrichment. For service out under the traditional jurisdictional rules, R.S.C. Order 11 rule 1(1)(t) requires that:

— the claim itself be for forum restitutionary relief that is due from a constructive trustee defendant, without any further requirement as to the way in which trusteeship may have arisen;[212]
— the liability arises substantially within forum jurisdiction.[213]

Where the proprietary claim concerns movable property, jurisdictional implications are much less of an issue than they are in relation to immovables; in the latter case, Article 16(1)(a) of *the Brussels Convention* gives exclusive jurisdiction to the courts of the situs in the interests of effectiveness of judgments disposing as to rights in rem, and of jurisdictional propriety. A sound proposition would be that "when the plaintiff claims a proprietary interest in immovable property as a means of reversing the defendant's unjust enrichment, it matters not whether he claims to be legal or equitable owner or, in the case of the latter, whether he claims to be beneficiary under a resulting trust or a constructive trust. In every case, Article 16.1(a) should be applied."[214] Where the facts are governed by a non-forum law which characterizes the restitutionary obligation differently, the forum's preparedness to impose a constructive trust must significantly depend on how functionally related are the merits to the

[211] [1750] 1 Ves Sen 444; relied on by the High Court in *Webb* v. *Webb* [1991] 1 WLR 1410, at 1419.

[212] Cf. A. Briggs, "Juisdiction under Traditional Rules" in Rose (ed.), *op. cit.*, at 61–63.

[213] See, e.g., *Polly Peck International plc* v. *Nadir*, 17th March 1993 (C.A.); this evidently is to be objectively interpreted to mean that substantial and efficacious acts giving rise to liability will have occurred in England, as was noted by Hoffmann LJ in *Metall & Rohstoff* [1990] 1 QB 391, at 437, pointing out similarity with sub-rule (f). Leave is of course now not required in respect of claims under the *Brussels Convention*.

[214] Peel, *loc. cit.*, 36.

imposition, as may be discerned from *Chase Manhattan*.[215] What may well be the most telling view of the scope for constructive trusts in restitution conflicts is one adapted from Lord Millett's writing.[216] Consonant with the argument for "a unified and comprehensive restitutionary response to unjust enrichment", it runs that the inadequacy or undiscriminating tenor of equity's terminology favours the use of restitutionary principles and terms instead. One major consequence of this view is that the constructive trust effectively becomes de-institutionalized as a vindicatory proprietary response to subtractive unjustifiable enrichment, and leaves the way for the resulting trust. That this could take root is much a matter to be anticipated. For one thing, it is not so straightforward to relate "unified restitution" with "resulting trust", nor does it further cause for accepting the remedial constructive trust, e.g., as it exists under United States law. Furthermore, relief in damages for breach of constructive trust or conversion—as was inquired into by the plaintiffs in *Macmillan Incorporated* v. *Bishopsgate Investment Trust plc (No.3)*[217]—is unlikely to become de-prioritized relief in order to suit the foregoing. Discussion or restitutionary revesting of property under a breached or an avoided transaction[218] would add little. Transactional rescission is rarely resorted to because restitution is often impossible at the given stage. If restitution in specie is possible, equitable judicial assistance to revest title unjustifiably acquired may be necessitated.[219]

CONCLUSION

There is much to commend the private international lawyer's focused attention to the remedial forms of restitution, emulating the view that the inclusive underlying causa is indeed not solely to be identified in the terms of unjustifiable enrichment, and taking the sound operational terminology for the purpose of exploratory substantivist enquiry on board. Although the forum is constructively predisposed to transnationalism in the particular context of enquiry as to formal redirection of improper cross-border transfers of value, restitution conflicts do not strictly speaking necessarily comprise choice-of-law, rather that there are requirements of precision in local or (and) transnational litigation (in particular, what the parties state to be the causa, the applicable law and the relief, and how the forum localizes and characterizes the claims) in much the same way that further clarification is essential as regards the formulation of forum policy (as is distinct from public policy),[220] e.g., as to limitation or as to

215 Cf. *Dicey & Morris*, *op. cit.* (12th ed.), at 1477–1478.

216 *Loc. cit.*, at 407–408 *et seq.*

217 [1996] 1 All ER 585.

218 Cf. H. McGregor, *Contract Code Drawn Up On Behalf of the English Law Commission* (Milan, Giuffre Editore and Sweet & Maxwell; 1993), at 155–159 (paras. 470–471).

219 Cf. earlier discussion, under personal restitution, of the decisions in *El Ajou* and *Re Goldcorp Exchange Limited*.

220 Cf. Reinicke, *op. cit.*, at n. 42 above.

the scope of its local restitution law analogues. Inter-system divergence has been found not to be the bugbear it has often seemed in the literature to be, nor has comparativism shown itself to have an unassailable immediate practical purpose beyond situations where the applicable restitution law is not forum law and thus needs to be proved. An individual case approach, that features judicial flexibility and inventiveness, is to be preferred, given that remedial liability in restitution will frequently overlap with liability in compensation in the way that the formal contexts of reasonable recompense and the remedy of account have illustrated. As is to be expected, these issues are a great deal more forgiving where the claimant succeeds in representing the action, and thus the relief sought, in terms of forum law wherein, at any rate, any consequential development of the legal and policy issues necessarily must begin.

Part D

Relief in Rem

11

Remedial declarations and other relief in rem

JURISDICTIONAL AND OTHER FACTORS OF GENERAL APPLICATION

IT IS SOMETIMES sufficient for a claimant to seek and obtain an authoritative judicial statement of the legal position as it obtains in relation to any type of right asserted against a defendant, with neither an alteration of the legal position necessarily ensuing nor the requirement for an accompanying remedy. Being a remedy in rem, a remedial declaration is good against all legal enquiry. Although some other type of relief, e.g., the coercive orders dealt with in Part C, will often be sought together with a declaration,[1] it is usual for this somewhat understated but regularly used remedy to be pursued in conflicts cases, for example, in an action for negative declaration in the context of pending litigation in which the defendant is in the capacity of claimant, as in the *Laker* litigation discussed in the Chapter of this book dealing with antisuit injunctions. It is useful to be reminded:

> "[It] is easy to make too much of the difference between a declaratory and a coercive judgment. In the first place, all judgments, even if they can be directly enforced, inevitably contain, expressly or by implication, a declaration of the rights and duties of the parties; but, secondly, it will usually be found that if a party acts at variance with what has been declared, he may make himself liable to have a coercive order given against him. Indeed...unless some contingent liability of that kind can be envisaged, a court is very likely to issue a declaratory judgment."[2]

However, should the claimant be entitled to other relief, a declaration will not issue as it will be superfluous in the circumstances. Nor is it permissible for a claimant to reclaim declaratory relief if it was obtainable but not claimed first time around.[3] The wholly domestic case of *Slough Estates Ltd.* v. *Slough*

[1] RSC Order 15 r. 16 (previously Ord. 25, r. 5 of the 1883 Rules of Court): "No action or other proceeding shall be open to objection on the ground that a merely declaratory judgment or order is sought thereby, and the Court may make binding declarations of right whether or not any consequential relief is or could be claimed." For an early application, see *Guaranty Trust Co. of New York* v. *Hannay & Co.* [1915] 2 KB 536. A declaration may be sought by originating process: Order 5 r.7 and Order 7 RSC.

[2] F. Lawson, *Remedies of English Law* (2nd ed., London, Butterworths; 1980), at 231.

[3] *The Supreme Court Practice 1997* (London, Sweet & Maxwell; 1996), Vol. 1 Part 1, in the notes to Order 18 r. 15 (at 323–324).

Borough Council and Another[4] is authority that the court may grant a declaration not specifically claimed as long as the merits have been argued and determined to justify the relief.

With its origins in the principles of equity, the declaration is described as "a formal statement by a court pronouncing upon the existence or non-existence of a legal state of affairs".[5] It has always been discretionary,[6] with its application primarily being in proceedings in which the parties' legal status or relationship is at issue (e.g. contractual disputes; marital causes; trusteeship situations) with neither party necessarily being aggrieved. A defining main consequence is that its enforcement is either unnecessary, to be separately pursued—the latter being a feasible option in the same action for declaration—or to be autonomously granted by the forum in the interests of justice between the parties. As it is res judicata, the declaration of itself is self-executing even though it may subsequently become necessary for the successful claimant to seek other relief such as a further declaration as to whether the first has been complied with. As is the case with all remedies, the jurisdiction cannot be ousted by parties' agreement because doing so would offend public policy.[7]

It is said on notable authority that the remedial declaration is "one of the most valuable contributions that the courts have made to the commercial life of this country."[8] The context was that of transnational shipbuilding contracts of which performance was delayed and unilaterally repudiated, with the result that it was considered necessary to clarify the nature and existence of the subsisting legal relationship between the parties. The declaration is especially useful for protecting diverse legally recognized interests. In *Société Anonyme d'Intermediaries Luxemboureois* v. *Faux Companie*,[9] concerning multi-layered re-insurance and retrocession arrangements, a plethora of parties' (i.e., as between themselves) as well as court declarations featured. The judicial declarations actually sought included those to clarify the validity and enforceability of the agreements, to identify the litigants and their respective interests. The decision also highlights the forum's inherent jurisdiction to rectify declaratory

[4] [1968] EGD 124 (Ch.D., per Megarry J).

[5] H. Woolf and J. Woolf, *Zamir & Woolf- The Declaratory Judgment* (2nd ed., London, Sweet & Maxwell; 1993), at 1 (para. 1.02).

[6] See generally, Woolf and Woolf, *op. cit.*, Chapter four; cf. *Russian Commercial and Industrial Bank* v. *British Bank for Foreign Trade Ltd.* [1921] 2 AC 438; but see *Chapman* v. *Michaelson* [1909] 1 Ch 238 in which the Court of Appeal held otherwise. More recently, Lord Denning, in *Pyx Granite Co.* v. *Ministry of Housing and Local Government* ([1958] 1 QB 554, at 571), stated that "if a substantial question exists which one person has a real interest to raise, and the other to oppose, then the court has a discretion to resolve it by a declaration, which it will exercise if there is good reason for so doing." In furtherance of the view that it is discretionary in nature, it is to be recalled that it is essentially dependent on the forum's sense of its appropriateness and is, in fact, excluded relief in some public law statutes (e.g., those which make clear that the remedy is not available against the Crown: *Dyson* v. *Attorney-General* [1911] 1 KB 410, on the *Finance (1909-1910) Act 1910*) which do not concern this book.

[7] *Lee* v. *Showmen's Guild of Great Britain* [1952] 2 QB 329.

[8] Atkin LJ, in *Spettabile Consorzio Veneziano di Armarto* v. *Northern Ireland Shipbuilding Co. Ltd.* (1919) 121 LT 628, at 635.

[9] 31st July 1996 (Transcript LEXIS-NEXIS ENGGEN/CASES).

claims to accurately meet the requirements from the facts. Another expository illustration of the nature of the jurisdiction is afforded in a domestic case[10] involving an unargued breach of contract claim for a Chancery declaration about the availability of the remedy, to indicate the discharge or termination of the contract at issue and, that the plaintiff is no longer bound by it, in view of the Chancery rule of practice against declarations being made in the course of judgments by consent or without trial.

Although a declaration does not aid a claimant who has a cause of action in progress, as was clarified in *Gouriet* v. *Union of Post Office Workers*,[11] in the right circumstances the action for declaration has the convenience of being inexpensive (partly because no evidence need be called nor do pleadings need to be filed), amicable, and available in circumstances of increased interaction in which parties' legal circumstances are much less certain and in need of formally binding authoritative statement. It should be positively ventured that, with the globalization of legal relations and activity, it has to be more than reasonable to recognize the facilitative pertinence of declaratory relief.

It may be disposed of at this point that there is little possibility of an interim or interlocutory declaration being made, because parties' relevant substantive private rights are basically immutable as between pre-trial and judgment[12] and, further, because the usual "balance of convenience" reasons applicable to remedies at that stage do not impact upon declarable rights.

As Woolf and Woolf[13] affirm, "[w]ith the development of declaratory relief the range of interests susceptible of legal protection has been greatly widened" notably to cover not only testamentary and trust deed construction for which the jurisdiction was originally developed,[14] but also typically matters of personal status, title to [local] property, the construction of commercial contracts and other written instruments (excluding court process), and the interpretation of the law of the European Union in national and international fora, e.g., under Article 177 of the *Treaty Establishing the European Economic Community*). However, in presently discussing and illustrating these and other features, it will be seen that the availability of a declaration is not at all necessarily lightly taken by the English forum. Not only must the claimant's interest be real and substantial as would be the case where there has been a breach of legal rights, as with all equity-grounded relief, the claimant's inequitable conduct[15] operates to deny the remedy. The conduct in question includes the

[10] [1991] 1 WLR 541.

[11] [1978] AC 435, at 501.

[12] *International General Electric Co. of New York Ltd.* v. *Commissioners of Customs and Excise* [1962] Ch 784. An exceptional contrary suggestion is expressed by Woolf and Woolf, *op. cit.*, at 83 (para. 3.092), based on "the sensitivity of the issues." See also *M* v. Home Office [1993] 3 All ER 537, at 564–565.

[13] *Op. cit.*, at 6–7 (para. 1.10).

[14] I.e. prior to the *Judicature Acts 1873–5* and Order 25 r. 5 RSC 1883, by which the High Court's general jurisdiction to declare was first statutorily provided for. Before this, S. 14 of the *Court of Chancery Act 1850* had provided for the making of declarations in Chancery, without consequential relief, whether or not the claim was brought against the Crown.

[15] *City of London* v. *Horner* (1914) 111 LT 512.

claimant's motives[16] and the expiry of an applicable limitation period, but not the inadequacy of legal remedies or the likelihood of grave loss or injury.[17]

Lord Dunedin made clear that "[t]he question must be a real and not a theoretical question; the person raising it must have a real interest to raise it; he must be able to secure a proper contradictor, that is to say, someone presently existing who has a true interest to oppose the declaration sought."[18] Likewise, Lord Diplock spelled out the jurisdiction as follows: "[T]he jurisdiction of the court is not to declare the law generally or to give advisory opinions: it is confined to declaring contested legal rights, subsisting or future, of the parties represented in the litigation before it and not those of anyone else."[19] There may thus be the question of proper parties to be resolved in the normal way in transnational litigation by recourse to either internal forum law[20] or the relevant governing law should this be justified. The Court of Appeal had little difficulty in finding that identification of the proper plaintiff in *Bumper Development Corporation* v. *Commissioner of Police for the Metropolis*[21] can be a matter for the relevant non-forum law where the party in question would otherwise not be capable of legal personality under forum law, with public policy and considerations of comity applying. In the context of multi-party interests, it is necessary that all who are interested be joined in the litigation if leave of court is to be unnecessary for its enforcement by or against persons not joined.[22]

What is required is that the particular aspect of the factual relationship between the parties, and on which the justiciable claim is based, is made clear in the claim. The rights or interests directly and immediately at stake can be either legal or equitable.[23] So it is that declarations have been granted as to the nature of the defendant's obligation toward the claimant as would constitute a basis for asserting the underlying legal relationship (*Rajbenbach* v. *Mamon*),[24] as to shipowners being in breach of a charterparty (*Louis Dreyfus et Companie* v. *Parnaso Compania Naviera SA*[25]), and in connexion with the claimant's lawful possession and occupation of particular foreign land (*Companhia de Mocam-*

[16] *Everett* v. *Griffiths* [1924] 1 KB 941, at 960 and 961.

[17] Cf. Woolf and Woolf, *op. cit.*, at 115–116 (para. 4.029).

[18] In *Russian Commercial Bank*, above, n. 6, at 448, concerning a successful claim as to entitlement to the redemption of bonds upon payment in Russian currency. *Mellstrom* v. *Garner & Others* [1970] 1 WLR 603 (per Harman LJ) emphasizes the unavailability of the relief in support of hypothetical circumstances.

[19] *Gouriet* v. *Union of Post Office Workers* [1978] AC 435, at 501. As to future rights, to be differentiated from hypothetical rights, see *Societe Maritime et Commerciale* v. *Venus Steam Shipping* Co. [1904] 9 Com Cas 289; for one thing declarations in furtherance of such rights avoid repetitious litigation.

[20] Cf. Woolf and Woolf, *op. cit.*, at 235–243 (paras. 6.01–6.17).

[21] [1991] 1 WLR 1362 (Purchas LJ).

[22] E.g., under *RSC* Order 15 r. 13–15; s. 47 *Administration of Justice Act 1985*; Order 85, r. 3(1),(2) and 4(3).

[23] *Re Farbenindustrie* [1944] Ch 41, at 43 (per Lord Greene M.R.)

[24] [1955] 1 QB 283.

[25] [1959] 1 QB 498 (reversed [1960] 2 QB 49). The claim was for a declaration that the defendant was in breach of contract and that the damages was for such and such a sum.

bique v. *British South Africa Company*).[26] Treitel[27] indicates that "[w]here a breach has occurred, there is normally no reason why the injured party should wish to confine his claim to such a declaration. But exceptional circumstances may justify such a course."

Having described the general characteristics of remedial declarations, and before going on to look at more specific conflict of laws applications, it is necessary to say that a declaratory action is available only if, as was stated in *Tito* v. *Waddell (No.2)*,[28] "the dispute is within the jurisdiction of the court in a territorial sense." Thus, for example, inasmuch as intellectual property disputes concerning rights registered under foreign law are subject to the law and to the forum of the particular country; they can not be the subject of an English declaratory judgment.[29] To a large extent, this is because to make this type of dispute so subject could amount to English jurisdiction to invalidate, by declaration, the relevant foreign legislation,[30] something which it cannot do in relation to local legislation. According to *Dicey and Morris' The Conflict of Laws*,[31] foreign judgments for recognition and enforcement are subject to the forum's declaratory jurisdiction.

The remainder of the discussion of remedial declarations in the conflict of laws deals with the typical subject matter: interpretation of European Union law, construction of legal instruments, family law and status cases, and negative declarations. As Kerr L.J. pointed out in *The Volvox Hollandia*,[32] "[c]laims for declarations...must be viewed with great caution in all situations involving possible conflicts of jurisdictions, since they obviously lend themselves to improper attempts at forum shopping." It is against this type of backcloth that the following necessarily brief practical analyses are to be understood.

INTERPRETATIONS OF EUROPEAN UNION LAW

It has to be said that interpretations of European Union law may be made not only by the institutional courts of the Union but also by national courts, although the jurisdiction invoked in this regard arises when references for conclusive interpretation are made to the European Court of Justice, or to the Court of First Instance if it is appropriate to do so. References may be made either by national courts of the Member States or by individuals seeking final

[26] [1893] AC 602 (H.L.)

[27] In *Remedies for Breach of Contract: A Comparative Account* (Oxford, Clarendon; 1987), at 5.

[28] [1977] 1 Ch 106, at 260 (per Megarry V.-C.)

[29] Cf. *Tyburn Productions Ltd.* v. *Conan Doyle* [1991] Ch 75, following the Australian decisions in *Potter* v. *Broken Hill Pty. Co. Ltd.* [1906] 3 CLR 479 and *Norbert Steingardt* v. *Meth* [1961] 105 CLR 440.

[30] Woolf and Woolf, *op. cit.*, at 102 (para. 3.124).

[31] L. Collins *et al. Dicey & Morris The Conflict of Laws* (12th ed., London, Sweet & Maxwell; 1993), at 495; see also Woolf and Woolf, *op. cit.*, at 102 (para 3. 125).

[32] [1988] 2 LlR 361, at 371.

clarification of either (or both) the relevant aspects of Union law and how it affects their legal entitlements and of the validity of institutional acts.

It is significant to the present work to identify the salient aspects of European private transnational law which can be the subject of the procedure. One need only recall the decisions involving requests for preliminary interpretation of either the *Brussels Convention* or the *Rome Convention* variously referred to in this book. A prime example is the House of Lords' reference to the European Court of Justice in *Kleinwort Benson Ltd.* v. *Glasgow City Council*,[33] in connexion with whether Article 5(1) of the former *Convention* by definition covers restitutionary claims deriving from a void contract. This and other decisions need not be reviewed here; others turn up in due course of the Chapter. It is to be recalled that the range of topics can extend to any matter provided for in the legislation and, perhaps, also that these rulings are remedial only in the sense in which a right of action may also be generally classified as such.

The nature of the relevant law, in particular the intrinsic requirement that it be uniformly developed and applied in the Member States, makes it a matter of course that the pronouncements of national courts must necessarily be less authentic than those of the courts of the Union. The main provision to be relied on, as was pointed out earlier, is contained in Article 177 of the *E.E.C. Treaty*, dealing with requests for preliminary rulings. There are broad similarities between the jurisdictional competence of an international forum to render advisory opinions on request on the one hand and, on the other, to declaratively interpret procedure and substantive law: the rulings are not quite declaratory of rights in the English sense,[34] because the procedural consequence of a ruling is for national courts to then take further the content of a ruling presumably prior to the making of a declaration of its own as to facts which may or may not have been presented to the European Court of Justice. It is for this less reason, and the widespread recourse that is had to the Article 177 procedure, that more need not be made of it for the present purpose.[35]

THE CONSTRUCTION OF LEGAL INSTRUMENTS

The law applicable to the construction of legal instruments is of course the proper law of the obligation, whatever be the obligation, of which the particu-

[33] *The Times Law Report*, 30th October 1997.

[34] But see L. Brown and T. Kennedy, *The Court of Justice of the European Communities* (4th ed., Sweet & Maxwell; 1994), e.g., at 108 and 118–119, on the scope for declaratory judgments almost routinely entered against Member States in the early years. These are not of concern to this book. See also H. Abraham, *The Judicial Process—An Introductory Analysis of the Courts of the United States, England, and France* (7th ed., New York, Oxford; 1998), at 392–393.

[35] For a full discussion of the general procedure under the article, see, e.g., L. Collins, *European Community Law in the United Kingdom* (4th ed., London, Butterworths; 1990), Chapter Three; further, see J. Bengoetzea, *The Legal Reasoning of the European Court of Justice- Towards a European Jurisprudence* (Oxford, Clarendon; 1993), at 218 *et seq*.; and, not least, D. Lasok and P. Stone, *Conflict of Laws in the European Community* (Oxford, Professional Books; 1987), at 75–81.

lar instrument is a record, subject to proof of any interpretive contexts that may become necessary where the proper law is not, or is not in any part to be determined by, forum law.[36] As was mentioned earlier, it is not part of the forum's jurisdictional competence to declare as to the validity, rather as to the meaning following satisfactory proof, of foreign law, so that legal instruments that may be declared upon in the present context do not include statutes or other written records of foreign law. The interpretation or construction which follows proof is restricted to the particular case and is not subsequently applicable as a precedent except, within the meaning of Section 4(2) of the *Civil Evidence Act 1968*, as an auxiliary to proof. The process of proving a foreign proper law significantly depends on the evidence of experts on the foreign rules of construction.

It is settled[37] that should a foreign document be comprised in part of a foreign statute, the forum is required to avoid the foreign rules of construction unless the parties intended that the rules are to be applied for the purpose. In *Stafford Allen & Sons Limited* v. *Pacific Steam Navigation Company*,[38] a bill-of-lading clause which set out a provision of the United States *Carriage of Goods by Sea Act 1936* fell to be construed by the Court of Appeal. In describing the forum's independent role, Parker L.J. held: "[W]hen one is construing a contract or other written document,...in every case it is for the court to bear in mind the context in which the words were used, including the position of the parties, the nature of the transaction, the object of the venture."[39] In the passing off case of *Rouyer Guillet et Compagnie* v. *Rouyer Guillet & Company Limited*; *Rouyer Guillet* v. *Jackson Knowland & Company*,[40] Lord Greene M.R. held that the forum's construction of a private document may be assisted by permissible evidence especially a judgment of the relevant foreign court; in interpreting a foreign statute, expert witnesses with the persuasion of decisions in point, would be appropriate.

It goes without saying that the burden of proof lies on the party seeking to rely on a particular foreign context. The declaratory relief which may issue is then based on whatever independent conclusions the forum reaches. Should the pertinent foreign law not be proved to the satisfaction of the forum, forum law in point becomes applicable either as a consequence of the usual default conflicts rule or because the forum must then form its own conclusion as to the meaning to be ascribed to that law. Any erroneous construction is reversible on appeal, as in *Russian Commercial and Industrial Bank* v. *Comptoir dEscompte de Mulhouse*.[41] Standard texts on the conflict of laws should be consulted for a fuller discussion of these precursory aspects of the jurisdiction. To reiterate, the jurisdiction does not extend to the documentary process of a foreign forum.

[36] Cf. *Dicey and Morris* Rule 18, *op. cit.*, at 226 *et seq.*; *Bumper Development Corporation* v. *Commissioner of Police for the Metropolis* [1991] 1 WLR 1362, at 1369 (C.A.); cf. the *Société Anonyme* case, n. 9, above.

[37] *Dobell* v. *Steamship Rossmore* Co. [1895] 2 QB 408 (C.A.)

[38] [1956] 1 WLR 629 (C.A.)

[39] Ibid., at 637.

[40] [1949] 1 All ER 244 (C.A.)

[41] [1923] 2 KB 630, reversed [1925] AC 112 (cf. nn. 6 and 18, above, for cases on identical facts).

In the context of commercial or other contracts subject to the *Rome Convention* (Article 10(1)(a) in particular), and which contain a choice-of-law clause in favour of non-forum law, the forum law requirement that foreign law be pleaded and proved applies unless the parties do not look to rely on the foreign law as they are entitled to do by virtue of Article 3(2). This is because the particular requirement is characteristically procedural and evidential, and therefore outside the scope of the *Convention*: Article 1(2)(h). Indeed, it is increasingly apparent that most contracts subject to the jurisdictional competence of the courts of Member States are, by presumption, to be interpreted along similar lines. In *Sierra Leone Telecommunications Company Limited.* v. *Barclays Bank plc.*[42] a successful action was maintained for a declaration that a bank account not managed according to its holder's mandate continued to be subject to the mandate in accordance with its governing law which was forum law. *Aluminium Industrie Vaassen B.V.* v. *Romalpa Aluminium Limited*[43] is authority that identical considerations apply to contracts not regulated by the *Convention.* The net effect of this is that the forum construes transnational contracts by applying its own ordinary rules,[44] about which it has been said[45] of the English legal approach to commercial contracts that the objective and often inter-related issues of parties' common intentions,[46] the surrounding circumstances,[47] the reasonableness of results,[48] and market norms and practices[49] are central. Particular aspects of material validity of a contract are of course determined by the applicable law which may also be the proper law.

The approach to construing other types of legal document such as testamentary, trust and other deeds is essentially equivalent. The object of the declaration is always to assist the avoidance or resolution of the immediate dispute which surrounds or necessitates it. In the case of wills, *Dicey & Morris*'s Rule 141[50] is authority that a testator's intended applicable law is, if it is not expressed, to be taken to be his personal law at the time of executing the will

[42] [1998] 2 All ER 821, at 826–827 (per Cresswell J.)

[43] [1976] 1 WLR 676 (C.A.)

[44] Cf. The Giuliano-Lagarde Report [1980] OJ C282, at 18, and 35–36.

[45] Sir Christopher Staughton, "How Do the Courts Interpret Commercial Contracts?" (1999) 58 CLJ 303, especially at 304–312.

[46] Cf. *Total Gas Marketing Ltd.* v. *Arco British Ltd.* [1998] 2 LlR 209, at 223 (per Lord Hope of Craighead).

[47] Cf. Lord Wilberforce's speech, introducing the use of "the matrix", i.e. the factual background, in the local case of *Investors Compensation Scheme* v. *West Bromwich Building Society* [1998] 1 WLR 896, at 913; for subsequent applications of the phrase, see, e.g., Lord Hoffmann in *Mannai Investments Co. Ltd.* v. *Eagle Star Life Assurance Co.* [1997] AC 779.

[48] See, e.g., *Wickman Machine Tools Sales Ltd.* v. *L. Schuler AG* [1974] AC 235 (per Lord Reid, especially at 251: "The fact that a particular construction leads to a very unreasonable result must be a relevant consideration. The more unreasonable the result the more unlikely it is that the parties can have intended it..."); also, *Segovia Compania Naviera SA* v. *R Pagnan & Fratelli* [1977] 2 LlR 343, and *Charter Reinsurance Co. Ltd.* v. *Fagan* [1997] AC 313.

[49] Cf. *Roar Marine Ltd. and Others* v. *Bimeh Iran Insurance Co.* [1998] 1 LlR 423 (per Mance J., especially at 429: "For there to be any relevance in any custom or practice, whether in a strict or informal sense, it must be possible to identify the particular custom or practice with some certainty").

[50] *Op. cit.*, at 1038 *et seq.*

even if he acquired another domicile before his death: *Philipson-Stow* v. *Inland Revenue Commissioners*.[51] The lex domicilii rule applies to movable and immovable property, although the lex situs must be complied with as regards the actual implementation of dispositions that will have been construed by reference to the domiciliary law. According to forum law, a testator or settlor can oust the jurisdiction to make declaration on specified facts otherwise left to a nominee for the purpose of determining those facts: *Re Tuck's Settlement*.[52] In such circumstances, beneficiaries need not be parties to the action.

FAMILY LAW AND STATUS CASES

It is probably easy to hold that declarations as to status, constitutive and not just declaratory as they must be, in relation to the types of matter dealt with in this section are the prototype for declaratory relief, not least because the particular remedy, in the form of a decree, neatly lends itself to a conclusive resolution of the issues. There is always the likelihood that the resolution is to found subsequent entitlement or obligation on either party in a given case. The scope of the legal matters covers the existence, or otherwise, of marital relationships (validity; annulment; dissolution; divorce), parentage, legitimacy or legitimation of relationships and (or) of offspring, and the adoption of children overseas. In English law, these are dealt with predominantly in Sections 55–57 of the *Family Law Act 1986*.[53] A declaration can also deal with the nationality, presumption of death, identity, friendly or enemy status of the propositus (as a legal or as a natural person), frequently as issues connected to a private international law dispute. Forum jurisdiction depends on sufficiency of connecting factors and the claimant's genuine legal interest in the declaration. Personal law typically decides substantive issues of status.

Availability of the declaration depends, in a general sense, on verification of the data which is to be the subject of the relief, so that once this is settled in favour of a declaratory decree being granted, disapproving evidence will not be allowed unless considerations of public policy make manifestly different requirements:[54] Section 58(1). According to the remaining subsections, the

[51] [1961] AC 727, at 761 (per Lord Denning M.R.); see also S. 4 *Wills Act 1963*.

[52] [1978] Ch 49 (C.A., per Lord Denning M.R.), at 117; contra *Re Wynn* [1952] Ch 271 (Danckwerts J.)

[53] Section 55 deals with marital status (see also *Dicey & Morris*, *op. cit.*, at 765 *et seq.*); s. 56, on offspring, is from 4th April 1988 substituted by s. 22 *Family Law Reform Act 1987*; s. 57 deals with adoptions in conjunction with s. 72(2) and 38(1)(d) of the *Adoption Act 1976* (on overseas adoptions being on a par with local ones). Part III of the 1986 statute carries these provisions and implements the Law Commission Report No. 132 "Declarations in Family Matters" (London, H.M.S.O.; 1984). See generally N. Wall, G. Maple, M. Everall and A. Biggs, *Rayden & Jackson's Law and Practice in Divorce and Family Matters* (17th ed., London, Butterworths; 1997), Vol. 1, at 543–564, dealing with status and with questions of consent to treatment of adult and child patients.

[54] A good example is *Chaudhary* v. *Chaudhary* [1985] Fam 19, that a bare talak divorce which was pronounced and valid abroad without the need to notify the wife is not recognized in England for public policy reasons, especially because it would not be a divorce by judicial proceedings.

general consequence of a declaration is final and limited to what will have been claimed. Subsection (5) makes it impossible for a declaration to be issued to the effect either that a marriage was void from its inception, or that any person is or was illegitimate. The order operates to substitute pre-existing liabilities with those which may survive or be set up through ancillary orders, e.g., those dealing with financial and related maintenance.

Although by no means declaratory, such further orders, not being remedies discussed elsewhere in this book, deserve some mention.[55] The jurisdictional framework ensures that only sufficiently localized status cases can be heard by the forum and, consequently, be the subject of remedial orders thereafter. Internal law texts ought ideally to be consulted for the detail of the rules in these regards, but perhaps the following outline comments may be highlighted. It may be decided that matrimonial property be sold by court order for sale under Section 24A of the *Matrimonial Causes Act 1973*, by which a lump sum is provided for the needy party; the order cannot be interim. In the case of an overseas divorce, nullification or judicial separation, the financial relief claimable, e.g., under Sections 14, and 17–26 of the *Matrimonial and Family Proceedings Act 1984* are those which would have been claimable had the proceedings been wholly local, with Rule 3.18 of the *Family Proceedings Regulations 1991* governing the applications procedure to be followed in approaches to a judge in the Principal Registry of the Family Division of the High Court.

The issue of propriety of claimant is left as a general one, i.e., anyone may apply. The declaration sought is mainly positive—thus confirming the law's ethos in favour of marriage and legitimacy—in the sense that the order is to be expressed in the affirmative, unless it is aimed at, e.g., stating that a marriage in question did not subsist at a specified date or that the validity of a divorce, annulment or legal separation in respect of such a marriage is not good for English recognition and enforcement, or at stating that the subject of the declaration has not become legitimated in accordance with Section 2 or 3 of the *Legitimacy Act 1976* or Section 1 or 8 of the *Legitimacy Act 1926* or in accordance with a recognizable foreign order.

NEGATIVE DECLARATIONS[56]

A negative declaration is "a declaration as to the absence of a right or power in the defendant or, what usually amounts to the same thing, the absence of any

[55] See generally the clear account in *Dicey & Morris*, *op. cit.*, at 767–789, and the Law Commission Report No. 117, "*Financial Relief after Foreign Divorce*" (London, H.M.S.O.; 1982) now contained in Part III, S. 6, of the *Matrimonial and Family Proceedings Act 1984*. For local law and reciprocity-based arrangements, regarding foreign financial orders, see, e.g., S. Oliver *et al.*, *Enforcing Family Finance Orders* (Bristol, Jordans/Family Law; 1999), Parts 1–3 and 4 respectively.

[56] For a succinct account, see L. Collins, "The Marc Rich Case and Actions for Negative Declarations" in *Essays in International Litigation and the Conflict of Laws* (Oxford, Clarendon; 1994), Chapter V.

duty or liability in the plaintiff."[57] The jurisdiction applies to any type of case as long as the English court is forum conveniens the merits.[58] Even if it be stated in positive terms, a declaration is to be regarded as negative if it establishes that the claimant is not liable, and whether or not an infringement of the rights concerned has taken place. It is more readily available of course if there has been a repeatable infringement. A negative declaration can state, as it did in *Finnish Marine Insurance Company* v. *Protective National Insurance Company*,[59] that the claimant is not obligated to complete contractual performance. In *Guaranty Trust Company of New York* v. *Hannay & Company*,[60] a reluctance to grant negative declarations was identified in view of the fact that "in practically every case the person asking it will be left to set up his defence in the action when it is brought", so that Lord Wilberforce's dicta in *Camilla Cotton Oil Company* v. *Granadex SA*,[61] differentiating reluctance from competence, is to be taken on board for hard cases.

The context of jurisdictional conflicts, and with it the need to abrogate forum shopping, is one in which the claim for a negative declaration is noticeable. The context of the *Brussels Convention* in this regard is illustrated in the decision of the European Court of Justice in *Gubisch Maschinenfabrik KG* v. *Palumbo*[62] in which a pre-existing action for the recovery of a price paid by the one party was followed by an action by the other for a negative declaration that the international sales contract in question was not enforceable (it was allegedly revoked before the offer was accepted) and therefore rescindable or dischargeable. In the form of a reference for a preliminary ruling, the Rome Supreme Court of Appeals sought interpretative clarification of the relevant Article 21 by the European Court of Justice, particularly whether the Article's provision for jurisdiction allocation in favour of the court first seised is to be broadly construed or whether it narrowly refers to same party and same causa proceedings. It was held that the circumstances fell within the scope of the Article, and therefore that the declaration sought was in order. *The Maciej Rataj*,[63] is authority that it would be an abuse of process if negative declaration proceedings are brought simply to hinder proper proceedings imminent in another Contracting State.

In non-*Convention* cases, Lord Diplock's speech in *British Airways* v. *Laker Airways*[64] is instructive in that a negative declaratory claim is forthcoming if its object, with or without further relief, is in furtherance of the true legal position between the parties and is not superfluous. In the pre-*Convention* case of *The Manar, Northern Trust Limited* v. *Strachan Brothers*[65] a declaration was

[57] Woolf and Woolf, *op. cit.*, at 166 (para. 4.142).

[58] *First National Bank of Boston* v. *Union Bank of Switzerland* [1990] 1 LlR 32: English negative declaration proceedings stayed in favour of foreign forum conveniens. Also, *Sohio Supply Co.* v. *Gatoil (USA) Inc.* [1989] 1 LlR 588 (C.A.), in which the superficiality of foreign negative declaration proceedings did not justify an English stay.

[59] [1990] 1 QB 1078.

[60] [1915] 2 KB 536, at 564–565 (per Pickford LJ).

[61] [1976] 2 LlR 10, at 14.

[62] Case 144/86 [1987] ECR 4861.

[63] [1991] 2 LlR458.

[64] [1985] AC 58.

[65] [1903] 89 LT 218.

granted in furtherance of the claimants' action in a French court. Indeed, it is generally not discountenanced, all things being as they should, to avoid or deter anticipated proceedings by seeking a declaration.

A NOTE ABOUT OTHER RELIEF *IN REM*

It has been said in the present Chapter that the declaration is a judgment in rem: that is, its content is binding on all the world as to the particular parties' legal position. Several other remedies in rem have been discussed at various junctures in this book: e.g., the proprietary restitutionary remedies, typically money remedies of the particular category (and also liens, for example), and the reference to restitution *in specie* or in rem; the discussion and descriptive analysis of damages awards, e.g., when they are awarded in furtherance of the forum's jurisdictional competence *ad rem* (so-called because it is sometimes said figuratively that the only jurisdiction in rem which remains properly described as proprietary is that which subsists in Admiralty claims).

The typifying qualities of the judgment in rem are essentially that it is in principle enforceable as against the res itself alone; it affects personal interest(s) in the res to the extent of the interest. Albeit in the context of the recognition and enforcement of foreign judgments, *Dicey and Morris*[66] defines the judgment in rem in English law as "a judgment whereunder either (1) possession or property in a thing is adjudged to a person, or (2) the sale of a thing is decreed in satisfaction of a claim against the thing itself. The term is used also to describe (3) an adjudication as to status such as a decree of nullity or dissolution of marriage, and (4) a judgment ordering property to be sold by way of administration in bankruptcy or on death". A general note is in place about the remaining types of judgment where they are in fact administered by the English court in the conflict of laws. The main point of reference which ties the remaining types together is that the judgment can only be realized by a court order that the *res*—whatever it is[67]—should be sold.

The respective types of remedy in rem are therefore to be differentiated by the kind of liability which would justify the judicial imposition of the particular relief. In the case of adjudgment of property or possession to a named person, some initial resort may be had to the circumstances of *Webb* v. *Webb*[68] for a

[66] *Op. cit.*, at 495 *et seq*. Admiralty jurisdiction of itself (S. 6(1)(b) *Supreme Court Act 1981*) is discussed between 439–452 (Rule 33). The action *in rem* is to be differentiated from the judgment in rem, even though a right of action is definable as being remedial. A remedy ostensibly *in rem* can, as often it is, be the outcome of a claim in personam such as where, under the High Court's general admiralty jurisdiction provided for in S. 20 *Supreme Court Act 1981*, the defendant in an action in respect of which the *res* has been arrested secures the release of the res and incurs liability not limited to its value: "*The Nordglimt*" [1988] QB 183, at 200–201; "The Prinsengracht", *Financial Times*, 24th July 1992.

[67] It is usually a ship or aircraft, and may include goods carried on it as freight or cargo, the proceeds of selling the ship or aircraft or its cargo. Aircraft claims are extremely rare.

[68] [1991] 1 WLR 1410.

transnational illustration of relief to affirm possessory or other equitable interest that is good against the world. In the particular case, the relevant jurisdiction was had under Article 16(1)(a) of the *Brussels Convention* as was also the jurisdictional basis in *Rosler* v. *Rottwinkel*[69] concerning landlord and tenant obligations in relation to forfeiture or possession of the leasehold. It appears that land sale (or disposition), contracts or agreements for the disposition of landed interests within the meaning of Section 2 *Law of Property (Miscellaneous Provisions) Act 1989*, are specifically enforceable by court order in rem, as would be a declaration of trust: *Official Solicitor* v. *Stype Investments (Jersey) Limited.*[70] In this case, the proceeds of the sale of English land at the owner's direction under a bare trust were transmitted to Jersey after he had died. The overall circumstances fell well within the English forum's proper jurisdiction.

Where the land is question is foreign, the rule in *British South Africa Company* v. *Companhia de Mocambique*[71] naturally limits the jurisdiction of the English forum in these regards, lest the exercise be contrary to the relevant foreign jurisdiction's property rules, in particular such applicable local rules dealing with the registration of interests. In *Hesperides Hotels Limited* v. *Aegean Turkish Holidays,*[72] the jurisdiction-curtailing rule was justified by the claimant's motive in seeking access to the English forum for the purpose of access to land (not movables) abroad. The law of the situs as to capacity to engage in implementing a foreign order of sale, as to the formalities to be complied with in sale agreements generally, as to the validity of a contract of sale, are not to be taken lightly by the English forum, although it has been conceded that the antiquity of this jurisdictional position, is another of its most prominent rationales.[73] However, the fact that this position is reflected in the forum's own disposition toward foreign forum pronouncements[74] is indicative of the coherence and the importance of the connecting factor in these respects. For one thing, the English forum will in the correct circumstances enforce foreign judgments affecting property located within the jurisdiction of the awarding court.[75] In *Ibenekwa and Others* v. *Egbuna and Another,*[76] a declaration was granted to affirm title to land in a newly independent Commonwealth country. The central role and importance of the localizing matrix of the

69 [1986] QB 33. 70 [1983] 1 WLR 214. 71 [1893] AC 602.

72 [1979] AC 508. Cf. *Dicey & Morris*'s Rule 117 (*op. cit.*, at 960 *et seq.*)

73 In *Hesperides*, at 543–544, per Lord Fraser.

74 See, e.g., *Re Trepca Mines Ltd.* [1960] 1 WLR 1273, especially at 1277 (C.A.) Much the same attitude obtains elsewhere, e.g., in several Canadian provincial jurisdictions.

75 *Minna Craig Steamship Co.* v. *Chartered Mercantile Bank of India, London and China* [1897] 1 QB 55 (per Collins J.), in which an English company—the owners of the claimant ship—in liquidation with property in India, was subject to a German order of sale of the ship to meet prioritized creditors' claims. At 61–63, his Lordship considered the authorities on the effects of the in rem judgment as it affected the claimants assets generally; in particular, that "where an English creditor by process of law in a foreign country gets hold of assets which from the English standpoint would be divisible among the general body of the creditors, he cannot retain the proceeds as against the trustee." The importance of the forum's viewpoint was perhaps not better expressed.

76 [1964] 1 WLR 219 (P.C., per Viscount Radcliffe).

forum's jurisdictional competence is reliably illustrated. Indeed, where the preponderance of the facts and other considerations is in the direction of the forum, the applicable law has unavoidably to be forum law, and the inclination to consider the circumstances as being those of the conflict of laws must be much less. The types of action which have been described in Part C to be intrinsically forum-related (e.g., intellectual property disputes)[77] would be just as remediable as long as the justification is established.

[77] Cf. *In the matter of an application to the Comptroller-General by the Locroy Engineering Co. Ltd. under s. 56 of the Patent Act* 69 R.P.C. 3 (1951): a declaration of an employer's entitlement to profits and gains from an invention.

Part E

Envoi

Remedies and localism

I

IN THIS LAST Part and Chapter, it is not necessary or intended to summarize what has thus far been the subject matter of this book. But not quite. Rather, the object is to review private international law, as the book's primary context for the consideration of forum relief, as it may respond in its own turn to other broader contemporary themes that may have a profitable bearing on formal as well as substantive transnational remedialism. One of these themes is so-called globalization of legal relations. It has turned up in the course of the book, mainly in the guises of international civil justice and procedure. Although the conflict of laws and globalization both have a subtle self-evidently compossible area of classical or standard application—they respectively pertain to private activity which does not primarily or necessarily fall under the direct influence of formalistic state public regulation—it is hardly ever the case that they are extensively considered in terms of their mutuality. The one, essentially, consists of prescriptive formalism that is dictated through the legal institutions of the state (Parliament and the courts) and the latter is typically given to subsist (unwieldily, and often erosively) at the periphery of statehood and law. The contemporary scope of either is, in relation to territorial sovereignty, constantly subject to evaluation such that current formal legal problems of either are often a direct function or consequence of the lacunae thrown up by new trends and directions in transnational activity.

Legal responses in general transnational practice in the courts have variously been shown to look to comparativist,[1] regionalist and other disciplines (including those of under-utilized internal law) for conceptual and administrable solutions. Regionalism succeeds where the legal systems are comparable. A common juridical background facilitates cross-border adjudication. There is talk of a "global" jurisdiction and judgments Convention, as well as of a European Convention on the law applicable to non-contractual obligations (a "Rome II Convention"), which is to apply in any transnational circumstances and without the need for the applicable law to be that of a Contracting State.[2]

[1] See generally B.S. Markesinis, *Foreign Law & Comparative Methodology: a Subject and a Thesis* (Oxford, Hart; 1997).

[2] European Group for Private International Law, "Proposal for a European Convention on the Law Applicable to Non-Contractual Obligations" (1998) XLV *NILR* 465–471.

Fentiman has produced a blueprint for justifiably furthering the scope of relevance and application of foreign law generally.[3]

In the context of general jurisprudence, MacCormick has opined that contemporary legal theory and practice is, so to speak, "beyond the sovereign state", that "[o]ne thing which it is necessary for jurisprudence or the philosophy of law to do in the present state of affairs is to guard against taking a narrow one-state or Community-only perspective, a monocular view of these things."[4] Contemporary international law accordingly applies its policy foundations and, through the eyes of McLachlan,[5] is to be seen to exert not inconsiderable influence on forum jurisdiction, that most central of issues of the conflict of laws fundamentally relating to remedial competence. Indeed, Lowenfeld too has been persuasive in arguing for a pervasive "reasonableness"[6] (as a judicial balancing act) in international adjudication, on the primary basis that the received differentiation of public from private international law is perhaps not to be pursued as rigidly, or without recourse to function, as the differentiation normally conducts the deliberation and resolution of the issues.

Whether, and how, these broad strokes are identifiable in the remedialism of English courts is, however, a different matter. A reading of Rose on restitution conflicts[7] re-emphasizes legal discipline in the sense that the law must look within, to its own conceptual resources, in order to deal with legal disputes and problems arising in the globalized shape of things. Efficient judicial flexibility becomes a central feature of the class of responses from private international law which, for the sake of a complete overview, must include the success of private international arbitration particularly in the commercial sphere.[8] And arbitration is the logical precursor of international adjudication in either public or private law. Writing extra-judicially, Lord Steyn has shown that legal formalism in English Common Law must now be viewed as a dynamic concept by which new problems and horizons can constructively be broached: "[T]he modern trend is for English courts not to confine their reasoning to the narrow inner logic of law" especially at the appellate level where "the court is confronted with situations of choice in which deductive reasoning competes for supremacy with considerations of general principle, policy and justice."[9]

[3] *Foreign Law in English Courts* (Oxford, Clarendon; 1998).

[4] "Beyond the Sovereign State" (1993) 56 *MLR* 1, at 5.

[5] "The Influence of International Law on Civil Jurisdiction" [1993] *HYbIL* 125.

[6] *International Litigation and the Quest for Reasonableness: Essays in Private International Law* (Oxford, Clarendon; 1997), e.g., at 228–230.

[7] *Restitution and the Conflict of Laws* (Oxford, Mansfield; 1995).

[8] See, e.g., D.M. Cato, *Arbitration Practice and Procedure (Interlocutory and Hearing Problems)* (London, LLP; 1997), especially Chapters seven (common law arbitration), ten (damages), eleven (declaratory relief), eighteen (injunction), twenty-nine (rectification), and thirty-one (specific performance); also, A. Redfern and M. Hunter, *Law and Practice of International Commercial Arbitration* (London, Sweet & Maxwell; 1999), generally.

[9] "Does Legal Formalism hold sway in England?" in M.D.A. Freeman (ed.), *Current Legal Problems 1996* (Oxford Clarendon; 1996) 43, at 58 for the quotations in the main text above.

But what impact, if any, on remedies in the conflict of laws from the foregoing? A readymade method by which to usefully assess this query is forthcoming from the language of conflicts doctrine (i.e., the influential local law theory) and the discoursive terminology of globalization (i.e., the "global"/"local" interface). It is perhaps prudent, without being too selective about the parametric breadth of issues of globalization by which the economics and legal aspects often have prominently featured,[10] to focus on how legal localism adapts to transnational circumstances. Local law theory, with which Dicey grappled to produce his own theory of vested rights, has been identified as probably that which best explicates English conflict of laws. The subject and indeed its English context is not, nor has it been so given, to high theory or to abstraction. Similarly, the economic analysis of law,[11] with which conceptual overlaps with general globalization discourse could be associated, has neither been accepted as integral to English law, nor is it intended in this envoi to take it up, for the simple reason that to do so would be premissed on an association of the content and design of relevant jurisdictional and remedial rules of forum law on the one hand with, on the other, the postulates from economic analysis. The writer does not say that it may not be worthwhile to deliberate that association; rather that to do so would not quite belong in this book.

II

Localism is the counterpart of globalism and transnationalism. Their coexistence denominates the responsiveness of the legal system to external considerations. In the dualist jurisprudence of the Common Law, forum law that is sourced in bilateral or multilateral legal instruments is, for the prevalence of territorial sovereignty, usefully construed as local law, albeit that it is not relevant or applicable to domestic legal disputes. So it is that local law caters to extra-territorialism and to foreign law where the circumstances make these topics an integral part of remedialism in private international law. All the same, convergence criteria, at least at the level of transnational law, are increasingly impossible to overlook. In the context of remedies, the importance of local forms has been shown in this book to tie the primary issues of the context to forum law, that it is productive single bright line logic to adapt the substantivist considerations to those forms. In view of the currents and trends so far underlined in this closing Chapter, the range of vision in these regards continues to be pre-determined by the forum's disposition to those

[10] See generally G. Teubner (ed.), *Global Law Without A State* (Aldershot, Dartmouth; 1997).

[11] Cf. R.A. Posner, *Economic Analysis of Law* (2nd ed., Little Brown, Boston; 1977), at Chapters Four (contract rights and remedies), Six (tort rights and remedies), Nineteen (the market, the adversary system, and the legislative process as methods of resource allocation), Twenty (the process of legal rule-making), Twenty-one (civil procedure), and Twenty-two (law enforcement).

forms in their transnationalist application. Jurisdictional competence must not automatically translate as remedial competence but, without the former, the last mentioned is absent. Where remedial competence is the issue, there is every reason for the dedicated private international lawyer to anticipate new shapes of formal remedialism, not simply for its own sake or because the incidence of foreign law is a profound and characteristic justification for the conflict of laws but, because the internal consistency of local law as internal law may be inadequate to the requirements of judicial justice in the circumstances.

Yet the issue is not that disparate local laws ought to become uniform; there is far too much rational divergence to bear this out let alone to propose it. Therein lies the challenge, if at all it is a cogent one, from legal globalism. The Chapters of Part B have individually described the limits of a perspective by which remedialism is apropos of localization but not necessarily always of inward-looking localism. If prognosis were either right or permitted, it ought reasonably to be in the order of an adaptive preservation of remedial forms.

Harmonized, indeed unified, transnational substantive law approaches completion at many important levels, contractual as well as non-contractual. There remains much legal ground to be specifically dealt with at the international level. It would be unjustifiable ambition in a forum state which generalizes as to its own transnational remedial competence. Isolated fact-instances—e.g., in the area of transnational product liability, environmentalist liability, remedial restitution, intellectual property, and so forth—have to varying extents re-emphasized the role of judicial policies of legal certainty, consistency and predictability in the nature of the responses to the remedies aspects of these developments. It would appear to be reasonably accurate to anticipate any accretion, to a developed law on conflicts remedies, as being based primarily on consensual law and policy at the transnational level and on the individual case.

However one looks at remedialist theory and policy, much must depend, without looking unnecessarily far ahead, on what may be construed from the premiss in forum law or lex fori. It seems not so long ago that Graveson[12] spoke of an inherent inequality of applicable laws as a philosophical basis for conflict of laws applications. In today's globalized world, de Sousa Santos points out that "the core countries specialise in globalized localisms, while upon the peripheral countries is imposed a choice of localized globalisms."[13] All the same, basic remedial forms are relatively co-ordinate between or among jurisdictions, or so the acceptedly finite discipline of private international law makes clear and deals with. This book is about English conflict of laws in relation to comparable legal systems. The imposition that Santos identifies is, first, unpejorative and, second, a realistic reflexion of the design of the world's autonomous legal systems, existing without a central adjudicatory institution. It is a bonus

[12] In "The Inequality of Applicable Law" [1980] Vol. LI *BYbIL* 231.

[13] In *Toward a New Common Sense: Law, Science and Politics in the Paradigmatic Transition* (New York, Routledge; 1995), at 263.

to deliberation of remedial conflict of laws that, not only is the subject matter virtually indicative of the legal system's rachis and the immutability of forms, the issue of jurisdictional autonomy as the conceptual predicate of the topic means that concern has almost exclusively to be on the much more tangible aspects, as has been the case in this book.

The conflict of laws is thankfully not a controversial subject area, another consequence of the role of localism perhaps. However, the pace and facility of transnational activity enjoins a measure of consolidation. Reinecke[14] identifies the beginnings of global public policy, aimed at those shared aspects of the widest context from which private international law and adjudication must be viewed, not entirely dissimilar from Lowenfeld's characterization of "reasonableness"[15] if allowance is made for the former author's perspective in public policy and the latter's in judicial outlook and co-operation. Likewise, Maclean draws attention to the development of cross-border judicial activity and collaboration as a concerted but relatively underused facility in response to transnational legal transactions.[16] McLachlan and Nygh[17] have looked beyond the scheme of the EU for the groundwork for non-contractual obligations previously charted neither in the legal literature nor in the courts, or at least not quite outside the terms of instant adjudication. The shape of substantive conflict of laws, part-settled and partly requiring either legislative or judicial development especially in the avant garde subject areas at this millennium, firmly suggests to this dedicated remedialist that there is much to commend in the view that local as the policy justification for the conflict of laws is, it is attractive and helpful to regard the nexus between substance and remedy and to value the implications of law and localism as this book has done.

14 In *Global Public Policy* (Washington DC, Brookings; 1998).

15 *Op. cit.*, at 229.

16 *International Judicial Assistance* (Oxford, Clarendon; 1992).

17 *Transnational Tort Litigation: Jurisdictional Principles* (Oxford, Clarendon; 1996).

Index